# American
# Trial Judges

John Paul Ryan (Ph.D., Northwestern University) is Senior Research Associate at the American Judicature Society. He is co-author of *The Supreme Court in American Politics*.

Allan Ashman (J.D., Columbia University Law School) is Executive Director of the National Conference of Bar Examiners. He is co-author of *The Key to Judicial Merit Selection: The Nominating Process*.

Bruce Dennis Sales (Ph.D., University of Rochester and J.D., Northwestern University School of Law) is Professor of Law and Psychology and Director, Law-Psychology Program, at the University of Nebraska, Lincoln. He is the editor of the journal *Law and Human Behavior*.

Sandra Shane-DuBow (M.A., Loyola University) is Director of Criminal Justice Research at the Wisconsin Center for Public Policy. She is co-author of *Felony Sentencing in Wisconsin*.

# American Trial Judges

## Their Work Styles and Performance

John Paul Ryan
Allan Ashman
Bruce D. Sales
Sandra Shane-DuBow

THE FREE PRESS
*A Division of Macmillan Publishing Co., Inc.*
NEW YORK
Collier Macmillan Publishers
LONDON

Copyright © 1980 by The American Judicature Society

All rights reserved. No part of this book may be reproduced or transmitted in any form or by any means, electronic or mechanical, including photocopying, recording, or by any information storage and retrieval system, without permission in writing from the Publisher.

The Free Press
A Division of Macmillan Publishing Co., Inc.
866 Third Avenue, New York, N.Y. 10022

Collier Macmillan Canada, Ltd.

Library of Congress Catalog Card Number: 80-756

Printed in the United States of America

printing number
1 2 3 4 5 6 7 8 9 10

Library of Congress Cataloging in Publication Data
Main entry under title:

American trial judges.

   "Prepared with the support of National Science Foundation grant no. DAR76-14964 to the American Judicature Society."
   Bibliography: p.
   Includes index.
   1. Judges—United States.  2. Judicial process—United States.
I. Ryan, John Paul  II. American Judicature Society.
KF8775.A95     347.73'14     80-756
ISBN 0-02-927620-9

This book was prepared with the support of National Science Foundation Grant No. DAR76-14964 to the American Judicature Society. However, any opinions, findings, and conclusions are those of the individual authors and do not necessarily reflect the views of the American Judicature Society or the National Science Foundation.

# Contents

Foreword ......................................................................... xiii

Preface ............................................................................. xv

### Part I   Introduction

1. In Search of Judging ................................................... 3

### Part II   Organizational Influences on Judicial Work

2. The Work Patterns of Trial Judges ............................. 17
3. The Impact of Court Structure .................................... 47
4. The Role of Attorneys .................................................. 80
5. Judicial Resources in the Courthouse ......................... 101

### Part III   Individual Influences

6. The Recruitment and Socialization of Trial Judges ..... 121
7. Judicial Morale ............................................................ 146

### Part IV   Selective Views of Judicial Performance

8. Styles of Negotiation: Judicial Participation in Plea and Settlement Discussions ........................................... 173
9. The Social, Political, and Legal Environments of Courts: Judging in Chicago, Los Angeles and Philadelphia ..... 196

### Part V   Conclusion

10. Judging in America's Trial Courts ............................. 227

## Appendix A

Observing Trial Judges: A Note on Philosophy, Strategies, and Techniques — 249

## Appendix B

The Development and Administration of a Mail Survey — 267

## Appendix C

The Questionnaire — 278
**Selected Bibliography** — 286
**Index** — 288

# LIST OF TABLES

Table 2–1.  The Assignment of Trial Judges, 23
Table 2–2.  Variety of Judicial Work by Assignment, 25
Table 2–3.  Length of Judicial Work Days, 26
Table 2–4.  The Frequency of Jury and Nonjury Trial Work on Judicial Work Days, 30
Table 2–5.  Identification of Clusters of Judicial Tasks, 31
Table 2–6.  The Frequency of Jury and Nonjury Trial Work by Assignment, 33
Table 2–7.  Trial Judges' Allocation of Time on Their Work Days, 35
Table 2–8.  Patterns of Task Predominance on Judicial Work Days, 39
Table 2–9.  Trial Judges' Expenditure of Time on Community Relations Activities, 42
Table 3–1.  Proportion of Trial Judges by Size of Court, 48
Table 3–2.  Frequency of Judicial Rotation: The General Practice of Trial Courts, 51
Table 3–3.  Trial Judges' Perceptions of the Influence of Divisional Assignment Criteria in Their Courts, 52
Table 3–4.  Proportion of Circuit-riding Judges by Size of Court, 54
Table 3–5.  Trial Judges' Length of Assignment Under Statewide Systems, 55
Table 3–6.  Utilization of Individual and Master Calendar by Size of Court, 57
Table 3–7.  Variety of Judicial Work by Size of Court, 63
Table 3–8.  Trial Judges' Time on Community Relations Activities by Presence of Statewide Assignment, 70
Table 3–9.  Length of Trial Judges' Most Common Work Day by Presence of Circuit-riding, by Court Size, 70
Table 3–10. The Impact of Task Rationalization upon Trial Judges' Waiting Time, by Assignment, 74
Table 4–1.  Trial Judges' Evaluation of the Skills of Criminal and Civil Attorneys in Their Courtrooms, 84
Table 4–2.  The Impact of Civil Attorney Skill at Preparing Decrees upon Trial Judges' Preparation and Writing of Decisions, 88

| | |
|---|---|
| Table 4-3. | The Impact of Criminal Attorney Skills upon Trial Judges' Waiting Time, 89 |
| Table 4-4. | The Impact of Criminal Attorney Skill at Negotiation upon Judges' Nonjury and Jury Trial Work, 90 |
| Table 4-5. | Trial Judges' Estimate of the Stability of Prosecutors and Defense Counsel in Their Courtrooms, 91 |
| Table 4-6. | The Impact of Defense Attorney Stability upon Trial Judges' Plea Bargaining, Nonjury, and Jury Trial Work, 93 |
| Table 4-7. | The Impact of Prosecuting Attorney Stability upon Trial Judges' Plea Bargaining Work, 94 |
| Table 4-8. | Trial Judges' Estimate of the Concentration of Plaintiff and Defense Counsel in Their Courtrooms, 95 |
| Table 4-9. | The Impact of Community Size upon Civil Attorney Stability, 96 |
| Table 5-1. | Trial Judges' Level of Law Clerk Services, 105 |
| Table 5-2. | The Impact of Law Clerk Services upon Trial Judges' Preparing and Writing of Decisions, 107 |
| Table 5-3. | Trial Judges' Level of Secretarial Services, 110 |
| Table 5-4. | The Impact of Courtroom Personnel Efficiency upon Trial Judges' Waiting Time, 114 |
| Table 6-1. | Initial (and Interim) Selection Methods for Trial Judges in the States, 123 |
| Table 6-2. | Trial Judges' Report of the Method of Their Selection, 124 |
| Table 6-3. | Trial Judges' Immediate Prior Occupation, 125 |
| Table 6-4. | Occupational Paths to the Trial Bench by State, 126 |
| Table 6-5. | The Impact of Age upon Judicial Assignments, 132 |
| Table 6-6. | The Impact of Age upon Trial Judges' Interpersonal Tasks, 133 |
| Table 6-7. | The Impact of Immediate Prior Occupation upon Trial Judges' Frequency of Criminal and Civil Negotiation, 137 |
| Table 6-8. | Trial Judges' Length of Service on the Bench, 138 |
| Table 7-1. | Trial Judges' Perceptions of the Most Important Area of Job Satisfaction, 155 |
| Table 7-2. | The Impact of Court Politics upon Trial Judges' Perceptions of Their Work Environment, 159 |
| Table 7-3. | Trial Judges' Evaluation of Their Skills in Five Areas of Work, 162 |
| Table 8-1. | Trial Judges' Style of Participation in Plea Discussions, 175 |
| Table 8-2. | Trial Judges' Style of Participation in Civil Settlement Discussions, 177 |
| Table 8-3. | The Impact of Court Rules upon Trial Judges' Style in Plea Discussions, 180 |
| Table 8-4. | The Impact of Civil Attorney Skill at Settlement upon Trial Judges' Style in Settlement Discussions, 185 |

## List of Tables

| | |
|---|---|
| Table 8–5. | The Impact of Trial Time Pressures upon Judges' Style in Plea Discussions, *186* |
| Table 8–6. | The Impact of Trial Time Pressures upon Judges' Style in Civil Settlement Discussions, *187* |
| Table 8–7. | The Impact of Trial Judges' Skill at Negotiation upon Their Style in Plea Discussions, *187* |
| Table 8–8. | The Impact of Trial Judges' Skill at Negotiation upon Their Style in Civil Settlement Discussions, *188* |
| Table 8–9. | Causes of Variation in Judicial Styles in Plea and Settlement Discussions: A Summary, *191* |
| Table 9–1. | Judicial Perceptions of Community Pressures in Chicago, Los Angeles, and Philadelphia, *202* |
| Table 9–2. | Immediate Prior Occupation of Trial Judges in Chicago, Los Angeles, and Philadelphia, *205* |
| Table 9–3. | Judicial Assignments in Chicago, Los Angeles, and Philadelphia, *208* |
| Table 9–4. | Trial Judges' Style in Civil Settlement Discussions in Chicago, Los Angeles, and Philadelphia, *212* |
| Table 9–5. | Trial Judges' Level of Intervention in Nonjury Trials in Chicago, Los Angeles, and Philadelphia, *213* |
| Table 9–6. | Judicial Perceptions of the Work Environment in Chicago, Los Angeles, and Philadelphia, *215* |
| Table 9–7. | Trial Judges' Perceptions of the Influence of Court Politics on Assignments in Chicago, Los Angeles, and Philadelphia, *218* |
| Table 9–8. | Trial Judges' Perceptions of the Influence of Case Disposition Rate on Assignments in Chicago, Los Angeles, and Philadelphia, *219* |
| Table A–1. | Listing of Fifteen Trial Courts Selected for Field Observation, *259* |
| Table A–2. | Selection Criteria for Observations: Characteristics of Fifteen Trial Courts in 1976, *260* |
| Table B–1. | Response Rate by State and Region, *274* |

# LIST OF FIGURES

Figure 1-1.  The Impact of Organizational and Individual Influences on Trial Judges Work: A General Framework, 9
Figure 2-1.  Length of Trial Judges' Most Common Work Day, 27
Figure 2-2.  Proportion of Trial Judges Reporting Specific Tasks on Their Most Common Work Day, 29
Figure 2-3a. Time Spent in Jury Trial Work on Judicial Work Days, by Type of Assignment, 36
Figure 2-3b. Time Spent in Nonjury Trial Work on Judicial Work Days, by Type of Assignment, 37
Figure 3-1.  Distribution of Trial Judges by Court Type, 60
Figure 3-2.  Frequency of Jury and Nonjury Trial Work by Size of Court, 64
Figure 3-3.  A Summary of the Relationships Between Frequency of Tasks and Size of Court, 65
Figure 3-4.  A Summary of the Relationships Between Time Spent on Tasks and Size of Court, 67
Figure 4-1.  Trial Judges' Differentiation of the Skills of Criminal and Civil Attorneys: A Spatial Analysis, 86
Figure 5-1.  The Impact of Law Clerk Services upon Trial Judges' Keeping Up with the Law, by Size of Court, 108
Figure 5-2.  The Distribution of Law Clerk Services by Size of Court: Actual Distribution Versus Distribution Based upon Estimated Need, 109
Figure 5-3.  Trial Judges' Perceptions of the Efficiency of Their Courtroom Personnel, 113
Figure 6-1.  Distribution of the Current Age of Trial Judges, 129
Figure 7-1.  Trial Judges' Perceptions of Their Skill Utilization, 149
Figure 7-2.  Trial Judges' Perceptions of Their Control over Work Time, 150
Figure 7-3.  Trial Judges' Perceptions of Their Caseload Pressures, 151
Figure 7-4.  Trial Judges' Perceptions of Their Caseload Variety, 152
Figure 7-5.  Trial Judges' Perceptions of Their Salary, 153
Figure 7-6.  The Impact of Size of Court upon Trial Judges' Perceptions of Their Work Environment, 156
Figure 7-7.  The Impact of Civil Attorney Skill at Case Preparation and Management upon Trial Judges' Perceptions of Their Work Environment, 158

# List of Figures

Figure 7-8.   Centrality of Skill Areas to Trial Judges' Perceptions of Skill Utilization, *164*

Figure 8-1.   Frequency of Judicial Participation in Plea and Settlement Discussions by Size of Court, *182*

Figure 8-2.   The Impact of Prosecutor Stability upon Trial Judges' Participation in Plea Discussions, *184*

# Foreword

The life of a judge can be lonely and burdensome. On appointment or election to the bench, the judge faces a traumatic transition from lawyer to judge, from partisan advocate to impartial magistrate. Often, this is not an easy metamorphosis, particularly if the person has followed an aggressive, gregarious, political career in the community. Inevitably, isolation displaces fraternalization, and barriers emerge to establish restraints on everyday behavior.

Surprisingly, little authentic writing has appeared to document the life and times of a judge, his work and environment, his work patterns and styles of judicial performance, and what it means to be a judge in America's trial courts. There have been occasional biographies and studies of judges in the aggregate, but none have explored the world of trial court judges.

At long last, with the publication of this book, a deliberate and conscientious investigation of judges in action becomes available. Myths give way to facts, and intuition—sometimes right but more often wrong—is replaced by the revelations of the 3,032 trial judges who returned questionnaires to the American Judicature Society in 1977.

This study of general jurisdiction judges contains surprising disclosures. Only 12 percent of all trial judges sit exclusively on criminal cases; the greater number of judges deal with the spectrum of civil and criminal matters. Only judges in criminal and specialized assignments have relatively little variety in their daily work; most identify different work days. Judges work longer hours than most court watchers generally report. The work patterns of trial judges are heavily influenced by court size: as the size of the court increases, the percentage of judges engaged in specific tasks similarly increases. The recurring controversy over whether the master or individual calendar produces a more effective use of judicial time is short-circuited by the conclusion from these data that there are no significant differences. The point may require further investigation. Rather than rely on guesswork, it is interesting to find an indication that attorneys play a major role in defining judicial work patterns: the "adversariness of attorneys" impacts on what and how much judges will do. Furthermore, the judge's work is often a reflection of the level of familiarity or stability of the total workgroup.

These are simply a handful of the fascinating and illuminating insights which can be gleaned from *American Trial Judges*. It is a pioneering attempt. Even though more complete documentation of much discussed here may have to await further research and probing, this book should be read by all who are concerned with the operation of one highly important component of America's justice system: the trial judges.

In a day when the public complains that the dispute resolution process costs too much, takes too long, and is never over, this book is indispensable reading for the chief justices of state supreme courts, court administrators, presiding judges, judicial educators, and bar association presidents—in fact, all those who are accountable for the management of America's courts. Here is a beginning for understanding, and with understanding perhaps the promise of finding ways to improve and elevate judicial performance.

ERNST JOHN WATTS<br>
Dean<br>
The National Judicial College

# PREFACE

This is a book about the work of American trial judges. It fills what we perceive to be a substantial gap in the growing literature on trial courts. Except for a few autobiographical accounts by judges themselves, there is precious little information on or analysis of the work trial judges do. Of the significant amount of literature on the role of the trial judge that has emerged in the last decade, most treats the judge in a highly abstract way with little reference to concrete tasks. In one sense, these studies place the cart before the horse. Meaningful role orientations probably cannot be developed without reference to the working world of trial judges. Indeed, a number of these studies look not to what trial judges do but to role characterizations of appellate judges for inspiration.

We have spent much time observing judges at work and collecting quantifiable information through a mail survey. We observed in the courtrooms and chambers of forty judges situated in eight states. We surveyed *all* the trial judges in the fifty states and the District of Columbia who serve in courts of general jurisdiction (and received a creditable 63 percent response). As a result, we have an extensive and unusually rich data base on America's trial judges. To our knowledge, it is the only such data base.

This book is intended for several audiences. It is, quite naturally, directed to researchers of the judicial process. We have attempted to apply the methods and analytic perspective of social science research to a legal setting. An organizational model, which draws upon the dominant contemporary perspectives on trial courts, has been adopted to explain variations in judicial work. Secondarily, we intend the book to be a useful reference work and supplementary reading in advanced undergraduate and graduate courses in the judicial process.

Beyond these academic audiences, the book is also directed to a variety of practitioner audiences—most notably, national and state judicial education programs and court administrative offices. Much of our data should assist planners of judicial education programs in designing their curriculum and courses. In more extended programs (such as the National Judicial College in Reno), the book can serve as a text or supplementary reading for specific courses. Similarly, state and especially local trial court administrators should find useful our analysis of various local management practices and their effects upon the performance of judicial work.

We wish to acknowledge many individuals for their assistance in the conduct of this research. Judges R. Paul Campbell of Bellefonte, Pennsylvania, and Robert Wenke of Los Angeles, and Professors Beverly Blair Cook, Herbert Jacob, and David W. Neubauer served ably on our advisory committee by offering suggestions in data collection and by reading portions or all of the manuscript. We are grateful for the comments of several formal reviewers of our manuscript, including Professors Wes Skogan and Lawrence Redlinger. Finally, we are indebted to our research colleagues at the American Judicature Society (AJS) who read and incisively critiqued portions of the manuscript: Jim Alfini, Rachel Doan, Chuck Grau, Marcia Lipetz, Lee Luskin, and Malcolm Rich. Without the supportive intellectual environment of a place like AJS, this book would not have been possible.

We are further indebted to the AJS librarian, Tim Pyne, who assisted tirelessly in bibliographic work; to Northwestern graduate student Andrew Van Esso, who served as the *de facto* project manager in the data management stages; to Northwestern graduate students Robert Harmel and Frances Gragg, who also assisted in data collection and management; to Northwestern undergraduate students Susan Barth and Sandra Berman, who completed by themselves the coding of 3,000 cases; and to Sharyn Eierman of AJS, who typed the entire manuscript in its many revised forms with flawless accuracy and perseverance.

We thank the judges who participated in the study, both those who responded to our long questionnaire and especially those who agreed to be observed in their courtrooms and chambers. These latter forty judges truly permitted a substantial invasion of privacy in order to facilitate our study; most did so not grudgingly but with patience, understanding, and good cheer.

Finally, we acknowledge the National Science Foundation, which funded this research under Grant APR76–14964, and the support of Law, Science, and Technology Program Manager Arthur F. Konopka.

All the assistance notwithstanding, we alone are responsible for the interpretations and analyses presented herein and for any errors of omission or commission.

JPR

# PART I

# Introduction

# CHAPTER 1

## In Search of Judging

THE American trial judge is a crucial figure in the business of dispensing justice, yet we know surprisingly little about the men and women who occupy this office. In particular, we know little of their habits, patterns, and styles of work.

Images of the role and working life of the trial judge abound in popular culture and research, but these are a curious mixture of fictions and half-truths. Judges look dignified, aloof, perhaps even irrelevant in courtroom dramas on television. Real judges who are portrayed on the evening news, or who are the subject of an investigative documentary, are often corrupt, senile, eccentric, or soft-hearted in their sentencing or bail-setting practices. Court-watching groups often leave the impression that most judges work only a few hours each day. Finally, researchers have all too frequently viewed trial judging as a poor stepchild of appellate judging, without coming to grips with the differences in the work and functions of appellate and trial courts.

Trial judges are all of these characterizations—in individual cases—and yet none of them as a group. A few sitting judges have been convicted of a crime. Some judges, old or physically incapacitated, have been removed from the bench by disciplinary commissions. Some judges do sentence defendants contrary to popular norms, or even very differently from their own colleagues on the bench. Some judges do work only a few hours on most days. And a few trial judges do perform tasks more closely akin to appellate judges, as in hearing only motions for new trials. Nevertheless, the functions as well as actual performance of American trial judges differ from these images and reflect much diversity.

It is the actions of criminal court judges that are most familiar to Americans, through the media and contemporary research. Most judges, however, do *not* sit in criminal court. In fact, only 12 percent of all trial judges in the country hear exclusively criminal cases. Some judges hear only civil matters, or some subset of civil cases—e.g., domestic relations or probate. Most judges hear the entire range of criminal and civil cases.

The diversity of trial judging extends beyond differences in the types of cases to be heard. Judges across America sit in all different-sized courts. In Los Angeles, a judge sits with more than one hundred fifty fellow trial judges. In Milwaukee, thirty-three judges serve side by side. In Omaha, twelve judges sit in the courthouse. Throughout the rest of Nebraska, though, one-judge courts predominate. Many judges ride circuit to fulfill their responsibilities, not in horse-drawn carriages but in the motorized trappings of the late twentieth century. Still, most judges, in large and small courts, stay put in one courthouse. Judges in some courts bear the entire responsibility for managing their caseloads, including the scheduling of cases and attorneys. Judges in other courts have yielded that case management responsibility to a centralized office under the supervision of the chief judge or court administrator. Judges are part of a stable workgroup in some courts by virtue of their working with the same (small) group of attorneys day in and out, whereas in other courts judges are part of a constantly shifting workgroup that rarely contains familiar faces. And in some courts judges must be law clerks, administrative assistants, and secretaries, as well as judges, while elsewhere trial judges have access to some or all such courthouse resources. These and other organizational elements of courts define the structure of judicial work in America.

The diversity of trial judging, then, is our most significant, if basic, finding. Yet it is not a finding that could easily be gleaned from the available materials on trial judges and courts. Accounts by trial judges themselves are little more than autobiographical case studies.[1] The stories are sometimes quite vivid, as Botein's description of how he got involved in club politics in New York or recollections from his first cases on the bench.[2] The descriptions are sometimes revealing of work patterns, as Gignoux's emphasis on the legal research tasks of a federal district judge.[3] Yet it is difficult to know whether, or how, to piece these disparate accounts together.

Outsiders who have looked into the world of trial judges constitute a much more significant literature. The most extensive and systematic is the work of Herbert Jacob.[4] His images on the nature of judging—analogizing the trial judge to a tax agent or factory worker—hold a dominant position in the literature of the social sciences. Other researchers and commentators have scrutinized trial judges in more specific contexts—e.g., plea bargaining,[5] sentencing,[6] and the conduct of trials.[7] In these task situations, the emphasis has centered upon the *diffusion* of judicial responsibility—to prosecutors, parole boards, and attorneys.[8] In an interesting way, these more specific views of the working life of the trial judge converge with Jacob's overall assessment. The metaphors of tax agent and, especially, factory worker are consonant with a low level of discretion and substantial diffusion of responsibility.

Why do judges, looking outside, see their work in a light different from those who observe and analyze them? In part, of course, it is a difference in perspective: the subjective versus objective, the experiential versus analytic. Yet it is also a function of the diversity of trial judges and their work. Botein began his judicial career in civil court; Gignoux was exposed to the intellectual complexity of cases in the federal trial courts. In contrast, most researchers have studied predominantly, if not exclusively, the criminal courts.

This brief inquiry into the literature of trial judging highlights the need to know much more about what judges do, what perceptions they hold, and how their work and perceptions interact. If we are interested in building or refining theories about the legal process, knowledge of the work of trial judges is essential. For example, it is important to know the working environment of judges as one basis for assessing the empirical validity of competing theories of the political functions of courts—"due process," "cooptational," and "conspiratorial" among others. How (and how much) are tasks and goals shared between judge and attorneys? In what organizational contexts is the judge most or least likely to be coopted by an experienced prosecutor or a knowledgeable attorney? Is judicial "independence" in work actually similar to isolation? The answers to these questions require more empirical information about what trial judges do.

Meanwhile, the general public is also beginning to ask about the nature of judicial work, though for different reasons. The perceived need to evaluate the performance of sitting judges is one reason. As courts become more visible in their communities, citizens and interest groups are asking hard questions about specific judicial actions. Sometimes such questions occur in the context of monitoring ongoing performance; in other instances, the questions are directed toward a coming election for judicial offices. In either case, it is essential for citizens to know more about the work of trial judges than how they sentence. Bar polling efforts (surveys of lawyers' opinions) provide the public with some additional information on specific judges, but information usually restricted in focus to "legal competence." The skills that trial judges are called upon to demonstrate on a day-to-day basis extend well beyond legal competence. Thus, the forums in which judicial performance may be evaluated—public, media, bar—can uniformly benefit from a comprehensive portrait of the work of trial judges.

Special publics, more intimately involved with the selection, education and training, and discipline and removal of judges, also have expressed a need to know more about the range of judicial work in the trial courts. Nonlawyer members of judicial nominating commissions, in their search for the proper attributes and mix of skills in potential judges, need to know what kinds of tasks their candidates are likely to confront. Planners of ongoing judicial education programs, especially at the national level, currently are required to design curricula without knowing much about the distribution of judicial work or even the characteristics of judges likely to attend. State discipline and removal commissions, designed to safeguard the public from extreme forms of abuse of judicial office, need to know the content of judicial tasks as well as the dynamics within which work takes place—especially organizational and ideological conflicts between bench and bar. For each of these special interest publics concerned with judges, the need to know more about the substance and style of judicial work has already been, or should soon be, well established.

On both theoretical and policy-related grounds, then, the gap between what we know about trial judges at work and what we should know is much too large. In the balance of this opening chapter, we provide a framework for studying judicial work in the trial courts, with attention to questions of focus, theory, analysis, and methods of data collection.

## A Framework for Studying Judicial Work

### FOCUS: CONCEPTUALIZING TASKS

The literature on trial judges typically focuses upon one slice of a judge's work. The judge is characterized as adjudicator, umpire, bureaucrat, docket manager, negotiator, or disposer of cases. These selective portraits of judicial work and functions need to be drawn together to permit a more accurate and comprehensive picture. Each trial judge, in a sense, is all of these characterizations (and others), in some mix.

Our eclectic view of judicial work encompasses six quite different task areas. These are adjudication, administration, community relations, legal research, negotiation, and affiliation. Most trial judges devote some time to each of these task areas, though the exact mix depends upon elements of court structure, the characteristics of attorneys, available courthouse resources, the characteristics of judges, and judicial perceptions of the work environment.

By *adjudication,* we mean formal legal decision-making in an adversary setting. This includes the tasks associated with presiding at a trial (ruling on objections, charging a jury, rendering a verdict or imposing sentence). Also included would be most tasks performed in pretrial settings—e.g., conducting preliminary hearings or ruling on motions—and tasks in posttrial settings—e.g., ruling on appeal motions or postconviction bond hearings. These are the tasks most commonly associated with judging, and they typically take place in the courtroom.

*Administration* refers to tasks involving the court with external agencies (e.g., state legislatures, county boards) as well as the development and regulation of internal procedures. Examples of the former would be budget discussions, liaison, and even subtle forms of lobbying (e.g., for a bill providing for more judges or higher pay). These tasks are likely to be performed by a presiding judge, elected by his peers to represent the court in questions that revolve around the self-interest and well-being of individual judges *qua* workers. Administrative tasks of an internal nature would include staffing of courtroom personnel, courtroom security, the assignment and scheduling of cases, and general correspondence, all of which have to do with facilitating the normal work of courts. The average trial judge is likely to be involved in doing some or all of these tasks, either directly or by contact with such intermediaries as assignment judges or a court administrator. These activities mostly take place outside the courtroom, usually far from public view.

*Community relations* refers to activities that bring the trial judge into contact with the general public or "selected" publics (i.e., civic and political leaders). Through speeches, informal talks and interviews, and press conferences, judges communicate to the public facts or images about judging and courts. A presiding judge may do the bulk of this work for a court, but individual judges involved in highly publicized cases may also share in such work. In a slightly different context, some judges also have contact with local community elites who may have been instrumental in their selection to the bench or who may seek their advice on matters of public policy. These are the tasks perhaps least often associated with judging, and they may be performed away from the courthouse in the institutions of the larger community (city hall, prisons, halfway houses).

*Legal research* includes the basic task elements of reading and writing. Written decisions and judgments are part of the work of the trial judge in state as well as federal trial courts. Reading—keeping up with the law through reporters, journals, statutes, court rules, and social science research—is an essential, if marginally visible, task of the contemporary trial judge. These activities are conducted in chambers when an occasional sound of silence sweeps by, or at home, where the distractions of the courthouse seem far away.

*Negotiation* refers to a range of tasks designed to resolve civil and criminal cases without recourse to a trial. This would include presence at, if not direct participation in, plea or settlement discussions, as well as interactions with other figures who seek to influence such discussions (e.g., insurance company claims representatives or probation officers). The forum for discussions may be a formally scheduled conference in chambers or casual meetings in hallways, cafeterias, or other places away from the glare of the courtroom.

Finally, *affiliation*-related tasks are part of the work of trial judges. Modern psychology has demonstrated that the morale of any workgroup is an essential ingredient in promoting productivity, and courts would seem to be no exception. Judges are required to spend at least a little time in keeping up the spirits of co-workers, especially court personnel who are usually hired and assigned by others. Many judicial tasks, particularly those related to negotiation and community relations, involve a significant interpersonal component.

This conceptual overview of the tasks trial judges perform reflects the breadth of our idea of judicial performance. It is, to be sure, an empirical idea, rooted in the realities of trial judging across the country on a day-to-day basis. Accordingly, individual judges can be expected to vary in the emphasis they give—in the allocation of their work time—to these six distinct task areas. But why?

## THEORY: SEARCHING FOR CAUSES OF WORK PATTERNS

The application of organization theory to trial courts provides a significant point of departure for identifying classes of variables which might influence trial judges' work patterns. Most recently, the focus of empirical research has been upon individual actors in criminal courts—prosecutors, public defenders, judges—and how they shape or adjust to the constraints of the court. Eisenstein and Jacob discovered, within individual courtrooms, the formation of stable workgroups whose primary purpose was to dispose of felony cases.[9] Heumann found adaptation, or learning, to be an important process for "newcomers"—be they prosecutors, defense attorneys, or judges—as each tried to cope with the realities of plea bargaining.[10] Whether these theories of interpersonal relationships extend beyond negotiation tasks in criminal courts remains to be determined.

More general notions of organization theory may also be applicable in the study of judging. The concept of "worker morale" seems especially ripe for transfer to court actors, particularly judges, given the imagery often associated with judicial tasks in trial courts ("boring," "mind-deadening"). The intellectual roots of morale can be found in early-nineteenth-century utopian thinkers who sought, among other things, to harmonize man with the environment in which he worked.[11] Contemporary perspectives draw upon this approach by utilizing the demon of science to isolate empirical phenomena—like decentralized decision-making and flexible working hours—that contribute to worker morale and (more important) to worker productivity.[12] Although judges work in organizations that are not highly structured, the basic idea—that morale is positively related to performance—is highly plausible and testable within courts. All too often, observers have been unwilling to ascribe to judges the potential range of motivations that characterize workers. Judges work, albeit not in factories or on assembly lines.

Attention to the structural characteristics of organizations is also in keeping with the growing literature of judicial administration that describes courts from a management perspective.[13] Though this literature contains few specific hypotheses or empirical findings about the relationship between structure and individual judicial performance, the variables highlighted—size, specialization, allocation of work—are those which are significant in most organizations. Such literature, although weak in theory, provides a proximate handle on how courts are organized in a formal or structural, rather than informal or interpersonal, sense. This complementary approach to courts—as formal and informal organizations—provides the essential contours of our theoretical framework for studying judicial work patterns.[14]

## ANALYSIS: DELINEATION OF A FRAMEWORK AND VARIABLES

Having described the focus of this book—the nature and patterns of judicial work in the trial courts—and a few potentially applicable theories for studying variations, we briefly turn to a description of our analysis strategy. Figure 1-1 sketches, in relational form, the key classes of variables that will be the subject of our inquiry.

The figure illustrates our view that the styles and patterns of judicial work are a function of several sets of variables. Our primary attention will be given to the *organizational* influences that are external to the judge but nevertheless a part of the court system. These influences include elements of court struc-

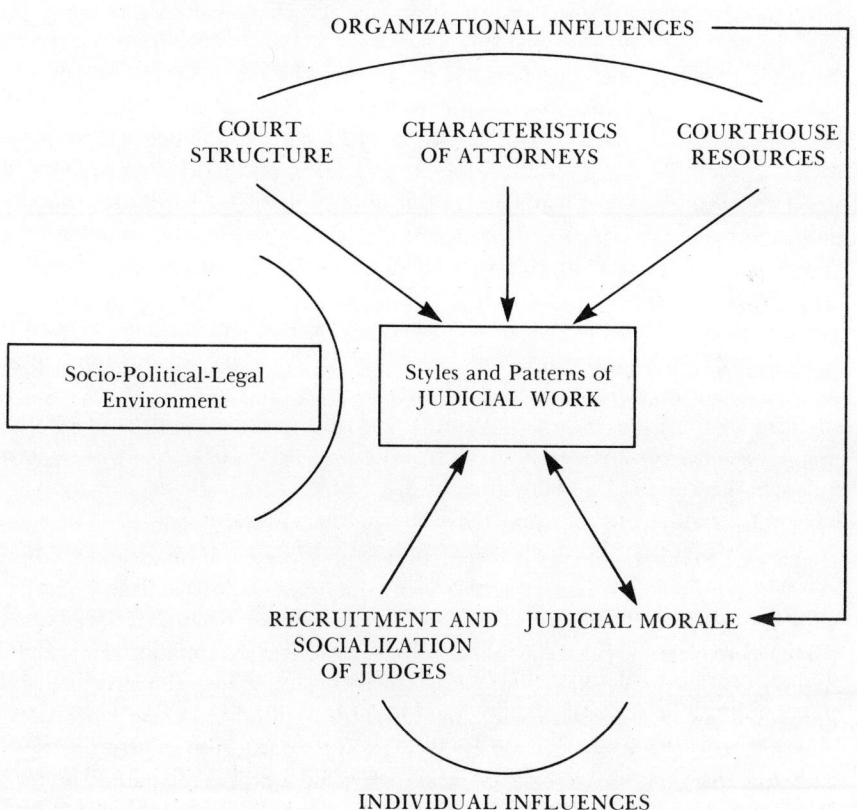

FIGURE 1-1  The Impact of Organizational and Individual Influences on Trial Judges' Work: A General Framework

ture, characteristics of attorneys, and the availability of human resources in the courthouse. Secondarily, we will examine the *individual-level* influences that inhere in the judge as a professional worker or human being. These include personal background and experiences, on-the-job learning and adaptation (socialization), and perceptions of the work environment (morale).

Judicial morale interacts with other variables in the model in a conceptually complex way. The perceptions of judges about their work environment are not independent of organizational influences. That is, elements of court structure, characteristics of attorneys, and courthouse resources affect how a judge will view his job; thus, the line drawn from organizational influences to judicial morale in Figure 1-1. Furthermore, there is a reciprocal relationship, or feedback, between morale and judicial work. Not only do elements of morale influence the way in which judges work, but that work will, in turn, influence how judges come to view their environment. This is visually represented by a double-headed arrow in Figure 1-1 between morale and judicial work.

Finally, it is important to remember that courts do not exist in a "work vacuum." The context of judging is influenced by the larger political, social, and legal environments of the communities in which courts are located. The political environment, for example, influences the salience of community relations work. Judges may need visibility, with the voters or the party, in order to be re-elected. In some communities, judges may be part of the local "ruling elite" by virtue of their personal friendships and political ties. Even the content of trial judges' decisions is likely to be influenced by the political environment, as Dolbeare demonstrated for urban zoning and land use cases.[15] The social or cultural environment of the community helps to shape the attitudes and perceptions of courtroom participants.[16] For example, the life-style of a community, its racial composition, and the mix of social classes shape professional as well as citizen views of crime and social justice. Finally, the legal environment—through case law, court rules, and the organized bar—influence judges' working relationships with attorneys.[17] These various environmental influences are important, indeed essential, for coming to a balanced understanding of the functions of trial courts. But they are rarely primary or proximate influences on the composition of judicial work. Rather, the environment provides the context or boundaries within which organizational and individual-level variables impact upon the work of trial judges.

Our chapter plan for the book flows directly from this framework. We first examine, in Chapter 2, what judges actually do, the work patterns of trial judges across the country. Then Chapters 3 through 5 analyze the impacts of organizational influences on work patterns. In Chapter 3, the reader is introduced to the diversity of trial court structures—notably, size, specialization, circuit-riding, and case assignment systems. Chapter 4 examines the characteristics of attorneys, including adversariness, skill, and courtroom tenure. Chapter 5 describes the range of courthouse and courtroom personnel potentially available to trial judges, giving special attention to the role of law clerks in facilitating legal research. Chapters 6 and 7 analyze the impact of the individual characteristics, attributes, and perceptions of judges upon their work. In Chapter 6 we examine the formal and informal recruitment processes for trial judges as well as the techniques of socialization utilized by trial courts. Chapter 7 explores judges' perceptions of their work environment, from which we draw inferences about their morale. Chapters 8 and 9 offer selective views of judicial performance, limited either by task area or by community. In Chapter 8 we analyze judicial styles of negotiation in criminal and civil cases. Chapter 9 examines the impact of political, social, and legal environments by comparing judging in three quite different communities: Chicago, Los Angeles, and Philadelphia. Finally, Chapter 10 provides a summary and highlighting of major findings, as well as a discussion of the theoretical and policy implications of our study.

A METHODOLOGICAL OVERVIEW

We limited our scope of data collection to trial judges serving in courts of general jurisdiction in the fifty states and the District of Columbia. Excluded are trial judges serving in the federal district courts. The work patterns of these judges have already been subject to some systematic scrutiny.[18] Further, federal courts are quite different from the state trial courts in structure and jurisdiction, making comparisons difficult. Also excluded are judges serving in the lower state trial courts and in specialized jurisdiction courts. These judges do not perform the same diverse range of work as their colleagues in the upper-level trial court. Our universe of inquiry, then, is the approximately five thousand judges serving in trial courts of general jurisdiction in the states.

We collected both observational and survey data. First, we set out to observe judges in as wide a variety of environmental and organizational settings as possible. To accomplish this, we observed (in 1976) some forty judges in fifteen courts across eight states, for a period of three to five days per judge. The observations were comprehensive in that we had access to judges not only in the courtroom but in chambers, other courthouse offices, and (sometimes) in the community. We attempted to be, as one newspaper characterized our observer, "the judge's shadow." For a more descriptive, analytic, and personal view of the observational process, see Appendix A.

Our survey instrument was grounded in, and guided by, the observational experience. In addition, a limited pretest was undertaken to sharpen the final instrument. We subsequently mailed an eight-page questionnaire, in May 1977, to all trial judges serving in courts of general jurisdiction in the states and the District of Columbia. Pursuant to several follow-up appeals, we received a healthy 63 percent response (n = 3,032). For a fuller description of the development and administration of the mail survey, including a sample of the final instrument, refer to Appendices B and C.

Taken together, our observational and survey-based data constitute a significant foundation on which to build and refine descriptions and theories of judging. We rely most directly on our survey data, because they are more readily quantifiable and statistically representative.[19] Nevertheless, we intersperse observational data throughout our analysis to provide in-depth focus or vivid example.

## Notes

1. See, for example, Bernard Botein, *Trial Judge* (New York: Simon & Schuster, 1952); Edward Gignoux, "A Trial Judge's View," *Massachusetts Law Quarterly*, 50 (1965); Charles A. Wyzanski, *A Trial Judge's Freedom and Responsibility* (New York: Association of the Bar of the City of New York, 1952).
2. Botein, *Trial Judge*, pp. 16-20, 25-38.
3. Gignoux, "A Trial Judge's View," p. 103.
4. Herbert Jacob, *Justice in America* (Boston: Little, Brown, 1965), and *idem, Urban Justice: Law and Order in American Cities* (Englewood Cliffs, N.J.: Prentice-Hall, 1973).
5. Albert W. Alschuler, "The Trial Judge's Role in Plea Bargaining, Part I," *Columbia Law Review*, 76 (1976), and Kathleen Gallagher, "Judicial Participation in Plea Bargaining: A Search for New Standards," *Harvard Civil Rights-Civil Liberties Law Review*, 9 (1974).
6. Marvin E. Frankel, *Criminal Sentences: Law Without Order* (New York: Hill & Wang, 1972), and Dean Jaros and Robert I. Mendelsohn, "The Judicial Role and Sentencing Behavior," *Midwest Journal of Political Science*, 11 (1967).
7. Stephen A. Saltzburg, "The Unnecessarily Expanding Role of the American Trial Judge," *Virginia Law Review*, 64 (1978).
8. Abraham S. Blumberg, *Criminal Justice* (Chicago: Quadrangle, 1967).
9. James Eisenstein and Herbert Jacob, *Felony Justice: An Organizational Analysis of Criminal Courts* (Boston: Little, Brown, 1977).
10. Milton Heumann, *Plea Bargaining: The Experiences of Prosecutors, Judges, and Defense Attorneys* (Chicago: University of Chicago Press, 1977).
11. The utopian communities founded by Robert Owen (New Lanark, New Harmony), Charles Fourier (Brook Farm), and John Humphrey Noyes (Oneida) are particularly good examples of institutionalized concern for the conditions under which workers labored. For a summary of these and other utopian communities, see Mark Holloway, *Heavens on Earth: Utopian Communities in America 1680-1880* (New York: Dover, 1966).
12. See, for example, Warren S. Bollmeier and Waino W. Suojanen, "Job Enrichment and Organizational Change," *Atlanta Economic Review*, 24 (1974); Daniel Katz and Robert L. Kahn, *Social Psychology of Organizations* (New York: Wiley, 1966); Edwin Locke, "Nature and Causes of Job Satisfaction," in Marvin Dunnette (ed.), *Handbook of Industrial and Organizational Psychology* (Chicago: Rand McNally, 1976); Edward Lawler III, *Motivation in Work Organization* (Monterey, Calif.: Brooks/Cole, 1973); and Barry M. Staw, Karl Weick and, Paul S. Goodman (eds.), *New Directions in Organizational Behavior* (Chicago: St. Clair Press, 1976).

13. See, for example, Ernest C. Friesen, Jr., Edward C. Gallas, and Nesta M. Gallas, *Managing the Courts* (Indianapolis: Bobbs-Merrill, 1971); Russell R. Wheeler and Howard R. Whitcomb (eds.), *Judicial Administration: Text and Readings* (Englewood Cliffs, N.J.: Prentice-Hall, 1977); Larry C. Berkson, Steven W. Hays, and Susan J. Carbon (eds.), *Managing the State Courts* (St. Paul: West Publishing, 1977).
14. See Edward Clynch and David W. Neubauer, "Trial Courts as Organizations: A Critique," paper presented at the Annual Meeting of the Midwest Political Science Association, Chicago, 1977, for a critical review of the applicability of organization theory to trial courts.
15. Kenneth M. Dolbeare, *Trial Courts in Urban Politics* (New York: Wiley, 1967). For a brief discussion of the role of the political environment in criminal justice systems, see Eisenstein and Jacob, *Felony Justice*.
16. The best examples of the potential influence of "culture" or life-styles may come from fiction. See, for example, Albert Camus, *The Stranger* (New York: Alfred A. Knopf, 1946), and, more recently, John Gardner, *The Sunlight Dialogues* (New York: Ballantine, 1972).
17. For a consideration of the role of the "legal subculture" in the decisionmaking of federal courts, see Richard J. Richardson and Kenneth N. Vines, *The Politics of Federal Courts* (Boston: Little, Brown, 1970).
18. Federal Judicial Center, *The 1969-1970 Federal District Court Time Study* (Washington D.C.: Federal Judicial Center, 1971).
19. In the analyses of the survey data to follow, we do not use tests for statistical significance. We have attempted to study the universe of general jurisdiction judges sitting at the time of the survey (1977). The consequences of our failure to achieve a 100 percent response rate cannot be measured or controlled by significance tests, because the problem of nonresponders cannot properly be viewed as a sampling issue. See Ramon E. Henkel, *Tests of Significance*, Sage University Paper Series on Quantitative Applications in the Social Sciences 07-001 (Beverly Hills and London: Sage Publications, 1976). Rather, the potential for error in interpretation of data is a direct function of the proportion of nonresponders. Our robust 63 percent response rate ensures, within a small margin of error, the accuracy of inferences made to the total population of trial judges serving in courts of general jurisdiction in 1977. For further tests regarding the amount of bias, see Appendix B.

# PART II

# Organizational Influences on Judicial Work

# CHAPTER 2

## The Work Patterns of Trial Judges

*"Knowledge is limited as to how judges spend their professional time. The extent to which time is misplaced is a matter for conjecture."*
Friesen, Gallas, and Gallas, *Managing the Courts* (1971), p. 154.

WHAT do trial judges do in the course of a work day? What is the nature of the tasks they perform in the courtroom and in chambers? How do judges organize their work days, in terms of the sequence and the mix of tasks? Finally, how do judges hearing civil cases differ in their work days from those who hear criminal cases or from those in general assignment who hear both civil and criminal cases?

These are a few of the questions we shall seek to answer, based upon our observational impressions and national survey data. The purpose of this chapter is to provide a comprehensive overview of judicial work patterns. We hope to make the work of the trial judge come alive, for the composition of that work is crucial to an informed analysis of both policy and theoretical issues. We first present a simplified summary of the work of a judge of criminal, civil, and general assignment by following the judge chronologically through the events of a typical day as we saw them in the field. We then provide a series of data focusing on the variety, length, and substance of judges' work days drawn from our survey. In so doing, we examine differences in work days as reported by judges in criminal, civil, and general assignments.

## The Judge of Criminal Assignment: Time Management and the Flow of a Typical Day

A typical day for the judge of criminal assignment began around 9:00 A.M., when the judge arrived in chambers, read his mail, and skimmed the day's case files. The call of criminal cases generally started soon after but might be delayed if the judge were in conference with lawyers, or if lawyers were in conference with each other. More times than not, the judge and the court were forced to wait while lawyers concluded bargains, talked with clients, or hurried from an appearance in another courtroom. In many courts the call itself tended to be a rather chaotic process, with attorneys coming in and out of court, whispered plea negotiations continuing throughout the room (and sometimes back in chambers), and a variety of people approaching the clerk's desk (usually immediately adjacent to the bench) for one reason or another. In most instances, the criminal call not only served an attendance-taking function but afforded a review of the status of each case. The call could also assume some legal importance as defense lawyers jockeyed for advantageous (i.e., later) trial dates, while the judge used the threat of immediate trial as his own form of bargaining leverage. Often, short hearings, arraignments, the taking of guilty pleas, sentencings, and probation violations were disposed of in the criminal call.

After the completion of the call (or the first round), the judge might attend to some minor administrative matters, socialize with attorneys or court personnel, take a coffee break, or participate in case-related discussions with attorneys. Then, the judge might begin formal court proceedings—a motions hearing, a bench trial, or (most likely), a jury trial. These proceedings would continue for the rest of the morning, with adjournment around noon for a lunch break. While some judges gulped sandwiches at their desks and worked through lunch, most criminal judges lunched with court or law enforcement personnel, lawyer acquaintances, former political associates, or other judges. Occasionally judges attended bar luncheons, spoke at civic meetings, or participated in more specialized meetings such as judicial seminars, advisory board meetings of a halfway house, and the like. Frequently lunch conversations included mention of past and current cases, and from time to time some judicial business of a minor nature was transacted (usually pertaining to scheduling). However, politics, financial affairs, and travel plans were also common topics of conversation.

Returning to chambers somewhere between one hour and ninety minutes later, the judge might meet with some lawyers, catch up on correspondence, sign orders, or glance through the "advance sheets" (early publication of recent appellate cases) before the afternoon court session. After the court was reconvened, unfinished matters of the morning might again be taken up, whether continuation of the call or of a bench or jury trial. Jury proceedings were planned to begin and end for juror convenience; but while there might be a half-hour comfort break during the afternoon, many judges preferred to finish as much of the scheduled proceedings as possible before leaving for the day. Departure ranged anywhere from 3:00 to 6:00 P.M. or later, though the majority probably left sometime around 4:30 or so. The judge might attend to some minor matters after adjourning court or go to a meeting of the judiciary before leaving the building, but such activities were generally infrequent and not very lengthy. Most of the criminal judges whom we observed did not take case files or journals home, though some may have read the latter at home.

There were, of course, *variations* from the typical day described above. Some judges were restricted in their assignment to a more specialized set of tasks—e.g., hearing only pretrial motions and possibly the taking of guilty pleas, or conducting only nonjury trials. The repetition involved in these kinds of assignments could be truly characterized as "mind-deadening."[1] A seventy-three-year-old judge in one court tolerated a criminal motions assignment by looking forward to his impending retirement (within a few months) and by whimsically noting to the observer that these were the only types of proceedings that his fellow judges trusted him to conduct effectively. A fifty-two-year-old judge in another court recognized the relative "slowness" with which he proceeded on the criminal bench, no doubt explaining his assignment to nonjury work where his lack of speed would do the least damage to systemwide caseflow. In some of these courts, frequent rotation of assignments (every six months) spared continuation of such monotony, but in other courts rotation was much less frequent.

## The Judge of Civil Assignment: Time Management and the Flow of a Typical Day

A typical day for the judge of civil court usually began similarly to that of the criminal judge. The civil judge also arrived at his chambers around 9:00 A.M. and checked his mail and the day's docket. But since civil cases more frequently settle at the very last moment before, or even during, trial, judges regularly confirmed case status reports with their clerk early in the day. If a significant portion of cases had settled, many judges immediately attempted either to schedule other matters or to request additional cases from a central pool, depending upon what kind of case assignment system prevailed in their court. In general, early morning was filled with formal and informal settlement conferences. Although various locales assigned different titles to scheduled pretrial conferences, most judges at least mentioned settlement at any meeting of opposing lawyers—in the ready room, in chambers just before trial, and even at chance meetings in the hall.

Around mid-morning the civil judge convened court, sometimes conducting a call, which, like its criminal counterpart, served an attendance-taking as well as a scheduling function. Frequently, short hearings were disposed of, including the ratification of uncontested divorces, adoptions, name changes, etc. After the call, the judge might take a coffee break, socialize with courtroom personnel (he was less likely to know individual attorneys than the criminal court judge), or, because case settlement was an ever present goal, meet with assembled lawyers in yet another attempt to catalyze agreement between parties. If a jury trial were scheduled, the judge would try to begin before 11:00 A.M. To begin much later was regarded as pointless since a lunch break would intrude so early in the proceedings. If nearing lunchtime and no trial were ready, the judge might fill his time by reviewing orders, reading case files, meeting with his law clerk, or handling minor administrative tasks. Civil judges lunched with other judges more than they did with court personnel or lawyers, but conversation topics and actual lunchtime activities were similar to those of criminal judges. A higher percentage of civil than criminal judges, however, were involved with a variety of professional luncheon meetings.

After lunch, the civil judge might begin (or resume) a trial, but usually only after a brief conference with counsel to determine if they had agreed on anything during their lunch break. If not, trial might continue for the afternoon, two small cases might be heard, or a new, longer trial might begin. Because one lawyer or another might request a recess at any point in the proceedings, intimating that recent testimony or a phone call to an insurance representative could lead to a speedy settlement, most civil judges spent a fair amount of time either waiting for recessed lawyers to report or engaging in negotiations themselves, sometimes while the rest of the assembled courtroom waited. The late afternoon (after adjournment for the day) was reserved for business of a drop-in nature, catching up with opinions, legal research, and the like. Several civil judges had developed rather esoteric legal specialties and willingly reviewed all motions or matters on their specialties, either in this late afternoon period or at home. Most civil court judges left the courthouse about 4:00 or 4:30 P.M., with perhaps fewer very early or very late departures than criminal court judges. In part, this is a reflection of civil judges' greater ease in working in chambers. If the calendar fell apart, civil judges had a wider set of interests to fall back upon for productive time in chambers. In contrast, criminal judges often seemed driven by the "action" syndrome of the criminal courts. In quieter moments, those judges not interested in keeping up with criminal case law appeared to have little to occupy themselves.

The *variations* in the typical day of civil court judges stem primarily from the different case-types which constitute the heterogeneous category "civil."[2] For example chancery court judges hear cases involving disputes that cannot be resolved by the awarding of monetary damages. While in some states the distinction between "law" and "equity" has been eliminated by statutory reforms, in other states (particularly in the south) the distinction remains. By the nature of their cases, equity judges are rarely, if ever, involved with jury trials. The one equity judge whom we observed (in Chicago) did not even have any nonjury trials during the three days of observation, though this was not typical, according to his perceptions. He spent his time with a morning call (short hearings and motions) and some informal negotiations, and in the afternoons divided his time among case-related research, drafting of a decision in a highly publicized case, and preparation of materials for teaching a seminar for newly elected judges in the state's judicial education program.

The domestic relations judge is another whose work is entirely restricted to nonjury matters. We observed only one judge whose sole jurisdiction was devoted to this area, but we also observed at least two other judges whose civil caseload included a significant portion of family law work. The domestic relations judge observed in Philadelphia heard only issues relating to the children involved in divorce proceedings—i.e., custody and child-support payments. These narrow hearings, in open court, constituted his entire workload. A second judge, located in Nashville, heard a substantial amount of divorce trials and all related issues (alimony, property, custody, etc.). A third judge, in Los Angeles, was on a one-month "tour" of domestic relations cases and proudly announced to the observer that he had not taken one word of testimony in resolving an entire month's cases. Reflecting his informal style and administratively rooted desire to conserve time, he had brought the parties to mutual agreements on property settlement in chambers, with litigants themselves present. In general, the wide variation in family law statutes and case law from state to state sharply affected the substance and format with which judges in domestic relations assignments performed their tasks.

We observed still other variants of the civil court judge. One judge served in a division that hears only mental health proceedings and election disputes; another judge fulfilled a more widespread function—the law and motions (discovery) calendar. This latter judge, for example, heard an intensive morning call devoted to clarifying the issues at an early stage in the litigation of a case and then spent the rest of long days reading case files to prepare for the next day's call. An infrequent negotiation session in chambers would be the only activity to break the routine for this particular judge.

In sum, "civil" assignment is not a very descriptive characterization of judicial work. The great variation in types of civil cases affects the kinds of tasks that judges perform and the style in which they are performed.

## The Judge of General Assignment: Time and Task Management

Because the work of the general assignment judge (i.e., one hearing both criminal and civil cases at the same time) is so broad, it is necessary to describe the range of tasks routinely handled by these judges. The variation in their days is then somewhat more understandable.

The usual tasks included in the day of general assignment judges were amazingly diversified with respect to both types of cases heard and other duties. For example, in rural Vermont one judge heard all criminal matters (except homicide), all civil cases up to $5,000 (including small claims), all traffic matters, juvenile proceedings, and mental health commitments. A circuit-riding Nebraska judge heard all criminal and civil matters in five counties; in addition, he was responsible for filling vacancies on county mental health boards, writing rules for county jails, and hearing prisoners' complaints. A general assignment judge in Madison, Wisconsin heard criminal and civil cases, petitions, and appeals from decisions of state agencies. Only in suburban areas were generalist judges restricted to criminal and civil casework. One striking distinction, then, between judges of general assignment and their counterparts on either the criminal or the civil bench is that the generalist performs a much wider array of tasks, including those not performed at all by judges in more urban locales. As a result, judges of general assignment in smaller towns and rural locales become involved, on a more personal basis, with a larger segment of the community.

The "typical" day for a general assignment judge was too varied to permit a recounting of the flow of events. Sometimes the variation was reflected in the scheduling of different kinds of cases by day of the week, as in one rural Pennsylvania court where miscellaneous criminal matters were heard on Mondays and Thursdays, probate on Tuesdays, "civil" cases on Wednesdays, and juvenile proceedings on Fridays. Other courts, as in Amarillo, Texas, and Clinton, Tennessee, established separate weeks to hear jury and nonjury trials. When general assignment judges heard only criminal or civil matters exclusively on a given day, that day was still rather unlike the day of a criminal or civil court judge in a larger community. The pace was usually less hectic (except in one visibly overworked suburban court). Informality and familiarity with attorneys and litigants were more prevalent. Events were less tightly scheduled; a breakdown in the appearance of one or two attorneys did not cause general havoc. On balance, there was a greater flexibility or elasticity to the working day of a general assignment judge.

These portraits of the working world of trial judges are little more than glimpses, however. They do not capture the full variety of work environments, nor do they give precise answers to questions about individual judicial performance. Ascertaining what proportion of trial judges spend how much of their day doing what kinds of tasks requires a broader data base, which only our national survey can provide. Before turning to these issues, we look first at the distribution of judicial work by mix of cases heard.

What proportion of judges nationally sit in criminal assignment, in various types of civil assignment, and in general assignment? Table 2–1 provides these data from our survey.

Judges serving in general assignment—hearing both criminal and civil cases—are by far the most prevalent in trial courts. About three of every five judges across the country currently sit in a general assignment. Of the remainder who do specialize, most sit in some kind of civil court, usually one

TABLE 2-1.  The Assignment of Trial Judges

|  | Percent |  | Number |  |
|---|---|---|---|---|
| General | 59.1 |  | (1763) |  |
| Criminal | 13.7 |  | (409) |  |
|    Criminal |  | 12.2 |  | (363) |
|    Juvenile |  | 1.5 |  | (46) |
| Civil | 26.8 |  | (801) |  |
|    Civil—mixed |  | 21.1 |  | (631) |
|    Civil—jury |  | 1.9 |  | (57) |
|    Domestic relations |  | 1.8 |  | (54) |
|    Chancery |  | 1.4 |  | (41) |
|    Probate |  | 0.6 |  | (18) |
| Miscellaneous | 0.4 |  | (11) |  |
|    Law and motions |  | 0.3 |  | (8) |
|    Appellate |  | 0.1 |  | (3) |
|  | 100.0 |  | (2984) |  |

that hears several types of civil cases ("civil—mixed"). The proportion of judges hearing exclusively criminal cases is not large, only about 12 percent. Finally, it should be noted that juvenile, domestic relations, and probate judges in most states serve in limited jurisdiction or specialized courts, not in courts of general jurisdiction. Therefore, relatively few of these types of judges appear in our survey.

The distribution of judges by type of assignment is significant for interpreting both previous research on trial judges and the data to be presented in this book. To the extent that previous studies have focused on criminal court judges, as we suggested in Chapter 1, knowledge about the species of "trial judge" appears that much more selective and incomplete. As for the data in our study, what is true for general assignment judges is also likely to hold for all judges when analyzed in the aggregate, because general assignment judges comprise such a substantial proportion of the total trial judge population. In contrast, we can expect to find variations from the overall picture when we examine criminal or civil court judges separately. It is to the detailed portrait of judicial work, and its variations by assignment, that we now turn.

*Asking Judges About Their Work:*
*A Brief Note on Method*

To develop meaningful and accurate responses to questions about the performance of judicial work, we experimented with alternative question formats in a pretest version of our survey. (For details, see Appendix B.) Based upon those results, we concluded that it was best *not* to ask judges what they did on a particular day (e.g., the day they received the questionnaire!) Rather, we asked judges to enter a level of abstraction in their responses and to characterize their different work days in terms of patterns—i.e., mixes of tasks and time allocations. Accordingly, judges were asked to identify what their "most common" day consisted of, from a list of fourteen specific activities representing each of the six task areas described in Chapter 1 and including such work as "reading case files," "plea negotiation discussions," or "presiding at nonjury trial."[3] The assignment of time, in quarter-hours or more, to each of the activities performed on their most common day completed the description for that type of day.

Judges were also provided similar space for completing a description of a second, third, fourth, and fifth most common day. To the extent that a judge's work days differed sufficiently, in reality and in his own mind, to constitute two or more different days, he completed information for such days.[4] Because we wished to know the relative frequency of an individual judge's most common and less common work days, we asked judges to estimate the percentage of days, over the course of a year, that would account for each type of day.[5] This format also permitted judges to attribute some percentage of days to a "random" category.[6]

## The Nature of Judicial Work Days

### VARIETY

One of the defining characteristics of a trial judge's working environment is the variety, or lack of variety, in his job. Variety can be viewed in several different ways: the range in types of cases heard, in kinds of tasks performed, or even in the mix of tasks performed from one day to another. To some extent, variety in one area is related to another.

Why is the question of variety important at all in examining the working environment of trial judges? Its significance is reflected in two lines of argument, one focusing on the consequences of too much variety, the other on those of too little variety. Since judges are professionals and come to the bench with (if not because of) identifiable interests and skills, it is argued that utilizing a judge in too many ways (especially types of cases) is inefficient for the court system and creates undue pressure on the individual judge.[7] In a contrary vein, it is argued that too little variety for the trial judge leads to intellectual boredom and frustration resulting in low job morale.[8] Furthermore, the repetitive and tedious nature of tasks that many trial judges perform may make it difficult to recruit lawyers of high quality to the state trial bench.[9] To the degree that both of these lines of argument have some merit, finding the optimal level of case and task variety becomes an important policy concern, at least for courts that can actively manipulate the variety of work that their trial judges perform.

In our observations we saw judges who differed not only in the breadth of cases heard but also in the task composition of their work days. For some judges, one day seemed almost exactly like the next, and the next, and the next. For example, a judge in a civil division that heard only jury cases might have one morning settlement conference followed by an all-day or multiday jury trial for a week or more. Or a judge in a criminal division might have a long calendar consisting of arraignments, guilty pleas, sentencings, and probation violations followed by a jury trial, for a series of consecutive days. In contrast, judges in general assignment, which included both criminal and civil cases and a variety of quasi-judicial duties, sometimes had no two days that seemed similar. One day might require extensive circuit-riding, another might involve mostly trial work, and a third might be spent in research.

Our survey data also shed light on the amount of variety trial judges encounter. Almost equal proportions of judges report one, two, three, four, and five different kinds of work days. Of course, it is important to remember that these are judges' *perceptions* of their work patterns, and there is no feasible way of determining an individual judge's frame of reference as to what constituted a work pattern sufficiently distinct to be described as another type of day.[10] Nevertheless, there is no reason to believe that perceptual differences in this area are subject to systematic bias.

Observational impressions about the impact of different assignments on day-to-day variety in the life of the trial judge are confirmed by our survey data. Table 2-2 demonstrates the limited variety reported by judges in criminal and highly specialized civil assignments.

Judges in general assignment report the widest variety of work patterns; nearly half indicate four or five different types of work days. Judges hearing a mixture of civil cases report almost as much variety from day to day. At the other extreme, judges who hear only domestic relations or only probate cases indicate the least variety in their day-to-day work patterns; the majority report only one type of work day. Judges in chancery, criminal, civil—jury, and

**TABLE 2-2. Variety of Judicial Work by Assignment**

| | \multicolumn{5}{c}{Number of Different Work Days} | |
| | 1 | 2 | 3 | 4 | 5 | Number |
|---|---|---|---|---|---|---|
| *High variety assignments* | | | | | | |
| General | 11.1% | 16.2% | 24.8% | 17.1% | 30.8% | (1418) |
| Civil—mixed | 19.6 | 20.4 | 24.5 | 15.7 | 19.8 | (491) |
| *Moderate variety assignments* | | | | | | |
| Chancery | 35.4 | 19.4 | 25.8 | 9.7 | 9.7 | (31) |
| Criminal | 36.5 | 27.3 | 21.3 | 7.9 | 7.0 | (315) |
| Civil—jury | 38.5 | 28.8 | 21.2 | 7.7 | 3.8 | (52) |
| Juvenile | 45.4 | 22.7 | 20.5 | 0 | 11.4 | (44) |
| *Low variety assignments* | | | | | | |
| Probate | 53.3 | 26.7 | 13.3 | 6.7 | 0 | (15) |
| Domestic relations | 59.2 | 20.4 | 8.2 | 2.0 | 10.2 | (49) |

juvenile assignments fall in between, but closer to the low end of the variety continuum. In sum, judges in different assignments experience quite different levels of variety in the tasks they perform from one day to another.

There is another side to the question of variety: How varied is any one work day? For even if a judge reports only one kind of work day, that day may be a chaotic assortment of different tasks. Each day, in other words, might be a repetition of variety. There is some hint of this in our data. The number of different tasks that judges report doing on their most common day is greatest for those with only one type of work day ($\bar{x}$ = 7.6) and drops slowly but consistently to those indicating five types of work days ($\bar{x}$ = 6.5). Thus, there appears to be some task variety even for judges who report only one type of work day.

LENGTH

The length of judicial work days has become a matter of increasing concern to a number of different audiences. In an occupation where the product is as amorphous and elusive as "justice," it is perhaps understandable that so many observers have latched onto time as a surrogate measure of judicial performance. Newspaper reporters, hungry for a scoop, have been known to stalk the (sometimes empty) corridors of courthouses on Friday afternoons.[11] Local television stations, anxious to cover the details of a sensational or sadistic crime, sometimes stumble upon courtrooms without judges at apparently normal business hours. Court watchers, unconcerned though they usually are with what judges do in chambers, are puzzled at the "banker's hours" that judges keep in the courtroom proper. Even presiding judges sometimes place substantial reliance upon hours worked, at least when they have reason to believe the accuracy of the data.[12]

Although the number of hours worked is not a very good measure of productivity, either in judging or in other professions, it is one characteristic that helps to define the working environment of the trial judge. How long do judges report that they work on their most common and less common work days? Table 2-3 presents these data.

Subtracting an hour for the average reported lunch, judges as a group in-

TABLE 2-3. Length of Judicial Work Days[a]

|  | MOST COMMON | 2ND MC[b] | 3RD MC | 4TH MC | 5TH MC |
|---|---|---|---|---|---|
| Mean | 9.2 hrs | 9.1 hrs | 8.9 hrs | 8.9 hrs | 8.7 hrs |
| (Standard deviation) | (1.6) | (1.7) | (1.7) | (1.8) | (1.7) |
| Number | 2502 | 2019 | 1529 | 946 | 584 |

[a] Includes time for lunch.
[b] MC where it appears in tables and figures stands for "most common day." With ordinal numbers it means "second" or "third most common day," etc.

dicate working about eight hours per day. Such a figure does not distinguish judges from most other American workers, but it may strike some readers as higher than expected in light of the reports and investigative work referenced above. Several factors should be kept in mind, however, when interpreting these data. Some judges work at home, especially reading or writing. This kind of work would be reflected in Table 2-3 but not in the reports or studies of most "court watchers." Also, the number of hours worked declines slightly as judges move farther away from their most common day. The relatively few judges who report a fifth most common day work, on the average, a half-hour less on such a day than judges on their most common day. Finally, these figures are *averages,* around which there is significant variation. Some judges do work much shorter hours, but an equivalent or greater proportion work longer hours. The distribution of working hours reported by all judges on their most common day is presented in Figure 2-1.

The most striking feature of Figure 2-1 is the absence of a sharp dropoff at the very upper end. A small but significant percentage of judges report thirteen and even fourteen hours of work on their most common day. Every profession has its share of "workaholics," and it is possible that many of these judges do fall into that category.

**FIGURE 2-1.** Length of Trial Judges' Most Common Work Day

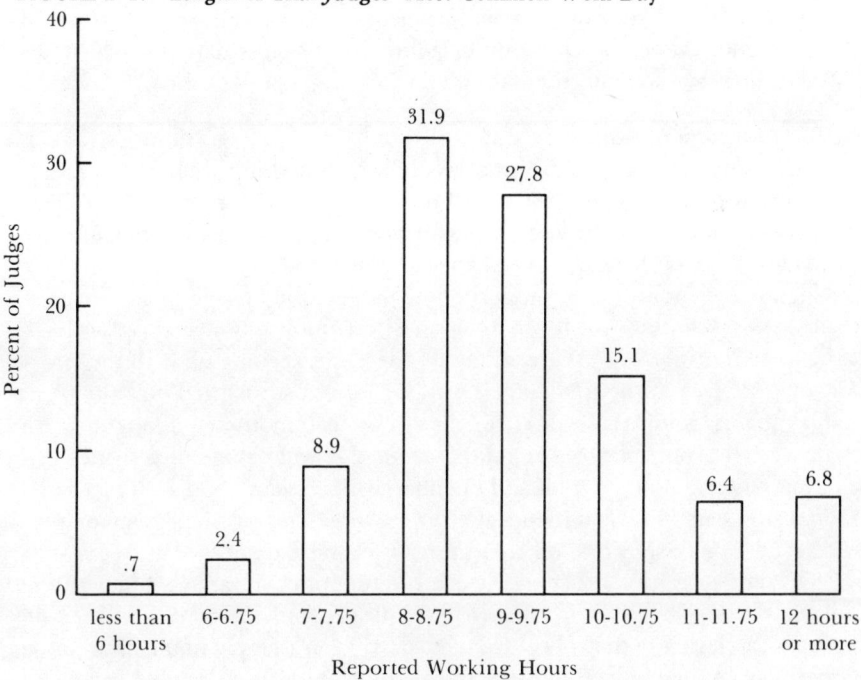

| Reported Working Hours (including lunch) | Percent of Judges |
|---|---|
| less than 6 hours | .7 |
| 6-6.75 | 2.4 |
| 7-7.75 | 8.9 |
| 8-8.75 | 31.9 |
| 9-9.75 | 27.8 |
| 10-10.75 | 15.1 |
| 11-11.75 | 6.4 |
| 12 hours or more | 6.8 |

N = 2502

Our observations of judges provide a useful comparative frame of reference here.[13] We observed judges in their courtrooms and chambers (but not at home) to work an average of 7.5 hours per day, including one hour for lunch. The difference, then, between what we observed and what judges self-report (about one and one-half hours) is sizable. It can partly be explained by work done at home, partly by the rounding principle attached to the survey question,[14] but partly also by conscious or accidental exaggeration.

We observed no obvious pattern between length of work day and the current assignment of the judge. We saw long hours worked by criminal judges in metropolitan areas, by civil judges in metropolitan areas, and by generalists in both suburban and rural localities. Our survey data similarly reveal few significant patterns. Criminal assignment judges generally report slightly longer hours (up to one half-hour above the average); and probate judges somewhat shorter hours (up to one hour below the average). The remaining groups of judges—generalists, juvenile, and a variety of civil assignments—fall close to the average for each day.

It was not the length of time worked so much as the *quality* of time utilization that seemed to differentiate the criminal and civil judges whom we observed. Perhaps because the criminal judge works in close and continuing contact with a small number of prosecuting and defense attorneys, some judges do not cope very effectively with interludes of peace and quiet in their chambers. This, like many important issues related to the utilization of judicial time, cannot be answered or addressed by gross data on total hours worked, however accurate the data might be.

## SUBSTANCE (TASKS)

The variety and length of work days tell us something about the contours of trial judges' working environment but not about its substance. What kinds of tasks do judges actually engage in, for how long, and in what mix or combinations? It is to these questions which we now turn.

Figure 2-2 indicates the proportion of judges who engage in each of thirteen tasks (excluding lunch) on their most common day. Three activities—general administrative work, reading case files, and keeping up with the law—are a typical part of the trial judge's working day. A substantial majority of all judges report doing these tasks on their most common day, though, as we shall see later, not for great amounts of time. A wide range of activities, including jury and nonjury trials and calendar work, engage about half of all trial judges on their most common day. Fewer judges report settlement of plea discussions, or travel time, on their most common day.

The data in Figure 2-2 generally conform to our observations, but with the following exceptions. We saw many fewer judges (only 26 percent) "keeping up with the law," perhaps because most do this on the way home or at home rather than in the noisy atmosphere of the courthouse. We also observed many more judges (81 percent) to have "case-related" discussions with attorneys

| Task | Percentage |
|---|---|
| General administrative work | 71.2% |
| Reading case files | 70.1% |
| Keeping up with the law | 68.1% |
| Preparing/writing decisions, judgments, orders | 56.2% |
| Civil or criminal calendar | 52.0% |
| Case-related discussions with attorneys | 47.5% |
| Presiding at nonjury trial | 44.5% |
| Presiding at jury trial | 44.3% |
| Waiting time | 42.4% |
| Socializing with attorneys et al. | 38.9% |
| Settlement discussions | 32.0% |
| Plea negotiation discussions | 18.9% |
| Travel time | 17.1% |

N = 2502

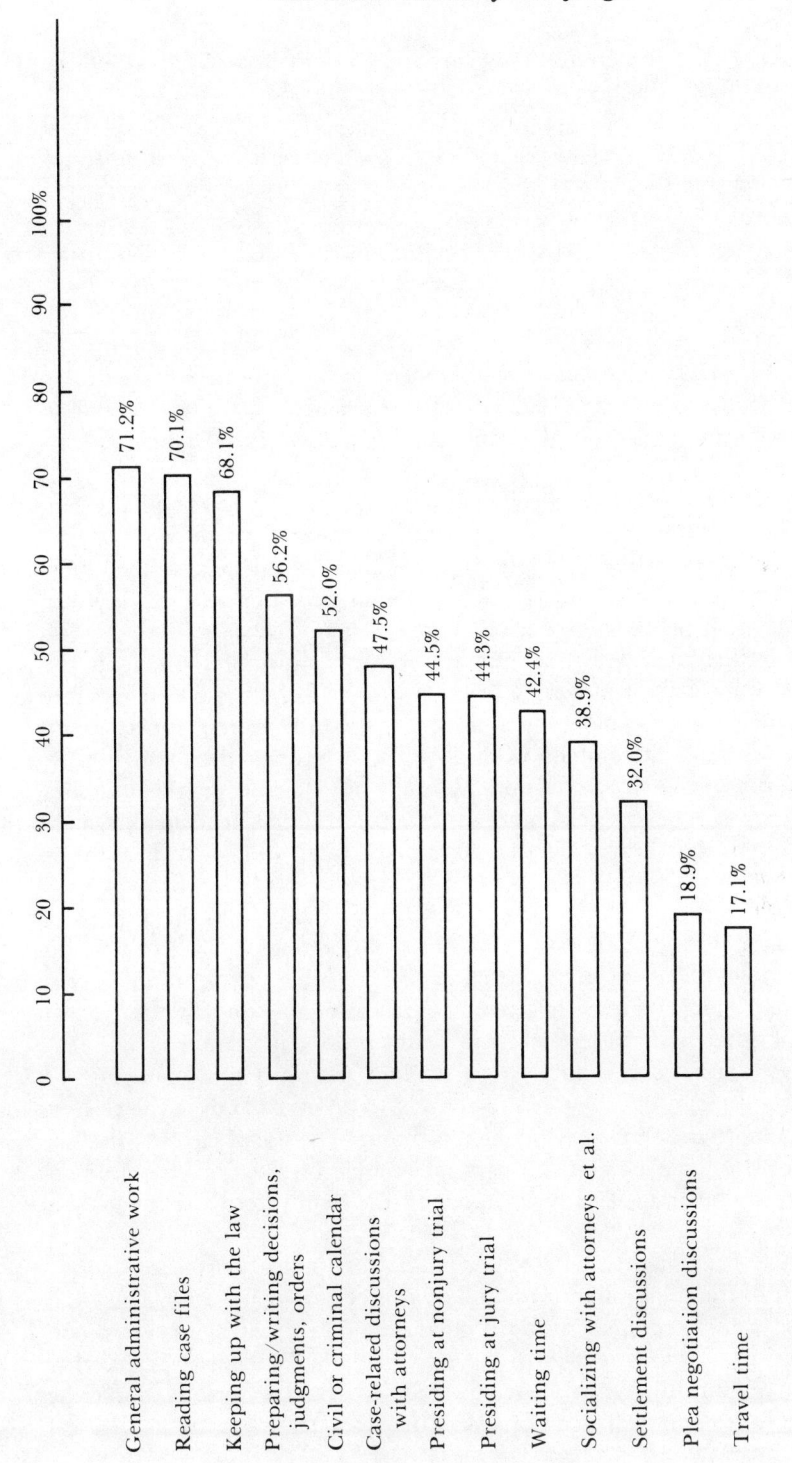

**FIGURE 2-2.** Proportion of Trial Judges Reporting Specific Tasks on Their Most Common Work Day

TABLE 2-4. The Frequency of Jury and Nonjury Trial Work on Judicial Work Days

|  | Presiding at Jury Trial | Presiding at Nonjury Trial | Number |
|---|---|---|---|
| Most Common | 44.3% | 44.5% | (2502) |
| 2nd MC | 32.9 | 44.2 | (2019) |
| 3rd MC | 25.8 | 30.9 | (1529) |
| 4th MC | 21.5 | 28.6 | (946) |
| 5th MC | 20.4 | 25.0 | (584) |

(not related to plea or settlement) and to socialize with attorneys or courtroom personnel (fully 66 percent). These disparities are likely to be attributable to judges' misperceptions about the frequency and nature of conferences with attorneys.

The proportion of judges doing one or another of these tasks typically does not change from the most common to the fifth most common work day. A slightly higher percentage of judges engage in many of the tasks on their most common day, but the differences are sizable only for jury and nonjury trial work. Table 2-4 presents these data.

Trial work, particularly the jury trial, occurs much less often on the peripheral work days of judges. Whereas nearly half of all judges report jury work on their most common day, only one judge in five presides over a jury trial on his fifth most common work day. The percentage decline is similar, though not quite so sharp, for nonjury trial work. In essence, this indicates that judges use jury and/or nonjury work as a perceptual benchmark against which to assess whether or not they have many (e.g., four or five) different kinds of work days.

Now that we have examined the tasks that trial judges, in the aggregate, perform on a given type of day, a second set of questions directs our focus to the mix, or combination, of tasks that *individual* judges perform on a given day. No judge engages in every activity on his most common day; the average number of different activities reported is seven. More important, the combination of tasks performed is not entirely random. Judges who do one kind of thing are also more (or sometimes less) likely to do other things. The clearest way of demonstrating this phenomenon is through the use of factor analysis, a technique which can point to clusters, or groups, of activities that are performed in combination.[15] Table 2-5 presents the results from a factor analysis of judicial tasks.

Note first from Table 2-5 that these four factors[16] together account for only 46 percent of the total variance among the thirteen task categories. There is a substantial *random* component to the organization of a judge's most common work day, when viewed from the perspective of the tasks themselves. In other words, we cannot fully explain why a judge does one task but not another by looking only at the organization of tasks. (In subsequent chapters we shall ex-

TABLE 2-5. Identification of Clusters of Judicial Tasks

| Most Common Day | ROTATED FACTORS: OBLIQUE SOLUTION[a] |  |  |  |
|---|---|---|---|---|
|  | Factor 1 | Factor 2 | Factor 3 | Factor 4 |
| Reading case files | .43 | −.08 | .16 | .02 |
| Keeping up with the law | .65 | .02 | .01 | .04 |
| Preparing/writing decisions, judgments, orders | .57 | −.07 | −.05 | .03 |
| General administrative work | .32 | −.09 | .24 | −.06 |
| Plea negotiation discussions | .02 | .02 | −.02 | .56 |
| Settlement discussions | .22 | .00 | .10 | .07 |
| Socializing with attorneys et al. | −.04 | −.07 | .59 | .01 |
| Case-related discussions with attorneys | .08 | −.02 | .45 | −.01 |
| Waiting time | −.06 | .07 | .45 | .19 |
| Travel time | −.14 | −.06 | .01 | −.01 |
| Presiding at nonjury trial | .06 | −.68 | −.04 | .03 |
| Presiding at jury trial | .02 | .80 | −.01 | .07 |
| Civil or criminal calendar | .07 | −.09 | .10 | .18 |
| (% of total variance explained) | (19.5) | (11.0) | (8.3) | (7.6) |

[a] See note 16 at the end of this chapter.

amine this question by looking at court structure, attorneys, courthouse resources, etc.)

What we can learn by viewing a summary of the relationships among the various tasks, as portrayed in Table 2-5, is that there are *clusters* of activities that are likely to be performed in combination with each other. Factor 2 illustrates the exclusion or displacement of tasks: if a judge conducts a jury trial on his most common day, he almost certainly will *not* also conduct a nonjury trial. These two activities are all but mutually exclusive; in fact, only 7 percent of all judges indicate that they engage in both activities on their most common day. There are also differences in the variety and length of work days that stem from jury versus nonjury patterns of work. Specifically, judges reporting jury trial work on their most common day also report working longer hours (by about a half-hour) and performing fewer different tasks than judges reporting nonjury trial work. These consequences are a reflection of the greater amount of time judges allocate to jury, as opposed to nonjury, work on their most common day. Otherwise, however, there are no differences between jury and nonjury days revealed in our data. While days on which judges do jury trial work may involve fewer different tasks, no one specific task (except nonjury trials) is more likely than others to be excluded or included.

An examination of Factor 1 reveals that four activities are particularly likely to occur in combination—reading case files, keeping up with the law, preparing or writing decisions/judgments/orders, and general administrative work. If a judge performs any one of these tasks, he is more likely to do each of the others. The four tasks are clearly of different kinds, involving as they do elements of legal research, administration, and pretrial adjudication. But the tasks do share one thing in common: They are rarely interpersonal in nature. The trial judge, alone in chambers, performs these tasks in whatever moments of peace and solitude he can find. Thus, if he has the requisite level of quiet to do one of these tasks, he can probably do several of the others.

In contrast, an examination of Factor 3 reveals the clustering of three tasks that are interpersonal in nature—case-related discussions with attorneys, socializing, and waiting time. Indeed, it might well be difficult to isolate any one of these tasks from the other, based upon our observations. Socializing often serves as a prelude or conclusion to a conference or discussion with attorneys. And many, though not all, judges utilize waiting time by socializing with whoever is available, in chambers or en route to the courtroom. What is surprising is that neither plea discussions nor settlement discussions are a part of this cluster, for these also seem to generate possibilities for socializing and waiting.

It is in Factor 4 that plea negotiation discussions emerge, but for the most part isolated from all other activities. In other words, when judges do attend plea discussions with attorneys,[17] these sessions are likely to occur at almost any time, on any kind of day, regardless of what other tasks might be performed. The comparatively *ad hoc* occurrence of plea discussions is tempered only by a very small relationship with the presence of calendar work and waiting time (see dotted boxes in Table 2-5). The relationship between plea discussions and calendar work is obvious, since "calendar" duties include the taking, in court, of guilty pleas that have been agreed to, usually on the same day, in chambers. That waiting time is slightly associated with plea discussions but not, for example, with jury trials, is counter-intuitive[18] but also supported by our observations. Some of the longest stretches of waiting time we saw occurred when judges were "forced" to wait for prosecutor and defense counsel to finalize bargains in which they (the judges) may or may not have participated. Management problems in pretrial negotiations (on the criminal side) are only now being uncovered and researched,[19] and it appears that utilization of judicial time may be an important, if less visible, type of problem.

Finally, a similar mix, or clustering, of activities occurs on judges' less common work days. The factor structure presented in Table 2-5 is remarkably stable across all work days. In particular, the first three factors are nearly identical for the most common, second most common, and third most common days. This suggests that there is an essential commonality underlying the mix of judicial tasks—something that is more than day- or situation-specific. Interpersonal tasks are performed in conjunction with one another, with one task facilitating the completion of another. Similarly, "intrapersonal" tasks, or those which judges perform without relating to others, also tend to be performed in combination. In contrast, jury and nonjury trials are almost always mutually exclusive within the time span of one day, whereas plea bargaining sessions can occur on almost any occasion.

## DIFFERENCES IN THE SUBSTANCE OF WORK DAYS: CRIMINAL, CIVIL AND GENERAL ASSIGNMENT JUDGES

The frequency and mix of judicial tasks is generally similar for judges in criminal, civil, and general assignment. There are several elaborations and exceptions to be noted, however. For example, the number of judges engaging in plea or settlement discussions is underestimated in Figure 2–2 because some judges, by virtue of the restriction of their assignment to only criminal or only civil cases, do not have the opportunity to engage in such discussions. Nearly half (48 percent) of all criminal court judges report some time on plea discussions on their most common day, though only 19 percent of general assignment judges do. Similarly, almost half (47 percent) of all judges in civil—mixed assignments report some time spent in settlement discussions, a figure parallel for judges in more limited civil assignments but lower for general assignment (31 percent).

The balance between jury and nonjury trial work is also affected by type of assignment. Judges sitting in courts that typically do not hear jury cases (e.g., juvenile, chancery, domestic relations, probate) rarely, if at all, report time spent in jury trials on their most common or less common days. By contrast, judges in criminal assignment report a high frequency of jury work, much greater than judges in a civil—mixed or general assignment. Table 2–6 reports these data.

Criminal judges are much more likely to hear jury, as opposed to nonjury, trials, whereas judges in civil—mixed or general assignment are about equally likely to hear jury and nonjury matters. Though this imbalance in the types of trials heard by criminal judges does not persist beyond the most common day, for 37 percent of criminal judges their most common day is their *only* work day. How these figures for criminal judges relate to aggregate court data on the relative frequency of jury and nonjury criminal trials, at the felony level, is not fully clear. There has always been the impression that nonjury trials outnumber jury trials in most locales, especially big cities.[20] Such impressions are difficult to square with the data in Table 2–6, even if we assume that the average nonjury criminal case takes only a fraction of the trial time that a jury case takes. If there are so many nonjury criminal trials, who hears them?[21]

**TABLE 2–6. The Frequency of Jury and Nonjury Trial Work by Assignment**

|  | % Judges Reporting (MC) | | |
|---|---|---|---|
|  | Jury Trial | Nonjury Trial | Number |
| Criminal | 69.2 | 27.6 | (315) |
| Civil—mixed | 40.9 | 48.9 | (491) |
| General | 43.7 | 44.0 | (1419) |

There is a nonjury section of the criminal division in the Philadelphia Court of Common Pleas and in the Cook County (Chicago) Circuit Court; otherwise, we observed in the field no examples of the concentration of nonjury cases, on the criminal side, among a few judges.[22]

The mix of activities structuring judicial work days is similar for judges in all types of assignments. The clustering of interpersonal tasks, of intrapersonal tasks, and the exclusionary character of nonjury and jury trial work stays intact for judges in criminal, civil—mixed, and general assignments respectively. The relative isolation of plea discussions from any patterns of judicial activities is clearly exhibited in the factor structure where analysis is confined to criminal judges. For general assignment judges, however, both plea and settlement discussions cluster together. This suggests that many general assignment judges do not necessarily divide their workloads arbitrarily into criminal and civil "days." Rather, days on which negotiations with attorneys in criminal cases take place are likely to be the same days when negotiations in civil cases occur, possibly because of the unspecialized nature of attorney practice in smaller towns. Finally, for judges in civil—mixed assignments, settlement discussions do *not* stand in task isolation. Rather, settlement discussions cluster with jury trials and to the exclusion of calendar work. This is precisely what we observed in the field and recounted in our opening summary of the civil judge's day: The civil judge is constantly on the alert for opportunities to settle cases, even—especially—on the day of trial and throughout the course of a multiday trial.

## ALLOCATION OF TIME TO TASKS

A complementary perspective to judicial work can be provided by examining how much time is allocated to particular tasks. By analyzing the typical range of time consumed for different tasks, we move toward a composite picture of the judicial day. If a judge engages in a specific task, for how long might he be occupied? The answer to this question significantly depends upon whether we are speaking of the judge's most common, or some less common, work day, as Table 2-7 indicates.

Trial work accounts for much of the time of judges on days when it occurs. The 45 percent of judges who report jury trial activity on their most common day average slightly under five hours. Only a few judges indicate either less than three or more than six hours spent on jury trial work on any day. Hours in jury trial work could reflect the presence of more than one jury trial, but we believe this is generally unlikely in light of what we observed in the field and the estimated length of jury trials that judges report in our survey data.[23] One jury trial may end, and another begin, in the course of a day, but few jury trials begin and end on the same day early enough to enable the beginning of another jury trial.

The time required for nonjury trials is a different matter. Judges report spending anywhere from one and one-half to two and one-half hours *less* per

TABLE 2-7. Trial Judges' Allocation of Time on Their Work Days[a]

|  | MOST[b] COMMON | 2ND MC | 3RD MC | 4TH MC | 5TH MC |
|---|---|---|---|---|---|
| Reading case files | .8 hrs. | .9 hrs. | 1.0 hrs. | 1.0 hrs. | 1.1 hrs. |
| Keeping up with the law | .8 | .9 | 1.1 | 1.2 | 1.4 |
| Preparing/writing decisions, judgments, orders | 1.0 | 1.2 | 1.7 | 2.3 | 2.0 |
| General administrative work | .9 | .9 | 1.0 | 1.1 | 1.2 |
| Plea negotiation discussions | .7 | .9 | 1.0 | .9 | 1.0 |
| Settlement discussions | .8 | 1.0 | 1.3 | 1.5 | 1.3 |
| Socializing with attorneys et al. | .4 | .5 | .5 | .5 | .6 |
| Case-related discussions with attorneys | .6 | .7 | .8 | .9 | .9 |
| Waiting time | .6 | .6 | .6 | .6 | .7 |
| Travel time | 1.5 | 1.6 | 1.6 | 1.8 | 1.8 |
| Presiding at nonjury trial | 3.5 | 4.1 | 3.9 | 3.9 | 3.2 |
| Presiding at jury trial | 4.9 | 5.5 | 5.6 | 5.4 | 5.2 |
| Civil or criminal calendar | 1.7 | 2.2 | 2.7 | 2.3 | 2.3 |

[a] Figures are means based upon only those judges who report performing the task for a given day.
[b] Columns cannot be summed to total hours worked, because each of the figures represents a different subset of judges.

day on nonjury trial work. In addition, it is quite likely that more than one nonjury trial might take place on the same day. This may occur because no time is needed for jury selection or jury deliberation. It is also related to differences in the adversary character of jury and nonjury trials, a point we shall elaborate upon when comparing judges in criminal and civil assignment.

Calendar work—the hearing of motions, default judgments, guilty pleas, sentencings, etc.—comprises a significant portion of time, which increases after the most common day. In many civil courts, Friday mornings or afternoons are set aside to hear motions. The criminal calendar is more typically called every day, though here too some days may be set aside to facilitate the gathering together of probation officers, psychiatrists, and other professionals who are not regularly present in the courtroom.

Travel also constitutes a significant expenditure of time for that small proportion of judges who report traveling on a particular day. Our data indicate that most travel time reflects *circuit-riding* across county lines, a phenomenon we shall address in the next chapter.

Waiting occupies a relatively small segment of time; nevertheless, thirty minutes in which a judge does nothing while waiting for someone or something should not be treated lightly. Its causes, some of which we have already alluded to, may be quite varied. Waiting time may reflect judges' inability to work productively in the absence of cases, the failure of a court administrative office to assign cases expeditiously, the frenetic courthouse practices of attorneys, the inefficiency of courtroom personnel, or some combination of these and other factors.

Finally, the remaining activities each take up only a small amount of time, at least on judges' most common and second most common days. On less common days, however, such activities as preparing and writing decisions and keeping up with the law account for an hour or more, indicating that trial judges occasionally, but not regularly, are able to do some case-related or general legal research.

## DIFFERENCES IN THE ALLOCATION OF TIME TO TASKS: CRIMINAL, CIVIL AND GENERAL ASSIGNMENT JUDGES

Our description of time allocations applies equally well for criminal, civil, and general assignment judges in all tasks except trial work. There are some sizable and consistent differences in the time spent in jury and nonjury trials

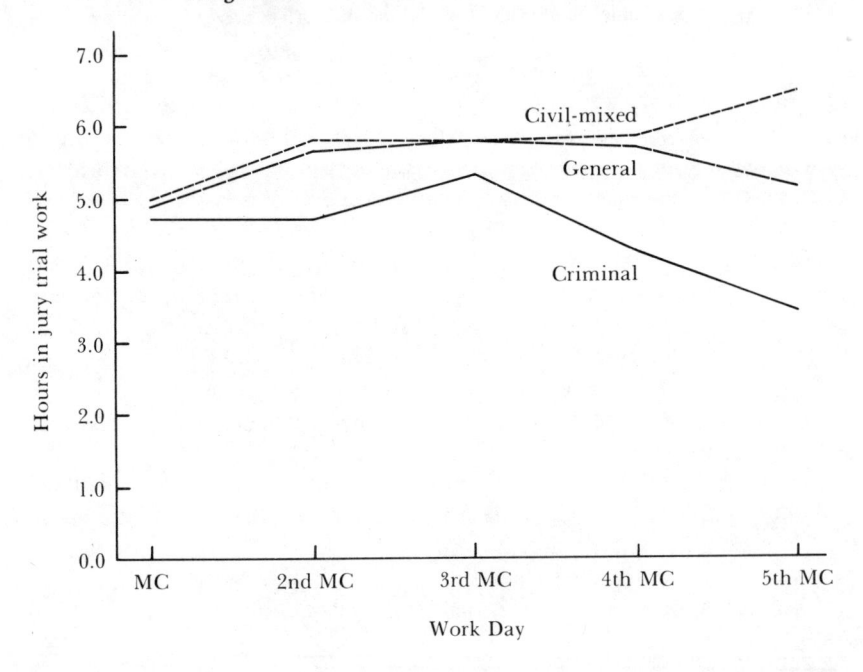

**FIGURE 2-3a.** Time Spent in Jury Trial Work on Judicial Work Days, by Type of Assignment

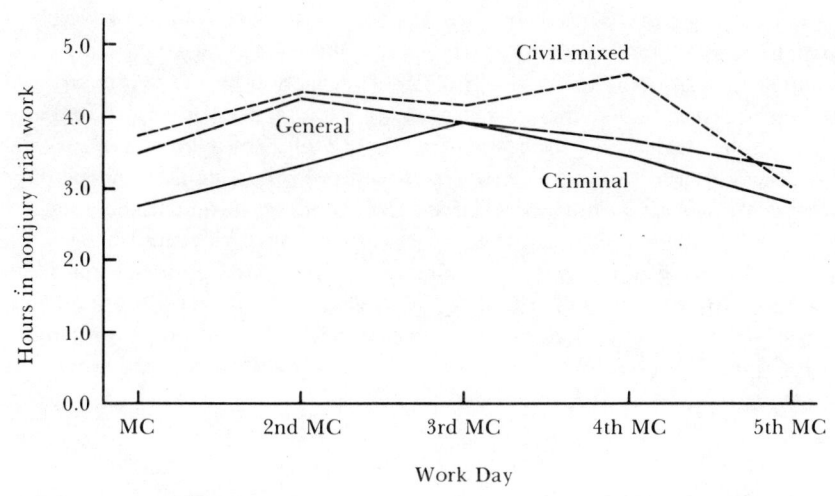

FIGURE 2-3b. Time Spent in Nonjury Trial Work on Judicial Work Days, by Type of Assignment

on a given day, depending upon the judge's assignment. Figures 2-3a and 2-3b display these differences.

From Figure 2-3a, we see that judges in criminal assignment spend less time on jury trial work, beginning with the second most common work day. For the most common day, there are no differences among criminal, civil, and general assignment judges; all spend about five hours in jury trial. On less common days, criminal judges average anywhere from one hour to several hours less time in jury trial than their counterparts in civil—mixed and general assignments.[24] Yet there are no obvious explanations as to why criminal judges often spend fewer hours on a given day in jury trial work. In light of the ever increasing caseload pressures on criminal courts, one might expect these judges to spend *more* hours per day in jury trial work. Perhaps this paradox is best resolved by referring to an earlier finding: Criminal judges are much more likely to report *jury* trial work on their most common day (Table 2-6). Thus, because more criminal judges are faced with jury trials, day in and day out, they may be forced—or choose—to devote less time each day to such work, in order to do other things or simply to preserve their own peace of mind in the face of monotonous work. It is no doubt easier, psychologically, for a judge in a civil or general assignment to spend six or even eight hours one day in jury trial work knowing that the next day (or the day after) will bring something different to do.

Criminal assignment judges also typically spend significantly less time (one hour or more per day) in nonjury work than civil—mixed or general assignment judges. These differences, as illustrated in Figure 2-3b, are much more likely to be attributable to the different nature of nonjury criminal and civil cases. Nonjury criminal trials tend to be short of duration and less adversarial than their civil nonjury counterparts.[25] In some locales, a bench trial in a criminal case amounts to a "slow plea"—a realization by the defendant and his counsel that the likelihood of conviction is too high to risk a jury trial and the possibly heavier sentence upon a finding of guilt. This type of nonjury trial enables counsel to "earn his keep" in the eyes of the defendant and perhaps to reveal to the judge mitigating circumstances of fact or defendant character in a depth not possible amid chaotic plea discussions.[26] In still other courts, bench trials in criminal cases may merely be "recycled" guilty pleas—pleas agreed to in chambers but ritualized as trials for public consumption.[27] Of course, the waiver of a jury in a criminal case may reflect calculated preference in a highly adversarial context,[28] but even here the result should be fewer hours of trial time than if a jury were present.

In contrast, nonjury trials in civil cases are often highly adversarial. The waiver of jury is much more due to the legal complexity of the issues at hand and to what degree (if at all) facts, as opposed to interpretations of law, are in dispute. When the primary issue to be resolved is the amount of "pain and suffering," injured plaintiffs almost always prefer juries. But when the ground shifts to contractual disputes, for example, attorneys for both plaintiff and defendant prefer arguing before a judge. We observed nonjury cases of this type to consume five or six hours of a judge's time for several days. Generalizations are difficult to draw for judges in civil—mixed assignments, however, for time spent in nonjury work may also reflect a series of short domestic relations or small claims "trials." Our data do not permit us to distinguish among these kinds of civil nonjury trials.

In sum, the differences between criminal and civil judges' allocation of time to trial work seem to be a reflection of a complex network of variables, including the nature of the case, variety and repetition levels in day-to-day work, demands of other courtroom actors, and the individual judge's own personality. We are not able to sort out the relative influence of each of these variables, but we can suggest their importance.

## TOWARD SUMMARIZING JUDICIAL WORK DAYS

Thus far, we have looked at judges' work days in detail, yet often at an aggregate level. In this section, we try to pull together our data on work patterns. Thus, we frame the simple question: What do judges do with "most" of their work time on a given day? We also combine some tasks that are essentially similar in their functional nature in order to approach most of our conceptual categories for judicial tasks—adjudication, administration, negotiation, and legal research.

To reach a summary of the judicial work day, we have adopted a "50 percent guideline" with respect to the expenditure of time on tasks. If a judge works on one group of activities—e.g., reading case files and civil or criminal calendar—for 50 percent or more of the time reported for a particular day, we

TABLE 2-8. Patterns of Task Predominance on Judicial Work Days

|  | MOST COMMON | 2ND MC | 3RD MC | 4TH MC | 5TH MC |
|---|---|---|---|---|---|
| Adjudication | 59.3% | 64.0% | 55.7% | 42.6% | 35.8% |
| Jury | 32.1 | 27.1 | 21.5 | 16.7 | 15.1 |
| Nonjury | 18.6 | 24.5 | 15.2 | 13.0 | 9.1 |
| Motions | 8.6 | 12.4 | 19.0 | 12.9 | 11.6 |
| Legal research | 1.5 | 4.8 | 10.3 | 18.4 | 17.8 |
| Negotiation | .7 | 1.4 | 2.0 | 2.6 | 2.7 |
| Administration | .8 | .7 | 1.3 | 2.3 | 3.4 |
| General | .8 | .7 | 1.1 | 1.6 | 2.7 |
| Travel | 0 | 0 | .2 | .7 | .7 |
| Fragmented | 37.7 | 29.1 | 30.7 | 34.1 | 40.3 |
| Number | (2502) | (2019) | (1529) | (946) | (584) |

labeled it that kind of day ("motions"). In all, there are eight possible kinds of days, given our grouping of tasks. Three involve adjudication: jury trial days, nonjury trial days, and motions days. Two relate to administration: general administrative days and travel days. One each involve research (preparing/writing decisions and keeping up with the law) and negotiation (civil and criminal). The eighth type of day is a "fragmented" day, in which no one group of activities reaches or exceeds 50 percent of a judge's work time. Table 2-8 indicates what proportion of judges experience the predominance of one type of task or another.

On the most common work day, about one-third of all judges experience a jury trial day—a day on which half or more of their work time is devoted to presiding at a jury trial. Indeed, for many of these judges much more than half their time is so occupied. Slightly less than one-fifth of all judges experience a nonjury trial day and about one-tenth spend their most common day predominantly in motions work. By comparison, only an infinitesimal percentage of judges experience research, negotiation, general administration, or travel days as their most common. The remaining judges (37.7 percent) do not predominantly do any one of these sets of activities on their most common day—thus, the label "fragmented."

Judges' second most common days are not too much different. Beginning with the third most common day, however, the proportion of judges experiencing a jury or nonjury trial day drops steadily. Motion days peak, in their frequency, on the third most common day, whereas legal research days continue to rise. Indeed, by the fourth and fifth most common day, research activities are more frequent than any other discrete task. It is important to remember, of course, that many judges do not have four or five different kinds of days *and* that for those who do, such days occur infrequently in their work schedules.[29] Nevertheless, these data suggest that for some significant percentage of judges trial work, as a predominant daily activity, does give way to other matters, particularly legal research.

We also are able to re-evaluate the variety in judicial work by comparing patterns of task predominance from one day to another. Regardless of what type of tasks predominate on a judge's most common day, a different set of tasks is likely to predominate on his second most common day. For example, only 10 percent of all judges who have a jury day as their most common *also* have a jury day as their second most common. Most judges (74 percent) have a different second day, which is likely to be a nonjury day. The situation is similar for judges with a "nonjury" most common day; many have a jury day as their second most common, but only a few (9 percent) repeat the same nonjury work. For judges with motions work predominant on their most common day, the majority experience some kind of trial work on their second day. Judges whose most common day is fragmented, or fractured into a number of elements, are much more likely than other judges to have a "similar" second day—similarly heterogeneous or unpatterned, that is.

To what extent these types of activities are "different" from one another is a separate question. This could be raised particularly with respect to jury and nonjury trial work. Both kinds of trial require that the judge listen to testimony and formal argument for some duration of time. Yet there would appear to be some meaningful differences. In a nonjury trial, the judge is a fact-finder—assuming the role of a jury—as well as law-applier. This may induce judges to be more active in their presiding role in nonjury trials, both to find the "truth" and to expedite the process. With no jury on hand (to prejudice), judges, as well as attorneys, have more freedom in their roles.[30] This became quite clear to us as we observed nonjury trials, particularly on the civil side.

Differences in task predominance among judges in criminal, civil, and general assignment follow directly from our earlier presentations of data. A higher percentage of criminal judges (46 percent) experience jury trial days as their most common, and a lower percentage (only 8 percent) nonjury trial days. Judges in general or civil—mixed assignments parallel the overall distributions of task predominance on the most common and subsequent days. Judges in assignments that do not require hearing jury trials—chancery, domestic relations, probate, or juvenile—are much more likely than others to have "fragmented" days. From 45 to 75 percent of these judges experience no task predominance on their most common day, which, as we have seen, is likely to be their *only* work day.

## A Note on Bar Association and Community Relations Activities

Some activities, by their very nature, require the time of judges on a periodic rather than patterned basis. These activities occur irregularly and are usually not under the control of the judge. Two important kinds of activities, based upon our field observations, fit this description: judicial involvement in bar association matters and in community relations work.

Many judges sever their active relationship with the local bar upon assuming the bench. They are no longer merely lawyers; more than that, their identification with any one group of lawyers or clique of the local bar could jeopardize their reputation for impartiality and fair-mindedness. Other judges continue some involvement with the local bar association, feeling that they can provide a unique perspective to questions of procedure or substantive law which ordinarily only practicing lawyers debate. Still other judges have little involvement with the bar association prior to their gaining the bench and do not change. We observed judges in all three categories.

In a section of the questionnaire separate from the inquiry into judicial work days, we asked judges how much time *per month* they spend in bar association and community relations activities. Regardless of whether the activities are intellectual, administrative, or affiliative (social) in nature, they are likely to occur in episodic frames which cannot be averaged or fitted into types of days.

Our data reveal that only a very small percentage of judges spend a significant amount of time each month on bar association matters. Twenty percent report *no* time spent, 50 percent said "1–2 hours," and another 20 percent reported "3–4 hours" per month. Thus, 90 percent of all trial judges indicate they spend the equivalent of one-half day or less per month with the bar. A judge's assignment bears no relationship to the level of activity in this area: Judges in criminal, civil, and general assignments all report about the same amount of time.

In contrast to bar association activities, community relations work—e.g., speeches, interviews, civic meetings—is more likely to attract the energies of trial judges once on the bench. The public's desire to know about the operations of courts and the status of the judge as a special actor in the community converge to bring judges into contact with the citizenry. We saw this in the field, not only in the settings described above but also in more mundane scenes—performing weddings, interacting with past or prospective jurors about service, accommodating visiting students, or lunching with a political figure at a local restaurant or with municipal firemen at the stationhouse.

Our survey data corroborate the frequency with which judges are involved in community relations activities, as Table 2–9 indicates. Almost one-third of all judges spend the equivalent of one-half day or more in community rela-

TABLE 2-9. Trial Judges' Expenditure of Time
on Community Relations Activities

| Time Spent per Month | Percent of Judges | Number |
|---|---|---|
| 0 | 13.2 | (392) |
| 1–2 hours | 31.0 | (921) |
| 3–4 hours | 25.5 | (757) |
| 5–8 hours | 16.8 | (499) |
| 9–12 hours | 6.8 | (202) |
| 13 hours or more | 6.7 | (199) |
|  | 100.0 | 2970 |

tions; more than one judge in ten spends a full day or more each month. For the most part, a judge's assignment is not related to the amount of time spent in community relations activities. Judges in juvenile assignment are the exception: More than half (51 percent) report one full day or more each month in the community. We observed no juvenile judges in the field, but might speculate that these judges find it useful, perhaps necessary, to generate community support and to identify and build community resources for the noninstitutionalized treatment of juvenile offenders.[31]

In sum, bar association and community relations activities taken together do not demand large expenditures of time from most trial judges. Nevertheless, the time they do require on a periodic basis—as well as the qualitative character of the tasks themselves—constitute an important adjunct to judicial work patterns.

## Summary

The working environment of trial judges is properly viewed in three contexts: the amount of variety, the amount of work, and the nature of the tasks that confront judges from one day to the next. Variety and duration of work provide a psychological framework within which the substance of judicial activities assumes meaning. Trial judges as a group report moderately varied work schedules, but with sharp differences by assignment. In criminal and highly specialized civil assignments, judges report little variety in the organization of their work from one day to the next. Most of these judges identify only one or possibly two different kinds of work days. By contrast, judges in general assignment or a diversified civil assignment report much more variety, often identifying four or five different work days.

Trial judges do not work the long hours, which some citizens have come to expect. Nor do they work the very short hours often charged by court-watching groups who restrict their monitoring of judicial work to the courtroom. Judges themselves report that they work an average of nine hours (including lunch) on their most common day, and slightly less on other days. We observed judges in the field to work seven and one-half hours per day (including lunch). The discrepancy between our observations and judges' self-reports can only partly be explained by judges who do some work at home. Nevertheless, even if our observationally based estimate of the length of a trial judge's work day is the more accurate, we cannot easily conclude that judges work "too few" hours. Judges do not establish work norms on their own; they require support and assistance from lawyers and courthouse personnel.

The substance of what trial judges do can be summarized by referring to routine activities, frequent and time-consuming activities, and occasional activities. Most judges do some administrative work, read case files, and keep up with the law on their most common day, but none of these activities typically consumes as much as one hour. These are routine, recurring activities, most appropriately measured in minutes. Frequently, but not on every day, judges preside at jury or nonjury trials and do calendar work. These activities, especially the jury trial, are likely to fill much of the day. Finally, some activities occasionally occupy the time of the judge. For example, preparing and writing decisions is a task that judges are better able to accommodate in their work schedules on their less common days. Also, judges occasionally engage in community relations or bar association activities. These occur episodically, usually for several hours at a time, and almost always outside the structure of a particular kind of day.

In one critical area, the judge's assignment affects the substance of his work. Judges in criminal assignment are much more likely to experience jury, rather than nonjury, trial work. Their counterparts in civil and general assignments, by contrast, are about equally likely to experience jury and nonjury trial work. Because jury trials require a lower intensity of work or involvement on the judge's part, some criminal court judges come to view their work as a "piece of cake," whereas others who miss the intellectual challenge of complex civil cases find their work "boring as hell." Whatever perspective is adopted, the world of the criminal assignment judge is observably different—in pace, style, and tone—from that of the judge in civil assignment.[32]

Trial courts are increasingly referred to as "settlement" or "plea bargaining" courts, because so few cases, proportionately, are disposed of by trial.[33] Though this is unquestionably true in criminal and civil courts, such an image conceals or distorts the nature of most of the work performed by judges (and probably also by attorneys). Avoidance of trials may be a prime motivation of courtroom actors, but trial work is what judges mostly do—in terms of their time. Little wonder, then, that judges seek to avoid more trials.

## Notes

1. Herbert Jacob, *Urban Justice: Law and Order in American Cities* (Englewood Cliffs, N.J.: Prentice-Hall, 1973), p. 67
2. For an excellent overview of the civil courts that describes some of these different jurisdictions, see William P. McLauchlan, *American Legal Processes* (New York: Wiley, 1977), pp. 62–103.
3. These activities were derived from a larger list of seventy discrete activities identified in our field observations.
4. Methods of data collection relying upon self-reporting are fraught with problems. Judges, like other people, undoubtedly like to view themselves as hard-working. In addition, the hectic nature of the courthouse environment may make it difficult for some judges to perceive accurately *how* they spend their time. These caveats are necessary but do not challenge the basic reliability of the data to be presented. For example, 83 percent of all respondents completed the section on the description of work days, and 66 percent of these expressed "full" or "reasonable" confidence in the accuracy of their answers.
5. On the average, the most common day accounts for 58 percent of judges' total working days in a year. This figure ranges from 95 percent for judges who report only *one* type of work day to 38 percent for judges who report *five* types of work days.
6. Most judges (88 percent) attributed "0" percentage to the random category, indicating that the work days which they described account for all of the variation in their work days. For those few judges who did attribute some percentage to random work days, the average was thirty days over the course of a year. This ranges from forty-five random days for judges reporting only *one* type of work day to twenty-four random days for judges reporting *five* types of work days.
7. These arguments are summarized in Ernest C. Friesen, Edward C. Gallas, and Nesta M. Gallas, *Managing the Courts* (Indianapolis: Bobbs-Merrill, 1971), pp. 175–179, and McLauchlan, *American Legal Processes*, pp. 204–211.
8. Jacob, *Urban Justice*, p. 67.
9. See Herbert Jacob, *Justice in America*, 2d ed. (Boston: Little, Brown, 1972); also Jacob, "The Effect of Institutional Differences in the Recruitment Process: The Case of State Judges," *Journal of Public Law*, 13 (1964).
10. We did adopt a coding rule that two types of days reported by a given judge that actually were identical in the allocation of time to each task were coded as one type of day.
11. See, for example, Jeffrey Perlman, "Are County Judges Earning Their Pay? The Jury Is Still Out," *Los Angeles Times*, Orange County ed., July 26, 1976.
12. See David Pike and Thomas Crosby, "Judging the Judges," Parts 1–7, *Washington Star*, January 8–14, 1978. The *Star* series is one of the very few to move beyond hours worked as a measure of performance, no doubt prompted in part by the presence and sophistication of the District of Columbia Commission on Judicial Disabilities and Tenure.

13. Recall that we observed only forty judges in courts selected by purposive, not random, criteria.
14. Respondents were directed in the question to round to the nearest quarter hour, which probably meant rounding *upward* for a number of peripheral activities that consume only minutes on a given day.
15. The correlation matrix, upon which the factor analysis is based, is derived from the intercorrelations of dichotomous variables—i.e., whether or not the judge engaged in the specific activity (for a quarter-hour or more) on his most common day.
16. Factors were rotated to an oblique solution. The choice of an oblique solution is consonant with the moderate degree of intercorrelation among variables and among factors. For a discussion of rotation options, see Harry H. Harman, *Modern Factor Analysis* (Chicago: University of Chicago Press, 1967), or R. J. Rummel, *Applied Factor Analysis* (Evanston, Ill.: Northwestern University Press, 1970).
17. The majority of trial judges do not attend or participate in plea discussions. For a fuller treatment, see Chapter 8.
18. For suggestions of waiting time associated with jury trials, see Maureen Solomon, *Management of the Jury System*, American Bar Association Commission on Standards of Judicial Administration, Supporting Studies, 3, 1975, p. 5, and Bird Engineering–Research Associates, Inc., *A Guide to Juror Usage* (Washington, D.C.: Law Enforcement Assistance Administration, 1974), pp. 2-3, 4-6. We do not intend to suggest here that jury trials never cause judges to experience waiting time, but rather that the magnitude of the problem may be overstated, especially when compared to the effects from plea discussions.
19. See, for example, Raymond T. Nimmer and Patricia Ann Krauthaus, "Plea Bargaining: Reform in Two Cities," *Justice System Journal*, 3 (1977).
20. See, for example, Donald M. McIntyre and David Lippman, "Prosecutors and Early Disposition of Felony Cases," *American Bar Association Journal*, 56 (1970), reprinted in Jacob, *Justice in America*, (note 9 above), pp. 174-175.
21. The proportion of criminal judges who report nonjury trial work remains low until the fifth most common day, when 64 percent (of twenty-two judges) report nonjury work.
22. An analysis by state indicates only four states in which a higher percentage of criminal judges report nonjury than jury work on their most common day—Illinois, Pennsylvania, Virginia, and Wisconsin. Interestingly, this analysis comports quite well with selected state court data which indicate the proportion of nonjury trials (to all trials) to be very high in Virginia (93 percent) and Pennsylvania (81 percent) and moderately high in Illinois (58 percent). No data are reported for Wisconsin. See National Center for State Courts, *State Court Caseload Statistics: Annual Report, 1975* (Washington, D.C.: Law Enforcement Assistance Administration, 1979).
23. For a discussion of judges' estimated times for criminal and civil jury trials and the relationship to attorney characteristics, see Chapter 4.
24. What we do not know for general assignment judges is whether time spent in jury trials differs between their civil and criminal cases.

25. Our observational data reveal the following averages for length (in minutes) of nonjury trials:

   |                       | MEAN  | SD   | (N)  |
   |-----------------------|-------|------|------|
   | Criminal assignment   | 113   | 50   | (5)  |
   | Civil assignment      | 173+  | 123  | (17) |
   | General assignment:   |       |      |      |
   |   Criminal  | 94    | 49   | (6)  |
   |   Civil     | 189   | 186  | (7)  |

   For judges in civil assignment, a number of multiday nonjury trials concluded sometime *after* our observer departed.
26. For a discussion of the "slow plea," see Lynn M. Mather, "The Outsider in the Courtroom: An Alternative Role for Defense," in Herbert Jacob (ed.), *The Potential for Reform of Criminal Justice* (Beverly Hills and London: Sage Publications, 1974), pp. 265–266.
27. See James Eisenstein and Herbert Jacob, *Felony Justice: An Organizational Analysis of Criminal Courts* (Boston: Little, Brown, 1977), pp. 67–96.
28. See, for example, Harry Kalven, Jr., and Hans Zeisel, *The American Jury* (Chicago: University of Chicago Press, 1966), p. 380. A recent study of the Chicago courts reported that defendants (in 1977) were much more likely to be acquitted in a bench trial than in a jury trial (53 percent v. 29 percent). See "Defendants Are Better Off with Bench Trial, Study Says," *Chicago Tribune*, April 10, 1978.
29. On the average, the fourth most common day accounts for 12 percent of judges' total working days in a year. The fifth most common day, on average, accounts for only 9 percent of judges' total working days.
30. The most common grounds for appellate reversal of a trial court's decision are related to the jury—particularly, improper charge (instructions) by the judge. See Robert G. Nieland, *Pattern Jury Instructions: A Critical Look at a Modern Movement to Improve the Jury System* (Chicago: American Judicature Society, 1979), pp. 16–17.
31. Rubin notes that the juvenile court judge's greatest frustration "is the absence of readily available resources to meet the educational, counseling, supervision, treatment, and residence needs of his juvenile clients." See H. Ted Rubin, "The Eye of the Juvenile Court Judge: A One-Step-Up View of the Juvenile Justice System," in Malcolm W. Klein (ed.), *The Juvenile Justice System* (Beverly Hills and London: Sage Publications, 1976).
32. See Abraham S. Blumberg, *Criminal Justice* (Chicago: Quadrangle, 1967), p. 118.
33. Milton Heumann, *Plea Bargaining: The Experiences of Prosecutors, Judges and Defense Attorneys* (Chicago: University of Chicago Press, 1977), p. 1.

# CHAPTER 3

## The Impact of Court Structure

TRIAL judges, like other professional and occupational workers, are influenced in their day-to-day activities by the structure, operational characteristics, and norms of the organization of which they are a part. In this chapter, we seek to describe the key formal and informal structures of trial courts in America and analyze their impact on judicial work patterns.

We shall examine the role of court size, divisions of labor, and management practices, elements that define a major part of the judge's relationship with his work environment. Specifically, we focus on two questions: (1) How specialized is the judge's work? (2) How stable is his contact with the court? Size of court and, correlatively, size of community, as well as the degree to which courts formalize divisions, bear decisively upon the amount of specialization a judge will encounter. Our data indicate that judges in urban locales, larger courts, and courts that divide criminal from civil case work are more specialized in what they do. The stability of a judge's relationship to his working environment, by contrast, is directly a function of whether he must travel to different courthouses to do his work. In many rural and some relatively urban places, judges ride circuit across several counties or commute from their homes to courthouses far away. Stability is further influenced by the amount of "sharing" of work required in a particular circuit: The more judges who belong to a circuit, the less stable will be the relationship of each judge to the (many) courthouses because of the vagaries of rotational or assignment patterns within the circuit.

These diverse elements of court structure represent a curious mix of historical and contemporary ways of organizing work in entities we come to call "courts." In some instances, different approaches to organization reflect the special needs of rural and urban courts today. Rural places rely upon grouping together labor to hear cases, while urban locales foster specialization of work and workers. In other instances, though, idiosyncratic structures or procedures persist from custom, especially in regions of the country where adhering to tradition is a social and political value.

We now turn to a description of each of these structural and operational elements of trial courts, to a discussion of how they interrelate in forming types of courts, and to an analysis of their respective impacts on the judicial work patterns which we described in Chapter 2.

## Size of Court

The most far-reaching characteristic of most organizations is their size, and courts are no exception. Size of court, or the number of judges sitting in the local trial court of general jurisdiction, influences—even dictates—other structural and operational characteristics, such as the feasibility of divisions of work by case specialization, the appropriateness of one or another case assignment system, and the efficacy of cyclical work routines. Table 3-1 shows the percentage of judges serving in different-size courts, ranging from the solo-judge court to courts in which there are forty or more judges.

The most striking feature of these data is the small portion of the nation's judges who sit in large courts. Although these judges have been the focus of most previous research efforts, four-fifths of all judges sit in small or intermediate-size courts. A breakdown reveals that in only a few states do more

TABLE 3-1. Proportion of Trial Judges by Size of Court

| Size of Court (Number of Judges)[a] | Percent | Number |
|---|---|---|
| Small | | |
| 1 | 14.7 | (436) |
| 2 | 13.7 | (410) |
| 3–4 | 14.4 | (430) |
| Intermediate | | |
| 5–9 | 16.2 | (485) |
| 10–15 | 12.3 | (368) |
| 16–25 | 8.6 | (256) |
| Large | | |
| 26–39 | 9.1 | (272) |
| 40 or more | 11.0 | (329) |
| | 100.0 | (2986) |

[a] Categories represent those provided to survey respondents.

than one-third of the judges sit in large courts. In contrast, most states have a significant percentage of judges in one-judge courts; this is true, even pronounced, in some rather populous states such as Indiana, Texas, and Wisconsin, where one-third or more of the trial judges serve by themselves.

## Divisions in Urban Courts

In courts that do have more than a few judges, the opportunity for specialization along divisional lines arises. This much is clear from our data: As size of court increases, the likelihood that its judges will be generalists—hearing both criminal and civil cases—decreases sharply. Whereas 73 percent of judges in courts with three or four judges are generalists, only 14 percent of judges in the largest courts hear both criminal and civil cases in their current assignment.

Divisionalization within court systems is not an easy phenomenon to study or describe. There are many ways to effect divisions of labor in courts, as we observed in the field. In addition, specialization by case type is *not,* from an administrative view, the same phenomenon as divisionalization. We define divisions to be present in courts that "assign judges to hear only certain types, or stages, of cases for a period of time." Only if judges are elected or appointed to a court whose presiding judge makes *assignments* to specific divisions—e.g., a criminal division, civil division, or juvenile division—does the opportunity exist to serve in a number of different assignments (divisions).

Among our observational sites, Houston and Nashville are examples of work specialization without divisions. In Houston, there are some thirty-seven district court judges whose case jurisdictions are specified by statute. These include criminal, civil, domestic relations, and juvenile courts.[1] In Nashville, there are twelve criminal, circuit (civil), and chancery court judgeships to which judges are directly elected.[2] In both places, judges become and stay specialized in one area for the duration of their term of judgeship. In contrast, the Los Angeles Superior Court is one administrative unit that contains divisions to which judges are assigned by a presiding judge; these include one criminal division and several civil divisions (e.g., eminent domain, domestic relations). The Cook County (Chicago) Circuit Court is also one administrative unit, but with more highly specialized divisions of work. Judges in Chicago might be sitting in "gun court," "women's court," the law–jury division, the pretrial (civil) division, the chancery division, a "county" division, which hears a mix of mental health cases and election disputes, or a number of other specialized divisions.

The Orange County (California) Superior Court and the DuPage County (Illinois) Circuit Court are examples of divisionalization by *stage* of case, rather than by type of case. In both of these courts, most judges sit in a "trial" division where they might be assigned a criminal trial one day and a civil trial the next. Most of the pretrial work is handled by a series of "calendar" judges who do specialize, e.g., in criminal, probate, or domestic relations cases.

Still other courts we observed had no divisions whatsoever. For example, the Dane County (Madison, Wisconsin) Circuit Court has four judges, each of whom may hear any type, or stage, of case. And in one-judge courts, as in rural Nebraska, where we observed a circuit-riding judge, that judge hears everything.

Slightly less than half (46 percent) of our respondents report that they sit in courts with divisions. As would be expected, they are concentrated in the large multijudge courts of a few urban states. For these judges, we wished to determine whether or not they had served in other divisions, as well as their perception of practices underlying the rotation of judges from division to division in their court. From such information, the context within which divisionalization operates can better be understood.

More than half (58 percent) of judges in courts with divisions have served in some different division from their current one. Judges' most recent prior assignment was likely to have been criminal, civil—mixed, or domestic relations. Currently assigned criminal judges most frequently report civil or domestic relations as their previous assignment, wheras currently assigned civil judges report criminal, (other) civil, or domestic relations as their previous assignment. Generalists, on the other hand, are much less likely to have heard a different (i.e., narrower) range of cases, since most of these judges serve in courts without divisions.

Overall, we can detect little in the way of patterns from the assortment of current and previous divisional assignments that trial judges report. Most criminal division judges (63 percent) have served in the civil divisions of their court. Most civil division judges (65 percent) have also served in other civil divisions and/or the criminal division of their court. Similarly, most judges (70 percent) currently serving in juvenile, domestic relations, or probate divisions are likely to have served elsewhere in their court.[3] It is nearly impossible to disentangle which judges served where for how long, except to note that our field-based hunch that new judges are especially likely to be assigned to the criminal division is probably not true. Nevertheless, the data do indicate that most judges in courts that specialize work through divisions are exposed to several kinds of cases over the course of their service on the bench.

The general pattern of rotational practice which judges characterize for their courts is reported in Table 3-2. The perceived practices of courts vary widely, with respect to the frequency with which judges are typically rotated from one division to another. Almost half (43 percent) of the judges in courts with divisions report rotation on an annual or more frequent basis, offering judges in these courts the opportunity to sit in a number of different assignments. Conversely, more than one-third of judges report rotation patterns of two-year or longer intervals, suggesting that in other courts judges may

TABLE 3-2. Frequency of Judicial Rotation: The General Practice of Trial Courts[a]

|  | PERCENT | NUMBER |
|---|---|---|
| Six months or more frequent | 19.5 | (257) |
| Annual | 23.5 | (309) |
| Two to five years | 16.0 | (211) |
| Rarely | 19.0 | (251) |
| No discernible time pattern | 22.0 | (290) |
|  | 100.0 | (1318) |

[a] Judges sitting in courts without divisions have been excluded.

become frozen into particular specialties. Finally, almost one-quarter of all judges could detect "no discernible time pattern" to rotational practices in their courts.

Differences in the rotational practices of courts are partly explained by size of court. Annual rotation occurs most frequently in intermediate-size courts, where about one-third of the judges report its use. In larger courts, annual rotation gives way to less frequent rotation. In the largest courts, annual rotation probably does not take place because of sheer logistics: In these courts, judges most often report difficulty in discerning any time pattern to rotation. The experience and practices of large courts would suggest that decisions to rotate judges depend also upon criteria other than variety and specialization. We believe that at least four other criteria are sometimes, if not regularly, applied.

Technical expertise of the judge is one such criterion. If judges, because of their past legal practice or current interests, are more knowledgeable in certain areas of law, it makes intuitively good sense to utilize their expertise.[4] The case disposition rate of a judge may be another factor in assignments. Judges who agonize over decisions, who are reluctant to negotiate actively, who work short hours, or who are "slow" for whatever reasons may not be assigned to divisions requiring the processing of a high volume of cases quickly—e.g., the criminal division in a state having a speedy trial provision.

The sentencing philosophy of individual judges may influence a presiding judge's decision to assign or not to assign a particular judge to the criminal division. We saw two vivid examples of this criterion in action. In one urban court, a recently assigned civil division judge whom we observed remarked that he had really hoped for assignment to the criminal division but could not pass the sentencing "test" imposed by the presiding judge. A critical conversation went something like, PJ: "Would you ever send anyone to the state penitentiary?" J: "Well . . . I . . . I don't know." And in Orange County, California, a recent presiding judge-elect announced to local reporters that he would seek to increase the proportion of criminal cases disposed by guilty plea by sending the recalcitrant nonpleaders to trial before a "murderer's row" of judges known to be tough sentencers.[5]

The fourth criterion for judicial assignment to divisions is something of a residual category, which we have termed "court politics." In some courts, it could refer to the influence of *partisan* politics, as Eisenstein and Jacob have asserted for Chicago.[6] In other courts, it could stand for seniority or "clout." While it is difficult to pinpoint examples of the influence of politics, two recently publicized reassignments in the Chicago courts lend credence to its existence in that court and undoubtedly elsewhere. One judge was reassigned from juvenile to housing court in the wake of her ongoing battle with local child welfare agencies.[7] Another judge was reassigned from criminal to small claims court one day after he granted an appeal bond to a convicted drug dealer whom he characterized as an "upstanding" citizen in the community.[8] Needless to say, neither housing nor small claims court is regarded as a desirable assignment.

How do judges nationally view the significance of these criteria for rotational practices in their courts? Table 3-3 reports the findings for each of these criteria, including regular rotation. Our data indicate that regular rotation is most often perceived to have substantial influence on the assignment of judges, followed closely by the technical expertise of the judge. Case disposition rate and court politics are less often thought to be substantial influences, and sentencing philosophy was least frequently cited. It is nevertheless an interesting commentary upon the process of assignment that *as many as* 30 percent of all trial judges acknowledge some influence for sentencing philosophy, and almost 40 percent perceive some influence for court politics. Neither of these criteria would be regarded as fully legitimate by chief judges or the judicial rank-and-file.

An examination of the relationship between court size and the perceived importance of these criteria for assignment corroborates our earlier analysis. In larger courts (especially forty or more judges), the influence of regular rotation

TABLE 3-3. Trial Judges' Perceptions of the Influence of Divisional Assignment Criteria in Their Courts[a]

|  | SUBSTANTIAL INFLUENCE | SLIGHT INFLUENCE | NO INFLUENCE | NUMBER |
|---|---|---|---|---|
| Regular rotation | 47.6% | 18.1% | 34.3% | (1191) |
| Technical expertise | 39.3 | 27.0 | 33.7 | (1184) |
| Case disposition rate | 20.2 | 28.2 | 51.6 | (1164) |
| Court politics | 14.7 | 24.2 | 61.1 | (1163) |
| Sentencing philosophy | 5.8 | 25.2 | 69.0 | (1145) |

[a] Judges in courts without divisions have been excluded.

declines sharply, whereas each of the other factors—particularly case disposition rate and court politics—increases in significance.

## Moving Courts: The Rural Analog

In lightly populated areas, judicial specialization is usually not feasible. Rather, the pressing problem is how to get cases and judges together relatively quickly and economically. A central courthouse may not accomplish these goals because of its distance from some parts of a multicounty district or circuit. In fact, some very rural counties still may not have a pool of resident lawyers from which a judge could be selected.

The most frequently used administrative solution to this kind of problem is circuit-riding, which is anything but a relic from some bygone era. One-third of all judges serve in *multicounty* jurisdictions requiring some circuit-riding. Nearly half (47 percent) of circuit-riders report "travel time" on their most common day; the average time is 1.5 hours. These figures are similar for less common days. There is a significant overlap between those reporting travel time on their most common day and on less common days. This suggests that most circuit-riders frequently engage in travel, while a few are required only infrequently to travel.

Circuit-riding is also widely distributed across the country. Unlike divisions, which typically are present only in large courts in highly urban states, circuit-riders can be found in nearly every state. For example, a substantial percentage of judges report circuit-riding responsibilities in urban states such as Florida (34 percent), Illinois (33 percent), and Missouri (52 percent). In twenty states, more than *half* of all judges engage in some circuit-riding across county lines.

There are two different structures within which circuit-riding takes place, stemming directly from the number of judges in a given circuit. In the states of Arkansas, Kentucky, Mississippi, Nebraska, and Texas, among others, only one judge typically belongs to a circuit, so that he alone is responsible for traveling to the several locations within the circuit. In other states, such as Alabama, Florida, Illinois, Iowa, Louisiana, New York, South Dakota, and Virginia, a number of judges—perhaps as many as five or even ten or more—belong to a circuit and share, in some mixture of ways, responsibility for covering all the locations withing the circuit. Table 3-4 shows the number of judges sitting in different-size circuits.

Most judges who ride circuit do so in conjunction with one or more fellow judges. Only 25 percent of circuit-riding judges serve by themselves. Of the remainder, most belong to small circuits: two, three, or four judges. Yet a significant percentage belong to larger circuits, found primarily in Florida and New York. In urban states, some counties are circuits unto themselves—e.g.,

TABLE 3-4. Proportion of Circuit-riding Judges by Size of Court

| SIZE OF COURT (NUMBER OF JUDGES)[a] | PERCENT | NUMBER |
|---|---|---|
| Small | | |
| 1 | 25.2 | (213) |
| 2 | 22.3 | (189) |
| 3–4 | 20.4 | (173) |
| Intermediate | | |
| 5–9 | 14.5 | (123) |
| 10–15 | 9.6 | (81) |
| 16–25 | 6.0 | (51) |
| Large | | |
| 26–39 | .7 | (6) |
| 40 or more | 1.3 | (11) |
| | 100.0 | (847) |

[a] Categories represent those provided to survey respondents.

Cook (Chicago) and Dade (Miami). But in less populated areas within these states, circuits may comprise more than one central courthouse, in different counties, and may differ only in degree from circuits in sparsely populated states.

Another kind of administrative solution to the problem of matching cases with judges, also of considerable vintage, is the use of "statewide assignment," that is, dispersing judges from a central pool to locations throughout the state. Although a number of state court administrative offices occasionally shift judges around, on a temporary basis, to fill acute needs in one part of the state (usually from rural to urban locales), only a small number of states use this as the exclusive mode of utilizing judicial manpower in the trial courts.[9] All six New England states—Connecticut, Maine, Massachusetts, New Hampshire, Rhode Island, and Vermont—as well as Delaware, North Carolina, and South Carolina, use statewide assignment in this way. (It is no accident that virtually all of these states do, or once did, select their trial judges by gubernatorial appointment. In states where trial judges are elected locally, it is difficult to imagine that statewide assignment could be implemented without public uproar.) In some of these states there are only a few different locations to which judges can be assigned (three in Delaware); in other states there are as many as thirty districts, or areas, to be covered (North Carolina).

One characteristic of statewide assignment systems in operation is that judges move from one geographic location to another rather frequently.[10] Table 3–5 provides a state breakdown of the typical length of assignment to any one location.

In most of the nine states using statewide assignment, judges are assigned

TABLE 3-5. **Trial Judges' Length of Assignment Under Statewide Systems**

|  | \multicolumn{6}{c|}{Months} |  |
|---|---|---|---|---|---|---|---|
|  | 2 OR LESS | 3-5 | 6 | 7-11 | 12 | 13 OR MORE | Number |
| Connecticut | — | 100.0% | — | — | — | — | (19) |
| Delaware | — | 37.5 | 12.5 | 12.5 | 12.5 | 25.0 | (8) |
| Maine | 100.0 | — | — | — | — | — | (6) |
| Massachusetts | 95.5 | 4.5 | — | — | — | — | (22) |
| New Hampshire | 16.7 | 83.3 | — | — | — | — | (6) |
| North Carolina | — | — | 100.0 | — | — | — | (21) |
| Rhode Island | — | 50.0 | — | — | 20.0 | 30.0 | (10) |
| South Carolina | 28.6 | 21.4 | 50.0 | — | — | — | (14) |
| Vermont | — | 50.0 | 50.0 | — | — | — | (6) |

to a specific location for a rather short period of time—usually not more than six months, and often significantly less. In Maine and Massachusetts, for example, judges move from one assignment to another every two months or more frequently. Similarly, in most states policies of assignment are rather consistently applied to all trial judges within the state.[11] In Delaware and Rhode Island, the very high proportion of judges assigned to the most populous location in the state probably precludes uniform rotation.

One wrinkle to the use of statewide assignment is that some circuit-riding can still be involved. Judges may be assigned to an *area,* rather than one specific court, and accordingly be required to cover more than one courthouse. Our survey data and field observations in Vermont suggest this is more likely to occur in predominantly rural states, like Vermont and South Carolina, and less likely to occur in predominantly urban states such as Connecticut and Rhode Island.

Travel, then, may also be an important feature of judicial work in statewide assignment systems, either through circuit-riding, "commuting" (from home to assigned location), or both. In fact, 62 percent of judges serving in statewide assignment report travel time on their most common day, for an average of 1.6 hours. In the small states of Delaware and Rhode Island, which have only a few locations and a less frequent rotation pattern, no judges report travel time. In contrast, most judges in the remaining states using statewide assignment indicate travel time on their most common and less common work days.

## Case Assignment Systems

Once the essential structure of a court system is framed, a number of operational questions arise whose resolution bears upon the organization of work. Perhaps the most important of these management practices is the basis on which cases are to be assigned to judges.

Historically, cases were filed with an individual judge whose responsibility extended to the entire life of that case in the trial court. This is referred to as an "individual" calendar. But with the advent of large, multijudge courts and new theories of management, some courts adopted what is referred to as a "master" calendar. Under this system, at the conclusion of one or more stages of a case, the case is returned to a master or central pool for subsequent assignment to the next available judge. From the individual judge's perspective, he is hearing only one or more stages of any and all cases—e.g., pretrial motions, settlement conferences, or the trial itself. From a courtwide perspective, the master calendar represents an innovation designed, in part, to adjust for the inevitably different speeds at which judges process their own caseloads.[12]

There are variations in the actual operation of calendaring systems, which result in less pure distinctions. For example, some courts may elect an individual calendar principle through all pretrial events (discovery, motions, settlement conferences), but then revert to reassignment to a different judge at trial. Other courts, in contrast, may send cases back to the central pool after each distinct stage. Another variation lies in the number of cases simultaneously assigned to one judge, especially at the trial stage, in master calendar systems. Some courts may rigidly send down one case at a time, while other courts will send down several cases ready for trial, thereby granting some scheduling discretion to the judge. In still other courts, some divisions operate under a master calendar while other divisions use an individual calendar (for variations in our observation sites, see Table A-1 in Appendix A). Despite these variations, the individual and master calendars embody quite different general philosophies about court management, including the desirability of introducing specialization by *stage* of case.

A substantial majority of all judges report operating under an individual calendar, but some judges (in single-judge courts) necessarily so. When single-judge courts are excluded, 57 percent of the remaining judges have an individual calendar while 43 percent serve under a master calendar. Size of court makes a substantial impact upon the feasibility of effecting a master calendar system, as Table 3-6 demonstrates.

The significant points at which the use of a master calendar increases occur in intermediate-size courts (with five or more judges) and again in large courts (with twenty-six or more judges). In the latter courts, a majority of judges report a master calendar system. Nevertheless, these figures are a bit difficult to interpret precisely, because one calendaring system may not always be employed courtwide. Thus, the scale of the court as a whole may not be so decisive in the choice of a calendaring system as the size of a particular division, or even the types of cases heard in a division.[13]

The use of calendaring systems also varies quite sharply from state to state. The use of the master calendar is widespread in only a few states. In many other states its use is restricted to one or a few urban courts. In still others there are no courts or judges using a master calendar.[14] But virtually all judges under

TABLE 3-6. Utilization of Individual and Master Calendar by Size of Court[a]

| SIZE OF COURT (NUMBER OF JUDGES) | INDIVIDUAL | MASTER | NUMBER |
|---|---|---|---|
| Small | | | |
| 1 | 100.0% | 0% | (436) |
| 2 | 76.6 | 23.4 | (158) |
| 3–4 | 66.5 | 33.5 | (194) |
| Intermediate | | | |
| 5–9 | 58.7 | 41.3 | (286) |
| 10–15 | 57.2 | 42.8 | (222) |
| 16–25 | 56.6 | 43.4 | (159) |
| Large | | | |
| 26–39 | 41.6 | 58.4 | (219) |
| 40 or more | 41.6 | 58.4 | (245) |

[a] Excludes judges who ride circuit or who are located in statewide assignment systems.

statewide assignment report a master calendar. This initially puzzling description of their case assignment system is best understood by recalling that judges in these states are rotated from one geographic location to another quite frequently—*faster* than the life of most cases, either civil or criminal. Thus, while cases are stationary in these states—staying in the same courthouse—judges are not. The result is that one judge may hear pretrial matters in a case, but by the time that case is ready for trial another judge will be sitting in the courthouse. This "moving master calendar" is clearly a quite different organizational principle from that which exists in larger (stationary) multijudge courts.

## Work Cycles and Procedures

One final group of management issues that help to define the working environment of trial judges concludes our introduction of key elements of court structure. For lack of a better term, we call these "work cycles" because they typically involve a routinization of work on a periodic or cyclical basis. Most of these work cycles represent the decisions of the court as a whole, but some may reflect the preferences of individual judges within the court.

The use of weekly or monthly "terms"—to divide the work of jury trials from nonjury trials or criminal cases from civil cases—is quite common. Sometimes there is nothing more than historical custom behind such a division of work. Indeed, the use of lengthy criminal and civil terms (say, two months) is now criticized for contributing to some courts' inability to meet the mandates of speedy trial provisions in criminal cases.[15] In other instances, the use of weekly terms—particularly jury/nonjury weeks, as we observed in the

Nashville civil courts—can contribute to efficiency by reducing attorney scheduling conflicts.

Across the country as a whole, 40 percent of trial judges report the use of jury/nonjury terms, and 32 percent indicate the operation of criminal/civil terms in their courts. There is a sharp regional pattern to the use of terms suggesting a historical link: Terms appear to be dominant in the Northeast and South, but infrequent in the West. Size of court is also related: In small and intermediate courts, almost half of the judges report terms in their courts, but that percentage drops dramatically for judges in large courts. Finally, terms are more likely to occur in courts with circuit-riding judges. In some lightly populated areas, the "court" may be a periodic rather than continuous entity, depending upon the presence of its judge (e.g., three or four times per year, one month at a time) for activity.

Rationalization of work by day of week, setting aside part or all of one day for one kind of task (e.g., motion hearings), is also rather common.[16] Fifty-six percent of judges report that they rationalize tasks in this way, either on their own initiative or in response to a courtwide policy. There are no significant regional patterns, but rationalization of tasks drops off sharply in the very largest courts. This may reflect, in part, the fewer time management options available to judges in these courts. Perhaps the pressures of caseload are perceived to be sufficiently great so that no day of the week can be set aside exclusively for one type of matter (usually nontrial work).

One particular form of rationalization—setting aside an entire week for settlement conferences in civil cases—is used in some very large courts (notably Philadelphia), though it is not common nationwide (9 percent). Under this work plan, all judges in an entire division might be removed from trial work in order to help reduce backlogs. This type of work rationalization is clearly one over which the individual judge (in large courts) has no control.

Finally, some courts use extra manpower on a regular or periodic basis to hear certain kinds and stages of cases. The Philadelphia Court of Common Pleas, for example, has an active arbitration program, which utilizes lawyers on an *ad hoc* but frequent basis. The Orange County (California) Superior Court makes considerable use of "pro-tem" judges (volunteer lawyers) to conduct settlement conferences in civil cases. And the Los Angeles Superior Court uses full-time commissioners in its eminent domain division. Twenty-seven percent of judges nationally report "active" use of one or more of these kinds of supplements to manpower in their courts. As our observations suggested, this is much more likely to happen in the West and the Northeast than elsewhere in the country.

## Toward Synthesis: Court Types

These elements of court structure can be linked together in both functional and structural ways. The rubric of specialization and its rural face, geographic mobility, help to define the functional relationships among these variables.

But structural interrelationships also exist that result in a number of different ways of organizing courts, their work, and workers. It is to these structural interrelationships, which have been virtually ignored in the literature on court administration, that we turn our attention here.[17] Figure 3-1 displays the different types of court, including the approximate percentage of judges located within each.

As Figure 3-1 indicates, we have divided courts initially into three broad categories, one-judge courts, multijudge courts, and courts using statewide assignment. The overwhelming majority of trial judges are found in multijudge courts. Although nine states use statewide assignment, the number of judges serving in trial courts in these states is quite small.[18]

In one-judge courts, slightly more than half of the judges ride circuit, notably in Arkansas, Kentucky, Mississippi, Nebraska, and Texas. Other solo judges, likely to be located in the Mideastern region of Indiana, Ohio, and Pennsylvania, are permanently stationed in one courthouse. For judges serving by themselves, questions of case assignment system or divisionalization are not applicable.

Most judges (almost 80 percent) are located in multijudge courts. The bulk of these judges do *not* ride circuit. It is in these stationary courts that the presence of a particular type of case assignment system most clearly reflects a management choice. Applications of the individual and master calendars are almost equal here. Judges having an individual calendar and no circuit-riding responsibilities are most likely to be found in Arizona, Colorado, Florida, Michigan, Ohio, and Wisconsin. Judges serving under a master calendar who do not ride circuit are most likely to be found in California, New York, Oregon, Pennsylvania, and Washington. It is in multijudge courts without circuit-riding that divisionalization usually occurs.

For judges in multijudge courts who do ride circuit, most have an individual calendar. These judges are distributed broadly across a large number of states. In contrast, more than half of the judges who ride circuit and who report a master calendar are located in one of three states, Illinois, Iowa, and New York. In Iowa, this type of court predominates (representing about two-thirds of the state's trial judges); in Illinois and New York, it reflects the situation of only a small percentage of judges. In all three states, this configuration reflects a *localized* version of statewide assignment, i.e., multijudge, multicounty circuits with rotation (assignment) patterns within a circuit at a frequency faster than the life of a typical case.[19]

Finally, a small proportion of judges serve in statewide assignment systems, states in which judges are assigned to various locations from a central administrative office. Some of these judges, particularly in the more rural states, must also do some circuit-riding. Statewide assignment occurs, as we have already noted, in all of New England, Delaware, and North and South Carolina.

The diffusion of court types has a very sketchy and uncertain pattern. Only New England and the Pacific Coast states provide any support for a theory of

60    AMERICAN TRIAL JUDGES

**One-Judge Courts**[a]
(17.2%)[c]

- No Circuit-Riding (7.7%)
- Circuit-Riding (9.5%)

**Multi-Judge Courts**
(79.4%)

- No Circuit-Riding (58.7%)
  - Individual Calendar (32.8%)
  - Master Calendar (25.9%)
- Circuit-Riding (20.7%)
  - Individual Calendar (14.0%)
  - Master Calendar (6.7%)

**Statewide Assignment**[b]
(3.4%)

- No Circuit-Riding (2.7%)
- Circuit-Riding (.7%)

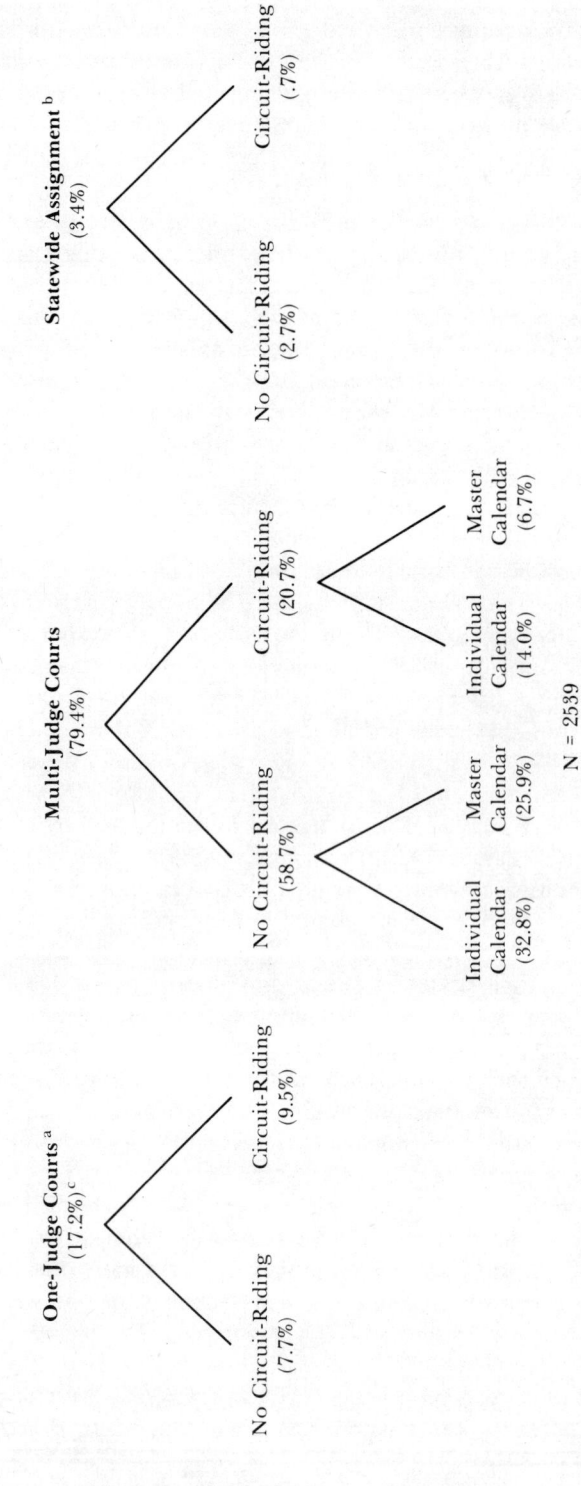

N = 2539

[a] By definition, individual calendar.
[b] By definition, (moving) master calendar.
[c] Percentage for one-judge courts varies slightly from Table 3-1 because of some missing data on the circuit-riding question.

**FIGURE 3-1.  Distribution of Trial Judges by Court Type**

diffusion on a regional basis.[20] Otherwise, the distribution of "court types" is fairly idiosyncratic and undoubtedly reflects differing attitudes toward the value of circuit-riding, local justice, and management innovations among each state's political and judicial elites.

## Questions of Impact

Having described the key elements of court structure and examined their interrelationships, we now turn to the question of their impact on judicial work patterns. What difference does each of these variables make in what judges do? Do judges in large courts have a different mix of tasks from that of judges in smaller courts? Are circuit-riding judges or those situated in statewide assignment distinctively different in their management of time and tasks from judges who stay in one courthouse? Through an analysis of these specific relationships, with appropriate statistical controls, we move toward a theory of judicial work. In the summary to this chapter, we return to a discussion of the linkages between individual structural variables and the larger themes of judicial specialization and stability.

THE IMPACT OF COURT SIZE

Based upon our field observations, we developed some general notions about the work patterns of judges in small and large courts. For example, judges in smaller courts clearly performed a wider variety of tasks from day to day. Judges in larger courts seemed more often occupied with settlement concerns on both the civil and the criminal side. Nevertheless, we could not develop a comprehensive description of, or theory about, the impact of court size by observing only forty judges.

Our survey data demonstrate that size of court influences trial judges' work patterns in a substantial way, much more so than for any other structural variable. In some instances, its impact is *linear:* As court size increases, so does the percentage of judges doing a specific task, for example.[21] In other instances, the impact is in the form of a *step-level* function: As court size increases, no change in the percentage of judges doing a specific task occurs until there are forty or more judges in a court, for example.[22] And in a very few instances, the impact is *curvilinear:* Judges in small courts and large courts behave similarly and, therefore, differently from judges in intermediate-size courts.[23]

One area in which size of court does not make much difference is among circuit-riding judges. This should not be surprising, given the theoretical underpinnings of the concept of organizational scale. Circuit-riding judges, regardless of the actual number of judges in their circuit, often perform their work alone. They are isolated from their judicial colleagues by the vagaries of geography. If they do work in a courthouse with other judges from the circuit, the relationship will not be constant. Different judges, and different numbers of judges, will be working together at various times and places. In the following analyses, then, data on the impact of court size pertain only to judges who do *not* ride circuit and, for parallel reasons, to judges who are *not* located in statewide assignment systems.

Size of court makes a difference in the contours of judges' working days, both variety and length. In two ways, judges in larger courts experience less variety than their counterparts in smaller courts. First, judges in larger courts hear a narrower range of cases, usually restricted to only criminal or only civil cases, or even some subset of civil cases (e.g., domestic relations, probate, or civil-jury). The less frequent divisional rotation patterns of large courts compounds, over time, this lack of variety. Secondly, judges in larger courts report fewer different kinds of work days in their current assignment, as Table 3-7 indicates.

The differences in work day variety by court size are striking. Fully half of judges in small courts report four or five different kinds of work days, whereas nearly half of all judges in the largest courts report only *one* type of work day. The impact of court size is uniform across types of assignment: For judges sitting in criminal, civil—mixed, and general assignments, the larger their court, the fewer different kinds of days reported.[24]

Judges in larger courts also report working longer hours on their most common day. The differences, however, are less dramatic than in the area of variety. The number of hours worked rises from a low of 8.6 hours on the average for judges serving by themselves to a high of 9.4 hours for those in courts with forty or more judges. This pattern holds on less common work days and for judges in civil, criminal, and general assignment. Why do judges in larger courts tend to work longer hours? We can only speculate, but two factors may be significant: relative caseload and accountability to an administrative structure. Judges in larger courts may be confronted with more cases *per capita,* or more "complex" cases, than their counterparts in smaller courts. Additionally, judges in large multijudge courts work within an elaborate administrative structure (chief judge, assignment judges, and court administrator), to which they are accountable by virtue of the sanctions that chief judges et al. possess. For example, in Philadelphia the court administrator's office has been known to call judges who are on vacation, but in town, back to the courthouse for emergency service. Perhaps for these or other reasons, judges in larger courts must work longer and more regular hours whether they wish to or not.

Judges in courts of different sizes also differ in the *substance* of what they do. Three task activities, in particular, are reported by more judges—on their most common day—in larger courts: keeping up with the law, presiding at a jury trial, and waiting time. The percentage of judges who "keep up with the law" rises from 63 percent in one-judge courts to 83 percent in the largest courts. Similarly, the percentage of judges who report some "waiting time" rises from 36 percent in one-judge courts to 55 percent in the largest courts.

**TABLE 3-7.** Variety of Judicial Work by Size of Court

| | \multicolumn{5}{c|}{Number of Different Work Days} | |
|---|---|---|---|---|---|---|
| Size of court[a] | 1 | 2 | 3 | 4 | 5 | Number |
| Small | 11.0% | 12.4% | 26.5% | 20.5% | 29.6% | (419) |
| Intermediate | 17.5 | 23.9 | 27.9 | 12.8 | 17.9 | (570) |
| Large | | | | | | |
| 26–39 | 28.9 | 36.4 | 20.5 | 5.3 | 8.9 | (190) |
| 40 or more | 43.8 | 30.3 | 13.2 | 6.1 | 6.6 | (228) |

[a] For tabular simplicity, the number of categories of court size has been reduced where distributions on number of work days are similar.

Each of these findings makes intuitive sense. The potential for complex litigation and for more active development of case law is undoubtedly greater in larger courts and communities. So much the greater is the perceived need for judges in these places to "keep up with the law." And it is almost to be expected that more judges will wait—for lawyers, litigants, and cases—in larger courts where work is organized on a more formalized and more rigid basis. It is also quite possible, of course, that judges in larger courts will tend to view "dead time" as waiting time (that is, wasted time). We noted in our overview of the generalist's working day that there seemed to be a greater elasticity or flexibility to scheduling in smaller courts. Adjustments to unexpected cancellations did not seem to wreak the havoc and dismay that accompanied "no-shows" in large courts.

The sharp increase in jury trial work as court size increases is not so readily explained, except initially by the concomitant decrease in nonjury trial work. Figure 3–2 displays these data. In one-judge courts, 60 percent report nonjury work, whereas only 25 percent report jury work, on the most common day. These figures are almost reversed in courts with forty or more judges. The graphic display also indicates that the slope is more pronounced between small and intermediate-size courts than between the latter and the largest courts. It is also useful in interpreting these data to recall that judges in small courts are much more likely to have second, third, and fourth common types of days (on which they might have jury work). Still, the comparative frequency of jury and nonjury trial work shifts considerably from smaller to larger courts, for reasons that are not entirely clear.[25] We can only speculate that perhaps a different mix of cases is heard in small and large courts (e.g., more personal injury cases, more serious criminal offenses in larger courts) or that litigants express different preferences between jury and bench trials. Also, very small communities may experience more difficulty in providing available jurors.[26]

In addition to these linear differences between judges in smaller and larger courts, judges in the largest courts differ from all others in the frequency with which they report certain activities, notably plea discussions, socializing, and administrative work. These relationships are best characterized as step-level

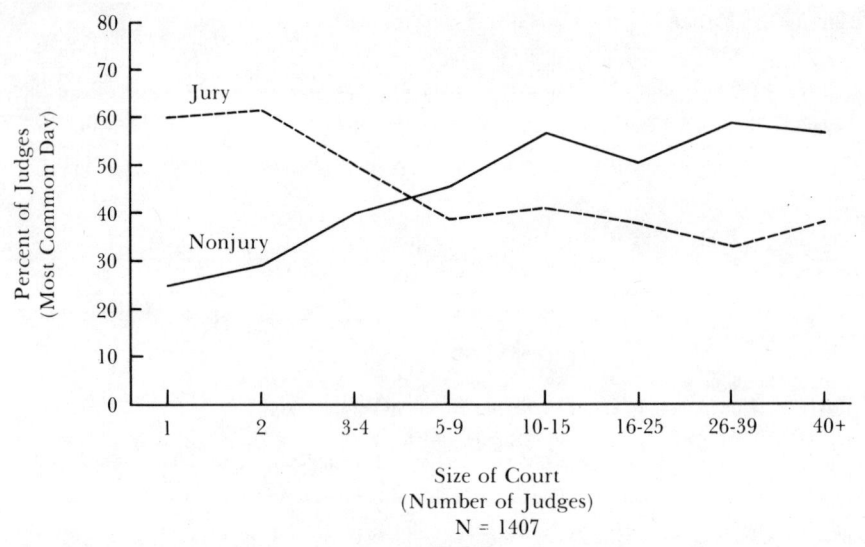

[Figure: line graph showing Percent of Judges (Most Common Day) on y-axis (0–80) vs Size of Court (Number of Judges) on x-axis with categories 1, 2, 3-4, 5-9, 10-15, 16-25, 26-39, 40+. Two lines: Jury and Nonjury. N = 1407]

**FIGURE 3-2.** Frequency of Jury and Nonjury Trial Work by Size of Court

functions, because there are no differences until courts with forty or more judges. For example, about 20 percent of judges report some plea negotiation activity on their most common day in all courts but the largest, where the percentage jumps to 33 percent. When we examine only judges in criminal assignment, a roughly similar pattern emerges: The percentages slowly rise, level off, then jump ten points (from 52 percent to 62 percent) in the largest courts. This increased involvement in plea discussions conforms to our observations and may reflect a similarly exponential increase in case pressures in these very large courts.

Administrative work and socializing reveal a downward step-level function. Judges in the largest courts are less likely to report doing these activities on their most common day. Whereas about 75–80 percent of judges in most courts report administrative work, the figure drops to 62 percent for judges in the largest courts. Socializing also takes a rather sharp drop, from about 40 percent in most courts to 27 percent in the largest courts. The drop in the proportion of judges doing administrative work is consonant with what we know of the characteristics of very large courts—case specialization, much jury work, and predominant use of the master calendar, characteristics which in combination militate against the occurrence of certain kinds of administrative work. We did not observe any noticeable dropoff in the occurrence of socializing by judges in very large courts; these judges may feel more comfortable in reporting "dead time" as "waiting" rather than "socializing" time where both may be happening and either may be an accurate description.

Figure 3-3 presents a summary of the relationships between court size and the occurrence of specific task activities on judges' most common days. Most of

## The Impact of Court Structure

**Most Common Day**

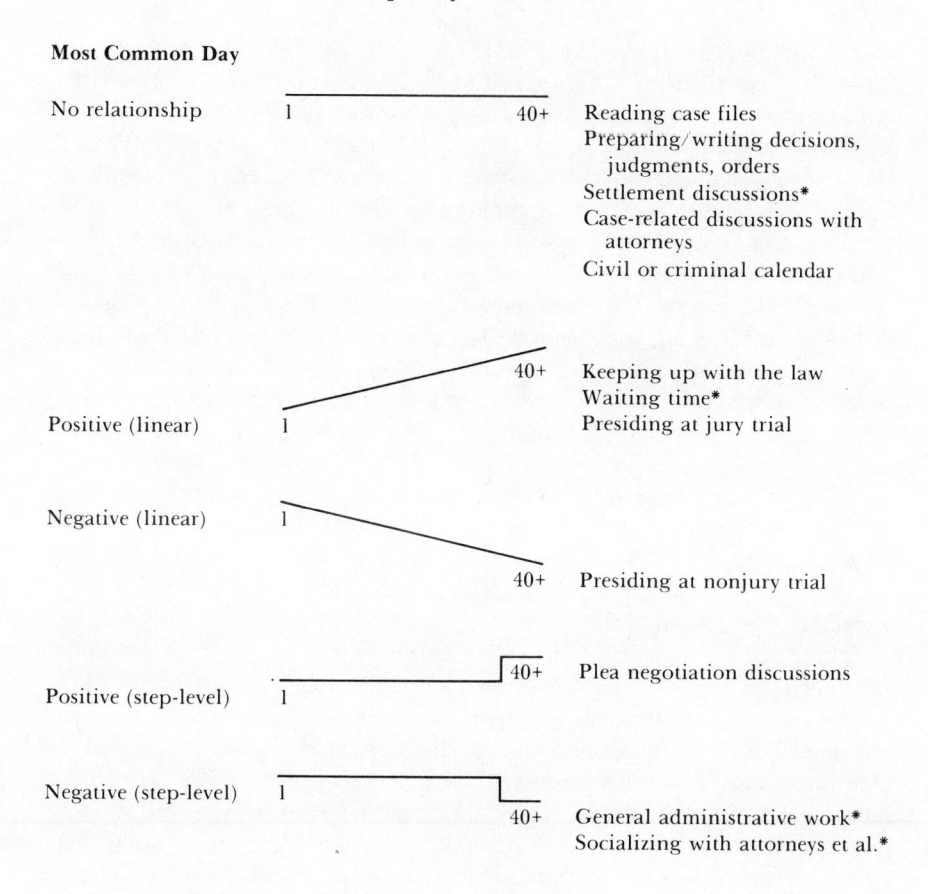

| Relationship type | | | Tasks |
|---|---|---|---|
| No relationship | 1 ——————— 40+ | | Reading case files<br>Preparing/writing decisions, judgments, orders<br>Settlement discussions*<br>Case-related discussions with attorneys<br>Civil or criminal calendar |
| Positive (linear) | 1 ⟋⟋⟋ 40+ | | Keeping up with the law<br>Waiting time*<br>Presiding at jury trial |
| Negative (linear) | 1 ⟍⟍⟍ 40+ | | Presiding at nonjury trial |
| Positive (step-level) | 1 ___⎾‾ 40+ | | Plea negotiation discussions |
| Negative (step-level) | 1 ‾‾‾⏌___ 40+ | | General administrative work*<br>Socializing with attorneys et al.* |

*Variations for judges in civil-mixed assignments

**FIGURE 3-3. A Summary of the Relationships Between Frequency of Tasks and Size of Court**

these relationships hold for the second most common day as well (except for the frequency of jury and non-jury work, where there are no differences). However, there are some variations to the overall picture when the relationships are analyzed within assignments. For judges in civil-mixed assignment, a number of the above-described relationships are different. Notably, frequency of settlement discussions increases with court size; waiting time shows a step-level function dropping off at the largest courts, and administrative work and socializing tend to reflect linear declines rather than downward step-level patterns. Court size appears to impact upon judges in criminal and civil assignments differently, a theme which we will develop more fully in the next section.

Not only do more judges engage in certain activities in different-size courts, but the *time spent* doing activities may also differ. As court size increases, so does the time judges spend in settlement conferences. Time on the most common day ranges from an average of forty minutes in small courts to slightly more than one hour in the largest courts. Both the complexity of litigation and its likelihood to result in more trial hours in large courts probably influence the judge to spend more time with individual cases.[27]

Time spent on preparing or writing decisions, judgments, and orders shows a steady decline as court size increases. In one-judge courts, judges average one and one-quarter hours on their most common day for this task, as against forty-five minutes in large courts. We believe this represents a different distribution of work between judge and attorneys in smaller towns and larger cities. In urban areas, the trial judge tends to give an abbreviated oral judgment (e.g., on property settlement in a divorce case), leaving the winning side's attorney to draw up a written order. Even in more sophisticated litigation, urban judges often ask the winning attorney (or both sides) to submit a recommended judgment. In rural areas, judges themselves take on these kinds of tasks, perhaps because they see the drafting of orders and judgments as a judicial task, but also quite possibly because they believe attorneys will not do a creditable or accurate job.

Three activities—keeping up with the law, plea discussions, and waiting time—show a step-level *increase* in time spent by judges in the largest courts. Just as a higher percentage of judges in the largest courts report plea negotiation activity on their most common day, these same judges spend more time in plea discussions than their counterparts in smaller courts (fifty versus forty minutes). By way of contrast, whereas keeping up with the law and waiting time reflect linear increases in the percentage of judges doing these tasks, they reflect step-level increases in time spent. Only in the largest courts do judges allocate more time to keeping up with the law (fifty versus forty minutes) and experience more waiting time (forty-five versus thirty minutes). This substantially increased waiting time in the largest courts is particularly revealing with respect to the efficacy of organizational size. While many organizations derive economies from increased scale (including courts in some instances), the utilization of professional time is not one of these economies. Attorneys, too, must often wait through lengthy calls of the criminal or civil calendar before their case is called.

Finally, time spent in jury trial work by judges on their most common day reveals a curvilinear tendency. Judges in intermediate-size courts spend the most time in jury trial work on their most common day, about five hours. That figure drops to four and one-half hours or less for those in small or large courts. It is probably for different, rather than similar, reasons that this phenomenon occurs, since these courts share so little in common. In large courts judges have so much jury work, day in and day out, that many of the activities in which judges in small courts engage on less common days must somehow be squeezed into that one predominantly jury day. If judges in large courts are to

# The Impact of Court Structure

keep up with the law or conduct settlement or plea discussions, for example, they cannot wait for "rainy days" that bring no jury trial customers. In contrast, judges in small courts who spend less time on jury trial work may be responding more to the exigencies of life in a rural community (e.g., slower pace, greater perceived need to ensure juror comprehension and prevent juror fatigue) and to the nature of the cases (shorter trial time) than to their own scheduling needs.

Figure 3–4 presents a summary of the relationships between court size and time spent on task activities, paralleling Figure 3–3's summary for the frequency of activities. Again, there are some variations to the overall picture

**FIGURE 3-4. A Summary of the Relationships Between Time Spent on Tasks and Size of Court**

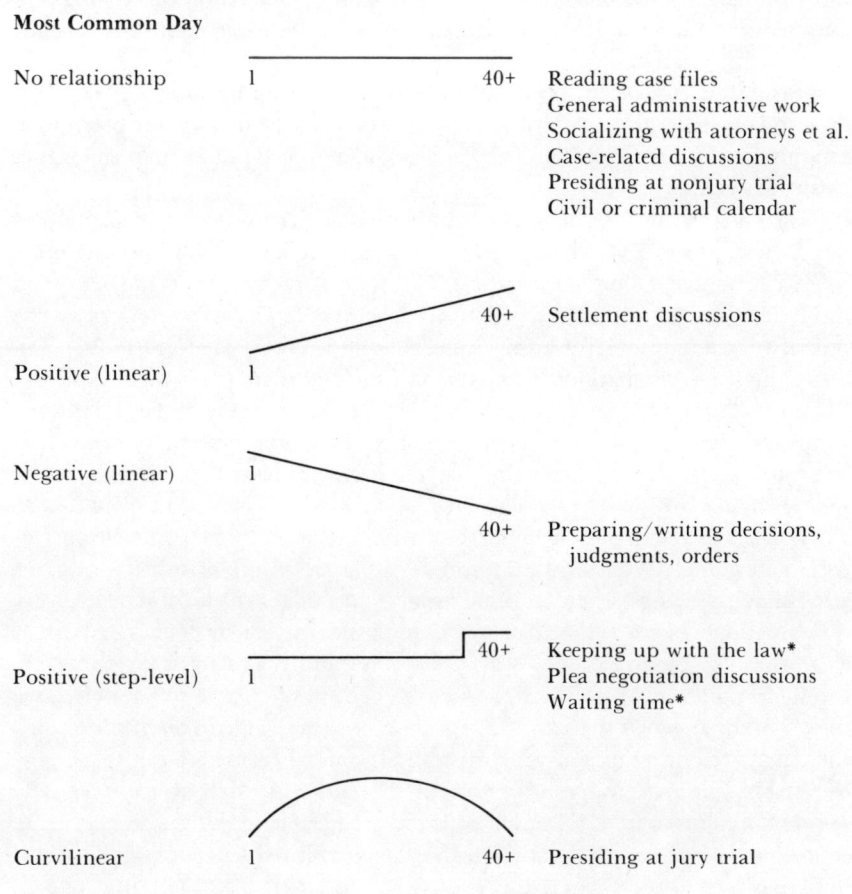

Most Common Day

| Relationship | Range | Tasks |
|---|---|---|
| No relationship | 1 — 40+ | Reading case files<br>General administrative work<br>Socializing with attorneys et al.<br>Case-related discussions<br>Presiding at nonjury trial<br>Civil or criminal calendar |
| Positive (linear) | 1 — 40+ | Settlement discussions |
| Negative (linear) | 1 — 40+ | Preparing/writing decisions, judgments, orders |
| Positive (step-level) | 1 — 40+ | Keeping up with the law*<br>Plea negotiation discussions<br>Waiting time* |
| Curvilinear | 1 — 40+ | Presiding at jury trial |

*Variations for judges in civil-mixed assignment

when relationships are examined separately for judges in criminal, civil—mixed, and general assignments. The three step-level functions do not apply for judges in civil—mixed assignments: There is no relationship between court size and keeping up with the law, and waiting time actually goes *down* as the size of court increases.

## THE SELECTIVE IMPACT OF COURT SIZE: THE DISTINCTIVE WORKINGS OF LARGE CRIMINAL COURTS

In large courts, judges experience less case and task variety on work days that are reported to be longer in duration. Further, judges in large courts are confined much more frequently to days predominantly taken up by jury trial work. Beyond these basic findings of judicial specialization—of cases and tasks—in large courts, however, lies a significant distinction between judges in criminal and those in civil—mixed assignment. Whereas court size usually reflects a linear relationship with the performance of various tasks by judges in civil assignment, it often shows a step-level relationship for judges in criminal assignment. It is in courts with forty or more judges that those in criminal assignment do specific tasks in frequencies and amounts unlike their colleagues in smaller courts.

The core of this task differentiation is the greater involvement in the plea negotiation process. We shall analyze the judge's role in plea bargaining more fully in Chapter 8, but it is sufficient to note here that more judges spend more time present at plea discussions in these very large courts. Related to the task of plea discussions is waiting time, a point we first made in Chapter 2 in analyzing the combinations, or mixes, in which tasks are performed. An extra fifteen minutes per judge of waiting time occurs in the very large criminal courts, but with less socializing taking place. Thus, the ratio of "unconstructive" to "constructive" dead time is very high, at least in the minds of the judges themselves.

What is it about these very large courts that mark them as transitional or threshold points? Why do the "normal" impacts, or lack of impact, of court size suddenly change when criminal assignment judges sit in courts with forty or more judges? Part of the answer, we think, lies in viewing court size both as a measure of organizational scale *and* community size. Just as there are threshold points at which the size of a class becomes too large to have effective discussion or at which the size of a group becomes too large to reach consensus, there may well be a point at which (criminal) courts become too big to manage effectively, vis-à-vis judges' time. Equally, however, size of court usually stands for community size. Some of the pressures facing judges in very large courts—e.g., to get involved more heavily in plea discussions—may result from external forces beyond the court's control. Notably, the crime rate in places like New York, Philadelphia, Chicago, Detroit, and Los Angeles may be increasing more steeply than in smaller cities and towns.

## THE IMPACT OF STATEWIDE ASSIGNMENT AND CIRCUIT-RIDING

At first view, statewide assignment and circuit-riding seem to share much in common. Both are examples of geographic uncertainty or instability in the judge's working environment; that is, judges travel from one place to another according to their assignment. Travel time is a regular part of the work of many judges in both settings. Nevertheless, the scope of their respective impacts on judicial work patterns is rather different.

Judges in statewide assignment systems do different amounts and kinds of work from other judges. The reported work day of statewide assignment judges is considerably longer (10.4 hours versus 9.1 hours); these differences narrow only slightly on the second and third most common days. Yet the differences, large as they are, can be directly attributed to travel time. When statewide assignment judges not reporting travel time are compared with other stationary judges, there are no differences in hours worked. Some sizable differences emerge *within* statewide assignment systems in length of work day, and these initially seemed traceable to frequency of rotation.[28] In fact, however, because the frequency of assignments is highly state-specific (see Table 3-5), it is more likely that judges work longer hours because they are located in certain states—e.g., Massachusetts and Connecticut—than because of differences in length of stay in a particular courthouse.

A substantially different mix of jury and nonjury trial work is the most distinguishing characteristic of their work day activities. Judges in statewide assignment systems are much more likely to report jury trial activity on their most common day and, correspondingly, much less likely to report nonjury work. Three-fourths of all statewide assignment judges report jury trial work on their most common day, compared with less than half (43 percent) of all other judges. Equally, many fewer judges in statewide assignment (17 percent) report nonjury work compared with all other judges (46 percent). This predominance of jury, as opposed to nonjury, trial activity roughly parallels the work experiences of judges in large courts. Not all or even most judges in statewide assignment systems, however, serve in the equivalent of large courts.[29] Thus, it is almost certainly something peculiar to statewide assignment systems, or the states in which they are located, which accounts for these differences. This is an instance where a causal inference between court structure and work patterns would be hazardous, however, because the differences may be attributable to the idiosyncrasies of states or regions.[30]

The most definitively *causal* relationship between use of statewide assignment and work patterns involves time spent in community relations activities, an area of work unaffected by size of court. One would expect that judges in statewide assignment systems spend less time in community relations—at least in self-initiated kinds of activities—because they are not permanently attached to any one community. This is precisely what our data indicate, as shown in Table 3-8.

TABLE 3-8. Trial Judges' Time on Community Relations Activities by Presence of Statewide Assignment

| Hours Per Month | Statewide Assignment | All Other |
|---|---|---|
| 0 | 23.4% | 12.7% |
| 1–2 | 37.9 | 30.8 |
| 3–4 | 23.4 | 25.5 |
| 5–8 | 10.5 | 17.1 |
| 9–12 | 2.4 | 7.0 |
| 13 or more | 2.4 | 6.9 |
| Number | (124) | (2846) |

Although the differences are modest, our data do indicate that almost twice as many judges in statewide assignment systems spend no time whatsoever in community relations. Also, these differences do not appear to be part of a smaller commitment generally to "outside" activities by statewide assignment judges, since they do report spending about as many hours as other judges in bar association activities. Judges serving in statewide assignment simply have less incentive than other judges to get to know, and become involved with, the community in which they currently happen to be assigned.

The impact of circuit-riding on judicial work patterns is less significant than what we have described for statewide assignment. Most of the few differences that do initially appear between circuit-riding and other judges are eliminated when a control for court size is introduced.[31] For example, circuit-riding judges report more kinds of work days (one-third identify five work days), but non–circuit-riders disproportionately serve in large courts. When circuit-riders and those who do not ride circuit are compared only in one-judge courts, or two-to-four judge courts, the differences mostly disappear.

The length of work days illustrates a slightly different situation. Whereas there are no apparent differences between circuit-riders and non–circuit-riders in the total hours worked on a given day, a control for court size reveals a different picture. Table 3–9 presents these data.

TABLE 3-9. Length of Trial Judges' Most Common Work Day by Presence of Circuit-riding, by Court Size

| Size of Court (Number of Judges) | Circuit-Riding[a] | No Circuit-Riding | Number |
|---|---|---|---|
| Small | | | |
| 1 | 9.3 hrs.[b] | 8.6 hrs. | 200/138 |
| 2–4 | 9.0 | 9.1 | 239/281 |
| Intermediate | 9.2 | 9.2 | 182/570 |

[a] Excludes judges in statewide assignment systems.
[b] Figures are mean hours worked, including lunch.

In one-judge courts, there is a rather sizable difference in the length of work day reported by circuit-riders and non–circuit-riders. The difference of nearly one hour is repeated for their second and third days. In larger courts (circuits), however, there are no significant differences in total hours worked. In part, this is a reflection that more circuit-riders report travel time on their most common day in one-judge courts than in larger courts.[32] Primarily, though, it is a reiteration that size of court has different effects among circuit-riding judges. Increased numbers of judges in a circuit *facilitate* sharing of work, including travel. It is the judge who rides circuit alone—without any potential backup—who must bear the brunt of the psychological and physical burdens commonly associated with circuit-riding.

The frequency with which circuit-riding judges engage in specific tasks, as well as their duration, parallel to a remarkable degree their non–circuit-riding counterparts in similar-size courts. This is not to suggest that the life of a circuit-riding judge feels, from a subjective or experiential dimension, the same as that of a judge without circuit-riding responsibilities. Travel can be hard and unpleasant, especially in the winter months. Having to work with different courtroom personnel and possibly different record-keeping procedures in each courthouse can be confusing at best. These are some of the intangible factors associated with circuit-riding to which our data cannot speak. We can only note that the kinds and proportions of work do not depend to any significant degree upon whether the judge rides circuit or not.

## THE IMPACT OF CASE ASSIGNMENT SYSTEMS AND WORK CYCLES

Much has been written in the literature of judicial administration about the desirability or efficacy of particular case assignment systems.[33] Most of these writings, however, have been highly prescriptive, not based upon empirical research. Our data, on balance, suggest only small and piecemeal differences in judicial work patterns attributable to the presence of a master or individual calendar.

One area in which there has been debate about the respective value of master and individual calendars is the effective utilization of judge time. Master calendars have sometimes been criticized for contributing to "dead time"—time spent by judges waiting for a new case to be assigned.[34] Nevertheless, our data reveal no differences in the proportion of judges waiting, or time spent waiting, in individual and master calendar settings (in similar-size courts).[35] Actually, fewer judges report socializing time on their most common day in master calendar systems, a further indication that there is no positive relationship between "dead time" and utilization of a master calendar.

In our own field observations, we saw courts that used a master calendar very effectively, sending cases to judges immediately upon their becoming available. In other courts we observed, as much as several hours might elapse before a case reached the available judge. The efficacy of master calendars probably depends in large measure upon *in-court communication* (between the assignment judge and courtroom judges and their clerks) and *attorney practices* (how willing or able counsel may be to "hang around" the courthouse on days when their cases are in the reserve or backup category). Because these two phenomena—communication and attorney behavior—vary widely from one locale and court to another, it is probably not realistic to expect any *uniform* impact on waiting time attributable to the use of a master calendar.

Case assignment system is related to the frequency and duration of negotiation tasks, on both the civil and the criminal side. Judges operating under a master calendar are *less* likely to report plea negotiation activity on their first three work days. For example, on the most common day only 36 percent of judges under a master calendar (in large courts) report some time spent in plea discussions, as against 53 percent of judges with an individual calendar.[36] Differences in the amount of time spent in plea discussions are sizable in small and intermediate courts. In these courts, judges with individual calendars average ten minutes or more of additional time in plea discussions than judges under a master calendar.

By contrast, judges serving in a master calendar system are *more* likely to report settlement discussions in civil cases and to spend more time with them. The differences are particularly pronounced in large courts where many more judges report settlement discussions on their most common day (62 percent versus 50 percent) and second most common day (62 percent versus 40 percent). Similarly, judges under a master calendar spend much more time each day with settlement discussion (up to an additional twenty minutes).

Why should master calendars be less conducive to judicial time involvement in plea discussions but more conducive to involvement in civil settlement discussions? Part of the answer may lie in the different *timing* of plea and settlement discussions. As we noted in our overview of the typical work day for a civil assignment judge, settlement is always on his mind. Indeed, settlement is on the minds of nearly all civil-assigned judges in master calendar settings, regardless of what stage of cases they might be hearing (motions, pretrial, or trial). The civil court trial judge may try to settle the case just before, or even during, the trial itself. For a variety of reasons including the perceived legitimacy of judicial involvement in plea negotiations, this scenario is much less likely to take place on the criminal side. In master calendar settings, "trial" judges cannot easily get involved in plea discussions. Cases have been assigned to these judges for *trial* (having failed to be disposed by plea before one or more "pretrial" judges). Defendants in criminal cases want to be tried in the court of a judge who has not been influenced or prejudiced by the prosecutor's "inadmissible gossip" during plea discussions.[37] This is not usually a problem in civil cases, since settlement discussions typically do not traverse beyond evidence that would be presented in a trial. Indeed, many of the civil settlement conferences we observed were highly pragmatic—focusing almost exclusively on the dollar amount of the settlement, with no more than a passing reference to the plaintiff's injuries.

Beyond these few highly specific impacts of case assignment system, the work patterns of judges in master and individual calendars—in similar-size courts—are quite similar. One observed judge, himself a former court administrator, perhaps most cogently addressed the issue of case assignment systems by remarking that "no one system is better . . . rather, we must keep frequently *switching* from one system to another in order to keep attorneys off balance."

Work cycles or procedures have only a very limited relationship with judges' work patterns. The utilization of terms—jury/nonjury or criminal/civil—bears no relationship to judicial work patterns. Rationalization of work and the use of supplements to regular judicial manpower do have some influence upon work patterns.

The active utilization of commissioners, referees, and pro-tem judges is *positively* associated with the proportion of judges who report settlement conferences on their most common and subsequent days. This might appear initially puzzling, since one of the prime functions that these extra "judges" perform is to conduct settlement conferences. Utilization of this additional manpower should, in theory, free regular judges from having to preside at so many (civil) negotiation sessions. But as early urban planners discovered, adding extra lanes to freeways does not always reduce traffic congestion. Demand grows in order to meet supply—in courts as well as transportation networks.

Rationalization of task activities by day (e.g., setting aside all or part of Fridays for motions, or Wednesdays for sentence hearings) shows little relationship to most activities. But its purpose, as articulated by more than one judge whom we observed, was primarily aimed at reducing judges' waiting time. Judges who were strong believers in this type of task organization, usually in criminal assignments, felt that getting all the principals together on one day served this purpose quite well. Particular frustrations in their courtrooms had resulted from the difficult schedules of "outsiders"—notably probation workers and psychiatrists.

Our data indicate some striking findings in this area, supportive of the efficacy of rationalization of tasks. Table 3-10 shows the percentage of judges in different assignments who experience waiting time, broken down by whether they report task rationalization.

For criminal court judges, rationalization of tasks appears to have substantial value. Judges who organize tasks by day are much *less* likely to report waiting time, on their most common day (48 percent versus 68 percent), and on their second most common day (39 percent versus 66 percent). By contrast, neither civil—mixed nor general assignment judges report such a benefit. This is not to say that other kinds of benefits might not accrue from rationalization of tasks in the courts of civil or general assignment judges.

It strikes us as particularly interesting, in light of these data, that a much

TABLE 3-10. The Impact of Task Rationalization upon Trial Judges' Waiting Time, by Assignment

| Assignment | % Judges Reporting Waiting Time by Rationalization of Tasks | | Number |
|---|---|---|---|
| | Yes | No | |
| *Criminal* | | | |
| MC | 48.0 | 67.8 | 98/202 |
| 2nd MC | 39.0 | 65.8 | 77/114 |
| *Civil—mixed* | | | |
| MC | 40.3 | 36.9 | 253/225 |
| 2nd MC | 33.6 | 29.6 | 217/169 |
| *General* | | | |
| MC | 40.7 | 41.0 | 878/529 |
| 2nd MC | 35.6 | 31.4 | 815/440 |

*smaller* percentage of criminal judges (33 percent) than civil—mixed (53 percent) or general assignment (62 percent) judges actually organize tasks by day. Yet it is in the criminal courts that the most direct or obvious benefit (reduction in the likelihood of experiencing significant waiting time) occurs. This is one of several "management irrationalities" we have discovered in the course of our data analysis.

## Summary

Elements of court structure bear considerably upon the kinds and amounts of activities in which judges engage during their work days. Size of court is by far the most decisive determinant. It exerts both linear influences and, for courts with forty or more judges, step-level influences. It cuts across judges in criminal, civil—mixed, and general assignments, though sometimes producing different patterns for those in civil as opposed to criminal assignment. Judges in small courts experience a quite different work environment from their colleagues in large courts, who face longer hours, repetitive jury work, more frequent negotiation, and more waiting time.

The remaining structural variables reveal only a limited or highly selective impact on judicial work patterns. The impact, for example, of case assignment system is not nearly so pervasive as the often heated management debates might suggest. Contrary to revisionist thinking, the master calendar does not seem to be more "inefficient" in utilization of judge time than the individual calendar. Case assignment does, however, structure the judge's involvement in negotiation tasks. Its impact here is contextual (affecting judges in criminal and civil assignments differently), and is explained only in part by the different case-processing strategies of criminal and civil courts.

Techniques to match cases with judges in a structural sense—circuit-riding, statewide assignment, and divisionalization—reveal surprisingly little relationship to actual work patterns. Circuit-riders are different from non–circuit-riders in the obvious way: travel time, but not in the mix of other tasks. Judges in statewide assignment systems are somewhat more distinctive in what they do, but in part perhaps because of "region effects." It is difficult to establish causal links when controls for such a large surrogate variable like region cannot be imposed. As with circuit-riding, though, judges in statewide assignment systems may *feel* very different in what they do, even if, objectively speaking, they work at much the same kinds of activities and allocate time to specific tasks similarly.

Judges serving in courts with divisions appear to have virtually identical work profiles to those not in divisions when a control for court size is introduced. This is probably true because the nature and manifestations of divisionalizing work are so diverse in practice. Furthermore, because specialization and divisionalization are not isomorphic (some courts without divisions are specialized), the theoretical significance of divisionalization is partially undermined. Nonetheless, from a descriptive standpoint the utilization of divisions is an integral part of how urban courts are structured.

The frequency with which judges are rotated from one division to another has no impact on work patterns.[38] Similarly, the application of principles by which judges are assigned to divisions (regular rotation, technical expertise of the judge, etc.) show no consistent relationship with work patterns. In part, this is so because judges in any one court do not necessarily *agree* as to which principles are operative. Indeed, all five criteria discussed earlier in this chapter may be used, in different combinations, in most courts.

Finally, we can also say something about the overall explanatory value of these structural variables for particular groups of tasks. The occurrence of jury and nonjury trial work, for example, is accounted for by the elements of court structure quite well. Judges in larger courts and in statewide assignment systems are much more likely to report jury work on their most common day, and much less likely to report nonjury work. These relationships are neither overlapping nor interactive; rather, they are cumulative in their contribution to explaining variation in the occurrence of jury and nonjury trial activity.

The occurrence of plea negotiation and civil settlement activities is also well accounted for by a number of structural variables. Judges in larger courts who have individual calendars are more likely to report plea negotiation activity and to engage in it at greater length. Similarly, judges in large courts who serve under a master calendar and judges whose courts set aside weeks at a time to hear settlement conferences are themselves more likely to report settlement discussions and to spend more time with them.

By contrast, variations in the occurrence and duration of administrative or legal research tasks are not well explained by differences in court structure. It is perhaps not surprising that the decision to do legal research might reflect an essentially "private" choice of the individual judge, unaffected by the kind of structure to which he and his court belong. If a judge wishes to "keep up with the law," however broadly defined, he will find some time to do this.

It is more difficult to reconcile the lack of impact with respect to administrative work. In particular, the lack of effect is surprising with respect to size of court and case assignment system. Judges in larger courts report about as much administrative work as those in smaller courts. Similarly, judges in master calendar systems report as much administrative work as those with individual calendars. It is as if the efforts of large courts to centralize administrative responsibilities by hiring court administrative staff and by adopting a master calendar have not materially affected the *time* individual judges must spend doing administrative work. In small courts, judges must do administrative chores themselves—e.g., picking a foreman for the local grand jury, setting the salaries of courtroom personnel, or providing for adequate courtroom security in a highly sensational trial. In larger courts, individual judges must interact, periodically or regularly, with intermediaries—court administrators, presiding judges, assignment judges—who perform administrative chores on behalf of the "court."

The impact of court structure, then, is highly variable. Size of court makes a significant difference across a wide variety of tasks. Correlatively, the performance of some tasks, particularly trial and negotiation-related activities, is quite substantially explained by reference to an array of structural factors. At a broader theoretical level, it is judicial specialization in its many faces (court size, case assignment system, and the type or breadth of cases heard) that leads to sharply different work patterns. By contrast, the stability of a judge's relationship to a particular community, constituency, or courthouse is a much less significant factor in shaping the composition of his work day.

## Notes

1. Other matters, such as probate, belong to the jurisdiction of the inferior trial courts in Texas.
2. A recent Tennessee court rule provides for the election of a chief judge (from among the several courts) who may exercise powers of case (re)assignment.
3. This finding provides support for our *a priori* decision to include, in our definition of the universe of general jurisdiction judges, judges who sit in these specialized divisions, which in some states are separate courts. For further discussion of these issues, see Appendix B.
4. The utilization of "expert" judges may not be a value-free decision, however. See, for example, Baum's discussion of the decisional tendencies of generalist and specialist judges in the U.S. Court of Customs and Patent Appeals. Lawrence Baum, "Judicial Specialization, Litigant Influence, and Substantive Policy: The Court of Customs and Patent Appeals," *Law and Society Review,* 11 (1977).
5. See Jeffrey Perlman, "Marathon Sessions Planned to Reduce Backlog of Civil Suits," *Los Angeles Times,* Orange County Ed., December 10, 1976.

6. James Eisenstein and Herbert Jacob, *Felony Justice: An Organizational Analysis of Criminal Courts* (Boston: Little, Brown, 1977), p. 112.
7. "Judge Hooton Is Reassigned," *Chicago Tribune,* November 9, 1977.
8. "Judge Frees Convict, Loses Post," *Chicago Tribune,* January 12, 1977.
9. For a description of the powers of state court administrators, see Robert G. Nieland and Rachel N. Doan, *State Court Administrative Offices* (Chicago: American Judicature Society, 1979).
10. Some judges have suggested that one rationale behind the use of statewide assignment is to ensure judicial independence from the very small bars of many communities in their sparsely populated states. Put another way, the purpose is "to avoid permanently inflicting on any one community the sentencing pattern, legal judgment, and foibles of a single judge." Robert Salter, "The Quality of a Judge's Experience," *American Bar Association Journal,* 65 (1979), p. 934. To the extent that this was ever a serious goal, our data in Table 3-5 suggest that this might be partially accomplished.
11. We refer here to the policy of the *frequency* with which judges are rotated. For example, an analysis of statewide assignments in North Carolina in the first six months of 1979 suggests that judges with high seniority were assigned to locations near their places of residence.
12. For a discussion of the master and individual calendars in theory and operation, see Maureen Solomon, *Caseflow Management in the Trial Court,* American Bar Association Commission on Standards of Judicial Administration, Supporting Studies, 2, 1973.
13. Judges in criminal divisions are less likely to serve under a master calendar than judges in civil or general assignments.
14. In Ohio an individual calendar has been mandated by state supreme court rules of superintendence (Ohio Sup. R. 4.). In California, by contrast, rules of the state judicial council provide for the use of a master calendar for all civil cases in courts having three or more judges (Cal. Super. Ct. R. 223a).
15. For example, in one study of the criminal caseflow process in a Pennsylvania county where terms are used, the authors noted: "The tradition of sitting in a fixed number of separate criminal and civil terms has little or no efficacy in the context of a modern judicial system. It offers no flexibility and tends to compound delay." See *Criminal Caseflow Management: Chester County, Pennsylvania* (Chicago: American Judicature Society, 1976).
16. The term "rationalization" of work (or tasks) is used in a value-free context to refer to the application of principles of "scientific management."
17. Solomon, *Caseflow Management,* makes no reference to unique problems or issues arising from the utilization of statewide assignment or extensive circuit-riding. Ernest C. Friesen, Edward C. Gallas, and Nesta M. Gallas, *Managing the Courts* (Indianapolis: Bobbs-Merrill, 1971) p.2, simply assert that the "need for circuit-riders has all but vanished." Indeed, virtually the only references to the existence or significance of these phenomena occur in the *National Survey of Court Organization* (Washington, D.C.: Law Enforcement Assistance Administration, 1973), and *Rural Courts: The Effect of Space and Distance on the Administration of Justice* (Denver: National Center for State Courts, 1977), pp.33–34.

18. Number of judges ranges from forty-seven in North Carolina to as few as thirteen in Delaware and New Hampshire. The response rate in these states was somewhat below the national average, thereby underestimating slightly the actual percentage of judges in statewide assignment systems.
19. There is a substantial positive correlation between size of court and utilization of the master calendar among circuit-riding judges. This suggests that as circuits contain more judges they parallel the rotational patterns of statewide assignment systems.
20. There is an extensive literature on the diffusion of innovations in sociology and political science. For an analysis of the diffusion of statutory innovations from state to state, see Jack L. Walker, "The Diffusion of Innovations Among the American States," *American Political Science Review,* 63 (1969).
21. There is one caveat to the assertion of "linear" relationships between court size and various judicial tasks. The intervals between categories of court size (1, 2, 3–4, 5–9, etc.) are unequal, thereby rendering the variable "ordinal" in level of measurement. This problem is essentially intractable, because even if "interval-level" data on court size had been collected, some grouping of court sizes would be required to cope with the hundred or more discrete categories. Any collapsing or grouping of categories, in theory, limits the use of mathematical functions such as linear, curvilinear, or step-level.
22. "Step-level" is intended to be a generic term suggesting a change in the nature of a relationship at a particular court size (e.g., forty or more judges). This change may be a change only in intercept, not in slope; or a change in intercept *and* slope. Both of these functions could accurately be labeled "step-level." Alternatively, the change could be one of slope, but not intercept. This function would more accurately be termed "nonlinear" or "curvilinear," rather than step-level. Our data do not permit these distinctions, primarily because the category "forty or more judges" is infinite.
23. There are a variety of "curvilinear" functions; the one referred to in the text is parabolic.
24. The extreme lack of variety for judges in courts with forty or more judges is partially a reflection of the disproportionate percentage of these judges who sit in a criminal assignment (45 percent). Recall from Chapter 2 that judges in a criminal assignment report fewer different types of work days than those in a civil—mixed or general assignment.
25. These data are not confounded by the greater proportion of criminal judges in larger courts (who report more jury work on their most common day; see Table 2–6). The relationship between size of court and jury work is equally large among civil—mixed judges as it is among criminal judges.
26. Our field observations in rural Nebraska indicated a jury trial was generally unavailable during harvest time.
27. On a typical day, observed judges in the larger courts did *not* conduct more than one settlement conference. Thus, we interpret these data to indicate that it is generally time spent with individual cases, which increases with court size.
28. Judges who move from one assignment to another frequently (every five months or more) work longer hours than those who move less frequently (every six months or less).

29. The concept of "size of court" proved meaningless in statewide assignment systems, as our respondents indicated by their confusion in describing the number of judges in their courts. Some simply referred to the total number of judges in the state for their response.
30. Kalven and Zeisel suggest that a major determinant in the defense's decision to choose a jury or nonjury trial is "simply regional custom . . . [which] varies enormously from one part of the country to another." Unfortunately, the data they present are inconclusive as to which region is most likely to have jury trials. See Harry Kalven, Jr., and Hans Zeisel, *The American Jury* (Boston: Little, Brown, 1966), p. 24.
31. It is essential to control for court size not because it makes a difference in the work patterns of circuit-riding judges (it generally does not) but because court size makes a large difference among non–circuit-riding judges. These latter relationships, described earlier in this chapter, would confound comparisons without a control.
32. Fifty-eight percent of circuit-riders serving in one-judge courts report travel time on their most common day; this figure drops slowly to a low of 30 percent in 16–25-judge courts. The pattern is similar for less common days. There are no differences in amount of time reported traveling by size of circuit, however.
33. See, for example, Eldridge Adams, *The Feasibility of Measuring and Comparing Calendar Effectiveness* (Springfield, Va.: National Technical Information Service, 1971); Solomon, *Caseflow Management;* and Friesen, Gallas, and Gallas, *Managing the Courts* (note 17 above).
34. See *Criminal Caseflow Management* (note 15 above), p. 44.
35. It is necessary throughout this section to control for size of court, since that variable is related to the presence of a master or individual calendar (see Table 3–6) as well as to work patterns. The analysis is appropriately restricted to judges who do *not* ride circuit.
36. This analysis is restricted to judges serving in a general, criminal, or juvenile assignment.
37. One of the rationales behind the American Bar Association's recommended prohibition of judicial involvement in plea discussions is the fairness question raised in cases where judges have been exposed to inadmissible, but sentence-relevant, evidence before trial. See American Bar Association Project on Standards for Criminal Justice, *Standards Relating to Pleas of Guilty* (Chicago: American Bar Association, 1968).
38. The frequency of judicial rotation may, however, bear significantly upon other factors—e.g., the formation and disruption of workgroups. For a discussion of this and possible consequences therefrom, see Eisenstein and Jacob, *Felony Justice* (note 6 above).

# CHAPTER 4

# The Role of Attorneys

THE public estimation of attorneys may be at an all-time low. The role of lawyers in the Watergate scandals contributed to much disillusionment. And Jimmy Carter took the opportunity during his presidency to paint the legal profession as elitist and unsympathetic to social justice. Yet is it likely that most Americans have always been ambivalent about attorneys, whether because of contact (direct or vicarious), class consciousness, or simply the pragmatic skepticism often reflected in fictional literature.[1] Judges have a far different basis on which to evaluate attorneys. Judges themselves are lawyers who once acted in the capacity of attorney. Furthermore, attorneys are the working associates of judges in court. The professional skills and personal characteristics of attorneys help to shape the content and the process of litigation in criminal and civil courtrooms. Our interest in this chapter is to describe some of the skills and characteristics of attorneys and to analyze their effect on the trial judge's work.

Which characteristics of attorneys and their behavior are most likely to impact upon the trial judge? From our observations and the organizational literature on trial courts, we identified four characteristics. First, the background and experience of individual attorneys undoubtedly shape the quality and efficiency of their interactions with judges. The kind of legal training received, the number of years as a practicing attorney, and the number of years in one's current role all are believed to be related to competence in either general or specialized work.[2] Second, adversariness, or attorney combativeness, is a key element of the courtroom work environment. Attorneys are expected to represent their clients competently, but not too argumentatively or in an obstructionist manner. Lawyers may respond to these ambivalent cues about their role in quite different ways. Third, the working skills of attorneys help to define what kinds of work can most easily be accomplished by the courtroom workgroup. Are attorneys good at trial argument or negotiation? Or are they equally good at all phases of litigation? The actual mix of attorney skills may influence which tasks judges will emphasize. Finally, the extent to which attorneys are familiar to the judge and with one another influences the processing and disposal of cases in courts.[3] Stable workgroups where actors know one another quite well tend to be less combative, though not necessarily less skilled, than workgroups that function in unfamiliar interpersonal terrain.

The amount and reliability of data we can bring to bear upon these four sets of attorney characteristics differ considerably. We can do no more than mention the important role of lawyers' backgrounds and professional experience; we have no data relating to them. We have limited observational data on the adversariness of attorneys in different parts of the country. We have quantifiable survey data relating to the work skills of attorneys, through the subjective eyes of judges. Finally, we have data reported by judges that bear upon the level of familiarity or stability of attorney members of the workgroup. It is these latter three attorney characteristics—adversariness, work skills, and familiarity—and their impact on judicial work that we examine in this chapter.

## Representation, Adversariness, and Legal Ethics

How adversarial must attorneys be in order to represent their clients effectively? The relationship of lawyers to the court and their clients has become the subject of increasing public and professional concern. Political activists outside and within the legal profession challenge the dominance of the lawyer in lawyer–client relationships, suggesting that the goals of lawyers and clients do not always converge in individual cases.[4] By retaining control over the direction of litigation, clients may be able to achieve political ends more important to them than the legal outcome itself. Such political ends might include educating the general public or attracting the attention and sympathies of specific referent groups.[5]

The lawyer–client relationship has also been examined from the perspective of the individual consumer.[6] Douglas Rosenthal found that clients who keep fully abreast of the facts and progress of their case—who *participate* actively with the lawyer in the development of strategies or the maintenance of information—are more likely to have successful outcomes. In addition, the U.S. Supreme Court recently boosted the potential power of clients by ruling that bans on lawyer advertising violate the public's right to critical information (about lawyer specialization, costs, etc.).[7]

The relationships among lawyer, client, and the *court* bring into full perspective the issues of representation and legal ethics. The legal profession long ago (in 1908) promulgated a set of standards (Canons of Professional Ethics) to guide attorney behavior.[8] But these standards do not reconcile, or perhaps even address, conflicts between attorney as "officer of the court" and attorney as full advocate for his client. It is this tension revolving around attorney "adversariness" that Monroe Freedman raises in his controversial work, *Lawyers' Ethics in an Adversary System*.[9] Though this issue has been indirectly addressed by "outsiders,"[10] Freedman's book is an unprecedented acknowledgement by a leading member of the legal profession that the full representation of clients sometimes directly collides with established canons of legal ethics or the interests of society.[11]

In focusing empirically upon attorney adversariness, we must therefore be cognizant that actors define and view the consequences of adversariness in different lights. Based upon our observations, these issues surround attorney adversariness in both plea negotiation and trial settings. It was in the plea negotiation setting that we most vividly observed conflict between client interest and the interests of the court *qua* public. The most obvious example occurred in a criminal courtroom in Nashville, Tennessee. The scene was a sentence hearing, following immediately upon a plea of guilty to drug possession charges by a youthful white defendant. The judge, a veteran of many years on the criminal bench, told the defendant that in order to receive probation he would have to reveal the name of his supplier in open court. The defendants's attorney *concurred* in the appropriateness of the judge's request (a "sign of rehabilitation," defense attorney and judge muttered to one another). This defense attorney openly proclaimed his obligation to the court and society as justification, but therein abandoned "full" representation of his client. Had he chosen to challenge the judge's request, however, we can surmise that the defense attorney would have been castigated as an "enemy of the people," willing to leave unscrupulous drug pushers free to roam the streets of the community.

It strikes us as no accident that this scene occurred in Nashville and not, for example, in Los Angeles. This is not to say that all or most Nashville defense attorneys capitulate to domineering judges or that all criminal court judges in Nashville are domineering. Neither is true. Rather, it is to recognize that differences exist in the legal training, experience, and attitudes of attorneys between those two cities (and others) and that such differences may be reflected in the combativeness or adversariness with which attorneys conduct criminal defenses.

Attorneys also vary, within and across communities, in the level of their adversariness in arguing trials. Specifically, we observed attorneys to differ in the choosiness with which they selected juries, in the repetitiveness of their questioning and cross-examination of witnesses, in the amount of corroborating testimony presented, in the use of "expert" witnesses, and, therefore, in the sheer length of time needed to complete a trial, from beginning to end. Because some judges intervened actively to curb excesses of adversariness (or sometimes merely simple-minded repetitiveness) by attorneys in *nonjury* trials, we believe attorney adversariness may best be viewed and compared across communities in *jury* trials.

We have observational as well as quantitative data relating to the length of jury trials in different locales. Through this measure, we can partially gauge the different levels of attorney adversariness in various communities. Jury trials were routinely held and quickly completed in rural areas, in both civil and criminal cases. One personal injury trial observed in rural Tennessee required but one work day (seven hours) to complete, from jury selection through verdict. In urban areas, especially outside the South, jury trials were often feared, avoided wherever possible (by repeated settlement efforts), and slowly completed where not avoided. In the Chicago courts, a personal inury trial comparable on the surface to the one observed in rural Tennessee was barely under way after one day's work. Variations in the conduct of jury trials in criminal cases paralleled those in civil cases. In a few instances, jury selection in serious criminal cases took longer in some urban courts than the entire trial in rural areas.

Our survey data confirm these observational impressions. Judges in metropolitan areas estimate that the typical jury trial in a personal injury (auto accident) case in their courtroom requires 17.0 hours, compared with only 14.9 hours for judges in nonmetropolitan areas, and 14.1 hours for judges in rural areas. Geographic region discriminates even more strongly. Judges in Southern states estimate only 11.7 hours for a typical personal injury trial, as against 16.6 hours by judges outside the South, differences which remain after controls for community size. Parallel differences occur in judges' estimates of actual trial time for a typical armed robbery jury trial. Though a number of factors may influence how many hours a jury trial consumes before a particular judge,[12] our observations strongly suggest that attorney adversariness plays a key, perhaps a decisive, role.

What impact, then, does the level of attorney adversariness have upon how trial judges manage their work day? Because our data are of a limited and mostly qualitative nature, we can only speculate. Judges who are frequently confronted with highly adversarial attorneys may have to work longer hours to complete the same amount of work and may have to hear more adversarial events (e.g., jury trials, motion hearings). Indeed, our data from Chapter 3 provide support in this regard. It is judges in larger courts, that is, in urban areas, who work longer hours on their most common day and who preside more often at jury trials (see Figure 3-2). Thus, one part of the explanation for the impact of court size lies in the characteristics of the attorneys who practice in large and small courts.

## Attorney Skills and Their Impact

How good are attorneys at what they must do in trial courtrooms? Do they prepare cases adequately? Draw up intelligible decrees? Negotiate settlements or pleas efficiently? Argue their cases effectively before judge or jury?[13]

These are at best difficult questions even for judges to answer. Different standards of excellence and competence exist. Some judges regard highly the tough, combative attorneys who fight for their clients to the last, whereas other judges hold these same attorneys in low regard. Measuring the quality of attorneys, then, is a highly inexact and subjective science on the part of judges, and yet still useful for our purposes. For if judges believe that the attorneys who surround them are quite good, or quite poor, they will act upon those beliefs and perceptions, thereby constructing a reality.[14] In the strictest sense, it is this reification process we study by examining—as we do later in this section—the *impact* of judges' beliefs about the qualities and skills of attorneys upon their own work patterns.

First, we turn to a description and assessment of attorneys' skills, as seen through the eyes of judges. Because the criminal and civil bars of many communities are quite distinct, judges were asked to rate separately the skills of criminal and civil attorneys. Table 4–1 presents these data.

Our data suggest that judges are cautiously complimentary of the skills of attorneys practicing in their courtrooms. Many more judges are willing to characterize attorneys as "above average" than "below average." This con-

TABLE 4–1.  Trial Judges' Evaluation of the Skills of Criminal and Civil Attorneys Their Courtrooms

| SKILL | EXCELLENT | ABOVE AVERAGE | AVERAGE | BELOW AVERAGE | POOR | NUMBER |
|---|---|---|---|---|---|---|
| *Criminal Attorneys*[a] | | | | | | |
| Case preparation and management | 4.4% | 32.9% | 47.8% | 11.9% | 3.0% | (2168 |
| Plea negotiation | 7.6 | 38.3 | 46.6 | 6.0 | 1.5 | (2101 |
| Trial | 5.2 | 34.8 | 47.1 | 10.2 | 2.7 | (2173 |
| *Civil Attorneys*[b] | | | | | | |
| Preparation of decrees | 7.7 | 39.5 | 46.8 | 5.0 | 1.0 | (256. |
| Case preparation and management | 3.8 | 38.4 | 46.5 | 10.0 | 1.3 | (255 |
| Settlement | 5.7 | 36.4 | 48.6 | 8.3 | 1.0 | (253 |
| Trial | 6.4 | 39.2 | 43.9 | 8.9 | 1.6 | (256 |

[a] Excludes judges in civil assignments.
[b] Excludes judges in criminal or juvenile assignments.

forms quite closely to the reported attitudes of judges in federal trial courts, where a substantial majority of attorneys' case performances were judged to be "good," "very good," or "first rate."[15] Furthermore, the quality of civil and criminal attorneys appears similar in the eyes of trial judges. Judges in criminal courtrooms look upon criminal attorneys in much the same light as judges in civil courts look upon civil attorneys. More important, generalist judges, who see both sides of the bar, rate criminal and civil attorneys comparably. Thus, the pervasive but little-documented suspicion that civil attorneys are better than criminal attorneys receives no support.[16]

This picture of general satisfaction with attorney skills is modified only slightly when specific skills are examined and compared. Judges are more likely to be critical of the case preparation and management skills of criminal attorneys than of their plea negotiation skills. This makes intuitive sense and conforms to our observations in criminal courts. Attorneys learn how to plea bargain fairly quickly[17] but never seem to learn quite how to manage their sometimes overburdened caseloads. On the civil side, the perceived differences among skills are even smaller, though here too judges are most likely to be critical of the case preparation and management skills of attorneys.

One ambiguity remains from the aggregate character of Table 4-1. How discriminating are individual judges with respect to the skill levels ascribed to attorneys in their courtrooms? Do judges who believe that attorneys are above average in trial skills also hold the same evaluation of these attorneys' negotiation skills, for example? In other words, is there a "halo effect" (attorneys are good, or bad, at all skills), or are judges able to differentiate the skills that the attorneys practicing before them possess?

Our data suggest that there is a limited amount of differentiation among attorney skills. Judges seem somewhat more able to discriminate among the skills of civil attorneys than those of criminal attorneys.[18] The extent to which judges rate similarly different pairs of attorney skills is visually represented by the spatial diagrams in Figure 4-1, which illustrates, through spatial proximity, which skills of attorneys are perceived to be most, and least, distinct from one another. Judges as a whole are most likely to see the plea negotiation skills of criminal attorneys in a light *different* from attorneys' other skills. Thus, an individual judge is more likely to rate the case preparation and management skills of criminal attorneys similarly to their trial skills (e.g., "above average") than to their plea negotiation skills. On the civil side, a parallel but more pronounced pattern exists. Judges rate the settlement skills of civil attorneys quite apart from their other skills, which are much more likely to be rated similarly.

This analysis suggests that judges perceive something distinctive about the task of negotiation in both criminal and civil cases. In judges' views of attorneys, negotiation skills do *not* necessarily coincide with other learned skills, such as trial advocacy or case preparation. In the eyes of some judges, attorneys in their courtrooms are generally best at negotiation. For other judges, attorneys as a group are perceived to be best at other skills.

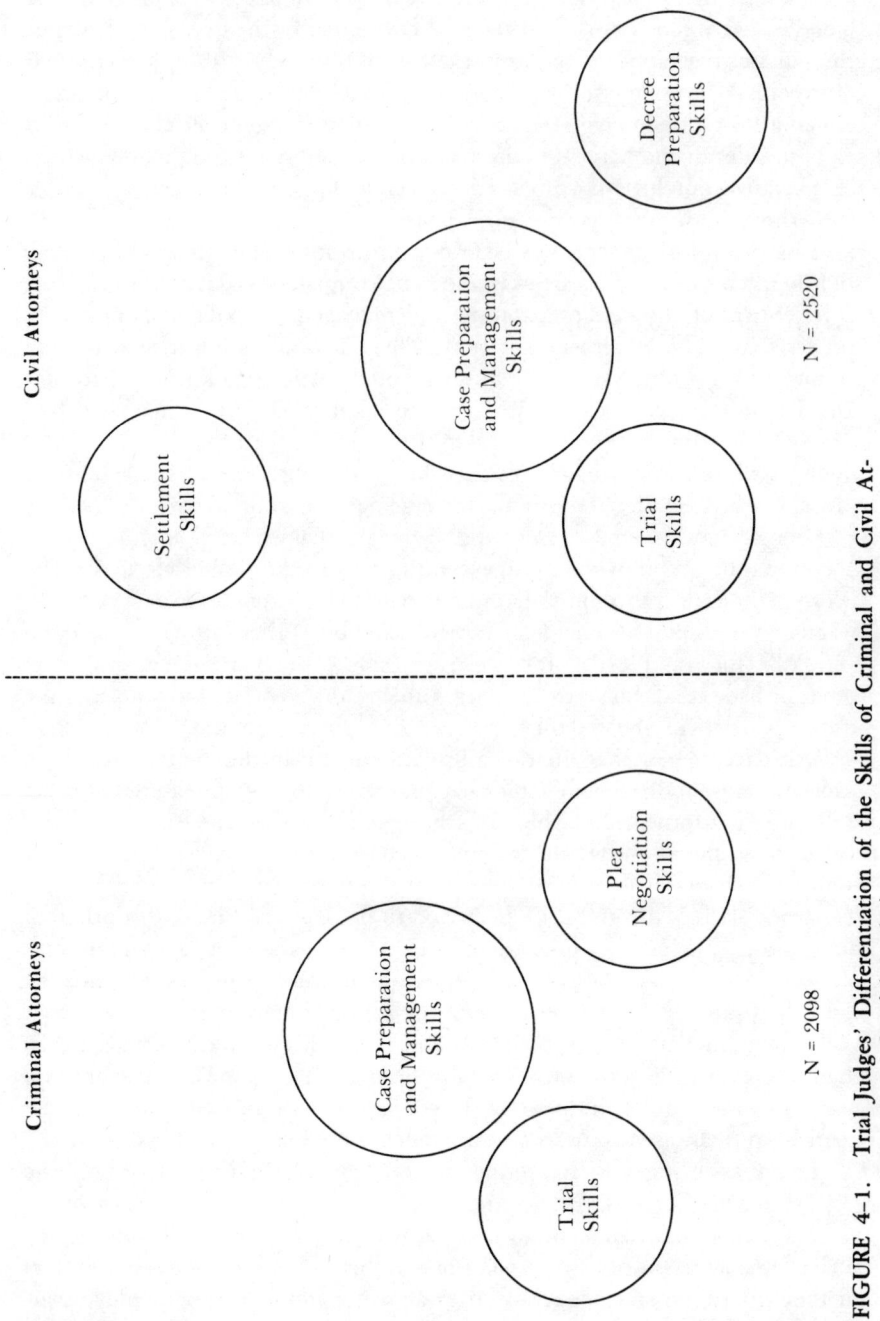

FIGURE 4-1. Trial Judges' Differentiation of the Skills of Criminal and Civil Attorneys: A Spatial Analysis

Before proceeding to an analysis of the impact of attorney skills on judges' work patterns, we need to consider the relationship of skills to size of community and other variables that define the structure of courts. In fact, however, we can speak of a lack of relationships. Judges in large cities evaluate the skills of the attorneys in their courts similarly to judges in smaller cities, suburbs, and rural places. Thus, although attorneys may be more adversarial in larger cities, judges do not seem to equate this trait by itself with a low level of skill. Equally, judges situated in different types of courts rate attorneys' skills similarly. In the following analysis, then, it is not necessary to control for any potentially confounding variables. We may look directly at the relationships between attorney skills and judicial work patterns.

## ALTERNATIVE THEORIES OF ATTORNEY–JUDGE WORK INTERRELATIONSHIPS

In assessing the impact of attorney skills, we draw upon two different theories of judicial response. Judges may do more of certain tasks to *compensate* for the poor skills of attorneys in these areas. For example, we suggested in Chapter 3 that judges, particularly in rural areas, may spend more time preparing orders and judgments because they believe that attorneys will not do a creditable job. Alternatively, judges may do more of certain tasks at which attorneys are relatively skilled. This phenomenon might occur either because attorneys recognize their own strengths and weaknesses and act accordingly (by emphasizing the skills at which they are good), or because judges try to draw upon the strengths of attorneys as they perceive them. For example, judges might hear more jury or nonjury trials where the local bar has strong trial skills. As more than one observed judge noted, a trial well argued by polished attorneys can be a very pleasurable event.

For civil attorneys, our data suggest some support for *both* theories. Judges are, in fact, more likely to report "preparing/writing decisions, judgments, and orders" and to spend more time doing so where they perceive attorneys to be below average or poor at preparing decrees. Table 4–2 presents these data.

Though the differences in Table 4–2 are small, they are consistent with a theory of compensation behavior. It is not that particularly good attorney skills in this area save judicial time, but rather that below average or poor skills require judges to become involved in drafting decrees more frequently and at greater length. These differences appear also on judges' second most common day, and for judges in civil—mixed as well as general assignment. As we would expect, attorney skill level in settlement or trial work does *not* influence judicial involvement in preparing and writing decisions, thus providing further confidence in the reliability of this finding.

Judges also more frequently perform tasks that are the strong points of attorneys. Settlement discussions are one such area. More judges are present at settlement discussions when they believe attorneys to be more skilled at settlement. Forty percent of judges who believe that attorneys are excellent or above

TABLE 4-2. The Impact of Civil Attorney Skill at Preparing Decrees upon Trial Judges' Preparation and Writing of Decisions

| Attorney Skill at Preparing Decrees[a] | % Judges Reporting Preparing/Writing Decisions (MC) | Number | ($\overline{X}$) Time Spent (MC) | Number |
|---|---|---|---|---|
| Excellent or above average | 56.2 | (985) | 1.0 hrs. | (554) |
| Average | 57.2 | (988) | 1.0 | (565) |
| Below average or poor | 61.8 | (123) | 1.2 | (76) |

[a] In this and subsequent tables, "excellent" and "above average" have been combined as have "poor" and "below average" because of the small numbers in the extreme categories.

average at settlement report settlement discussions on their most common day, as against 35 percent of judges who see attorney settlement skills as average, and 33 percent who believe attorneys are below average or poor in this area. A similar pattern emerges from judges' second most common work day. Trials represent a second area where good skills in attorneys are associated with a higher rate of work by judges. Judges do indeed seem to find a way to hear *jury* trials when attorneys have superior trial skills. There is a significant jump in the proportion of judges reporting jury trial work on their most common day, when attorneys are viewed as excellent or above average (46 percent) as opposed to average (38 percent) or below average/poor (36 percent). Again, this pattern repeats itself for judges' second most common day. It is interesting to note that the proportion of judges reporting *nonjury* trials is not affected by attorney skill level. Thus, attorneys with good trial skills do not necessarily prefer jury to nonjury trials. Instead, their trial skills seem to generate, and perhaps improve with, more frequent trial work.

A third pattern of work interrelationships between civil attorneys and judges emerges from our data: Judges do *less* of certain tasks because attorneys are good at particular skills. (This is the converse of compensation behavior). The relationships typically occur across all skill areas, suggesting an impact from general competence. Specifically, judges spend less time in case-related discussions with attorneys and in calendar work when they perceive attorneys to be generally skilled.

The underlying explanations for impact in these areas of work seem straightforward. Case-related discussions with attorneys may often degenerate into haggling, bickering, or time-consuming socializing where attorneys come unprepared or are unable to synthesize their arguments. This is true not only for settlement-oriented discussions but also for discussions focusing on administrative or adjudicative matters. Likewise, calendar work, which is often the formalization in the courtroom of what takes place in chambers, is a second

TABLE 4-3. The Impact of Criminal Attorney Skills upon Trial Judges' Waiting Time

| | % Judges Reporting Waiting Time (MC) | | | |
|---|---|---|---|---|
| Skill Level | Case Preparation and Management Skills | Negotiation Skills | Trial Skills | Number |
| Excellent or above average | 42.0 | 41.5 | 42.3 | 664/800/726 |
| Average | 43.1 | 43.7 | 43.2 | 847/803/825 |
| Below average or poor | 51.1 | 56.1 | 50.6 | 268/123/233 |

forum where good attorney skills can save judicial time. Attorneys who come unprepared to argue short motions or who appear late extend the time needed to call the calendar. We saw this phenomenon repeatedly in our field observations. Interestingly, the most expeditious call we observed—a law and motions calendar—occurred in a court that requires written submissions of argument. Though oral argument was crisp as a result, considerable judicial time of a preparatory nature (that is, reading files) was needed.

The consequences of civil attorney skill levels also reveal themselves in the length of the judicial work day. Where attorneys are relatively poor at preparation of decrees and case management, judges report working up to one-third of an hour longer on their most common and other days. This is likely to include more time in discussions with attorneys and calendar work. By contrast, where attorneys are poor at trial skills judges report working slightly shorter hours. Four or five hours of sloppy presentation of testimony may be just enough to send some judges packing for home, in the hope that the following day will somehow be better.

The work interrelationships of criminal attorneys and judges are quite different. There is no evidence to support a theory of compensation behavior. Judges are not more likely, for example, to report time spent in plea discussions where they view attorneys to be poor at negotiation. Equally, there is little evidence to support the idea that judges emphasize those tasks at which criminal attorneys are good. Above average trial skills in criminal attorneys do not lead to more frequent occurrence of jury trials.

Like their civil attorney counterparts, however, skilled criminal attorneys do save judges from unnecessary expenditures of time—in this instance, waiting time. In each of the areas examined for criminal attorneys—case preparation and management, negotiation, and trial—greater skill is associated with less frequent reports of waiting time by judges, as Table 4-3 indicates. For each task area, the proportion of judges who experience waiting time is much larger where attorney skills are below average or poor. The rela-

TABLE 4-4. The Impact of Criminal Attorney Skill at Negotiation upon Judges' Nonjury and Jury Trial Work

| Attorney Skill at Negotiation | % Judges Reporting (MC) | | |
|---|---|---|---|
| | Nonjury | Jury | Number |
| Excellent or above average | 42.9 | 45.2 | (800) |
| Average | 42.8 | 45.7 | (803) |
| Below average or poor | 32.5 | 54.5 | (123) |

tionship is particularly large for negotiation. If prosecuting and defense attorneys are not efficient in their bargaining sessions or wait to bargain until the last moment, a waiting judge and courtroom may often be the result. This is a phenomenon we observed in the field, as well as one which emerged from analysis of the *mix* of tasks which judges perform. Furthermore, judges who do wait are likely to spend more time waiting where criminal attorney skills in negotiation (or trial or case management) are below average or poor. These relationships between skill and waiting time are present among judges in both criminal and general assignment.

There is also a significant relationship between criminal attorneys' plea negotiation skills and the comparative frequency of nonjury and jury trial work reported by judges. As we might expect, where attorneys are relatively poor at negotiation the result is fewer nonjury trials and more jury trials. Table 4-4 presents these data. Where attorneys are below average or poor at negotiation, the balance between nonjury and jury work changes sharply. This finding is perhaps more understandable if we recall that nonjury trials in criminal cases are often "slow pleas"—i.e., opportunities for the defendant to have his hour (but not his week) in court.[19] In courts where plea bargaining breaks down—because of poor skills of attorneys or for any other reason—the ratio of jury to nonjury trials is likely to increase.[20]

Finally, poor criminal attorneys—like poor civil attorneys—generate longer working days for judges. Part of this extra time is likely to be spent in waiting, part in jury trial and related activity. If judges were asked to enumerate the causes of extra, especially unnecessary, work, most would almost certainly place poor attorneys near the top of their list. Our data indicate that these feelings are not mere prejudices or hallucinations from the bench. Such feelings have a degree of independent support.

## Attorney Familiarity and Stability

How familiar are judges with the attorneys who practice in their courts? To what extent are attorneys truly the "working associates" of judges? The relationships of attorneys to one another and the judge have become an underlying theme of recent criminal justice research.[21] Mutual interdependence of actors is viewed to be an important causal agent in the disposition of cases. But mutually supportive relationships do not simply happen; they are influenced, indeed built, by attorneys and judges who come to know each other on a regular working basis. Familiarity, then, is the essence of the concept of the courtroom workgroup.[22]

Familiarity is achieved primarily through the stability of attorney workgroup members. Where the same small group of attorneys regularly appear in a courtroom, familiarity develops. In criminal courts, the assignment policies of the prosecutor's and public defender's offices largely determine whether and to what extent workgroups will become stable and, therefore, familiar interpersonally. In civil courts, attorneys are not assigned to courtrooms; rather, they are "free-lancers" unaccountable to any sponsoring organization. Thus, stability amd familiarity are much more a function of the size of the lawyer pool in the community. In large cities, scores of civil attorneys can be expected to appear before a judge during the course of a few weeks or months.

In this section, we first describe the amount of stability which judges report for criminal attorneys, then analyze the impact on judges' work patterns. We shall proceed similarly for civil attorneys. Finally, we shall compare the accuracy and utility of the concept of a courtroom workgroup in criminal and civil courts.

### CRIMINAL ATTORNEYS

Eisenstein and Jacob assert that prosecutors in urban courts are more likely than defense counsel to stay in one courtroom.[23] Our data suggest that although this difference is sizable in metropolitan (and in rural) areas, it is not very large nationwide. Prosecutors, on the whole, are only slightly more likely to stay in the courtroom of a particular judge longer than defense counsel, as Table 4–5 indicates.

In the courtrooms of about half of all trial judges, neither prosecuting nor defense attorneys are assigned such that one or a few attorneys try most or all cases. In these courts, a number of different prosecutors or defense counsel appear over a short period of time. In other courts, the same prosecutors or

TABLE 4–5. Trial Judges' Estimate of the Stability of Prosecutors and Defense Counsel in Their Courtrooms

|  | PROSECUTORS | DEFENSE COUNSEL |
|---|---|---|
| 2 years or more | 29.9% | 23.7% |
| 1–2 years | 8.6 | 12.4 |
| 4–12 months | 11.2 | 6.8 |
| 1–3 months | 5.3 | 2.8 |
| No assignment | 45.0 | 54.3 |
| Number | (2172) | (2127) |

defense counsel do appear regularly, most often for two years or more. These data, however, give a very incomplete picture of the phenomenon of criminal attorney stability. Other variables prove to be significant influences upon the likelihood of stability, notably type of defense counsel, size of community, and the court's case assignment system.

Where public defender systems operate to represent the bulk of indigent cases, judges are much more likely to report stability of defense counsel. Sixty-five percent of judges report some stability for public defenders compared with only 23 percent where assigned counsel systems prevail. In these latter situations, it is judges themselves who influence the degree of stability through their appointments of counsel to represent indigents. Where judges choose to keep appointments to a small number of attorneys or are forced to do so by a small or unwilling bar, some stability will be achieved.

Community size also influences prosecuting and defense attorney stability. In rural areas, prosecuting attorneys are stable: Two-thirds of judges report that prosecutors stay two years or more in their courtroom. This is so because rural-based prosecutors rarely have deputies. The elected county prosecutor, serving a term of two or four years, becomes attached to the local court. By contrast, defense attorneys are not usually stable in rural areas. Assigned counsel systems are more likely to prevail in rural areas, and this leads to a fairly wide dispersion of cases under most judges. Defense attorney stability is more likely to occur in those few rural places where either (1) a public defender system is operative, or (2) the bulk of cases do not involve indigents, and instead bring together a small number of private counsel.

In metropolitan areas, stability takes on a quite different face. Rarely do judges in these courts report stays by prosecuting or defense attorneys of two years or more in their courts. It is assignment, by the prosecutor's office or the public defender's office, of deputies to courtrooms for a number of months that contributes to whatever stability may exist. Both prosecutors and public defenders tend to be assigned to one courtroom for more than three months but less than one year. This periodic rotation of attorneys is often viewed by their superiors as a learning process, an opportunity to try different types of cases (felonies, misdemeanors) before different judges.

Where stability for a period of time is not achieved in metropolitan courts, the reason is most likely to be the presence of a master calendar. If cases can be sent to any available judge, the attorneys for those cases must go with them. In large courts, for example, 70 percent of judges in master calendar systems report *no* stability of prosecuting attorneys, compared with only 13 percent of judges with individual calendars. Fewer judges under master calendars report defense counsel stability also, though the differences are not quite so large. For those few judges in larger cities who do report stability of criminal attorneys under a master calendar, this reflects the *adjustments* of prosecutor's and/or public defender's offices. In these instances, the offices assign deputies to *stages* of cases (e.g., arraignment, motions, trial), just as the court has assigned judges to stages of cases. Thus, specialized attorneys and specialized judges meet, in a "motions" or "trial" courtroom, for example.

This lengthy introduction to the distribution of criminal attorney stability suggests the difficulty inherent in subsequent analysis. Because attorney stability is related to a number of structural variables (which, in turn, affect work patterns), disentangling causal linkages becomes quite difficult. Attorney stability, size of community, and case assignment system are highly intertwined.

In analyzing the impact of attorney stability on judges' work patterns, we examine the potential influences of prosecuting and defense attorneys separately. Prosecutors and defense attorneys, after all, are not interchangeable. Their cumulative impact, therefore, is not likely to be a simple additive function. Furthermore, a comparative look at the respective impacts of prosecutors and defense attorneys is both interesting and useful from a policy perspective. Reformers and critics typically are quick to point the finger at defense attorneys for many of the court's case processing problems, notably delay.[24] Yet do defense attorneys influence the work patterns of trial judges—for better or worse—more significantly than prosecutors? Our answer is a cautious "yes."

The relative mix of plea bargaining, nonjury trial, and jury trial work of judges seems to be affected by the stability of the criminal defense attorneys appearing in their courtroom. This set of relationships is most clearly exhibited for judges in *metropolitan* areas. Table 4–6 clearly reveals that where there is no stability among the defense attorney members of workgroups, judges are much more likely to hear jury than nonjury work, and less likely to spend time in plea discussions. With some stability among defense attorneys, judges are usually more likely to spend time in plea discussions and to hear a more equal distribution of nonjury and jury trial work. This is precisely what we would expect in light of Eisenstein and Jacob's conclusions about the impact of stable workgroups on types of case disposition. If stable workgroups negotiate more dispositions and try (especially before a jury) fewer cases, then a judge's work

TABLE 4–6. The Impact of Defense Attorney Stability upon Trial Judges' Plea Bargaining, Nonjury, and Jury Trial Work[a]

| Defense Attorney Stability[b] | % Judges Reporting (MC) | | | |
|---|---|---|---|---|
| | Plea Bargaining | Nonjury | Jury | Number |
| 1–2 years | 47.8 | 37.0 | 56.5 | (46) |
| 4–12 months | 50.9 | 45.6 | 56.1 | (57) |
| 1–3 months | 27.6 | 48.3 | 41.4 | (29) |
| No stability | 37.2 | 27.9 | 70.0 | (290) |

[a] Includes only judges in metropolitan areas.
[b] Category "2 years or more" is not included here, because so few metropolitan judges reported such lengthy attorney stability.

day should reflect—as it indeed seems to—these differences of task emphasis. Of course, we cannot compare our data on judicial work *directly* with case disposition data, but the parallels are suggestive.

There are three elaborations to this thesis required by our data. First, the relationships reflected in Table 4-6 are not uniformly linear. In particular, where defense attorneys are assigned to a judge's courtroom for one to three months, the impact is less predictable. Judges in these courts are actually less likely to spend time in plea discussions, but nevertheless have a quite "favorable" nonjury to jury ratio of work. Defense attorneys assigned for such a short period of time may not have sufficient opportunity to learn the sentencing values and work preferences of judges, information critical to the plea bargaining process and to the risking of a jury trial. On the other hand, learning may take place quickly after three months, because the work patterns of judges with moderately and highly stable sets of defense attorneys are quite similar. Such a description of the socialization process of workgroup members—abrupt rather than incremental—is not inconsistent with extant accounts.[25]

Second, the presence of stability among *prosecuting* attorneys also contributes to a higher proportion of judges spending time in plea discussions. The relationship demonstrated in Table 4-7 is distinctly linear. Judges are increasingly likely to spend time in plea discussions with attorneys as the typical length of assignment for prosecutors increases. However, the level of prosecuting attorney stability does *not* influence the likelihood that a judge will be engaged in jury or nonjury trial work.

The defense attorney and the defendant must choose what kind of trial to pursue—before judge or jury—once the decision not to plead guilty has been made.[26] If the defense attorney feels comfortable with a judge, by virtue of having served in his courtroom for a period of time, he is more likely to opt for nonjury trial. Under these circumstances, the judge has become more predict-

TABLE 4-7. The Impact of Prosecuting Attorney Stability upon Trial Judges' Plea Bargaining Work[a]

| *Prosecuting Attorney Stability*[b] | % JUDGES REPORTING PLEA BARGAINING | |
|---|---|---|
| | MC | *Number* |
| 1–2 years | 56.4 | (55) |
| 4–12 months | 45.9 | (111) |
| 1–3 months | 43.1 | (65) |
| No stability | 27.8 | (205) |

[a] Includes only judges in metropolitan areas.
[b] Category "2 years or more" is not included here, because so few metropolitan judges reported such lengthy attorney stability.

able. In turn, defense attorneys who have become regular members of the workgroup owe a certain allegiance to the spirit of cooperation, a spirit potentially disrupted by an excess of jury trials. In these areas of judicial work, then, defense attorneys may make a more significant difference than prosecutors.

Third, these relationships can be demonstrated only for judges in metropolitan areas. In part, this is because only a small number of prosecuting and defense attorneys are assigned for a period of time to the courtrooms of judges in medium-size urban, suburban, nonmetropolitan, or rural locations. In these places, there is typically no stability among attorneys or, as in rural places, long-term stability (two years or more). It may also be, as Eisenstein and Jacob have suggested, that outside of metropolitan areas attorney familiarity is high *regardless* of actual stability of particular workgroups because the size of the lawyer pool is small. If this is so, we could expect to find significance from attorney stability only, or most clearly, in metropolitan areas.

CIVIL ATTORNEYS

The familiarity of civil attorney workgroup members cannot be measured in quite the same way as for criminal attorneys. Civil attorneys, as we earlier noted, are not assigned to particular courtrooms except on an individual case basis. Yet the idea of more and less stable sets of civil attorneys is not an empirically implausible one, if we recognize that rarely, if ever, will civil attorneys be as familiar with one another as are some prosecutors and public defenders.

We view the concept of civil attorney stability in terms of a continuum, ranging from a concentration of cases among a few attorneys to a dispersion of cases among many attorneys. In order to measure this concept, judges were asked to estimate how many *different* plaintiff and defense attorneys, respectively, appeared before them in their most recently concluded fifty civil cases. The results appear in Table 4-8.

There is considerable variability among judges regarding the number of civil attorneys appearing before them. For some judges, fifteen or fewer different attorneys represented the last fifty plaintiffs and defendants. Con-

TABLE 4-8. Trial Judges' Estimate of the Concentration of Plaintiff and Defense Counsel in Their Courtrooms

| Number of Different Attorneys[a] | Plaintiff | Defense |
|---|---|---|
| 1–15 | 12.8% | 23.2% |
| 16–30 | 42.2 | 45.0 |
| 31–45 | 33.8 | 24.0 |
| 46–50 | 11.2 | 7.8 |
| Number | (2512) | (2512) |

[a] Categories represent those actually presented to respondents.

versely, for other judges a different attorney in every case is the norm. The majority of trial judges report stability among civil attorneys to be somewhere in between, however. Judges tend to see slightly more stability, or concentration, to defense attorneys. This is understandable, especially in "personal injury courts," where a few large insurance companies are defendants in many cases. These companies are typically represented by one or two firms in a community.

There is a very substantial relationship between stability of plaintiff attorneys and stability of defense attorneys, more so than between prosecutors and defense counsel. This is partly the result of a less rigid distinction between plaintiff and defense bars. There is occasional interchangeability of roles on the civil side, especially in smaller towns. In addition, the distinction between plaintiff and defendant can become murky in civil actions where both sides seek some positive outcome—for example, in equity cases or domestic relations litigation, or in tort cases where countersuits are filed. For these reasons, we find it most sensible to analyze data bearing upon the impact of civil attorney stability through one variable, which represents the joint effects of the concentration of plaintiff and defense counsel.[27]

Before proceeding to an analysis of impact, however, we must first look at the distribution of civil attorney stability in urban and rural areas. Just as size of community influences criminal attorney stability, it also influences the stability of civil attorneys. The relationship, however, is much larger on the civil side. Table 4-9 reports these data.

In metropolitan areas, judges report very little stability in the flow of civil attorneys before them. In rural places, by contrast, more judges are likely to perceive high stability than low stability among civil attorneys in their courtrooms. In medium-size cities, suburbs, and nonmetropolitan areas, judges are most likely to report moderate levels of stability. Overall, the relationship is almost perfectly linear: As community scale increases, so does the proportion of judges who report a constant flow of different attorneys before the court. On the civil side, then, the size of the lawyer pool has a substantial influence upon the stability of courtroom workgroups.[28]

What impact on judges' work patterns does attorney stability in civil cases

TABLE 4-9. The Impact of Community Size upon Civil Attorney Stability

|  | CIVIL ATTORNEY STABILITY | | | |
| --- | --- | --- | --- | --- |
| Community Size | High | Medium | Low | Number |
| Metropolitan | 7.6% | 31.7% | 60.7% | (555) |
| Medium city | 18.9 | 45.9 | 35.2 | (366) |
| Suburban | 22.3 | 53.1 | 24.6 | (175) |
| Nonmetropolitan | 27.3 | 50.2 | 22.5 | (652) |
| Rural | 31.9 | 52.3 | 15.8 | (708) |

have? Is it comparable or analogous to the effects of courtroom workgroups in criminal cases? Our data suggest a negative answer. In fact, there appear to be effects directly opposite to those for criminal attorney stability. For example, whereas stability of criminal attorneys is associated with more judicial time in plea discussions, it is related to *less* judicial time in civil settlement discussions. This relationship holds across most types of communities, though the differences are small. Where attorneys are relatively unfamiliar with one another, judges may feel that attorneys are unlikely to initiate settlement discussions on their own. The presence of the judge may be required to force civil attorneys to be serious about possible grounds for settlement. More than one judge whom we observed expressed this sentiment, though some judges were unhappy that their time had to be "sacrificed" in order to bring attorneys together.

Our data suggest no consistent pattern between attorney stability in civil cases and the frequency of jury and nonjury work among judges. Neither the absolute frequency nor the ratio of such work seems to be a function of attorney stability. Again, this should not be surprising in light of our earlier discussion of jury and nonjury work in Chapter 2. Whereas nonjury trials in criminal cases are often "slow pleas," in civil cases nonjury trials are often full-blown adversarial events requiring many hours. The choice between nonjury and jury trial in civil cases is much more dependent upon such factors as the type of claim and the amount of delay that litigants (usually plaintiffs) are willing to tolerate.[29] Thus, comparatively stable workgroups in civil courtrooms do not fear jury trials, or relish nonjury trials, to the degree that workgroups in criminal courtrooms do.

## Summary

Attorneys play a significant role in defining the work patterns of trial judges. Though the relationships we find are not large, they provide the basis for developing theories of attorney–judge work interrelationships which can be tested in subsequent research. Furthermore, our data probably underestimate the role of attorneys by looking only at several characteristics through the eyes of judges.

We do find a subtle interplay between attorneys and judges. The adversariness of attorneys influences the amount and kinds of work that judges will do. Highly contentious attorneys, at the least, provoke more and longer motions hearings and jury trials. Indeed, the adversariness of attorneys partially explains why size of court is so important in determining the relative balance of jury and nonjury trial work. Attorneys tend to be much more adversarial in urban than in rural areas.

Judges also respond to the work skills of attorneys, at least as they perceive them, in selecting which tasks to emphasize in their work. This is especially true for civil attorneys. Sometimes judges do work to compensate for the inadequacies of civil attorneys, as in drawing up decrees, judgments, and orders. In other instances, judges draw upon the strengths of civil attorneys by emphasizing settlement or trial work where they perceive attorneys to be so skilled. And in a few instances, especially in criminal courts, judges see their own options regarding the utilization of time reduced by the (real or perceived) weaknesses of attorneys.

Finally, judges' work is shaped by the level of familiarity, or stability, of attorney members of the workgroup. The differences are more marked on the criminal side, where the balance among plea bargaining, nonjury, and jury trial work slowly tilts toward methods of quick disposition when stability of attorneys is high. These findings provide striking confirmation of the thesis that Eisenstein and Jacob could only assert from their observational data. On the civil side, however, the impacts are not at all parallel. Settlement work by the judge is actually more frequent where attorneys are part of less stable workgroups. These differences between the criminal and civil setting seem to be related *not* to dispositional philosophy (civil court actors want to get their work completed, too) but to the possibility that the *cost*—in judicial and attorney time—of settlement and nonjury dispositions may be comparatively higher in civil than in criminal cases.

The role of attorneys extends well beyond the characteristics we have examined in this chapter. Attorneys can influence the nature of judicial work through the kinds of litigation they generate and bring to the courtroom. Attorneys and the organized bar serve as gatekeepers to the courthouse, by shaping whose legal needs are to be heard, in what sequence, and with what outcomes. How attorneys manage their own work, then, is a crucial variable in the interactions between themselves and judges. In addition, the motivations, rewards, and sanctions that attorneys bring to their relationships with the judge and the court should not be overlooked. Judges and the attorneys who practice before them are uniquely accountable to one another.

# Notes

1. For a review of studies that focus upon public perceptions of lawyers, see Austin Sarat, "Studying American Legal Culture: An Assessment of Survey Evidence," *Law and Society Review*, 11 (1977), pp. 435–438, 464–465. Sarat concludes that attitudes toward lawyers are likely to be unstable and frequently shaped by personal experience.
2. For a brief discussion of the significance of prosecutors' backgrounds, see Lief H. Carter, *The Limits of Order* (Lexington, Mass.: D. C. Heath, 1974); for federal prosecutors, see James Eisenstein, *Counsel for the United States: U.S. Attorneys in the Political and Legal Systems* (Baltimore: Johns Hopkins Press, 1978); for defense attorneys, see Paul B. Wice, *The Endangered Species: America's Private Criminal Lawyers* (Beverly Hills and London: Sage Publications, 1978).

3. See James Eisenstein and Herbert Jacob, *Felony Justice: An Organizational Analysis of Criminal Courts* (Boston: Little, Brown, 1977).
4. See, for example, Jonathan Black (ed.), *Radical Lawyers* (New York: Avon, 1971), and Linda Medcalf, *Law and Identity: Lawyers, Native Americans, and Legal Practice* (Beverly Hills and London: Sage Publications, 1978.)
5. Michael Lipsky, "Protest as a Political Resource," *American Political Science Review*, 62 (1968).
6. See, for example, Douglas E. Rosenthal, *Lawyers and Client: Who's in Charge?* (New York: Russell Sage, 1974).
7. *Bates v. State Bar of Arizona*, 433 U.S. 350 (1977).
8. For a discussion of how individual standards apply to practicing attorneys, possibly inequitably, see Jerome Carlin, *Lawyers' Ethics* (New York: Russell Sage, 1966).
9. Monroe H. Freedman, *Lawyers' Ethics in an Adversary System* (Indianapolis: Bobbs-Merrill, 1975).
10. See Packer's discussion of the "due process" and "crime control" models of the criminal justice system. Herbert L. Packer, *The Limits of the Criminal Sanction* (Palo Alto, Calif.: Stanford University Press, 1968).
11. See also Jackson B. Battle, "In Search of the Adversary System: The Cooperative Practices of Private Criminal Defense Attorneys," *Texas Law Review*, 50 (1971).
12. Multivariate analysis confirms the significance of region and community size on judges' trial time estimates for typical civil and criminal cases. Two other variables also appear to affect trial times: prior occupational experience of the judge and specialization. Judges who come to the general jurisdiction trial bench directly from private practice rather than by way of a lower court judgeship report *shorter* trial times, as do judges who hear all types of cases, rather than only criminal or civil cases.
13. Chief Justice Warren Burger has long argued that attorneys appearing in trial courts are typically unprepared, by law school training, for the kinds of trial advocacy tasks they will confront. See Burger's remarks, "The Special Skills of Advocacy," delivered at the Fourth John F. Sonnett Memorial Lecture at Fordham University Law School (November 26, 1973).
14. See David W. Neubauer, "Judicial Role and Case Management," *Justice System Journal*, 4 (1978).
15. See Anthony Partridge and Gordon Bermant, *The Quality of Advocacy in the Federal Courts* (Washington, D.C.: Federal Judicial Center, 1978), pp. 13–20.
16. Partridge and Bermant, *ibid.*, found no differences in the overall performance ratings by judges of various types of criminal and civil attorneys in the federal courts.
17. See Milton Heumann, *Plea Bargaining: The Experiences of Prosecutors, Judges and Defense Attorneys* (Chicago: University of Chicago Press, 1977), pp. 75–78, 92–110.
18. The average intercorrelation among the (perceived) skills of civil attorneys is lower ($r = .48$) than for criminal attorneys ($r = .59$), indicating more discrimination, or differentiation, of the skills of civil attorneys by judges.
19. For a discussion of nonjury trials as "slow pleas," see Chapter 2.

20. It is surprisingly difficult to find empirical support for this proposition. Church, for example, found that an attempted abolition of charge bargaining in one Midwestern county led to a higher trial rate, but he fails to differentiate between jury and bench trials. See Thomas Church, Jr., "Plea Bargains, Concessions, and the Courts: Analysis of a Quasi-Experiment," *Law and Society Review*, 10 (1976). Eisenstein and Jacob, *Felony Justice* (note 3 above), imply but do not directly assert that choice of bench or jury trial is related to the success of plea negotiations in individual cases.

21. See Eisenstein and Jacob, *Felony Justice;* Heumann, *Plea Bargaining;* and Abraham S. Blumberg, *Criminal Justice* (Chicago: Quadrangle, 1967).

22. For a fuller discussion, see Eisenstein and Jacob, *Felony Justice,* pp. 35–37.

23. *Ibid.,* p. 33.

24. See, for example, Macklin Fleming, "The Law's Delay: The Dragon Slain Friday Breathes Fire Again Monday," *Public Interest,* 32 (1973); G. Joseph Tauro, "Court Delay and the Trial Bar," *Judicature,* 52 (1969); and Richard S. Miller, "A Program for the Elimination of the Hardships of Litigation Delay," *Ohio State Law Journal,* 27 (1966).

25. See Heumann, *Plea Bargaining,* pp. 78–89.

26. This choice is not entirely unfettered, however. In the federal courts and in many states, the prosecutor must concur in the waiver of a jury trial (in favor of a bench trial). See Dorothy W. Nelson, *Cases and Materials on Judicial Administration and the Administration of Justice* (St. Paul: West Publishing, 1974), p. 598.

27. The resultant variable was a scale which reflected the summation of two ordinal-scaled variables (plaintiff and defense counsel stability): 4 for "1–15;" 3 for "16–30;" 2 for "31–45," and 1 for "46–50." The scale was then divided approximately into tertials, to achieve the categories "high," "medium," and "low."

28. Specialization of the judge also appears related to the degree of civil attorney stability: Judges who hear a narrow range of civil cases report less stability among the attorneys before them than judges who hear a wider range of civil cases or both criminal and civil cases. We characterize this relationship as tentative, however. It is not possible to control for size of community, because that variable is highly correlated both with specialization of the judge (see Chapter 3) and with civil attorney stability.

29. For a discussion of the impact of choice of bench versus jury trial on litigant waiting time in the civil division of one court we observed, see John Paul Ryan, "Management Science in the Real World of Courts," *Judicature,* 62 (1978).

# CHAPTER 5

# Judicial Resources in the Courthouse

JUDGES do not perform the work of the court alone. They are assisted by a variety of courthouse and courtroom personnel who work to provide security, record-keeping, general administrative management, and legal research. These "lower participants" do more than assist the judge, however. They also serve as sources of information and wield power.[1] Courtroom personnel act as gatekeepers, both to protect the judge and for their own purposes.[2] When the goals of judge and personnel merge, a smoothly administered courtroom will probably result. But when goals collide, confusion is likely to run rampant.

In this chapter we first describe the potential range of personnel and their customary functions. Drawing upon our observations, we examine variations in the number and kinds of personnel from court to court, as well as how courtroom workers interact with one another. We move to survey-based data, and a representative national picture, in examining the availability of two specific kinds of assistance: law clerk and secretarial. We look at law clerks and secretaries because our observations suggested that (1) these positions are most likely to influence judicial work patterns and (2) significant variation exists in the availability of these two resources from judge to judge. For both resources, we examine their allocation as well as the impact of their availability on judges' work patterns. Finally, we view the skill, or efficiency, of courtroom personnel through the eyes of the judge (much as we did for attorneys), and assess the impact on judges' work.

## Courthouse and Courtroom Personnel: An Overview

In many American courts, the "courthouse" and the "courtroom" are distinguishable in that more than one courtroom and more than one judge occupy a courthouse. In these places, the courthouse acts as a coordinating mechanism with respect to records, case files, and sometimes the assignment of cases and personnel. Whereas the "clerk of court" once performed these functions, today the modern trial court administrator has usurped some of these functions, particularly those relating to planning and management.[3] By contrast, in one-judge courthouses the roles of clerk of court and court administrator are merged, as are most of the distinctions between courthouse and courtroom. It is within this larger framework that the availability and assignment of courtroom personnel is best viewed.

Most individual courtrooms are staffed by one or more bailiffs, a court reporter, and a clerk. Each of these positions represents an identifiable, essential function. Bailiffs provide security in the courtroom, particularly in criminal courts, where they monitor, and sometimes restrain, the behavior of defendants. Bailiffs also perform juror-management functions in criminal and civil courts. Court reporters record and transcribe the verbatim proceedings of trials and other adversarial hearings. Clerks are responsible for the docket or calendar, at least insofar as calling the cases, having available the case files, and (often) taking notes or minutes for subsequent incorporation into the files. In some courts, clerks may also play a larger managerial and liaison function vis-à-vis the judge, attorneys, and other courtroom personnel.[4]

Additionally, individual judges may have access to a full- or part-time secretary and a full- or part-time law clerk. A secretary may assist the judge not only by doing correspondence but also by scheduling the judge's time. Law clerks can aid the judge not only in case-related research but also in generally keeping abreast of the law and in outside activities such as committee, bar, or judicial education functions. These positions are "luxuries," however, in the sense that not all trial judges actually have access to secretarial or, especially, law clerk services.

VARIATIONS IN COURTS

We observed wide variations among courts in the number and types of personnel available and in the permanency of their assignment to particular courtrooms.

In rural areas and smaller cities, there was an interchangeability of individuals and functions. In rural Tennessee and Nebraska, for example, the court reporting and secretarial functions were performed by one person. In Omaha, the bailiff and secretarial functions were merged. Such "multiple-hat" assistance may occur because there is insufficient work to keep three or four persons busy or because of a lack of financial resources.

In larger cities, there was an almost astonishing degree of variability from one community to another in the sheer number of personnel. In Los Angeles,

Houston, and Milwaukee, comparatively spartan crews supported the judge: usually one bailiff (sometimes two), a courtroom clerk, and a court reporter. Access to secretarial services was limited to sharing in a pool. Legal research assistance was even more limited: Only one judge among the twelve observed in these three cities had so much as a part-time law clerk. By contrast, in Nashville, Chicago, and Philadelphia, the courtroom work force typically comprised anywhere from six to eight individuals. For the Nashville criminal court judge we observed, there were five bailiffs—one who served as a personal assistant to the judge, four in the courtroom—and a full-time secretary, in addition to a clerk and court reporter. In Chicago, some criminal court judges had a "personal bailiff" (bodyguard), in addition to one or more courtroom bailiffs. For civil judges in Chicago, access to secretarial and legal research assistance was often substantial. In Philadelphia, all judges had every conceivable type of assistance. Three bailiffs, a court crier, a "tipstaff" (chauffeur-bodyguard-valet), a full-time secretary, and a full-time law clerk joined the courtroom clerk and reporter in each judge's court.

The differences in the number of courtroom personnel, especially bailiffs, from one city to another are clearly not random. Los Angeles, Milwaukee, and Houston, though different in some respects, all share a "good government" ethos: decentralized municipal structure, strong civil service orientation, weak labor unions, and a relatively nonpartisan political climate.[5] The result, predictably enough, is the avoidance of the "worker abundance" found in cities such as Nashville, Chicago, and Philadelphia, where bailiff positions are typically political plums from successful campaigns. The work structure of courts, then, is very much a product of the local political environment, a theme to which we shall return in more detail in Chapter 9.

Variations in the number and kinds of personnel also occurred *within* courts. Consider the experience of judges in Philadelphia and Chicago as an example. In Philadelphia, every judge whom we observed had exactly the same support personnel regardless of assignment. That the principle of equity in the allocation of courtroom personnel is very important in Philadelphia is illustrated in field notes recorded by our observer in the courtroom of a highly senior judge:

> The judge's staff is similar to the others. The bailiffs in his court seem to be a little more efficient than in the other courtrooms, but this is probably due to his bent for organization and planning. Even so, my impression of over-staffing in the Philadelphia courts continues to hold. Perhaps the only significant aspect of his staff is his own feelings about them. When I ask about them, he glances at me shrewdly and says, "What I have is the same as every other judge."

It is clear that this judge is trying to convey the idea that he has no extra privileges in personnel, despite his substantial seniority and clout in the court.

In the Chicago courts, the story is quite different; it is one of significant inequity, particularly between judges in different assignments.[6] In the civil jury division, the judge whom we observed had little access to secretarial services and no access to law clerks, a pattern similar to other judges in his division. This judge grumbled about the lack of legal research assistance and cast an envious eye toward the adjacent chancery division, where each judge had at least one full-time law clerk. Within the criminal division, though, one judge had a part-time law clerk and a full-time secretary, whereas the other judge we observed had neither. Thus, it is difficult to attribute some discrepancies to the nature of the assignment; rather, they strike us as a likely case of seniority, status, or simply "court politics."

Courts also differed with respect to the permanency with which courtroom personnel were assigned. In courts as different as Philadelphia, Omaha, Amarillo (Texas), and DuPage County (Illinois), clerks were assigned to a courtroom from a central pool. They were in the courtroom only when needed (e.g., for a call of the calendar) and rotated from courtroom to courtroom. As a result, these clerks were likely to be loyal to the clerk's office rather than to any individual judge. Court reporters also were not necessarily permanent fixtures in a courtroom. In some states (e.g., Illinois and Tennessee), reporters are provided in criminal courtrooms but not in civil courtrooms, where private litigants must pay the cost of maintaining a record. In the Chicago criminal courts, the reporter was assigned from a central pool and rotated, sometimes daily. In general, we observed friction between permanent courtroom personnel and rotating clerks or reporters, who, lacking loyalty to one judge, often arrived late or were unfamiliar with, or unconcerned about, the norms of a particular workgroup.

ACCOUNTABILITY AND EFFICIENCY

For a variety of reasons, judges may have little control over their courtroom personnel. They are not merely "staffs" of individual judges, responding to their every call or whim. Bailiffs, clerks, and reporters, in particular, typically have independence from the judge; the judge cannot hire, promote, raise the salary of, or fire them. At best, he can request their transfer to another courtroom. Yet where courtroom personnel are stable and have been with a particular judge for a number of years, a mutual respect and accountability are likely to be present.

It is not surprising, therefore, that the most visibly efficient and cooperative "teams" were found in courts where all personnel were assigned to one courtroom on a permanent basis. This is not to say that justice was better served by such deployment, but rather that courtroom procedures flowed more smoothly, with less interpersonal tension, and with less time spent waiting for tardy personnel to appear. In addition, judges with only three or four permanent personnel tended to rely upon these individuals in predictable ways. The matching of work with worker seemed clearer. Unlike in locations where four or five bailiffs had trouble remembering whose turn it was to manage the jury, or where traveling clerks or reporters were pressed to arrive at court in time for trial, courtroom personnel who constituted a manageably small and stable team knew what to do and were the only ones responsible for doing it. Perhaps the best example of the superiority of small, stable groups is the disintegration that occurs when several members take vacations. In one Los Angeles court with a normally stable workgroup, we observed two or three substitutes to wreak havoc in one afternoon courtroom session by engaging in audible conversations, smoking, and even autograph-seeking, all while court was in session.

But what impact do courtroom personnel, as individuals and as a group, have upon the work patterns of trial judges? Do they have any impact, or are they merely an interesting, even at times colorful, appendage? Our data suggest that courtroom personnel *do* influence the work of judges, for better and worse. We turn in the following sections to a view of law clerk and secretarial assistance, and how the availability of these resources impacts upon what judges do.

## Law Clerks and Their Impact

Legal research assistance is the most distinctive, least readily duplicated, resource for which trial judges have need. Bailiffs or court reporters may, in a pinch, be able to double as secretary, but not as law clerk.[7] The law clerk, however, is not a homogeneous entity. Some clerks are law school graduates, even members of the bar, and serve on a full-time salaried basis. Others are part-time only, while attending law school; some of these may be paid, others may receive academic credit as part of an internship. Thus, the motivations and very quality of law clerks can be highly variable.

How much of law clerk services do trial judges across the country have? The data in Table 5-1 suggest that the majority of trial judges have no access to law clerks, not even on a part-time or shared basis. For these judges, whatever legal research they do—decision-writing, preparation, or reading—they do themselves. Among the remaining judges, some share a law clerk with fellow judges, and somewhat fewer have their own part-time law clerk. Finally, one judge in six has his own full-time law clerk, and a handful of judges (less than

TABLE 5-1. Trial Judges' Level of Law Clerk Services

|  | PERCENT | NUMBER |
|---|---|---|
| More than one full-time law clerk | .9 | (28) |
| One full-time law clerk | 16.6 | (497) |
| One (or more) part-time law clerk(s) | 8.6 | (259) |
| One (or more) shared law clerk(s) | 13.8 | (412) |
| None | 60.1 | (1797) |
|  | 100.0 | (2993) |

one percent) have even more assistance. Overall, though, it is a picture of meager support to do legal research, a viewpoint shared by many, though not all, of the judges whom we observed.

Which trial judges get this valued commodity of law clerk services? Judges in the very largest courts are more likely to have a full-time clerk; almost half report that they have one. Still, almost half of the judges in these very large courts have no access to law clerks. Judges who travel as a regular part of their job are much less likely to have full-time law clerk assistance; this is particularly true for judges in statewide assignment systems, who do, nevertheless, report a high frequency of shared law clerks. Judges in criminal assignment are actually more likely to have access to law clerks than their counterparts in civil or general assignment.[8]

The most critical determining factor in the distribution of law clerk services, however, seems to be the state in which the judge is located. Only in Maryland, New York, Pennsylvania, and the District of Columbia do the majority of judges have a full-time law clerk. In fact, in these states nearly all judges have a law clerk. In the New England states and Delaware, most judges share one or more law clerks with their fellow judges. In a few other states (notably Alaska, Idaho, Louisiana, Michigan, Minnesota, and Nevada), there is a fragmented pattern in which a majority of judges have access to some kind of assistance. In all remaining states (including such litigious states as California, Florida, and Illinois), the majority of judges have no help in legal research.[9]

Finally, what do law clerks actually do that may, in turn, have an influence upon the work patterns of trial judges? Law clerks have been used by Supreme Court justices for nearly a hundred years, and more recently by federal and state appellate court judges, to assist in the preparation of opinions.[10] In trial courts also, law clerks may help prepare "opinions" (decisions), as well as research points of law during the course of a trial (e.g., in response to motions), and serve as a sounding board to the judge.[11] The emphasis of a law clerk's duties and their impact upon the work of the trial judge vary by size of court.

In the largest courts, law clerks facilitate the writing of decisions, judgments, and orders. Substantially more judges report, on their first three most common days, preparing and writing decisions where access to law clerks is present. Table 5-2 presents these data. It is clear that the presence of a law clerk makes a difference in the likelihood that a trial judge located in the largest courts will write decisions, judgments, or orders. Without a law clerk, judges must do all the digging and background work themselves if they are to write up a decision. Accordingly, only a minority of all judges without a clerk actually write decisions on any given work day. As clerking assistance becomes available, many more judges (up to two-thirds) write decisions, judgments, or orders. Similarly, it is in the largest courts that the presence of a full-time law clerk makes a significant difference in the time judges spend preparing and

TABLE 5-2. The Impact of Law Clerk Services upon Trial Judges' Preparing and Writing of Decisions[a]

| | % JUDGES REPORTING PREPARING/WRITING DECISIONS | | | |
|---|---|---|---|---|
| Law Clerk Services | MC | 2nd MC | 3rd MC | Number |
| Full-time | 68.8 | 64.5 | 68.6 | 128/76/35 |
| Part-time or shared | 59.0 | 52.0 | 61.5 | 39/25/13 |
| None | 48.8 | 36.4 | 37.9 | 192/66/29 |

[a] Includes only judges in courts with forty or more judges.

writing decisions. Judges in the largest courts average about one-half hour *more* time doing this on a given day, if they have a full-time clerk. Though one might initially expect law clerks to "save" judicial time writing decisions, we infer from these data that judges with full-time clerks write certain decisions or judgments that they might not otherwise write.

In small courts, judges with law clerk assistance neither perform decision-writing duties more frequently nor spend more time in writing than their counterparts without law clerks. Indeed, judges in smaller courts tend to spend more time preparing and writing decisions than judges in larger courts, regardless of their level of law clerk resources. Rather, the presence of a law clerk in small courts facilitates the judge's keeping up with the law. Figure 5-1 demonstrates these data.

In small courts, fully 78 percent of judges report "keeping up with the law" on their most common day, as do 75 percent of judges with part-time clerks, compared with only 62 percent having no law clerk. These differences persist on less common work days. In intermediate and large courts, however, there are no significant differences. Thus, judges in small courts are uniquely able to keep up with the law through access to legal research assistance.

Why are law clerks utilized differently in small and large courts? We believe the key lies both in judicial role perceptions and in the requirements of the litigation. In large courts, judges themselves must keep up with the law—be familiar with current case law—if they are to rule correctly on the many motions argued before and during trials. Particularly on the criminal side, these motions are rooted in an ever changing body of constitutional law. Law clerks cannot do this work for judges, who must often make instant rulings without benefit of consultation. Furthermore, judges may keep up not only by reading but by exchanging ideas with fellow judges. What law clerks can do for judges in large courts is the background work, and even initial drafting, for decisions and orders that must or should be written up, either because of their policy significance or because they are likely to be appealed.

The effective utilization of law clerks in large courts seems attributable primarily to judges in civil, rather than criminal, assignment. Writing decisions, judgments, and orders is not something readily associated with trial judging in criminal courts.[12] The law clerks assigned to judges whom we observed in specialized civil divisions (e.g., equity and mental health) performed precisely this background work. In contrast, law clerks assigned to judges in criminal divisions often sat around "learning," unless (as in Philadelphia) they assisted judges in researching motions assigned from the civil division.

In small courts, law clerks could help judges write decisions, but instead these judges appear to utilize their law clerks in a more general rather than a case-related way—to keep current with the law, to reduce the intellectual isolation which is a significant part of judging in small courts and small towns. Given the potential range of cases (criminal, civil, juvenile) with which most judges in small courts are confronted, it is not surprising that they keep up with the law in these many substantive areas through the assistance of, and interactions with, their law clerks. The law clerk becomes an important sounding

**FIGURE 5-1.** The Impact of Law Clerk Services upon Trial Judges' Keeping Up with the Law, by Size of Court

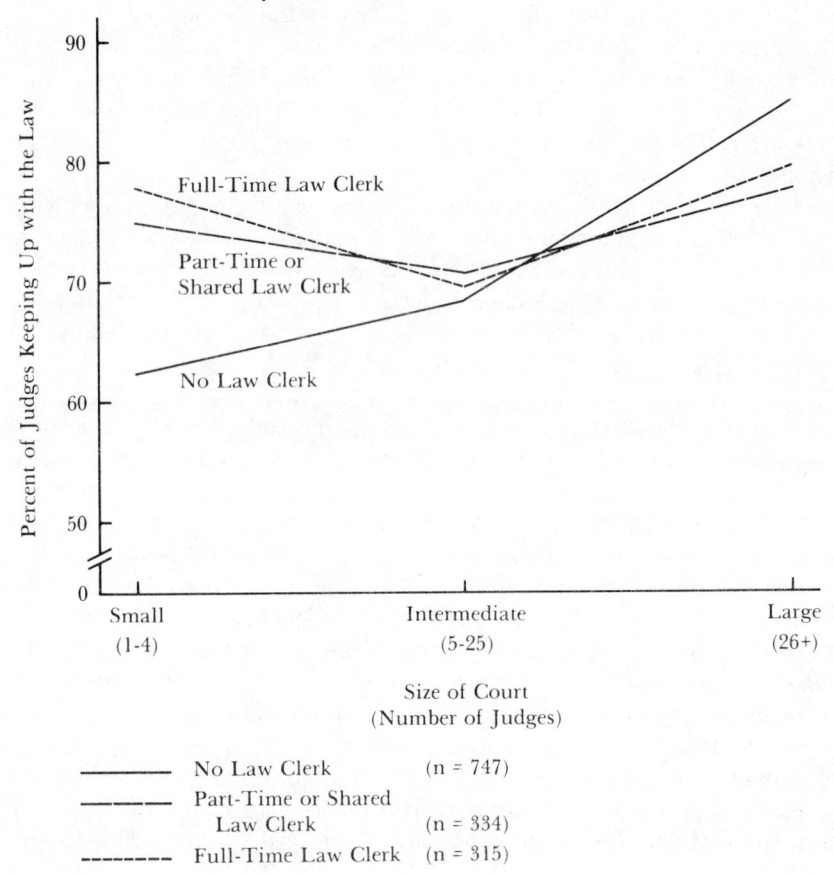

[Graph showing Percent of Judges Keeping Up with the Law (y-axis, 0 to 90) vs. Size of Court (Number of Judges) on x-axis: Small (1-4), Intermediate (5-25), Large (26+). Three lines: Full-Time Law Clerk, Part-Time or Shared Law Clerk, No Law Clerk.]

———— No Law Clerk (n = 747)
– – – – Part-Time or Shared Law Clerk (n = 334)
- - - - - Full-Time Law Clerk (n = 315)

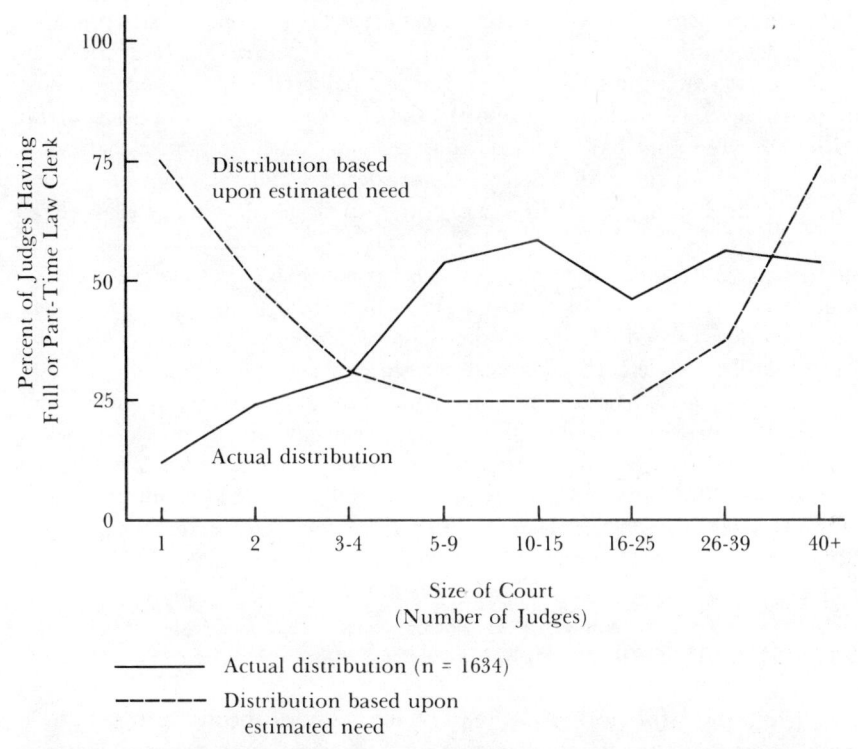

**FIGURE 5-2. The Distribution of Law Clerk Services by Size of Court: Actual Distribution Versus Distribution Based upon Estimated Need**

board, a link to the modern law. He fulfills a role that judges play in larger, multijudge courts. By contrast, writing decisions and orders is viewed as a *judicial* activity, one not to be shared with attorneys or clerks.

In both small and large courts, then, law clerks perform "luxury" work, that is, work that the judge would like to do but quite often cannot. In small courts, the luxury work is keeping current with the law, because attorneys expect written decisions but do not argue complex motions. In large courts, where attorneys' expectations and behavior are different, the luxury work is preparing and writing decisions.

But how do law clerks assist judges sitting in intermediate-size courts? Concrete benefits are not readily apparent from our survey data. There are only the slightest traces of additional legal research being accomplished by judges with access to law clerks; the relationships are neither sizable nor consistent. There is an equally slight trace of increased time being spent in bar association–related activities by judges with access to law clerks in these courts. Overall, though, our data simply suggest that judges' work patterns are not influenced by the presence or absence of law clerks in intermediate-size courts. Whatever clerks may do in these courts, it is not central to the ongoing work of the judge.

If we compare the actual distribution of law clerk services by size of court, with a distribution based upon "need," as could be inferred from the foregoing analysis, we would find that judges in small courts, as a group, are most disadvantaged. Figure 5-2 presents these actual and speculative data. Although we do not have sufficient data to determine the precise shape of a law clerk "need" function, Figure 5-2 provides an estimate of its shape, based upon certain assumptions.[13] In small courts, where our data suggest law clerks do have an impact, few judges have access to law clerks. Conversely, the highest proportion of judges having access to law clerks (mostly part-time or shared) occurs in intermediate-size courts, where little or no significant impact can be documented. It is in the larger courts where actual resources (mostly full-time clerks) and projected need come closest to matching.

This shortage of resources in small courts and abundance in intermediate-size courts is partly, no doubt, a function of the availability of law clerks. Small courts located in rural areas are typically quite removed from law schools. Nonetheless, differences in the tax bases of rural as opposed to suburban and medium-size communities also determine to what extent "luxury" will be indulged or need will go unmet.

## Secretarial Assistance

Secretarial assistance—including typing, miscellaneous administrative work, and scheduling of appointments—is needed, in some measure, by every trial judge. Not all judges, though, have enough of this type of work to keep one person busy throughout the work day or week. These realities are reflected in the distribution of secretarial assistance on a national basis, as reported in Table 5-3.

A substantial proportion of judges—more than one-third—have their own personal secretary on a full-time basis. A smaller number have a part-time secretary, and a similar proportion have access to a secretarial pool (though the number of judges drawing upon the "pool" may be quite large). Another

TABLE 5-3. Trial Judges' Level of Secretarial Services

|  | PERCENT | NUMBER |
|---|---|---|
| Full-time secretary | 36.7 | (1070) |
| Part-time secretary | 12.3 | (360) |
| Shared (in pool) | 14.8 | (431) |
| Clerk, bailiff, or court reporter acts as secretary | 32.6 | (951) |
| None | 3.6 | (106) |
|  | 100.0 | (2918) |

one-third of all judges report using their clerk, bailiff, or court reporter as secretary. Only a very small percentage of judges report no access to secretarial services. The availability of secretarial assistance, then, is considerably greater than for law clerk services.

Under what circumstances are trial judges more likely to have a particular kind of secretarial assistance? Judges in very large courts are much more likely to share in a pool and much less likely to use the services of a bailiff, reporter, or clerk. A formal division of the work of courtroom personnel occurs in larger cities, accounting for the paradoxical and sometimes frustrating situation in which five bailiffs read paperbacks in the courtroom while the judge searches frantically for someone to type a letter.[14] It is also in the very largest courts that more judges (10 percent) have *no* access to secretarial assistance. Judges who ride circuit are more likely to draw upon bailiff, reporter, or clerk for secretarial duty, reflecting the substantially rural character of circuits.

Once again, however, the state in which the judge is located is the single most critical determinant of the type of secretarial services, as it is for law clerk services. In nineteen states—mostly Southern and Southwestern, but also including the Northern industrial states of Michigan, New York, and Pennsylvania—the majority of judges have a full-time secretary. In eighteen states—mostly the Rocky Mountains, plains, and Midwest—the majority of judges use a bailiff, clerk, or reporter as secretary. In five states—urban New England and California—the predominant pattern is one of sharing in a secretarial pool. In the remaining few states a mixed pattern prevails.

Thus, there is some correlation between the availability of law clerk and secretarial services. In Maryland, New York, Pennsylvania, and the District of Columbia, most judges have *both* full-time law clerks and full-time secretaries. In New England, sharing both law clerks and secretaries is the norm. By contrast, judges in Southern states are rich in secretarial assistance but poor in law clerk help. The lack of a well-developed case law and a lower level of attorney adversariness in Southern states may have much to do with the pervasive absence of law clerks.

What impact do different amounts and types of secretarial assistance have upon judges' work patterns? In particular, how is a judge's administrative work affected by the availability of secretarial services? Our data indicate that similar proportions of judges spend about the same amount of time doing general administrative work, regardless of whether they have full-time, part-time, shared, or "multiple-hat" secretarial assistance. Only if judges have no assistance whatsoever is there a difference, in a curious direction: These judges are *less* likely to report doing administrative work on their several work days. We can surmise that having secretarial assistance requires a minimum initial investment of a judge's time each day (e.g., fifteen minutes), in order to provide direction or instructions for the particular work to be done. If a judge has no assistance whatsoever, he need not commit this time, though of course certain work may not get done. That most judges do have to invest some time each day in instructing, and probably socializing with, a secretary suggests how important it is that this person be reasonably efficient. An efficient individual easily repays the judge's investment of a few minutes each day; an inefficient individual can waste both the judge's and the court's time. It is to this question of efficiency of courtroom personnel generally that we now turn.

## The Efficiency of Courtroom Personnel

The availability of courtroom personnel, which we have described in some detail, may tell little about their actual effectiveness or efficiency. In many of the locations we observed, the number of personnel bore no relationship to how much assistance was actually provided to the judge. Indeed, the relationship often appeared to be inverse: The greater the number of personnel, the *less* work *per capita* each member accomplished; sometimes, the less work the entire group accomplished.

How effective, in the minds of judges, are the courtroom personnel who work with them? Figure 5-3 displays these data, derived from responses to a semantic differential question focusing upon how well personnel facilitate the day-to-day work of judges. The figure demonstrates that judges, as a group, regard quite highly the work of their courtroom personnel. Five judges out of every six, or about 83 percent, rate their personnel on the positive side (5, 6, or 7) of the ineffective–effective continuum, and fully one-quarter of all judges rate their personnel in the highest category of effectiveness. Only a small percentage of judges characterize their personnel as ineffective, to one extent or another.

These data should not suggest that the work of courtroom personnel is typically stellar. That inference would not quite conform to our field-based impressions, where we observed at least a substantial minority of personnel to be visibly indifferent to the court's work. Rather, judges seem to accept the human limitations of their personnel and the political constraints under which they and their personnel often operate. Nevertheless, the presence of political factors does influence judges' perceptions of the quality and efficiency of their personnel. Where judges perceive "court politics" to be a substantial influence in the procedures by which they themselves are assigned to divisions, they are much less happy about their personnel ($\bar{x} = 5.1$) than when they perceive political influences to be slight ($\bar{x} = 5.6$) or not at all present ($\bar{x} = 5.9$). If court politics is a primary basis on which judges are assigned to particular divisions within their court, it might be expected that the allocation of (limited) courthouse resources would also be made on political grounds. It may also be that personnel are more likely to be *selected* for political reasons, rather than for their skills and efficiency, in courts where internal politics directly affect administrative decisions.[15]

In addition, elements of the court structure make a difference in the effec-

## Judicial Resources in the Courthouse

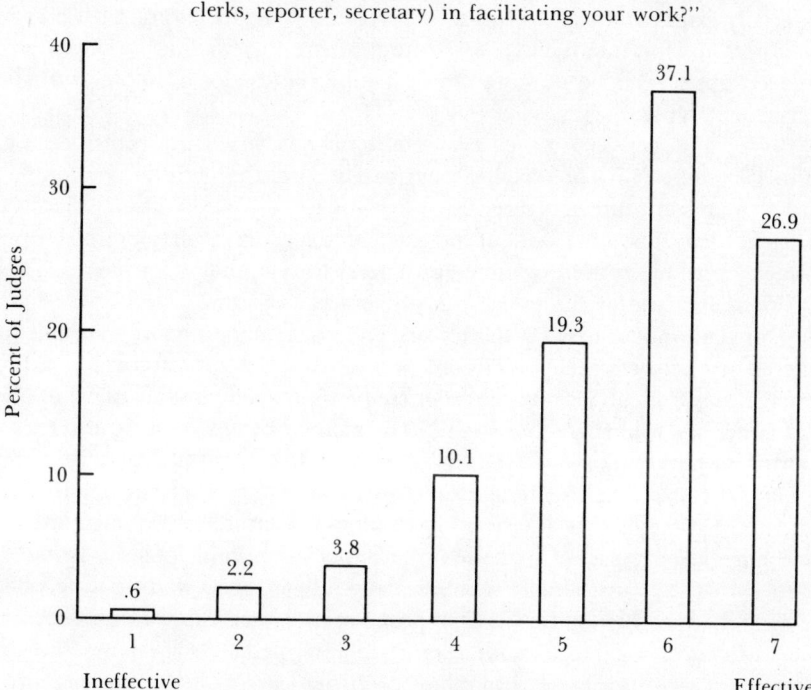

"How effective are the personnel in your courtroom (bailiffs, clerks, reporter, secretary) in facilitating your work?"

[Bar chart: Percent of Judges vs. scale 1 (Ineffective) to 7 (Effective)
1: .6
2: 2.2
3: 3.8
4: 10.1
5: 19.3
6: 37.1
7: 26.9
N = 3000]

FIGURE 5-3. Trial Judges' Perceptions of the Efficiency of Their Courtroom Personnel

tiveness with which personnel are viewed. Judges who travel as part of their regular duty rate their personnel somewhat less effective, both judges in statewide assignment systems ($\bar{x} = 5.1$) and judges who ride circuit ($\bar{x} = 5.3$), compared with judges who do not travel ($\bar{x} = 5.8$). This is probably, in part, a problem of communication. The schedules of judges who travel are often uncertain. When they arrive at a particular courthouse, personnel may be less well prepared because the judge was not expected for another hour or day. It may also be related to a lower level of familiarity with the various personnel in several courthouses. Judges who do not work with the same personnel day in and out may come to feel a weaker sense of commitment or loyalty to these different individuals, just as rotating clerks or court reporters probably feel weaker ties to individual judges.

Size of court also makes some difference in the effectiveness with which judges view their personnel. The relationship, however, is not linear; it is curvilinear. The effectiveness of personnel gently rises to a peak in intermediate-size courts and then drops off rather abruptly in large courts. Indeed, judges in the largest courts are least laudatory of their personnel, though it is in these courts that judges are most likely to have a large number of personnel, especially extra bailiffs and a full-time law clerk. Judges are most satisfied with their personnel in intermediate-size courts, where the relationship of resources to need appears to be most favorable to judges (as, for example, with law clerks; see Figure 5-2).

In sum, judges vary in their evaluations of the efficiency of courtroom personnel in some fairly predictable ways based upon the political environment and elements of court structure. But what impact, if any, do different levels of efficiency have upon the work of judges? Our data suggest that ineffective personnel contribute to waiting time and longer working hours for judges. Table 5-4 presents data for the impact on judges' waiting time.

Our data indicate that a higher percentage of judges report waiting time where they perceive their courtroom personnel to be less effective. The percentage rises from about one-third (where personnel are most efficient) to one-half (where personnel are inefficient). The amount of time waiting also rises as courtroom personnel are viewed to be less effective. A similar pattern of differences occurs on the second and subsequent work days, underscoring the persistence of the effects of inefficient personnel upon judges' waiting time.

The negative impact of inefficient personnel varies in its intensity by size of court. In large courts, almost twice as many judges report waiting time where personnel are highly inefficient as opposed to highly efficient. In small courts, the differences are more modest, and in intermediate-size courts the differences in waiting time attributable to efficient versus inefficient personnel are very slight. These findings reinforce earlier data regarding the availability and utilization of courtroom personnel in intermediate-size courts. These courts have the most efficient personnel overall (in the eyes of the judges), and here the availability of law clerk services has the least visible impact upon what judges do. It is as if judges located in intermediate-size courts have sufficient resources to withstand flurries of inefficiency from (some of) their courtroom personnel. This is not the case in small and, especially, large courts, where inefficient personnel are likely to cause judges to wait.

TABLE 5-4. The Impact of Courtroom Personnel Efficiency upon Trial Judges' Waiting Time

| Efficiency of Personnel | % JUDGES REPORTING WAITING TIME | |
|---|---|---|
| | MC | Number |
| 1 (Ineffective) | 50.0 | (16) |
| 2 | 49.1 | (57) |
| 3 | 53.0 | (100) |
| 4 | 43.1 | (248) |
| 5 | 47.4 | (477) |
| 6 | 41.9 | (927) |
| 7 (Effective) | 36.9 | (655) |

Inefficient courtroom personnel also lead to longer working hours for judges. On the average, judges report working one-half hour longer on their most common day where personnel are relatively or highly inefficient. Again, however, the differences vary by size of court. Judges in small courts and in the largest courts appear to suffer a substantial loss of time through the inefficiencies of their courtroom personnel. In small courts, judges report working fully one hour longer on their most common day when their personnel are inefficient, and in courts with forty or more judges more than one hour longer, and these differences persist across less common work days. Just as the effects of inefficient personnel are minimal upon the waiting time of judges in intermediate-size courts, so also are they minimal on the length of these judges' work days.

Why do judges with inefficient personnel sometimes work longer hours? What is different about the composition of their day, compared with judges who have more efficient personnel? Once again, the answer depends significantly upon size of court. In the largest courts, judges with inefficient personnel work longer on the day's jury trial—by almost one-half hour—than judges with more efficient personnel. Bailiffs and court reporters, in particular, can impair the efficiency of a jury trial by being late or simply inattentive to the proceedings. This behavior may be more likely to occur in some larger courts where workers enjoy greater job security through union or political protection. In small courts, judges having inefficient personnel spend up to one-half hour additional time in traveling. This linkage is not quite so clear, but it may be that the amount of traveling is not a fixed entity. Perhaps judges sometimes must retrace their steps to find papers, case files, or other documents as they move from one courthouse to another.

## Summary

The availability and efficiency of courtroom personnel vary quite sharply across courts and judges, and this contributes to differences in judicial work patterns. Most often the impact of personnel is contextual, depending upon size of court.

Judges in small courts have the fewest human resources: A court reporter or bailiff is likely to serve several functions, including secretarial, and law clerks are rare. By contrast, judges in large courts typically have the most, if not the best, workers. Extra bailiffs, including ones personally attached to the judge, are frequent. Law clerk and especially secretarial assistance, however, are not much greater in large courts than in intermediate-size courts, where judges feel best about the efficiency of their personnel. Politics—the political environment outside of and within the courts—also appears to impact upon the allocation of skilled resources. Both our observational and survey data indicate that court politics and partisan politics reduce the likelihood that a manageable team will complete its tasks competently.

Law clerks are the most distinctive and influential resource of the trial judge. They facilitate the performance of legal research tasks, at least in small and very large courts. In the largest courts, law clerks enable judges—especially in civil assignment—to produce written decisions in selected cases by doing background research and perhaps initial drafting. In small courts, law clerks assist judges in less conventional or expected ways, by facilitating their keeping abreast of changing substantive law. It is in intermediate-size courts, and sometimes in large criminal courts, that law clerks appear to be poorly utilized or not utilized at all.

The general efficiency level of courtroom resources also influences what judges do. Judges must work longer hours, at least in small and large courts, when their personnel are relatively ineffective. In large courts, the inefficiencies are particularly likely to occur in jury trials, where typically a delicate balance exists between organization and confusion. In most courts, judges feel they often wait because of inefficient personnel, a belief supported by survey data and our own observations.

The story of courtroom personnel, then, is inextricably interlinked with size of court. Resources and observable need vary by court size. And the impacts of personnel vary substantially, and asymmetrically, from small to intermediate to large courts, and thus modify some of the relationships we initially discovered in Chapter 3. The relationships between size of court and legal research tasks, for example, are strongest where no law clerk assistance is available, but much smaller among judges with a full-time clerk. This is to say that courthouse resources—law clerks or other personnel—can often ameliorate or even eliminate inherent disadvantages in the work environments of large and small courts.

## Notes

1. See David Mechanic, "Sources of Power of Lower Participants in Complex Organizations," *Administrative Science Quarterly*, 7 (1962).
2. Clerks in some large courts have been known to operate the call of the calendar mostly for their own (corrupt) purposes. A five- or ten-dollar bill slipped to the courtroom clerk by an impatient attorney can quickly alter the order of cases to be called.
3. For a discussion of potential conflicts between trial court administrators and clerks of court in Florida, see Larry C. Berkson and Steven W. Hays, "The Unmaking of a Court Administrator," *Judicature*, 60 (1976).
4. For a discussion of clerks in this larger capacity, see Marc G. Gertz, "Influence in Court Systems: The Clerk as Interface," *Justice System Journal*, 3 (1977). In our view, Gertz exaggerates the real or potential power of clerks as courtroom managers. For example, in most larger courts, scheduling functions are undertaken by an "assignment office" directly accountable to the presiding judge. In these courts, the clerk's office is often regarded as a feudal vestige. It may be that in statewide

assignment states like Connecticut, where Gertz studied, clerks assume more importance because judges frequently are rotated from courthouse to courthouse. Nevertheless, Feeley does not ascribe much significance to the work of courtroom clerks in New Haven, where he notes that "the clerk's passivity allows prosecutors considerable freedom to manipulate the docket to their own purposes." See Malcolm M. Feeley, *The Process Is the Punishment* (New York: Russell Sage, 1979).

5. For a discussion of urban political cultures in the context of public policy, see Robert L. Lineberry and Edmund P. Fowler, "Reformism and Public Policies in American Cities," in James Q. Wilson (ed.), *City Politics and Public Policy* (New York: Wiley, 1968); see also James Q. Wilson, *Varieties of Police Behavior* (Cambridge, Mass.: Harvard University Press, 1968).

6. Our observations on the allocation of courthouse resources are supported by survey data from Chicago judges. Variation between assignments is much greater than within assignments.

7. On rare occasions, bailiffs may be students working their way through law school.

8. We believe this has more to do with Law Enforcement Assistance Administration (LEAA) funding patterns than actual need. Some criminal judges had law clerks funded through one or another LEAA program. Though criminal assignment judges may have an extensive case law to keep abreast of, it is judges in civil and general assignment who write decisions, judgments, and orders. See note 12 below.

9. Law clerks are more typically funded by either the state or the county. In some instances, allocation of full- or part-time law clerks to judges in a particular court may be a compromise in lieu of additional judgeships.

10. Paul R. Baier, "The Law Clerks: Profile of an Institution," *Vanderbilt Law Review*, 26 (1973).

11. Loran L. Lewis, "Judges Need Law Clerks," *Judges' Journal*, 7 (1968).

12. Judges in civil assignments, especially chancery and probate, report spending more time preparing/writing decisions on their various work days than judges in criminal assignment.

13. The assumptions are: (1) 75 percent of judges in one-judge and forty- or more-judge courts could effectively utilize law clerk services; (2) 25 percent of judges in 5-9-, 10-15-, and 16-25- judge courts could effectively utilize law clerk services; and (3) the need function in between these points is curvilinear rather than step-level. These assumptions, of course, are estimates inferred from our observations and, primarily, from the results of our analysis of the impacts of law clerks in different-size courts. The choices of the 75 percent and 25 percent figures for effective utilization of law clerks are arbitrary but not unrealistic, in light of our analysis.

14. In fact, this scenario only infrequently occurs, because most courtrooms having an overabundance of bailiffs also have full-time secretaries.

15. The political climate *external* to the court also seems to be related to effectiveness of personnel. In states where trial judges are selected by nonpartisan election, judges rated their personnel higher ($\bar{x} = 5.8$) than where judges are selected by partisan election ($\bar{x} = 5.5$) or by gubernatorial appointment ($\bar{x} = 5.2$).

# PART III

# Individual Influences

# CHAPTER 6

# The Recruitment and Socialization of Trial Judges

In previous chapters, we have analyzed factors external to the judge that may influence how he manages his work day. The structure of the local court and the qualities of the attorneys and courtroom personnel with whom the judge interacts help to define judicial work patterns. But what about the judge as an individual?

In this chapter we look at the judge as an individual who brings certain backgrounds, experiences, and interests to the bench. Broadly speaking, the process through which judges arrive at the bench is termed "recruitment."[1] Judges are selected through formal methods prescribed by law, such as election (in a partisan or nonpartisan contest) or appointment (usually by the governor). Formal selection, however, is only the culmination of a process of attracting prospective candidates for judgeships. How and why individuals become candidates, and the ranks—social, occupational, and political—from which they are drawn are important issues that highlight the elite and homogeneous character of the trial bench.

We also examine the judge as an individual who is shaped by the experience of judging over time. Broadly speaking, this is the socialization or adaptation process.[2] Judges come to the bench with little formal training for the job and sometimes with unrealistic expectations about the operation of courts. On-the-job learning takes place, sometimes facilitated by orientation or continuing education programs for judges. Over time, judges confront the tensions between security and conformity, growth on the bench and mobility to higher judicial or political office, and those of career ambitions generally.

We turn first to the recruitment process by examining the variety of formal selection methods used in the states to select trial judges and the occupational ranks from which judges have been drawn. We then look at (1) the impact of recruitment on the social characteristics of America's trial bench, in particular the age, race, gender, and legal heritage of judges, and (2) the impact of these social characteristics on judicial work. Finally, we analyze the socialization and adaptation processes, first by discussing the transition from lawyering to judging, then by focusing upon later stages in the judicial career and the impact of judicial tenure on work.

## Recruitment

### FORMAL SELECTION SYSTEMS

Most states are authorized, by constitution or statute, to select their trial judges in one of four ways: partisan election (thirteen states), nonpartisan election (16 states), gubernatorial appointment (eight states), or gubernatorial appointment based upon screening by a nominating commission, usually referred to as "merit selection" (eight states). Two states utilize selection by the legislature, and a few other states have hybrid systems in which the method varies by locale.

These differences in formal selection method often reflect the evolution and change of political traditions and, in particular, the dominance of one of those traditions at the time of statehood. More recently, however, some states have undergone the cumbersome process of changing selection methods, usually away from partisan election and often to merit selection.[3] Table 6-1 presents a complete listing of selection methods by states, as of 1977.

The way in which judges in the states are actually selected is complicated by the presence of vacancies and the corresponding need for *interim* selection methods. Today, gubernatorial appointment and merit selection predominate in filling vacancies, and the occurrence of vacancies is so common in some states that the predominant method of selection is the method for interim selection.[4] In populous California, for example, 88 percent of the trial judges were selected initially to fill a vacancy (that is, by gubernatorial appointment) rather than by the "normal" method provided by law, nonpartisan election. Overall, in states utilizing nonpartisan election only 43 percent of the judges were initially elected; the majority were appointed by the governor or through merit selection. In partisan election states, however, fully 70 percent of the judges were initially elected.[5]

It is, therefore, this combination of initial and interim selection methods that accounts for how trial judges actually first arrived at the bench in the

**TABLE 6-1. Initial (and Interim) Selection Methods for Trial Judges in the States**

| Partisan Election | | Nonpartisan Election | | Gubernatorial Appointment[a] | |
|---|---|---|---|---|---|
| Alabama | (G or M)[c] | California | (G) | Connecticut | (G) |
| Arkansas | (G) | Florida | (M) | Delaware | (G-M) |
| Georgia | (G-M) | Idaho | (M) | Hawaii | (G) |
| Illinois | (SC) | Kentucky | (M) | Maine | (G) |
| Louisiana | (SC)[d] | Maryland | (G-M) | Massachusetts | (G-M) |
| Mississippi | (G) | Michigan | (G) | New Hampshire | (G) |
| New Mexico | (G) | Minnesota | (G) | New Jersey | (G) |
| New York | (G-M) | Montana | (M) | Rhode Island | (G) |
| North Carolina | (G-M) | Nevada | (M) | | |
| Pennsylvania | (G-M) | North Dakota | (M) | (n = 8) | |
| Tennessee | (G) | Ohio | (G) | | |
| Texas | (G) | Oklahoma | (G-M) | | |
| West Virginia | (G) | Oregon | (G) | | |
| | | South Dakota | (G-M) | | |
| (n = 13) | | Washington | (G) | | |
| | | Wisconsin | (G) | | |
| | | (n = 16) | | | |

| Merit[b] | | Legislative Selection | | Hybrids | |
|---|---|---|---|---|---|
| Alaska | | South Carolina | (G or LS)[e] | Partisan or Merit, depending upon locale | |
| Colorado | | Virginia | (G) | | |
| D.C. | | | | | |
| Iowa | | (n = 2) | | | |
| Nebraska | | | | Indiana | (G) |
| Utah | | | | Kansas | (G) |
| Vermont | | | | Missouri | (G or M) |
| Wyoming | | | | | |
| | | | | (n = 3) | |
| (n = 8) | | | | | |
| | | | | Nonpartisan or Merit, depending upon locale | |
| | | | | Arizona | (G) |
| | | | | (n = 1) | |

[a] Two of these states—Massachusetts and Delaware—currently use merit selection, by executive order, for initial selection.
[b] All states utilizing merit system for initial selection also utilize merit for filling vacancies.
[c] Codes for interim appointments: G = gubernatorial appointment; G-M = gubernatorial appointment, but merit system currently in effect by executive order; G or M = gubernatorial appointment or merit depending upon locale; SC = state supreme court appointment; LS = legislative selection.
[d] In Louisiana, the supreme court fills vacancies until an election is called by the governor, but the interim appointee is ineligible to run in the election
[e] In South Carolina, if the unexpired term is less than one year, the Governor appoints; if more than one year, the legislature selects.

**TABLE 6-2. Trial Judges' Report of the Method of Their Selection**

|  | Percent | Number |
|---|---|---|
| Elected: Partisan ballot | 27.0 | (806) |
| Elected: Nonpartisan ballot | 16.6 | (495) |
| Appointed by governor | 45.1 — 11.7 (P)[a] / 22.2 (NP) / 6.5 (GA) / 4.7 (NA) | (1349) |
| Merit selection | 7.6 | (228) |
| Legislative selection | 1.8 | (53) |
| Appointed by state supreme court | 1.9 | (58) |
|  | 100.0 | (2989) |

[a] P = in partisan election state; NP = in nonpartisan election state; GA = in gubernatorial appointment state; NA = in states utilizing a mixture of methods or in which there has been a recent change in method of selection.

various states. Table 6-2 presents these data in summary form. Our data reveal that the proportions of trial judges initially elected and appointed are almost equal (each slightly under 50 percent). Most of the appointed judges (perhaps three-fourths) were initially selected to fill vacancies. A relatively small percentage of judges have been chosen through merit selection, in part because this reform has not been diffused to many populous states. Nevertheless, the percentage will probably rise over time, as merit selection becomes a more frequent method of interim selection in the states. The number of judges selected by state legislatures is predictably small, as is the number appointed by state supreme courts to fill vacancies.

In sum, the states' various methods of selection result in a trial judiciary formally recruited in quite diverse ways. But what about the informal recruitment process, the occupational and political ranks from which trial judges are drawn?

## INFORMAL RECRUITMENT

How do men and women become trial judges in this country? What occupational experiences are most likely to bring them to the attention of selectors (governors, voters, etc.)? What political characteristics and experiences do judges bring with them? Is the office of trial judge a starting point for a political career, a springboard to higher judicial posts, or a capstone to a long legal career? These are the questions upon which we will focus in this section.

### Prior Occupation

The prior occupation(s) of a judge is (are) likely to be particularly important not only in the eyes of selectors but in his own eyes in framing his perceptions of the job. It is the point of departure from which the individual will

TABLE 6-3. Trial Judges' Immediate Prior Occupation

|  | PERCENT | NUMBER |
|---|---|---|
| Private legal practice | 53.8 | (1616) |
| Lower court judge | 24.0 | (720) |
| District attorney's office | 10.1 | (303) |
| Federal or local government lawyer | 2.5 | (76) |
| Other public official | 8.9 | (268) |
| Other | .7 | (22) |
|  | 100.0 | (3005) |

make a transition to judging. Table 6-3 reports the immediate prior occupation of trial judges.

The majority of trial judges come directly from private legal practice. Of this large group, about 60 percent report a general practice (without specialization) and most of the remainder specialized in civil matters. Only a total of fifty-three judges (3 percent) in our survey come from a private practice in which they specialized in criminal law. A substantial percentage of judges—about one in four—rose from a lower court judgeship (e.g., municipal, juvenile or probate court). A smaller group of judges come from the district attorney's office, either having been the elected district attorney from a smaller county or an appointed assistant in a larger community. Finally, some judges come directly from other public positions, including the state legislature, city council, state or local administrative agencies, and the public defender's office. In a few instances, some of these public officials (or even lower court judges) also maintained a part-time legal practice, where law or local custom permitted.

There are no straightforward regional patterns that delineate occupational roads to the trial bench. It is possible, however, to group states according to the predominant and secondary paths by which lawyers in those states achieve a trial judgeship. Accordingly, we find three groups: (1) states in which judges are drawn predominantly from the ranks of private practice (two-thirds or more); (2) states in which judges are drawn substantially from private practice (between 50 percent and 65 percent) but also significantly (20 percent or more) from the lower courts; and (3) states in which judges are drawn about equally from private practice and the lower courts. These three groups, which account for three-fourths of the states, are listed in Table 6-4. The table reveals a tendency among smaller states to recruit private practitioners and for larger states to draw significantly or substantially upon the lower courts (in New York and Connecticut, *most* judges rose from the lower courts). There are, however, some clear exceptions. In populous Pennsylvania, for example, most judges come from private practice, because the lower court traditionally has been staffed by nonlawyer judges.

TABLE 6-4. Occupational Paths to the Trial Bench by State

| Private Practice Dominant | | Private Practice Substantial and Lower Courts Significant | Private Practice and Lower Courts (balanced) |
|---|---|---|---|
| Alaska | Montana | Colorado | California |
| Arizona | New Hampshire | Idaho | Florida |
| Arkansas | North Carolina | Kansas | Hawaii |
| Delaware | Pennsylvania | Maryland | Illinois |
| Indiana | Tennessee | Massachusetts | Michigan |
| Iowa | Utah | Nebraska | Minnesota |
| Louisiana | Vermont | Oregon | Ohio |
| Maine | Virginia | Texas | Oklahoma |
| Mississippi | Washington | | South Dakota |
| Missouri | Wisconsin | | |
| (n = 20) | | (n = 8) | (n = 9) |

States not listed in the table have an atypically high percentage of judges—about 20 percent or more—drawn from the ranks of either district attorneys (Alabama, Georgia, Kentucky, Nevada, New Mexico, North Dakota, West Virginia), public officials (Rhode Island, South Carolina, Wyoming), or government lawyers (District of Columbia). The recruitment of district attorneys is relatively high in Southern and border states, where law enforcement (including sheriff) has been a key part of the local folk culture. Former politicians are heavily represented in two states with atypical selection systems, Rhode Island (where the governor appoints judges for life tenure), and South Carolina (where the legislature selects). These states, which depart from the mainstream of judicial recruitment, particularly well highlight the intersection of professional and political experiences that typically occurs in most states.

## Political Characteristics

The partisan political affiliation of the nation's trial judges reflects the dominance of the Democratic party at state and local levels for the last fifty years. Fifty-five percent of trial judges identify themselves as Democrats, 36 percent as Republicans, and 9 percent reported no affiliation. A regional perspective provides a fuller picture, however. In the South, most judges (82 percent) are Democrats, whereas in the other regions there is a highly competitive balance between Democratic and Republican judges. In general, state-by-state variations (often quite sharp within regions) reflect recent gubernatorial or electoral dominance by one party or the other.

We do not have any measure of the degree to which judges were politically *active* in their party prior to seeking a judgeship. This is an important question to consider but an area for which it is, in practice, difficult to collect meaningful data. Studies of federal judges, sitting as long ago as the early nineteenth century or as recently as the 1970s, suggest that perhaps half or more were "politically active" prior to their appointment.[6] Whatever the actual figure might be for federal judges, it is likely that the extent of partisan political involvement is higher among state trial judges, where the methods of formal selection are more varied and often more explicitly political.

AGE AT SELECTION

The age at which a judge is initially selected to the bench is probably the best indicator of the "career meaning" of judgeships in a state or community. Where trial judges are, for example, fifty years of age or older when first selected, it is reasonable to assume that they intend to conclude their professional career on the bench, possibly in an appellate seat some day, but probably on the trial bench where they began. Of course, some of these judges were once political officeholders. On the other hand, where judges are routinely selected at age forty or younger, the available career opportunities should prove much greater. For many of these individuals, the trial bench can be a stepping stone to a higher judicial post or other political office. A number of former trial court judges, for example, moved *directly* from their judgeship to the U.S. Congress. Examples include Senator Abraham Ribicoff of Connecticut (municipal court to the U.S. House of Representatives), Senator John Stennis of Mississippi (circuit judge to the U.S. Senate), former Senator Sam Ervin of North Carolina (superior court to the U.S. House), and former Representative Wilbur Mills of Arkansas (county court to the U.S. House). Mobility from a trial judgeship to state offices, including attorney general and even governor, also occurs. Governor Brendan Byrne of New Jersey was elected from his base as assignment judge for the state's superior court.

Trial judges in our survey were initially selected, on the average, at the age of forty-six. Twenty-nine percent were over fifty when selected, and almost as many (27 percent) were under forty when first selected. The variation in selection age and, therefore, career opportunity is quite substantial. Some states, for example, tend to attract judges at a younger age: In Alabama and Alaska, trial judges were typically forty or younger when selected whereas judges in Maine, Connecticut, and New York were typically fifty or older when selected.

Surprisingly, differences in political and occupational experience are *not* associated with the age at which individuals arrive at the bench. Different selection systems, for example, do not recruit judges at different career stages. This contradicts some conventional thinking that partisan systems "award" judgeships only, or mostly, to "old warriors."[7] In fact, partisan systems attract judges of the same age range as other selection methods. Likewise, judges coming to the bench from political or public office are generally not older than their counterparts from other occupations.[8]

We are missing too many key pieces of data to be able to speak conclusively about the career patterns of the nation's trial judges. We know their occupations immediately prior to their current judgeship, but not the positions previous to that. We know of their political party affiliations, but not of their partisan activity and involvement. We know the formal methods by which they were initially selected, but not why. Nevertheless, our primary purpose here has been to establish a descriptive picture of formal and informal recruitment processes. We now turn to a discussion of the consequences of recruitment.

## THE CONSEQUENCES OF RECRUITMENT: SOCIAL CHARACTERISTICS

We collected data on several variables which help to profile the American trial judge: age, race, gender, and legal heritage or ancestry. Though these variables are by no means exhaustive, they do provide a glimpse into key aspects of the sociopolitical representativeness of the judiciary. In particular, data on race and gender speak to the debates over the application of affirmative action principles to judicial selection.[9]

### RACE AND GENDER

Overwhelmingly, America's trial judges are white and male. The variation in race and gender is very small. Fully 96 percent of state trial judges are white; most of the remainder are black (n = 80), though a few are Oriental (n = 12) or Indian (n = 12). Similarly, 98 percent of trial judges are male. The number of women judges in our survey is only seventy-three.[10]

The distribution of "minority" (nonwhite or women) judges is by no means evenly spread across the country. Black judges are heavily concentrated in a few metropolitan courts outside the South. Though blacks in the South have been able to secure some political offices, the trial bench does not seem to be one of them.[11] Likewise, women judges are disproportionately found in metropolitan courts, particularly in the Northeast and West. These variations in minority accessibility to the trial bench appear to reflect different cultural perspectives as to the proper role of blacks and women in society.[12]

### AGE

The average age of judges sitting at the time of our survey (in 1977) is 53.4 years. The total range runs from a youthful twenty-nine to an elderly eighty. Figure 6-1 displays the distribution across groupings of age, based upon five-year intervals. The figure reveals a "normal" distribution of judges across age groups. Most typically, a trial judge is likely to be in his fifties, though one judge in four will be in his forties or sixties. Only a very small percentage of judges are under forty (7.3 percent) or seventy or older (2.6 percent).

From these data, we suggest that images of judges hanging onto the bench years after society's usual retirement age of sixty-five have been exaggerated. Though state and federal appellate judges, particularly U.S. Supreme Court justices, often stay well beyond age seventy, this appears rarely to be the case for state trial judges. Some states have mandated a retirement age for their trial

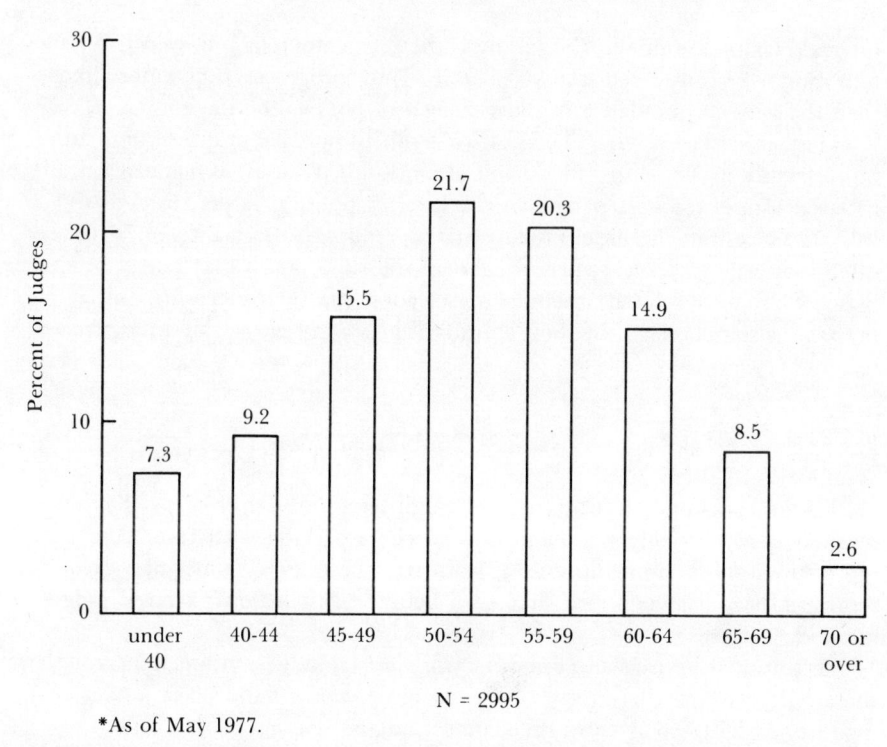

## The Recruitment and Socialization of Trial Judges

[Bar chart showing percent of judges by age group:
- under 40: 7.3
- 40-44: 9.2
- 45-49: 15.5
- 50-54: 21.7
- 55-59: 20.3
- 60-64: 14.9
- 65-69: 8.5
- 70 or over: 2.6

N = 2995]

*As of May 1977.

**FIGURE 6-1. Distribution of the Current Age of Trial Judges**

judges, and others have used a declining pension formula to encourage retirement.[13]

There is much variation in the average age of trial judges from state to state, reflecting, in part, the different career uses to which judgeships are put. Contrast the youngest benches, Alaska ($\bar{x}$ = 45.8), Vermont ($\bar{x}$ = 46.0), and Alabama ($\bar{x}$ = 46.9), with the oldest benches, Maine ($\bar{x}$ = 61.5), New York ($\bar{x}$ = 58.3), and Connecticut ($\bar{x}$ = 58.2). As the individual state data suggest, there is some regional variation: Judges sitting in the Northeast are about three years older, on the average, than elsewhere in the country.

### Legal Heritage

Individuals are not born to be judges, but some start with a decided advantage by virtue of the visibility of their family names in social, legal, or political circles.[14] More than once, we came across judges in our field observations whose fathers had been judges before them. Still more had come from families of lawyers. Our survey data corroborate the significant frequency (beyond chance levels) with which sitting judges come from legal or political families. One in ten judges reports a grandparent who was a lawyer, judge, or elected public official. One judge in five reports that a parent served in one of these careers. Having a judge in the family is the least common, but even this pattern cannot be considered statistically rare. Thus, judges are much more likely than the general population to have a legal or political heritage.

The "inheritance" of judicial office is much more common in rural communities and in the South. In North Carolina and Arkansas, as many as half of the trial judges report a parent with a legal or political career. In Alabama, fully 10 percent of the judges report that a grandparent was a judge. The frequent appearance of this phenomenon in the rural South may partly be explained by the dominant method of selection (partisan election), but it is probably also related to the local cultural values and practices of an ascriptive society.[15]

## RECRUITMENT, SOCIAL CHARACTERISTICS, AND WORK PATTERNS

The processes of recruiting trial judges, different though they may be, have resulted in a relatively homogeneous bench, especially with respect to the representation of nonwhites and women. There is a somewhat greater representation of generations, but even here the vast majority of trial judges are middle-aged.

Recruitment impacts also upon the work of trial judges, indirectly, through the effects of social characteristics. For example, women and black judges appear to be highly involved in their job of judging. Aging, too, has its impact on judicial work by restricting and redefining what judges choose to do and what their court system asks them to do. It is to these two themes—the impacts of minority status and aging—that we now turn.

### MINORITY JUDGES AND JOB INVOLVEMENT

Women and black judges comprise only a very small group, but one characterized by a high commitment, in time, to the work of trial judging. Women judges, for example, report working 9.7 hours, on average, on their most common day, compared with 9.2 hours for their male counterparts. This difference persists across less common work days. Similarly, black judges report working about one-half hour longer on their first three most common days. These differences remain *after* controls for size of court. Thus, women and black judges work longer hours not because they are predominantly located in large courts but for other reasons.

Interest in, and commitment to, the ancillary work of trial judging is also evident among black and women judges. This is particularly true for community relations work. Almost one-third of black judges, but only 13 percent of white judges, spend as much as one full day per month in community relations activities.[16] The figures are roughly parallel for female and male judges. Interestingly, these differences cannot be attributed either to the effects of court size[17] or to differences in assignment. Black and women judges, for example, are *not* more likely to be assigned to the juvenile division of a court (the division where judges spend much more time in community relations work). Furthermore, black and women judges report slightly *more* time spent in bar association activities, belying any notions that the local bar has effectively eliminated minority participation.[18]

Why are women and black judges as a group so highly involved, in terms of time commitment, in their job? We could speculate that they are more likely to feel "on display," easily identifiable to outsiders or even courtroom regulars, and therefore feel the need to exhibit or report a tendency to hard work. Actually, though, black judges are not likely to serve in isolation from one another. A number of black judges—as many as seven or eight or more—serve together in a few large metropolitan courts and therefore probably provide one another mutual support and security. As for women judges, Beverly Cook argues that they are highly committed to their work because they must "survive the barriers of the traditionally male-oriented profession."[19] In both situations, more politically based explanations may be equally relevant. For example, the relatively few minority judges may find themselves in great demand for public relations and committee work by courts seeking to invoke symbols of representativeness. Alternatively, women and black judges may develop, cultivate, or maintain community contacts as a buffer against the uncertainties of selection/retention/re-election politics.

AGING AND ITS IMPACT ON WORK PATTERNS

The age of a sitting judge plays a surprisingly large role in defining the amount and nature of the work he will do. It is evident from our survey data that older judges (over sixty-five) do not always "choose" to work differently. Rather, court systems often adapt to the perceived or real needs of older judges. In the analyses to follow, we compare the work of youthful judges (under forty), early middle-age (forty to forty-nine), later middle-age (fifty to sixty-four), and older judges (sixty-five or over).

One manifestation of a court's sensitivity to the aging process can be found in the types of assignment given to older and younger judges. As judges grow older, they are increasingly likely to be in some kind of civil, rather than criminal, assignment. This relationship is a modest one across all courts but quite sharp in large courts, as Table 6-5 indicates.

A smaller percentage (22 percent) of older judges sit in criminal assignment, compared with their younger colleagues (32-35 percent). The effects of court adaptation are best seen, however, in large courts which have the operating discretion—through divisionalization and administrative unification—to assign judges. In courts with forty or more judges, for example, the percentage shifts from 71 percent (of the youngest judges) in criminal assignment to only 46 percent (of the oldest judges) in criminal assignment. In courts with twenty-six to thirty-nine judges, a parallel drop occurs in the percentage of judges in criminal assignment (from 63 percent of those under forty to 29 percent of those sixty-five or older). Though there are only a small number of cases in a few cells, the pattern is unmistakable.

**TABLE 6-5.** The Impact of Age upon Judicial Assignments

PERCENTAGE OF JUDGES IN CRIMINAL ASSIGNMENT[a]

| Age | All Courts | | 40+ Judge Courts | | 26-39 Judge Courts | |
|---|---|---|---|---|---|---|
| Under 40 | 34.9 | (85) | 71.4 | (7) | 62.5 | (8) |
| 40–49 | 35.1 | (354) | 56.4 | (62) | 50.0 | (36) |
| 50–64 | 32.3 | (864) | 51.7 | (141) | 35.6 | (90) |
| 65 or over | 21.7 | (202) | 45.9 | (37) | 28.6 | (14) |

[a] Excludes judges in general or juvenile assignment; thus, 100 percent – cell figure represents the percentage of judges in a civil assignment.

Why do courts assign older judges more often to civil assignments? One part of the answer has to do with individual preference. Judges generally seem to prefer civil assignments because they are more varied, more challenging, and draw more directly upon their prior training and experiences. Older judges are likely also to be relatively senior judges, and therefore in a position to be rewarded. Yet assignments are made on bases other than individual preference, as we discussed in Chapter 3. Notably, case disposition rate is an important factor. If older judges are perceived to be slower in disposing of cases, court systems will feel more comfortable in assigning them to the civil division, where there are fewer pressures to move the docket.

Courts also provide older judges with more resources to do their work, especially law clerk assistance. Among judges over the age of sixty-five, one in four has the services of a full-time law clerk. This proportion compares quite favorably to middle-age judges (one in six) and to youthful judges (one in nine). Interestingly, these differences are not at all a function of seniority on the bench or other potentially confounding variables such as region. Older judges also evaluate the effectiveness of their courtroom personnel more favorably than does any younger age group.

Differences in the ways in which courts utilize judges presage variations in work patterns. Indeed, the work patterns of younger and older judges are strikingly different, sometimes because of differences of assignment or resources, but usually in spite of them. In some instances, differences are related to the aging process itself rather than adaptation to it by the court.[20] We turn to a discussion of these first.

As judges grow older, they report engaging much less often in tasks having a significant *interpersonal* component—socializing, case-related discussions with attorneys, and waiting time. Table 6-6 presents these data. For all three interpersonal tasks, the proportion of judges reporting the activity declines with each increment of age grouping. The differences are particularly large for socializing: 60 percent of the youngest judges report some time on their most common day for socializing, but that figure drops to a mere 27 percent for judges who are sixty-five or older. The frequency of case-related discussions with attorneys also declines, though not quite so sharply, with increasing age.

TABLE 6-6. The Impact of Age upon Trial Judges' Interpersonal Tasks

| | % JUDGES REPORTING (MC) | | | |
|---|---|---|---|---|
| Age | Socializing | Case-Related Discussions with Attorneys | Waiting Time | Number |
| under 40 | 59.6 | 58.5 | 50.0 | (188) |
| 40–49 | 42.9 | 53.0 | 45.1 | (632) |
| 50–64 | 36.3 | 45.2 | 40.8 | (1416) |
| 65 or over | 27.3 | 38.4 | 40.0 | (245) |

The differences in waiting time are the smallest and the most likely to be attributable to assignment differences. By contrast, the declines in socializing and discussing cases with attorneys are present among judges in civil and criminal assignment.

We interpret these data in light of the comparative ages of judges and attorneys. When judges are young (under forty), they are nearly the generational peers of the attorneys who practice before them, especially criminal attorneys (prosecutors and public defenders). It should not be surprising, therefore, that the young judges and young attorneys find common ground on which to socialize—children, sports, etc. As judges grow older, however, they become increasingly removed from the generational experiences of the attorneys typically before them. By the time judges reach the age of sixty-five, they are often old enough to be not the parents but the *grandparents* of most of the attorneys in court. This increasing age differential—which is especially likely to be the case in criminal courts in the larger cities—renders informal interpersonal contact much less likely and much less egalitarian where it does take place.[21]

A second arena in which older judges probably choose to do less is legal research. Specifically, older judges are less likely to report "preparing and writing decisions, judgments, or orders" on their first three most common work days, than their younger counterparts. Though the differences initially seem small (54 percent versus 62 percent), they assume added significance when the predominant assignment (civil) and available resources (additional full-time law clerks) of older judges are also considered. Despite the fact that judges in civil assignment and, especially, those with a full-time law clerk tend to do more preparing and writing of decisions (see Table 5-2), older judges do less. In sum, the marginal benefit of a full-time law clerk *diminishes* as the age of the judge increases. By age sixty-five, those judges with a full-time law clerk report no more decision-writing activity than those without assistance.

By contrast, other differences in the work of older and younger judges are attributable to the adaptations of courts. For example, consider the area of calendar work: motions, short hearings, etc. Judges over sixty-five are less likely (43 percent) to report this kind of work than younger judges (57 percent among judges under fifty), and where reported are likely to spend less time doing it. As one metropolitan criminal division judge noted to our observer, "judges like myself—the younger ones—get an essentially administrative calendar" (lots of routine criminal cases which need to be pushed toward final disposition). By contrast, he characterized the calendars of older judges as less harried but consisting of more complex cases that occasionally require lengthy motion hearings.

Older and younger judges also differ in the ratio of jury to nonjury work. The differences primarily occur in civil assignment, where judges under forty are three times more likely to report nonjury than jury trial work on their most common day, whereas judges sixty-five or older are more likely to report jury trial work. Again, the pattern is linear: At each older age group, judges are increasingly likely to hear jury work and less likely to hear nonjury work. Though difficult to document, nonjury trial work on the civil side is probably perceived by courts to be more taxing, both physically and intellectually, on the individual judge. In nonjury cases, the judge must be fact-finder as well as law-applier. In addition, the nature of nonjury cases on the civil side—especially equity matters—can be highly adversarial and politically controversial, yet requiring speedy resolution. Just as older judges may be kept away from the "heat" of criminal courts, they may also be protected from the more contentious civil matters.

Our interpretation of differences in judicial work in the areas of calendar, nonjury, and jury trial activity implicitly suggests a benevolent (if invisible) hand guiding the distribution of work with flexibility. But how could this be so in individual calendar systems, which typically distribute cases by some kind of "blind-draw" principle? The answer is quite simple: These differences in the work of older and younger judges are almost entirely the product of master calendar systems. The proportion of judges reporting calendar work declines only slightly with increased age in courts utilizing an individual case assignment system (58 percent to 51 percent), but sharply in master systems (51 percent to 33 percent). The contextual importance of the master calendar is even greater in determining the balance of nonjury and jury trial work. Overall, an older judge (sixty-five or older) is about equally likely to hear jury and nonjury trial work in individual calendar systems but *three times* more likely to hear jury cases in master calendar courts.

Field observations strongly support our primary point—that courts, especially those operating under a master calendar, do adapt to the presence of older judges. One judge (about age seventy) whom we observed was working on an atypical criminal jury case which involved preliminary motions, substantial psychiatric testimony, and media attention. When there were lulls in the action (as frequently occurred), neither the judge not the master calendar coordinator sought one another; there was a tacit understanding that this judge would not be overworked. Another judge (in his early seventies) whom we observed was assigned to the criminal calendar, though in a less-harried suburban setting. This judge very clearly perceived his assignment to be based upon his age and (presumed dwindling) intellectual faculties. In fact, however, this senior and sometimes eccentric judge displayed a glittering command of contemporary constitutional law in his hearing of a lengthy motion to suppress evidence in a drug case.

In sum, older judges choose to do, and are asked to do, different amounts and kinds of work from their younger colleagues. In courts that have the resources, size, and flexibility, older judges can be assigned to divisions and cases where speed of resolution is less important. Our data, both quantitative and qualitative, suggest that courts that adapt themselves to the perceived needs of their judges are usually realistic in their appraisal of the strengths, weaknesses, and general capacities of aging judges.[22] Inevitably, though, there are individual exceptions: some judges who probably should no longer be on the bench as well as other judges whose strength of intellect and physical presence remain entirely undiminished by the flood of years.

## Socialization

Once individuals have been recruited to the bench with whatever experiences, backgrounds, and interests, on-the-job socialization begins. First, new judges must make the transition from lawyer to judge and the concomitant role changes that are implied. Formal instruction and informal learning may be part of this transition, depending upon the available resources and sophistication of local and state court systems. As judges stay on the bench for a number of years, they slowly confront the tensions from conformity but also the opportunities for growth and advancement on their own court. We will discuss several "stages" of organizational socialization and career development in light of the nature of judicial education programs, available research on the socialization of judges, and our own survey data.

### THE TRANSITION FROM LAWYER TO JUDGE

The most traumatic and bewildering time in a judge's career is almost certainly the first few weeks and months, the period that constitutes his transition typically from a role of advocacy to one of impartiality. In addition to a change in roles, new judges, especially ones serving in criminal assignment, are confronted with demands of substantive law and procedure for which they typically have never been trained. In his Connecticut study, Heumann's interviews with new judges reflect their concerns about the need to develop patience, listen, process paperwork, and relate to a wide variety of courtroom actors having different goals.[23] In addition to these needs, new judges also expressed frustration with their lack of concrete knowledge about the operation of criminal courts. Little wonder, then, that an initial sense of bewilderment set in.

In Connecticut, new judges receive some formal, structured orientation, amounting in early 1974 to a total of four days for a group of new judges appointed to the trial bench.[24] This particular orientation took the form of lectures, question-and-answer periods, and one simulated jail lockup.[25] Thirteen other states, mostly larger industrial states, also have structured orientation programs consisting of lectures, small group discussions, panels, workshops, films, and on-site visits to courts and other criminal justice agencies. Most of these, too, are short in duration, with the exception of California, where programs may run several weeks. A few states have "clinical" programs, consisting of on-the-bench training under the supervision of "adviser judges" or simply one-on-one discussions with experienced judges. Finally, three states have "self-learning" orientation programs, comprising reference manuals or audio/video cassette tapes. In all, a total of sixteen states have one or more types of orientation for new judges, focusing on substantive law and/or administrative procedures. In the remaining thirty-odd states, no formal orientation is provided to new trial judges.[26]

Judges learn how to be judgelike, of course, whether there is a formal program or not. They learn from interacting with more experienced judges, in casual conversations at lunch, at judges' meetings, and so forth. They learn from experienced courtroom personnel who can aid them in coping with paperwork and in establishing courtroom procedures and decorum. They learn from the attorneys who are before them, especially prosecutors assigned to their courtroom. Heumann found more than one prosecutor who attempted to "clarify [with the judge] the ways things are done."[27]

Not all judges necessarily require the same amount of teaching and learning. Though law school training is rarely perceived to be of much specific value, a judge's prior occupation may be. For example, in their research on the problems facing new federal trial judges, Robert Carp and Russell Wheeler found that prior state court judges fared better in coping with the administrative and psychological burdens of their new judgeship.[28] Our survey data, too, suggest that prior lower court judges, in particular, more easily adapt to certain aspects of their environment, notably in the area of negotiation.

Nowhere is the tension between lawyering and judging more obvious than in negotiations. A lawyer's role is well defined in negotiations: He must firmly advocate his client's interests. A judge's role (as we shall explore more fully in Chapter 8) is more ambiguous: Should he be a neutral arbiter or should he try to push the parties toward a disposition or settlement? Should he even be present at such discussions, where evidence inadmissible at trial might be discussed?

Our data suggest that the background of the judge—specifically, the nature of his immediate prior occupation—makes a significant difference in the likelihood that he will experience criminal and civil negotiation work. Table 6-7 presents these data. Two major findings emerge. First, trial judges who have come from a lower court are more likely to report time spent in

TABLE 6-7. The Impact of Immediate Prior Occupation upon Trial Judges' Frequency of Criminal and Civil Negotiation

| Immediate Prior Occupation | % Judges Reporting (MC) Criminal Negotiations[a] | Civil Negotiations[b] | Number |
|---|---|---|---|
| Lower court judge | 32.4 | 45.1 | 407/468 |
| District attorney's office | 29.4 | 29.0 | 187/200 |
| Public official | 23.2 | 47.2 | 138/176 |
| Private legal practice | 18.7 | 32.8 | 974/1178 |
|   Criminal specialization | (28.0) | (26.7) | |
|   Civil specialization | (17.6) | (38.4) | |
|   General practice | (19.0) | (28.6) | |

[a] Excludes judges in civil assignments.
[b] Excludes judges in criminal or juvenile assignments.

criminal and civil negotiations than former private practitioners. Second, former practitioners of criminal law (in the public or private sector) are more likely to report time in criminal negotiations than those who worked in civil law. Conversely, former practitioners of civil law (and former public officials) are more likely to report time in civil negotiations than those who worked in criminal law.

Thus, we might conclude that judges like to get involved in work in which they feel comfortable, for which they have been trained by prior professional experience. Equally, however, these data suggest the possible difficulties in role transition for private practitioners generally. An active resolution of differences by the judge may strike some former private practitioners as inappropriate. In their efforts to move completely away from an advocacy role, these former practitioners avoid or disengage from negotiations that seem to require an active judicial role. Interestingly, the passage of time appears *not* to alter this perspective. Private practitioners on the bench for many years are not more likely to report criminal or civil negotiations than those with less service. In some areas, then, judges may not adapt their behavior over time; the influence of prior experience and roles may be too great. It is to the full sweep of the judicial career that we now turn.

## LATER YEARS ON THE BENCH

Alpert, Atkins, and Ziller interviewed trial judges of varying tenures in order to develop a broader framework of judicial socialization.[29] They identify three stages in the process of "adjusting to life on the bench." Their first stage is "initiation/resolution," accounting for the first five years on the bench, and characterized by the process of learning about the job and finding ways to resolve problems of initial adjustment. Their second stage is "establishment," accounting for roughly the next ten years, and characterized in part by the necessity to make a career decision (stay or leave) at some point. Their third and final stage is "commitment," a period characterized by an increased sense of certainty, loyalty, and fraternity in the job. Of course, these are broad-brush stages at best. For some judges reaching the bench late in life, the three stages may run together. For other judges who enter a judicial career early, some will leave before the period of commitment—a few involuntarily, but most probably by choice.

We draw upon Alpert and her colleagues in arriving at a framework within which to analyze our data on the impact of years on the bench. We compare the work patterns of judges who have been on the bench (in a court of general jurisdiction) less than one year, one to five years, six to fifteen years, and sixteen years or longer. It will be possible, therefore, to view the "newcomer" judge (to use Heumann's phrase) as well as judges in Alpert's three stages of the judicial career.[30]

How long have judges been serving on a general trial bench? The average is slightly under eight years, a figure that does not vary significantly by size of court or other structural variables. Table 6-8 indicates the proportion of judges in each category of service, as well as their average age. Approximately one judge in nine was a newcomer to the bench at the time of our survey, having served less than one year. One-third of the judges had served between one and five years, and a somewhat higher percentage between six and fifteen years. Only one judge in eight had served sixteen years or more. As we would expect, the average age of judges rises sharply from one category of service to the next. Whereas newcomers are typically about forty-six years of age, veterans of sixteen or more years on the bench average sixty-one years of age. Thus, to use the variable "years on bench" as it is constituted in Table 6-8 would only serve to reintroduce the effects of age, which are quite substantial in some areas of work as we have already seen. Rather, we control for the effects of age by restricting the following analyses to judges between the ages of fifty and fifty-nine who have been on the bench anywhere from less than one to more than sixteen years.[31] In this way, we can gauge more accurately the effects of different lengths of service on judicial work.

We arrive at competing hypotheses about veteran judges and their commitment to their work. One strong impression we received from our observations

**TABLE 6-8. Trial Judges' Length of Service on the Bench**

| YEARS ON GENERAL TRIAL BENCH | PERCENT | ($\bar{X}$) AGE (YEARS) | NUMBER |
|---|---|---|---|
| Less than 1 | 11.0 | 46.6 | (328) |
| 1–5 | 32.7 | 49.9 | (973) |
| 6–15 | 43.5 | 55.5 | (1292) |
| 16 or more | 12.8 | 61.4 | (380) |
|  | 100.0 |  | (2973) |

was that judges on the bench for fifteen or twenty years had lost some of their zeal for the job. This mainfested itself in shorter hours worked[32] and in conversations with the observer about judges' disengagement from community, bar, and committee activities. By contrast, Alpert and her colleagues see these later years in terms of commitment to the job, years which hold real promise of intangible psychic rewards for those who stay on the bench.[33] The veteran judges whom they interviewed spoke of an increased sense of comradeship and community service. Which of these perspectives about veteran judges, then, receives support from our national survey data? In fact, neither hypothesis receives any support. Veteran judges (on the bench sixteen years or more) report working approximately the same hours on their work days as judges with fewer years of service. Similarly, veteran judges report the same amount of time in community relations and bar association activities as their counterparts with fewer years of service.

Our field observations suggested few clear-cut relationships between length of service on the bench and the mix of judicial work. One would intuitively expect, of course, that more experienced judges would somehow be "better organized" in the work they do, and that this would be reflected in their task emphasis. No support, however, surfaces for this proposition either. Veteran judges perform the same kinds and amounts of activities in their work as do judges with less experience, including newcomer judges. It is significant, for example, to note that veteran judges are no less likely to report waiting time than less experienced judges, nor do they report less time spent waiting on a given work day.

The lack of impact attributable to years on the bench reinforces what has been implicit from earlier chapters. Judges work in response to the demands of their work environment. They work within the confines of their court structure, the attorneys and courtroom personnel who surround them (and their perceptions of them), and the limitations of their own age (or, perhaps, how the court responds to their age). A socialization or "learning" model does not appear to be appropriate or accurate for describing how trial judges manage their time and tasks. To be certain, judges may learn, as their experience increases, that their time could be used more effectively, but the work environment severely constrains any efforts to utilize such learning.

## CONFORMITY, GROWTH, AND ADVANCEMENT ON THE BENCH

The themes of conformity, growth, and advancement are intertwined. Judges learn how to adapt their behavior in some ways, most notably to conform to the demands of their work environment. Heumann describes adaptation by newcomer judges in criminal courts as a process of conforming to the norms about plea bargaining.[34] This includes accepting the reality that most defendants are factually guilty and recognizing the benefits of guilty pleas (moving one's docket, avoiding appellate reversal, etc.). Mary Lee Luskin, also studying newcomer judges (in the Detroit criminal courts), demonstrates that these judges quickly learned to conform to the court's philosophy about the role of the preliminary hearing.[35] New judges who bound over either too high or too low a percentage of defendants altered their behavior—toward the courtwide average—within one year. Though limited to the criminal courts, both of these studies suggest that a socialization or adaptation model is appropriate in analyzing substantive judicial decision-making.

If judging is characterized by an inability to utilize learning about the organization of work and by pressures to learn how to conform in other areas, to what (if any) positive benefits can judges look forward? Courts clearly frustrate, at times, the interests and skills of their judges, but how do they accommodate them?[36] We would suggest two ways: career opportunity within the local court, and professional teaching opportunities outside the court.

In larger, multijudge courts, judges have the opportunity for limited advancement in assignments. Such advancements entail an increase in administrative responsibility, in informal political power, and in status, though not usually in salary. Some judges may look forward to becoming chief judge of their court, or the supervising judge of a division. This is quite analogous to the lures that other public bodies (e.g., legislatures) use to keep their "workers" interested and involved in a job with potentially long tenure and little upward mobility. Internal leadership posts, then, are one arena where the ambition of trial judges can be satiated.

In practice, only a few judges in large courts can hope to achieve positions of leadership. Furthermore, many will have no interest in these positions because they do not clearly draw upon the intellectual or substantive skills rooted in the job of judging. For these judges, the attraction of "outside" work—most notably, teaching—will be much greater.[37] On the basis of field observations and an openended question in the pretest to our mail survey, we identified three settings in which trial judges often participate in teaching: law school, judicial education programs for new or continuing judges, and police officer training programs. Teaching in judicial education programs is most common (34 percent), followed by police training programs (29 percent), and law school courses (15 percent). Law school teaching is by far the most time-consuming, typically a semester of evenings, as compared with the one- or two-day formats of programs of judicial education or police training. Hence its comparative infrequency.

Community size influences the opportunity that a judge will have to become involved in these settings,[38] but years on the bench has a much more decisive effect. In each of these settings, judges who have been on the bench for a longer period of time are more likely to have participated. The relationship is marked for teaching other judges (from 9 percent of newcomers to 59 percent of veterans) and for teaching police officers (from 9 percent to 43 percent), but smaller for teaching law students (from 5 percent to 21 percent). Though we cannot determine at what point of the judicial career these teaching experiences occur, we infer that it is mostly experienced judges who teach, especially in judicial education programs.

Judges who are, or have been, active in teaching are also the ones who report a relatively high level of commitment to their work. They report more hours worked on their most common and less common days, and more time devoted to community relations and bar association activities. Through these teaching experiences, and committee and community work, judges utilize one important opportunity for growth on the bench. The exchange of ideas in these settings almost certainly broadens the geographic and substantive provincialism so much a part of judging. Newcomer and junior judges do have something to look forward to in their later years on the bench: a positive role model of involvement which neutralizes, or at least makes less important, organizational pressures to conform, adapt, and finally to retire.

## Summary

The recruitment processes within which trial judges are selected are highly variable, particularly with respect to formal selection mechanisms and prior occupational experiences. Differences in political culture, often associated with identifiable geographic regions, have much to do with variations in recruitment. In the South, for example, most judges still make their way to the bench through partisan election. In states highly influenced by the Progressive era, usually in the Midwest or West, nonpartisan election, merit selection, and frequent use of interim appointment exist side by side. The career uses to which judgeships are put also vary across political cultures and regions. In the Northeast, where judges are generally older at the time of their selection, a trial judgeship is likely to be a reward for past political service or lower court apprenticeship, whereas in the South the office of trial judge has proven to be a potential stepping stone to higher political office. It is these variable political cultures, still viable in late-twentieth-century America, that render the idea of transforming judging into a lifetime occupation (as in civil law countries) fundamentally unworkable.

Despite diversity in the recruitment of judges, a homogeneous trial bench still exists. Very few women, black, or other minority group members sit in state trial courts of general jurisdiction. The eligible pool of lawyers from which minority candidates could be drawn has, until recent years, been quite small. Now, increasing numbers of women, in particular, are attending and graduating from law schools, giving rise to expectations that the trial bench will diversify significantly in the near future. In the meantime, courts struggle to sustain their legitimacy in the eyes of the citizenry.

The age of sitting judges is somewhat more variable, including a significant proportion of judges under forty-five (17 percent) as well as sixty-five or older

(11 percent). More interesting is the impact a judge's age has upon the work he will do. Though older judges (sixty-five and over) apparently choose to do less of certain tasks (especially interpersonal tasks), most differences in the work of older and younger judges are the result of court adaptations to the strengths and weaknesses of aging judges. Older judges are increasingly likely to be assigned to civil rather than criminal work and to be provided with additional resources. In addition, older judges are likely to be spared the potentially more harried nonjury trials and calendar work. Larger courts using a master calendar are the primary sources of these adaptations to older judges.

The socialization process involves a balance between court-initiated training of its trial judges, through judicial education programs, and on-the-job learning. The latter, which includes interacting with courtroom personnel, attorneys and especially fellow judges, is probably more important, even in the relatively few states that have sophisticated, intensive formal orientation and training. Though judges learn about various aspects of their work environment and are taught to conform to the norms of the courtroom workgroup, few differences appear in the organization and mix of work among veteran and less experienced judges. The most significant results of increasing service on the bench lie in the available opportunities to pursue professional teaching experiences outside the courtroom—in law schools or particularly police training programs and educational programs for new or continuing judges. It is through these kinds of experiences, and occasionally through advancement to a leadership post within the court, that judges come to draw upon their interests and experiences.

# Notes

1. See Lester G. Seligman, Michael R. King, Chong Lim Kim, and Roland E. Smith, *Patterns of Recruitment: A State Chooses Its Lawmakers* (Chicago: Rand McNally, 1974), for a discussion of approaches to studying the recruitment of political elites; for a limited empirical inquiry, see Mary Volcansek-Clark, "Why Lawyers Become Judges," *Judicature*, 62 (1978).
2. There is an extensive literature within political science focusing on the structuring and development of political beliefs and values in children and adolescents. For a discussion of the socialization process as a general phenomenon, see Dean Jaros, *Socialization to Politics* (New York: Praeger, 1973), and Richard E. Dawson and Kenneth Prewitt, *Political Socialization* (Boston: Little, Brown, 1969); for a more specific empirical discussion, see David Easton and Jack Dennis, *Children in the Political System* (New York: McGraw-Hill, 1969), and Robert D. Hess and Judith V. Torney, *The Development of Political Attitudes in Children* (Chicago: Aldine, 1967).
3. For a further discussion of recent trends in judicial selection systems, see James Alfini, "The Trend Toward Judicial Merit Selection," *Trial*, 13 (1977).
4. Observers have begun to note the frequency of interim appointments to state ap-

pellate and trial courts. See James Herndon, "Appointment as a Means of Initial Accession to Elective State Courts of Last Resort," *North Dakota Law Review*, 38 (1962), and Herbert Jacob, "The Effect of Institutional Differences in the Recruitment Process: The Case of State Judges," *Journal of Public Law*, 13 (1964).

5. For a fuller discussion of the disparity between initial and interim selection methods, see John Paul Ryan, Allan Ashman and Bruce D. Sales, "Judicial Selection and Its Impact on Trial Judges' Background, Perceptions, and Performance," paper presented at the Annual Meetings of the Western Political Science Association, Los Angeles, March 1978.

6. See Kermit L. Hall, "101 Men: The Social Composition and Recruitment of the Antebellum Lower Federal Judiciary, 1829–1861," *Rutgers-Camden Law Journal*, 7 (1975), and Sheldon Goldman, "A Profile of Carter's Judicial Nominees," *Judicature*, 62 (1978).

7. See Wesley G. Skogan, "The Politics of Judicial Reform: Cook County, Illinois" *Justice System Journal*, 1 (1975). Skogan (p. 20) asserts that "judgeships in Cook County are terminal positions to which warriors retire." This is something of an overstatement for Cook County, though there is some basis for his speculation. See Chapter 9 for a discussion of the backgrounds of Chicago judges.

8. The exception is in metropolitan areas, where judges coming to the bench from public office are several years older ($\bar{x} = 48.7$) than other judges ($\bar{x} = 46.5$).

9. See Robert J. Lipshutz and Douglas B. Huron, "Achieving a More Representative Federal Judiciary"; Katherine Randall, "The Success of Affirmative Action in the Sixth Circuit"; Sheldon Goldman, "Should There Be Affirmative Action for the Judiciary?"; and Peter C. Fish, "Evaluating the Black Judicial Applicant," all in *Judicature*, 62 (1979). These articles focus on affirmative action in the federal judiciary, where President Carter made it his policy to appoint significant percentages of black and women candidates, more than any of his predecessors.

10. We are reluctant to transfer these precise percentages to the national body of state trial judges of general jurisdiction because we do have nonrespondents to our survey and because a (very) small percentage of respondents did not answer the question on race (1.4 percent) or gender (.9 percent). However, the percentage of women judges in our survey (2.4 percent) conforms almost exactly to the percentage (2.5 percent) which Cook found in her 1977 study of women judges in state trial courts of general jurisdiction. See Beverly Blair Cook, "Women Judges: The End of Tokenism," in Winifred L. Hepperle and Laura Crites (eds.), *Women in the Courts* (Williamsburg, Va.: National Center for State Courts, 1978).

11. Only in two Southern states (other than the District of Columbia) do we have even one black respondent.

12. It is probably not coincidental that there are fewer women judges in those regions (especially the South) whose states have been slow to ratify the Equal Rights Amendment. Cook, "Women Judges," finds a positive relationship between indicators of a "feminist environment" and the number of women judges in a state.

13. Forty states currently have some form of a mandatory retirement system. The minimum age for mandatory retirement is sixty-five (in Mississippi, and then only if the retirement board does not authorize continued service for one-year periods until age seventy), while the maximum age set for mandatory retirement is seventy-five (Louisiana, Oregon, Texas, and Washington). Most states set a mandatory retire-

ment age at seventy. Four states, which ostensibly make retirement "voluntary," provide for forfeiture of all retirement benefits for judges serving beyond a certain age (Arkansas, Maine, North Dakota, and Wyoming). Additionally, four states (California, New Mexico, Tennessee, and Texas) use a declining retirement benefits formula to encourage retirement. In California, for example, both judges' and widows' benefits are reduced for retirement after age seventy. Challenges to the constitutionality of mandatory judicial retirement laws have been rejected in two cases. In *Trafelet* v. *Thompson,* No. 78 C 1036 (N.D. Ill. July 11, 1978), the district court held that an Illinois statute which mandated the retirement of state judges at age seventy did not violate the equal protection clause. Similarly, in *O'Neil* v. *Baine,* 568 S.W.2d 761 (Mo. 1978), the Missouri Supreme Court upheld that state's compulsory retirement law against equal protection and due process challenges. In both cases, the courts concluded that retirement of judges at age seventy was rationally related to legitimate state interests.

14. Hall, "101 Men," found that 17 percent of the judges serving in the federal district courts, for the years studied, had fathers who were judges; nearly half of all judges' fathers held "important legal positions."
15. See V. O. Key, *Southern Politics* (New York: Knopf, 1949) and Wilbur J. Cash, *The Mind of the South* (New York: Knopf, 1960).
16. One study of trial judges in a "large, northeastern urban center" (Philadelphia) also found black trial judges to have extensive community involvement, more than that of white judges. See Thomas M. Uhlman, *Racial Justice* (Lexington, Mass.: D. C. Heath, 1979), pp. 55–56.
17. There is no relationship between court size, or community size, and time spent in community relations activities.
18. In a number of large cities, however, there are alternative bar associations that seek to represent the interests of black and/or women judges. It may be to these minority associations, rather than the established bar, that some of these judges belong.
19. Cook, "Women Judges." In this regard, it is interesting to note that women and black judges are more likely to come from the public sector (especially, lower court judgeships and positions as government lawyers) than from private practice. These differences are not entirely a function of the states from which minority judges are disproportionately drawn (populous industrial states). When we compare the occupational backgrounds from which minority and white male judges come—in the nine states where private practice and the lower courts play a balanced role in recruitment—these differences generally persist.
20. For a discussion of aging as a political research question generally, see Neal E. Cutler, "Demographic, Social-Psychological, and Political Factors in the Politics of Aging: A Foundation for Research in 'Political Gerontology,'" *American Political Science Review,* 71 (1977); for a discussion specific to appellate judges, see John Schmidhauser, "Age and Judicial Behavior: American Higher Appellate Judges," in Wilma T. Donahue and Clark Tibbits (eds.), *The Politics of Age* (Ann Arbor: Department of Gerontology, University of Michigan, 1962).
21. In one criminal courtroom in a suburban court where we observed, an older judge (beyond seventy) did socialize extensively with the young criminal attorneys. Nevertheless, the contact assumed a socialization or teaching aspect in which the grand-

fatherly judge tried, in an informal way, to train the young and obviously inexperienced attorneys.
22. The assignment of scarce law clerks to older judges with the expectation of aiding in producing written decisions is one exception to realistic appraisal.
23. Milton Heumann, *Plea Bargaining: The Experiences of Prosecutors, Judges, and Defense Attorneys* (Chicago: University of Chicago Press, 1977), pp. 129–137.
24. See *Survey of State Judicial Education Programs, 1974-1976* (Washington, D.C.: American University Law Institute, 1978).
25. *Ibid.*
26. For a succinct argument in favor of expanded judicial education programs based upon the findings of a national study, see Sofron B. Nedilsky, "How Can a New Judge Know What to Do?" *Judges' Journal*, 18 (1979).
27. Heumann, *Plea Bargaining*, p. 135.
28. Robert Carp and Russell Wheeler, "Sink or Swim: The Socialization of a Federal District Judge," *Journal of Public Law*, 21 (1972).
29. Lenore Alpert, Burton M. Atkins, and Robert C. Ziller, "Becoming a Judge: The Transition from Advocate to Arbiter," *Judicature*, 62 (1979).
30. We will be analyzing our data within a socialization framework, but the reader should be cautioned that these data are cross-sectional, not longitudinal. We do not have the responses of the same judges over time, but of different judges at one varying point in their career. Thus, the findings must be treated tentatively.
31. This has the twin effects of restricting the age variation to 1.7 years across the four categories (53.6 to 55.3), but also reducing the number of cases to 1,238. If we were to examine only judges in their forties or sixties, insufficient cases would appear for one or more categories of the variable, years on bench.
32. Quantitative analysis of our observational data supports this impression, though the numbers are small (n = 40). Among judges between the ages of fifty and fifty-nine the hours we observed judges to work dropped steadily from an average of 7.0 hours for those on the bench five years or less to 6.2 hours for those on the bench between six and ten years, to only 5.8 hours for those on the bench eleven years or more.
33. Alpert, Atkins, and Ziller, "Becoming a Judge," p. 332.
34. Heumann, *Plea Bargaining*, pp. 127–152.
35. Mary Lee Luskin, "Determinants of Attitude and Decision Behavior of Criminal Court Judges," Ph.D. dissertation, University of Michigan, 1978.
36. For a further discussion, see Chapter 7.
37. Other outside work in which we observed judges to engage included service on various boards and committees (ranging from state commissions on mental health to local halfway houses).
38. Judges in metropolitan areas are much more likely to teach a law school course, somewhat more likely to teach in judicial education programs, but less likely than judges in rural areas to teach in police training programs.

# CHAPTER 7

## Judicial Morale

How judges feel about their job and their work environment constitutes one crucial area of inquiry. In this chapter we focus upon judicial job satisfaction, or "morale," in the belief that morale is related to performance and productivity.[1]

Judges are workers, albeit at a high professional level. Accordingly, we derive six elements from the environment of workers that seem applicable to trial judges. These elements are skill utilization, autonomy (of work time), volume of work (caseload pressures), variety of work (caseload mix), effectiveness of subordinates (courtroom personnel), and compensation (salary). We first present judges' own perceptions of these areas of the work environment and then analyze the influence of organizational variables upon their perceptions. Lastly, we examine the relationships between satisfaction with the work environment and judicial industriousness, for which we use the term "hardworkingness," a rough surrogate variable for productivity.

Skill utilization emerges, in the minds of the judges themselves, as the single most important element of the work environment. Thus, it is appropriate that we also focus upon judges' evaluations of their skills at adjudication, administration, community relations, legal research, and negotiation. Judges discriminate sharply in evaluating their own skills, much more so than in evaluating those of attorneys. Furthermore, judicial perceptions of their skills correspond to work patterns, suggesting that both courts and individual judges often make realistic assessments as to what tasks should be performed by which judges.

## Judicial Job Satisfaction: Conceptual and Measurement Issues

Much attention has been devoted to levels of job satisfaction among different kinds of American workers.[2] The focal point of this research, however, has been upon low-skilled workers: in factories, on assembly lines, and in lower levels of management. Where upper management workers are referenced, it is usually in the context of "change agents" or controllers of work practices that influence the job satisfaction of others. Perhaps this is to be expected, because worker dissatisfaction is concentrated in lower-skilled occupations. Indeed, one comprehensive review of empirical studies concluded that "elite" workers—professional, technical, managerial, and proprietors—are quite satisfied, as a group.[3]

Though most research has focused upon low-skilled workers, parts of the conceptual framework underlying these studies may be transferable to a study of judges. Trial judges are not similar in education or in economic or social characteristics to low-skilled workers, but they are subject to analogous organizational pressures. Judges typically work within the confines of a larger organization. Judges typically need to interact and cooperate with—even depend upon—fellow workers and subordinates. Judges, like other workers, are sometimes pressured regarding the amount of work to be performed. Lastly, judges, like other workers, are compensated according to a set of explicit or implicit criteria, though their salary "negotiations" take place in a more public and more political setting. Thus, general characteristics of the work setting structured our inquiry into judicial morale. We refined these characteristics by accommodating them to our understanding of the work of trial judging, including attention to the unusual discretion that judges have.

We inquired into "skill utilization," or how well judges feel that their interests, preferences, and skills are utilized by the larger organization of which they are a part. Presumably, skill utilization is particularly important to judges who (like most professional workers) have undergone years of extensive training for their work. We inquired into "control of work time": to what extent judges feel they are able to control their day-to-day schedules. Autonomy of one's time is likely to be particularly important in high-status occupations like judging. A major constraint on autonomy is work pressure; thus, we asked about the nature of the caseload pressures facing judges. After all, it is judges who frequently voice complaints about the size of their workload, by calling for new courts or additional judgeships.

We also examined the "variety" of cases coming before judges. Variety is an important ingredient in all jobs,[4] including judging. We inquired into the "effectiveness of courtroom personnel" (see also Chapter 5). Finally, we asked about the adequacy of salary, while recognizing that this is not likely to be uppermost in the minds of most judges. The salary of trial judges in the states ranged only from a low of $25,000 in Alabama and Montana to a high of $49,166 in California at the time of our study.[5] Many lawyers, particularly those who become judges, are able to make substantially higher salaries in other positions.

These six areas—skill utilization, control of work time, amount of caseload pressures, variety of caseload, effectiveness of personnel, and salary—constitute our focus on judicial job satisfaction. Though not exhaustive, these are important areas of the work environment suggested by the literature on workers. Furthermore, our observations impressionistically verified the salience of these areas to judicial morale.

Measurement of the elements of job satisfaction was achieved through the use of "semantic differential" scales presented to our survey respondents.[6] For example, judges were asked to rate how well their skills are utilized, along a seven-point scale from 1 ("ineffective") to 7 ("effective"). Judges also responded regarding control of work time (from "no control" to "full control"), caseload pressures and variety (from "too little" to "too much"), courtroom personnel (from "ineffective" to "effective"), and salary (from "underpaid" to "overpaid").

These are not straightforward measures of judicial job satisfaction, because we did not ask judges how "satisfied" they feel in one or another area of the work environment. That would only have clouded the interpretability of "dissatisfied" responses. (For example, are judges dissatisfied because of too much or too little case variety?) In other words, we preferred to obtain a clear picture of the *content* of judges' perceptions of their work and then draw inferences about how these perceptions relate to satisfaction. Ambiguities of inference will be addressed in the discussion of individual elements of job satisfaction.

## Elements of Job Satisfaction: An Empirical Analysis

### SKILL UTILIZATION

Judges as a group feel quite positive about the degree to which their skills are being utilized in the job of judging. Figure 7-1 reports these data. The distribution is clearly skewed toward the "effective" end of the skill utilization continuum. One-sixth of all judges believe their skills are being utilized to the fullest, and more than 80 percent fall on the "effective" side of the continuum (5, 6, or 7). Only a handful of judges are sharply critical about the utilization of their skills and interests. This may appear somewhat surprising, in light of our discussion in Chapter 6 regarding the socialization and pressures to conform that new and sitting judges encounter. Yet courts do succeed in adapting to the needs and preferences of judges, and not only older judges. Furthermore, many prospective judges have a realistic view of some of the skills

"In your judicial capacity, to what extent are you able to utilize your skills and preferences effectively?"

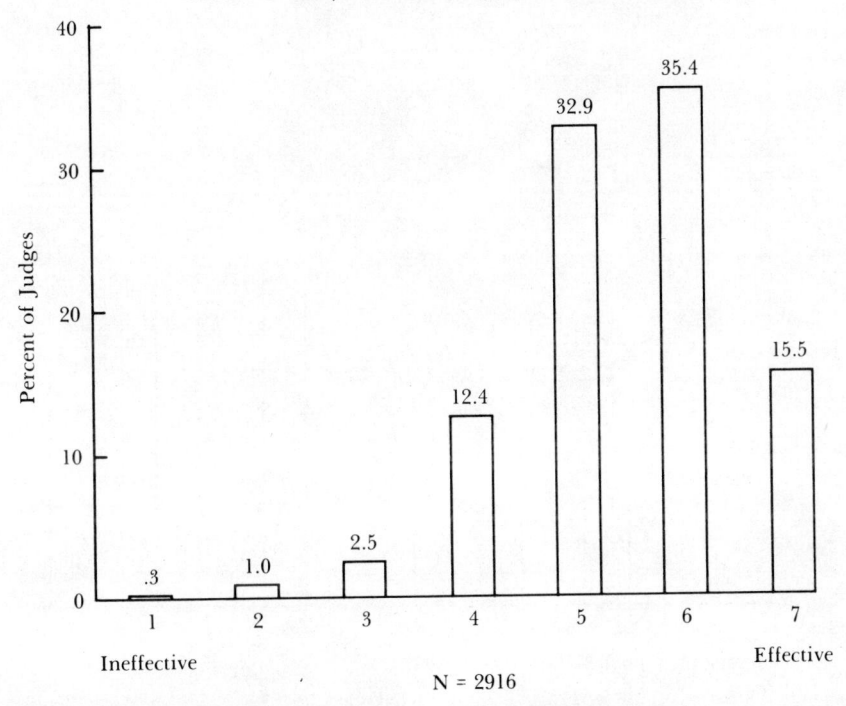

FIGURE 7-1. Trial Judges' Perceptions of Their Skill Utilization

(e.g., adjudication) that will be required on the bench, though they may be lacking in knowledge or understanding of others.

## CONTROL OF WORK TIME

Judges feel in control of their work time, typically from a moderate to full extent. Figure 7-2 displays the distribution of judicial responses. This distribution reflects a wider spectrum of responses, more evenly spread across the continuum. One-sixth of all judges fall into the highest category, perceiving themselves in "full" control of their work time. Almost two-thirds believe that they have more control than not, but a substantial minority perceive frequent lack of control over their work time. Sources that contribute to this lack of control are evident from our observations: tardy attorneys or courtroom personnel who keep judges waiting, poorly skilled attorneys who necessitate extra judicial work, heavy caseloads that prevent some judges from doing much else than presiding at jury trials, and perhaps especially the use of a master calendar, which removes docket management from the individual judge. Judges who sit in courts using a master calendar are placed in a *reactive* posture; they

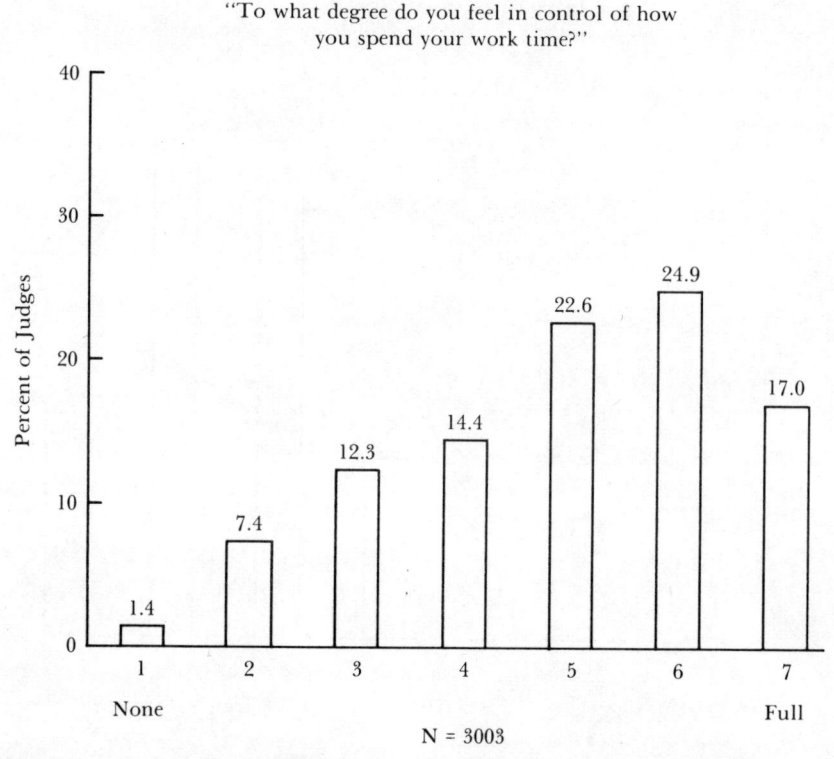

"To what degree do you feel in control of how you spend your work time?"

| Rating | Percent |
|---|---|
| 1 (None) | 1.4 |
| 2 | 7.4 |
| 3 | 12.3 |
| 4 | 14.4 |
| 5 | 22.6 |
| 6 | 24.9 |
| 7 (Full) | 17.0 |

N = 3003

**FIGURE 7-2.** Trial Judges' Perceptions of Their Control over Work Time

are much less able to set their own agenda or schedule of activities. Our survey data provide support here: Judges with individual calendars feel more in control of their time ($\bar{x} = 5.0$) than judges under a master calendar ($\bar{x} = 4.5$).

What is not clear from our data is how much control over work time judges actually *prefer*. Some judges, for example, may prefer *not* to have the additional responsibilities of case scheduling necessitated by an individual calendar. A number of observed judges indicated that they preferred operating under a master calendar, believing it to be "more efficient" in disposing of the entire court's workload. In some circumstances, then, judges may put aside or modify personal preferences (to have more autonomy of time) in favor of group goals.[7] Thus, satisfaction with control of work time may be somewhat higher than suggested by Figure 7-2.

## CASELOAD PRESSURES

Judges generally believe that they are under "too much" pressure to move cases, as Figure 7-3 demonstrates. The majority of judges believe that, to a greater or lesser extent, they are under "too much" pressure to move cases. About one-third perceive that their caseload pressures are about right, while

"Under how much pressure to move cases do you feel?"

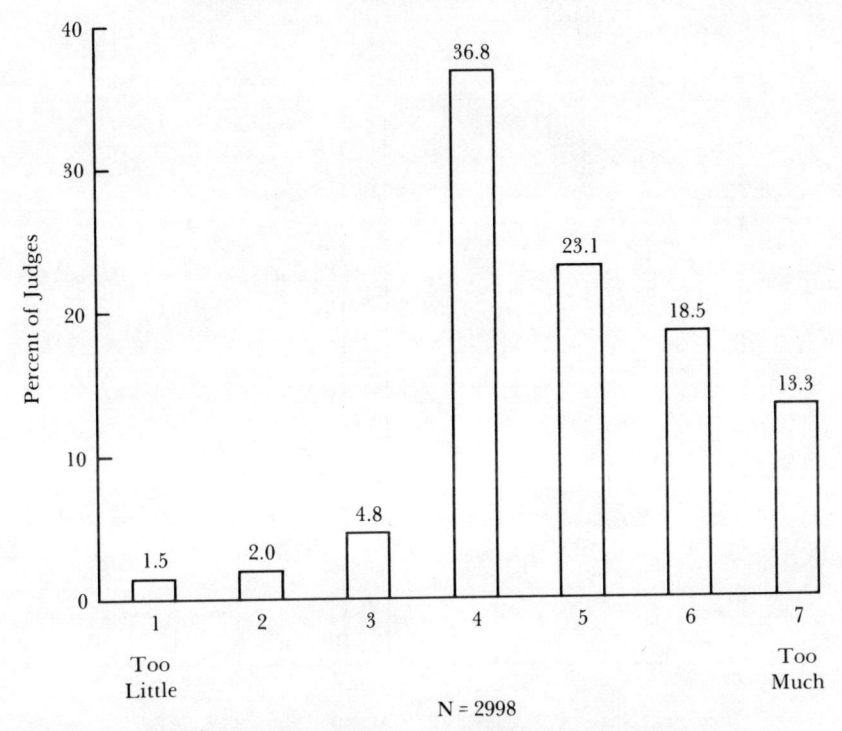

```
Percent of Judges
40 ┤                    36.8
30 ┤
                                    23.1
20 ┤                                        18.5
                                                    13.3
10 ┤
        1.5   2.0   4.8
 0 ┼────┴────┴────┴────┴────┴────┴────┴────
      1     2     3     4     5     6     7
    Too                                      Too
    Little                                   Much
                  N = 2998
```

**FIGURE 7–3.** Trial Judges' Perceptions of Their Caseload Pressures

only a very small percentage (8 percent) of judges report "too little" pressure to move cases. This is not to say, however, that most judges believe they are overworked. Case pressure may have more to do with the perceived *quality* of attention that can be given to individual cases.[8] The disposition of cases through negotiated settlement is viewed by many judges with an air of reluctant concession to necessity rather than outright glee. Judges are often not directly involved in the actual negotiations, especially on the criminal side. Thus, an orientation to "moving cases" may come to deprive judges of meaningful involvement in cases. It is this potential frustration, rather than sheer overwork, which may be the source of judicial discontent with the level of caseload pressures. Judges know that they are more likely to be evaluated by the quantity, not the quality, of their case dispositions, especially by their judicial superiors.[9]

## CASELOAD VARIETY

In contrast to perceptions of caseload pressures, judges seem highly satisfied with the variety of cases coming before them, as Figure 7–4 indicates.

"To what extent (if any) do you experience too much or too little variety in the cases coming before you?"

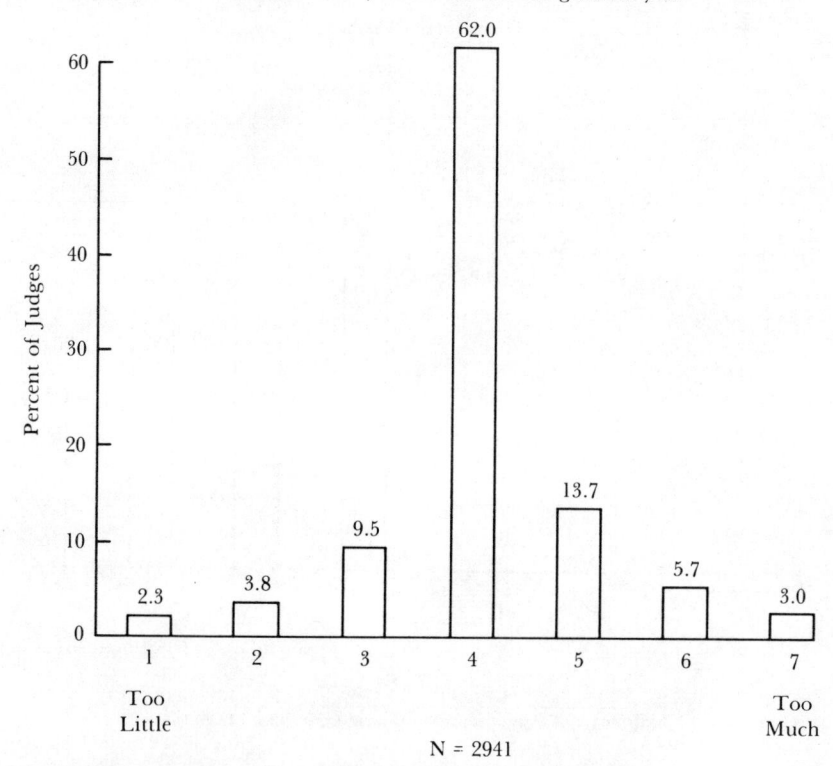

| Scale | Percent |
|---|---|
| 1 (Too Little) | 2.3 |
| 2 | 3.8 |
| 3 | 9.5 |
| 4 | 62.0 |
| 5 | 13.7 |
| 6 | 5.7 |
| 7 (Too Much) | 3.0 |

N = 2941

**FIGURE 7-4.** Trial Judges' Perceptions of Their Caseload Variety

This figure presents a dramatically different distribution from the previous ones. Fully 62 percent of all judges express complete satisfaction with the amount of variety in their caseload, by responding exactly at the midpoint of the continuum (4). Of the remaining judges, somewhat more are likely to perceive "too much" case variety than "too little." Though we have no way of directly determining this, we suspect that "too much" variety may be as damaging to morale as "too little," for reasons discussed earlier in Chapter 2.[10]

Suprisingly, type of assignment is only slightly related to perceptions of caseload variety. Criminal assignment judges, as we would expect, tend to perceive a bit too little variety ($\bar{x}$ = 3.7),[11] compared with judges in civil—mixed assignments ($\bar{x}$ = 4.1). General assignment judges edge farther toward too much variety ($\bar{x}$ = 4.2), but the differences among the three groups of judges are slight. The widespread perception that criminal judges feel quite bored with the variety of their work is more myth than reality.

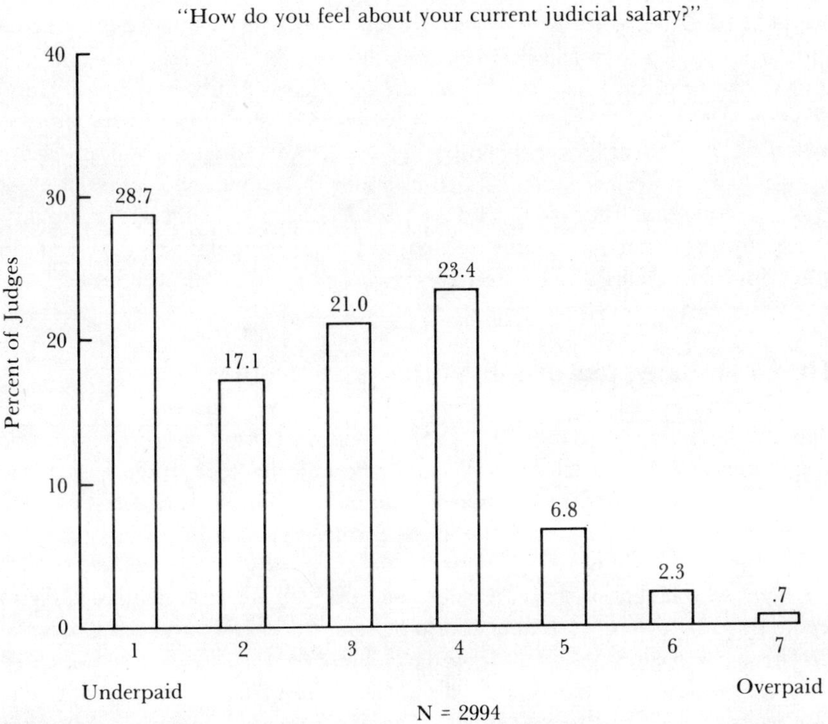

"How do you feel about your current judicial salary?"

```
Percent of Judges
40 |
30 |   28.7
20 |          17.1   21.0   23.4
10 |                              6.8
 0 |_____ 2.3 ___.7__
      1     2     3     4     5     6     7
   Underpaid                           Overpaid
                  N = 2994
```

**FIGURE 7-5.** Trial Judges' Perceptions of Their Salary

## COURTROOM PERSONNEL

Judges express great satisfaction with the performance of their courtroom personnel—bailiffs, clerks, court reporters, and secretaries. (See Figure 5-3 in Chapter 5). One-fourth of all judges rate their personnel in the highest category of effectiveness (7), and more than 80 percent are positive in their evaluation (5, 6 or 7). Though an outsider's assessment might be more critical of court personnel (especially in larger courts dominated by politics), judges seem to take these factors into account in assessing the work of personnel in their courtrooms.

## SALARY

Judges generally feel quite displeased about their salary, as Figure 7-5 indicates. Fully two-thirds of trial judges feel, in varying degrees, underpaid; 29 percent place themselves in the most extreme category of dissatisfaction (1). Most of the remaining judges feel about adequately compensated, while a small percentage (10 percent) perceive themselves to be overpaid.[12]

The actual salary judges are paid (determined by each state but sometimes supplemented by local jurisdictions) has much to do with feelings of being overpaid or underpaid. Although variation in salaries is relatively restricted (the majority of states pay between $30,000 and $45,000 for trial judges in courts of general jurisdiction),[13] there is nevertheless a substantial correlation between salary and feelings about its adequacy. Furthermore, such factors as region, salaries of judges in neighboring states, and cost of living appear to enter into an individual judge's calculus about the adequacy of his salary. For example, judges in Tennessee (who are paid $39,690) feel slightly "overpaid" as a group ($\bar{x} = 4.4$), no doubt influenced by the comparatively low salary in other Southern states and the relatively low cost of living in Tennessee.

## The Interrelatedness of Job Satisfaction Measures

Can these six elements of the work environment be collapsed into one overall measure of judicial job satisfaction? From a conceptual standpoint, the elements appear related to one general dimension. Empirically, however, the elements are not highly intercorrelated. Several—skill utilization, control of work time, and effectiveness of personnel—are slightly intercorrelated.[14] That is, judges who feel their skills are being well utilized are slightly more likely to feel in control of their work time and to believe that their courtroom personnel are effective. In contrast, the other three elements of job satisfaction—caseload pressures, variety of caseload, and salary—are almost entirely unrelated to one another or to the first three elements. Caseload pressure is related to control of work in the expected direction: Judges who feel more pressured to move cases feel less in control of their work time. It is not related to any other elements, however. Variety of caseload and adequacy of salary represent completely independent assessments by judges, without regard to any other elements of the work environment. Thus, there is no single empirical concept that we can term "job satisfaction" among trial judges.[15] Rather, there are at least three distinct components of the work environment. These would include salary, variety of work, and one general component including skill utilization, control of work time, courtroom personnel, and possibly caseload pressures. Because of the fractionalization of judicial job satisfaction, no one scale or summary measure can be developed. As a result, we shall discuss elements of job satisfaction individually.

One way of gaining some insight into overall judicial job satisfaction is by determining which of these elements is most important to individual judges. Are the most important areas of job satisfaction ones in which judges are generally satisfied or not? Through this approach, we can indirectly gauge judicial morale in a more composite way. Table 7-1 reports judges' perceptions of what single area is most important to their job satisfaction.

Overwhelmingly, judges indicate that skill utilization is the single most important variable contributing to their level of job satisfaction. A small but significant minority opt for caseload variety or control of work time. Only a

TABLE 7-1. Trial Judges' Perceptions of the Most Important Area of Job Satisfaction

"Which one of the following areas of your work is the most important area of job satisfaction?"

|  | Percent | Number |
|---|---|---|
| Skill utilization | 59.7 | (1443) |
| Variety of caseload | 15.3 | (369) |
| Control of work time | 14.7 | (352) |
| Caseload pressures | 5.4 | (129) |
| Courtroom personnel | 2.0 | (50) |
| Salary | 1.3 | (33) |
| Other | 1.6 | (40) |
|  | 100.0 | (2416) |

very small percentage rate caseload pressures, courtroom personnel, or salary to be most determinative of their morale. This comports quite well with our brief discussion of the literature on worker productivity and satisfaction. Professional workers are likely to be sensitive to more abstract qualities of the work environment, like skill utilization and autonomy of time. And judges, in particular, are not likely to view salary as a highly significant factor in their morale because of their lowered *expectations* about potential salaries. Few individuals seek judgeships to make (more) money; most have other professional or political motivations. The relatively low judicial salary is simply accepted, grudgingly if not willingly. It is perhaps a similar expectation of the inevitability of caseload pressures that reduces the importance of this variable in the eyes of working judges. By contrast, individuals surely come to the bench expecting that their skills will somehow be utilized effectively, that they will encounter a variety of cases across the run of their judgeship, and that they will have some control over their own work time. For the most part, these expectations seem to be well met. Thus, we can suggest that trial judges as a group are reasonably satisfied, that they possess a moderately high sense of job morale. On those aspects of the work environment which are most important to them, most judges have positive perceptions. Frustrations in the job of judging occur in places where they are to be expected and over which individual judges (or even judicial superiors) have little control.

## Sources of Job Satisfaction and Discontent

We have already noted a few variables that influence particular aspects of the work environment. In this section we take a broader and more systematic look at the impact of three variables which bear decisively upon most areas of the work environment: size of court, the (perceived) skill of attorneys, and court politics. Finally, we attempt to explode a few persistent myths, especially about the purported impacts of assignment and calendaring system, which permeate the literature of judicial administration.

## SIZE OF COURT

Size of court impacts upon four of the six areas of the work environment. Figure 7-6 displays these linear and nonlinear relationships. As court size increases, judges feel that their skills are being better utilized. The differences range from an average of 5.3 in one-judge courts to 5.7 in courts with forty or more judges. This finding might be intuitively expected, given that larger courts utilize more specialization and therefore enable individual judges to use their particular interests and substantive expertise more frequently.

Similarly, size of court is related to caseload variety. As court size increases, caseload variety goes down. The differences range from an average of 4.3 in one-judge courts (a bit "too much" variety) to 3.7 in courts with forty or more judges (a bit "too little" variety). Optimal variety occurs most frequently in intermediate-size courts. Again, this is a reflection of different levels of specialization in smaller and larger courts.

Caseload pressures increase as court size increases until the very largest courts, where a slight drop in perceived pressures takes place. The average scores increase from 4.5 in one-judge courts (a bit "too much" pressure) to a high of 5.2 in courts with twenty-six to thirty-nine judges (quite a bit "too much" pressure), then drop slightly to 5.1 in the largest courts. We would expect judges to be under more pressure to move cases in larger jurisdictions for a variety of reasons: larger backlogs resulting from more jury trials, longer jury trials resulting from more contentious attorneys, more scrutiny of individual work habits by administrative judges, etc. Why this trend would not continue

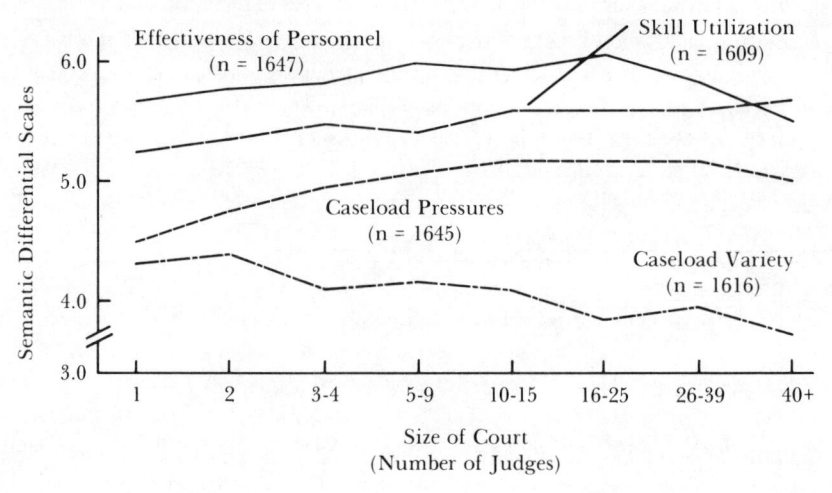

FIGURE 7-6. The Impact of Size of Court upon Trial Judges' Perceptions of Their Work Environment

in the very largest courts is unclear, though court politics may be a formidable competitor to goals of scientific management in a few large urban courts.[16]

Lastly, court size is related, in a curvilinear way, to perceptions of the effectiveness of courtroom personnel. The lowest evaluations of personnel occur in one-judge courts ($\bar{x} = 5.6$) and in courts with forty or more judges ($\bar{x} = 5.5$). In the largest courts, it is probably a case of too many bailiffs bumping into one another. In smaller courts, a bailiff sometimes doubles as clerk, reporter, or building janitor. Neither situation reflects adequate utilization of courtroom personnel.

In all, it is difficult to speculate whether judges are happier in large, small or intermediate-size courts. Each have their own advantages and disadvantages. We can say that judges in all sizes of courts rationalize, by highlighting in their evaluations of job satisfaction those characteristics inherent in their own courts. For example, more judges (70 percent) in the very largest courts rate skill utilization as most important, the same courts where judges are most likely to feel that their skills are effectively utilized. Similarly, in small courts, where caseload variety and control of work time are found in greater supply, judges rate such factors comparatively more important than do judges in larger courts. In sum, judges draw upon the sources of satisfaction that are available to them. In this sense, judges are basically an optimistic group of workers.

## ATTORNEY SKILLS

The skills of practicing attorneys, as perceived by judges, bear a substantial influence upon judicial morale. In four areas of the work environment, judicial satisfaction increases as the perceived skill of attorneys increases, especially the skill of civil attorneys. Although all skills measured—preparation of decrees, case preparation and management, settlement, and trial work—show some relationship with judicial satisfaction, the strongest relationships appear for case preparation and management, the core skill area identified in Chapter 4. Figure 7-7 displays these relationships.

Two general comments are appropriate. First, the relationships are substantial in magnitude, larger than between size of court and perceptions of the work environment. Second, the sharpest changes in perceptions among judges typically occur at the extremes of attorney skill level. That is, sharp increases in satisfaction occur as judges perceive attorneys to be "below average" rather than "poor." Nearly parallel increases occur as attorneys are perceived to be "excellent" rather than "above average." The differences from "below average" to "above average" are much smaller. Thus, judges seem affected, in their morale, negatively by very bad attorneys, and positively by exceptionally good attorneys. Of course, the bulk of practicing attorneys are perceived to be somewhere in between poor and excellent in all skill areas; thus, it is a relatively small percentage of judges whose morale is affected so sharply.

Judges feel their own skills are better utilized when they work with more skilled civil attorneys. Scores on skill utilization range from a low of 4.6 where

158                    AMERICAN TRIAL JUDGES

```
                    Skill Utilization
6.0 ─               (n = 2467)
        Effectiveness of Personnel
        (n = 2532)

5.0 ─
                                    Caseload Pressures
        Control of Work Time        (n = 2529)
        (n = 2533)
4.0 ─

3.0 ─
    Poor    Below Average   Average   Above Average   Excellent
        Civil Attorney Skill at Case Preparation and Management
```
(y-axis: Semantic Differential Scales)

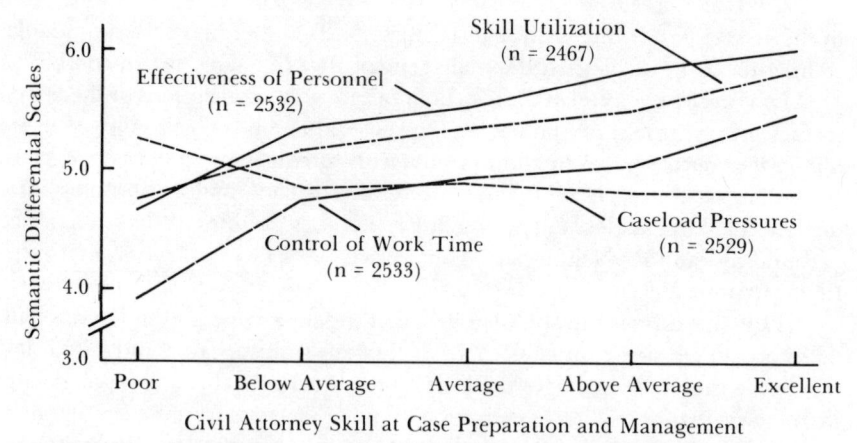

FIGURE 7-7. The Impact of Civil Attorney Skill at Case Preparation and Management upon Trial Judges' Perceptions of Their Work Environment

attorneys are perceived to be poor at case preparation and management to 5.9 where they are perceived to be excellent. This demonstrates that factors other than the court structure can affect judicial skill utilization. Regardless of how many rewards a judge may receive from his administrative superiors, he must still cope with attorneys—or his expectation of what attorneys should be like. Those judges who happen to be surrounded by low-skilled attorneys, especially civil attorneys who are inept at case preparation and management, or judges who are unusually critical of such skills in attorneys, will come to feel that their own skills are not being effectively utilized.

Similar but even larger differences occur in the area of control of work time. Scores range from a low of 3.8 where civil attorneys are perceived to be "poor" at case preparation and management to a high of 5.4 where they are perceived to be excellent. This is to be expected: Sheer judicial time is likely to be wasted when judges have to sort out managerial aspects of cases that attorneys should properly do. This might include instructions on filing motions, discovery practices, and preparation of routine decrees and orders.

A third area in which attorney skills make a difference is in judges' perceptions of the effectiveness of their courtroom personnel. Indeed, the differences are quite large, ranging from a low of 4.7 where attorneys are perceived to be poor to a high of 6.0 where they are perceived to be excellent. On the surface, such a relationship makes little intuitive sense. Surely, poor attorneys do not directly affect the quality of work performed by bailiffs, secretaries, or courtroom clerks. Perhaps poorly skilled attorneys make the work of courtroom personnel more difficult. We might further speculate that "attorneys" and "courtroom personnel" are not necessarily distinct in the minds of many judges. We observed a few vivid examples of judges who treated attorneys as if they were courtroom personnel in both social and professional ways. These judges treated attorneys as inferior subordinates and expected attorneys to share the goals of the court (e.g., to expedite a calendar call) rather than pursue the interests of their clients. Our survey data suggest that this blurring of roles may occur more often than our observations indicated.[17]

Finally, judges' perceptions of their caseload pressures are affected by the perceived skill of civil attorneys at case preparation and management. This relationship, however, is present only at one extreme. Where attorneys are perceived to be poor, judges report more caseload pressure ($\bar{x} = 5.3$) than where attorneys are below average or better ($\bar{x} = 4.8$). This suggests the possibility of a baseline level of caseload pressures (inherent in all courts, but varying slightly according to size), which cannot easily be lowered even by highly skilled attorneys. Factors external to the court itself, including the litigiousness of the community, undoubtedly influence real and imagined caseload pressures.

## COURT POLITICS

Court politics was introduced in Chapter 3 in the context of decisional criteria for assigning judges to divisions within courts. We suggested that courts heavily influenced by politics in this area are likely to be imbued with court politics, and perhaps partisan politics, throughout their operations. This idea receives further support when we examine the influence of court politics upon judicial morale. The impact is striking, as Table 7–2 indicates.

As court politics becomes more influential, judges become increasingly demoralized in five of the six areas of the work environment.[18] Where court politics are prevalent, judges feel (1) that their skills are less well utilized, (2) less in control of their own work time, (3) that their courtroom personnel are

TABLE 7-2. The Impact of Court Politics upon Trial Judges' Perceptions of Their Work Environment[a]

| | Judicial Perceptions of the Influence of Court Politics in Assignments (Semantic Differential Scales) | | | |
|---|---|---|---|---|
| | Substantial | Slight | None | Number |
| Skill utilization | 5.1 | 5.6 | 5.9 | (411) |
| Control of work time | 4.6 | 4.6 | 5.1 | (421) |
| Caseload pressures | 5.0 | 5.1 | 5.3 | (421) |
| Effectiveness of personnel | 5.1 | 5.6 | 5.9 | (420) |
| Caseload variety | 3.3 | 3.8 | 4.0 | (413) |
| Salary | 2.2 | 3.0 | 3.0 | (418) |

[a] Includes only courts with twenty-six or more judges, thereby controlling for size of court.

less effective, (4) that they have too little variety in their caseload, and (5) much more underpaid. Only in the area of caseload pressures does this generalization fail to hold. Judges in courts where politics have a substantial influence actually feel slightly *less* caseload pressure.

Our data suggest that court politics is a highly pernicious influence on the morale of many judges.[19] This influence is pervasive, not only affecting such explicitly political areas as courtroom personnel (who may be patronage workers), but infiltrating the assignment of cases (variety) as well as judges' own feelings about the more intangible qualities of their work (skill utilization, autonomy). That court politics and caseload pressures appear *inversely* related suggests a theme we shall develop further in our discussion of three urban courts in Chapter 9: Courts apparently often must choose between the interests of politics and the interests of management.

## MYTHS ABOUT JUDICIAL MORALE

A number of myths persist about factors that influence the morale of judges. One such factor is assignment. Criminal work has been widely viewed as less challenging than civil work.[20] Our survey data, however, suggest that judges do not share this view. Criminal assignment judges feel that their skills are as effectively utilized as judges in a variety of specialized or more general civil assignments. Our field observations suggest that civil judges received more and better courtroom personnel. But judges in criminal assignment do not perceive their personnel to be any less effective than judges in either general or civil assignments. Civil assignment judges appeared to us to be less harried and perhaps more in control of their work time. But again, judges themselves do not perceive this to be so. Only in the area of caseload pressure is there a significant difference. Here, criminal assignment judges, as we might expect, feel under slightly more pressure to move cases ($\bar{x} = 5.1$) than do judges in a civil—mixed or general assignment ($\bar{x} = 4.8$). It is in the large criminal courts that media attention has been focused on delays in prosecuting defendants. Chief judges respond to this pressure, no doubt, by placing additional pressures on judges in the criminal division to achieve many rapid dispositions.

A second myth revolves around case assignment system. One of the heated debates in judicial administration has concerned the relative efficacy of the master and individual calendars.[21] Though we cannot speak directly to individual judge (or court) performance, we can say that judicial perceptions of the work environment are typically unaffected by type of calendar.[22] Not only are there no differences in skill utilization or caseload variety, but there are no differences on caseload pressures either. Reformers had hoped the introduction of the individual calendar would stimulate more concern for individual caseloads and their speedy dispositions.[23] We have no evidence, however, to suggest that judges' consciousness about their caseloads is greater under individual calendars.

## Judicial Job Satisfaction and Hardworkingness

We do not have direct measures of judicial productivity, a phenomenon so elusive as to defy intelligent measurement. We do, however, have several measures of a judge's hardworkingness, including the total hours reported for his most common and less common days, involvement in community relations and bar association activities, and experiences in teaching in law school, police training, and judicial education settings. What relationship might exist between these indicators of hardworkingness and elements of job satisfaction? Are judges who work long hours likely to be more satisfied or more dissatisfied with their work environment?

Alternative hypotheses could be developed. For example, some might argue that judges who work long hours or engage in "extrajudicial" affairs are likely to be frustrated, perhaps even demoralized. Others might counter that hard work, in any professional setting, is likely to be a sign of job satisfaction and fulfillment. Only those who really like their work would labor at long hours and in arenas where rewards are intangible or nonexistent.

For both of these hypotheses, the causality underlying the relationship is not entirely clear. Perceptions of the work environment (which are shaped by such factors as size of court, attorney skills, and court politics) may help to determine levels of hardworkingness. Alternatively, hardworkingness may cause changes in judicial perceptions of the work environment. Almost certainly, the influences are reciprocal. Accordingly, for analytic purposes we shall simply compare levels of satisfaction with the work environment among judges who report working short hours (less than eight), below average (between eight and nine), above average (between nine and ten), and long hours (ten or more) on their most common day.[24]

Our data suggest some support for both of the stated hypotheses. Judges who work longer hours are more critical of their courtroom personnel, feel less in control of their work time, and believe themselves to be under more pressure to move cases. But these relationships are small. On the other hand, judges who work long hours feel that their skills are slightly better utilized than their colleagues working shorter hours. Thus, we are left with an ambiguity characteristic of our data on judicial morale. Those who work long hours feel better on the most important dimension, skill utilization, but consistently worse on other dimensions of the work environment (after controls for size of court). How these balance is not easily determined.

Judges who are heavily involved in community relations activities or who have taught in law school or judicial education programs feel that their skills are more effectively utilized. For example, among judges who report one-half day or more per month on community relations, the average score on skill utilization is 5.6, compared with 5.4 for judges who work less or no time in this area. Similarly small differences occur between judges who have and have not taught in a variety of educational settings, differences which remain after controls for size of court. On the other elements of job satisfaction, however, participation in these kinds of activities is not related.

In sum, our discussion of productivity and morale in the context of judicial work is necessarily limited by the nature of our data. We do not have measures of job satisfaction and hardworkingness at several points in time. We can say that there appears to be some *slight* relationship between the two phenomena, wherein hardworkingness is associated with a better feeling about skill utilization. Correspondingly, though, the lack of a large salary and of highly talented or motivated courtroom personnel become painfully obvious to the hardworking judge. Others do not always share his enthusiasm or appreciate, in any concrete way, his long hours at the courthouse or extra hours in the community.

## The Nature and Types of Judicial Skills

We have emphasized in this chapter the significance of skill utilization to judicial morale. It is the area of the work environment that judges believe to be most important to their overall sense of job satisfaction and one in which they generally feel satisfied. But precisely which skills are utilized in judging? How do judges evaluate their skills? In this section, we examine these questions as well as the relationships between judicial skills and the work of the trial judge.

Drawing upon our conceptual framework of judicial work, we identified five areas in which to inquire of skills—adjudication, administration, community relations, legal research, and negotiation. Each area constitutes some segment of the work of most judges, as we have seen in Chapter 2. Table 7-3 reports judges' assessments of their own skills in each of the five areas.

Trial judges rate their skill at adjudication substantially higher than in any other area. Almost one-third believe that they are excellent at adjudication, and most of the remainder rate themselves above average. Only a small percentage consider themselves average, and virtually no judges see themselves as below average or poor at the crucial work of adjudication. These data conform

TABLE 7-3. Trial Judges' Evaluation of Their Skills in Five Areas of Work

|  | ADJUDICATION | ADMINISTRATION | COMMUNITY RELATIONS | LEGAL RESEARCH | NEGOTIATION |
|---|---|---|---|---|---|
| Excellent | 31.0% | 18.4% | 21.7% | 17.1% | 16.7% |
| Above average | 54.1 | 39.4 | 35.2 | 39.1 | 34.2 |
| Average | 14.8 | 36.5 | 35.4 | 38.2 | 37.9 |
| Below average | .1 | 5.3 | 6.9 | 5.2 | 9.0 |
| Poor | 0 | .4 | .8 | .4 | 2.2 |
| Number | (2975) | (2960) | (2941) | (2966) | (2831) |

well both to expectations about what judging will entail (presiding over trials and other formal adversary events) and to what most judges actually spend the bulk of their time doing.

Among the other areas of work, there are few differences in judges' views of their skills. Smaller percentages of judges believe they are excellent in each of these areas, and some actually rate their skill to be below average or poor. This is especially true for negotiation, where 11 percent see themselves as below average or worse. Indeed, for negotiation more than one hundred fewer judges indicated any rating at all. This could point to an underestimation of the percentage of judges who perceive their skills to be inadequate in this area. Furthermore, it is important to emphasize that judges do *not* have a uniformly high view of their skills and talents. As a group, they acknowledge limitations, particularly in secondary but important areas of judicial work. Individual judges are able to differentiate—quite sharply—their skill in one area of work as opposed to another.[25] Few judges perceive themselves to be excellent in all areas; similarly, few judges rate their skills as average in all areas. Rather, individual judges distinguish their stronger areas from their weaker ones, particularly outside of adjudication. This stands in sharp contrast to their ratings of the skills of attorneys practicing before them, where judges do not sharply differentiate attorney skills in one area from skills in another. Clearly, judges know themselves better than they know the attorneys before them; they are able to identify their own strengths and weaknesses much more readily.

We can provide one additional perspective on the relative importance of each area of judicial work by examining the relationships between skill utilization and judges' assessments of their skill level in particular areas. In other words, how much difference in skill utilization results from judges' perceptions of their skill at adjudication, administration, community relations, legal research, and negotiation? The larger the difference, the more central a skill area is to the judge's overall satisfaction with his skill utilization. Figure 7-8 illustrates these data.

The figure suggests that some areas of work are perceived by judges to be more crucial to their overall skill utilization. Skill at adjudication and administration, for example, each account for differences of slightly under one full point on the skill utilization scale. Judges who rate themselves as excellent at adjudication have an average score of 5.8 on the skill utilization scale; this drops to 5.4 for judges who rate themselves above average, and to a rather low 4.9 for judges who believe they are only average at adjudication. A parallel decline occurs as judges rate themselves less skilled at administrative work. An almost equally large decline occurs as judges perceive themselves less skilled at negotiation.

By contrast, the areas of community relations and legal research seem less central to skill utilization in the eyes of judges. Differences between judges who rate themselves excellent as opposed to above average are very small, and the entire range of differences is noticeably constricted. It should not be sur-

```
                                                                5.9 ┐ Exc.
        5.8 ┐ Exc.    5.8 ┐ Exc.
                            Above    5.7 ┐ Exc.                       Above
                    5.5 ┤ Avg.             Above   5.6 ┐ Exc.   5.5 ┤ Avg.
                                    5.5 ┤ Avg.           Above
        5.4 ┤ Above                                5.5 ┤ Avg.
             Avg.   5.3 ┤ Avg.      5.3 ┤ Avg.                  5.3 ┤ Avg.
                                           Below   5.3 ┤ Avg.         Below
                                    5.1 ┘ Avg. or        Below  5.1 ┘ Avg. or
                            Below          Poor    5.1 ┘ Avg. or      Poor
        4.9 ┘ Avg.   4.9 ┘ Avg. or                       Poor
                            Poor
```

Perceptions of Skill Utilization (y-axis, 4.0 to 6.0)

Judicial Skills (x-axis): Adjudication, Administration, Community Relations, Legal Research, Negotiation

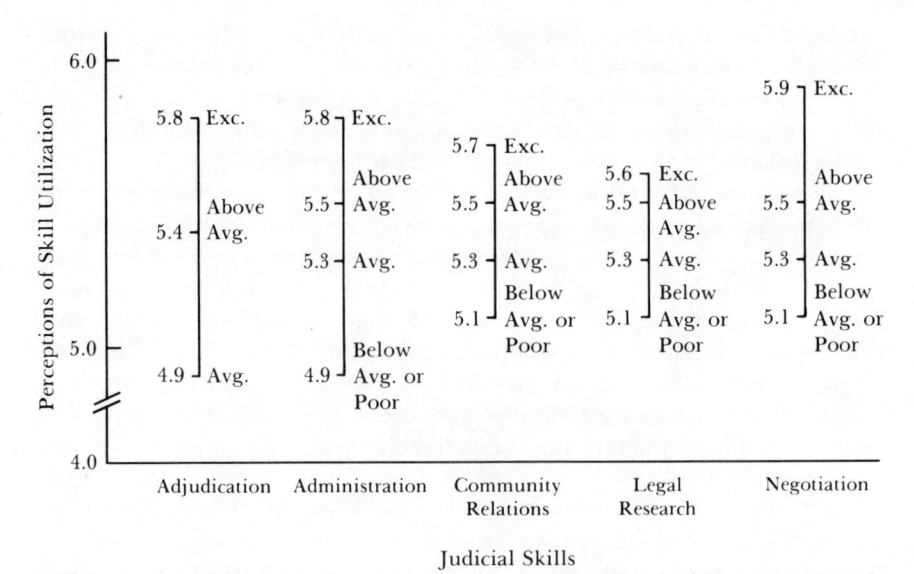

**FIGURE 7-8.** Centrality of Skill Areas to Trial Judges' Perceptions of Skill Utilization

prising that community relations is viewed to be more peripheral. For many judges, the idea that the court or justice system must be attractively "packaged" for consumption by other elites or the public at large is truly repugnant. These judges view their work in a narrower, more technical-legalistic framework. With regard to legal research, it is somewhat surprising that this task area is viewed to be more peripheral to the effective utilization of judicial skills. Trial judges report a small but nearly daily routine of "keeping up with the law," unlike their episodic forays into community relations. Furthermore, judges who are active in preparing and writing decisions spend much more time doing this (perhaps one day per week) than judges active in community relations spend in that pursuit (perhaps one day per month). Nevertheless, judges perceive that how good they are at legal research is only marginally related to how well they feel their skills are being utilized.

## THE DISTRIBUTION OF JUDICIAL SKILLS

Most elements of court structure (e.g., type of assignment, calendaring system, presence or absence of circuit-riding responsibilities) make little difference in judges' views of their own skills. The one notable exception is size of court. As court size increases, a higher percentage of judges believe they have superior skills. The impact of size of court is strongest in the area of adjudication. Seventeen percent of judges who serve by themselves rate their skill at adjudication as excellent, a figure which rises steadily and sharply to 46 percent of judges in the largest courts. Smaller linear rises also occur in the areas of community relations (15 percent to 31 percent), legal research (12 percent to

29 percent), and negotiation (10 percent to 32 percent). Only for administrative work is there no significant relationship with court size.

But why do judges in larger courts generally evaluate their skills in work areas to be higher than their colleagues in smaller courts? Are the differences real or only a function of the egotistical imaginations of urban judges? We would suggest that these perceptual differences are rooted in both self-image and reality. Judges in large cities are probably more likely to feel the need for greater self-esteem, in response to the more sophisticated, professional (perhaps pretentious) fiber of life in metropolitan places. Moreover, it is in highly urban areas that trial judges are more likely to come from "proprietary" or low-prestige law schools, giving rise to possible feelings of inferiority.[26] On the other hand, judges in larger cities may actually have superior skills in certain areas. Our observations suggest that this may be true for negotiation: Judges in urban areas feel more pressured to move cases and therefore develop more effective negotiation styles. The most aggressive of judicial negotiating styles observed in large courts were never seen in smaller courts, where judges were more likely to believe in, or to be able to implement their belief in, a person's right to his day in court.

## SKILLS AND WORK PATTERNS

We previously found that the judge with high morale tends to be a hardworking judge. There is similar evidence to suggest that the highly skilled judge is also hardworking. For each task area, judges who think they are highly skilled work up to one-half hour longer, on average, than their counterparts who see themselves as less skilled. Likewise, judges who are more self-confident of their skills are also more likely to spend time in community relations and bar association activities. This relationship is quite strong when judges believe they are highly skilled at community relations. In sum, skills, judicial job satisfaction, and hardworkingness go hand in hand.

Judges also emphasize different tasks in their daily work according to their perceptions of their own skills. This is particularly marked in legal research and negotiation. Judges who think they are excellent at legal research are more likely to engage in keeping up with the law and preparing/writing decisions, and they do so for greater lengths of time. Likewise, judges who think they are highly skilled at negotiation are also more likely to spend time in this activity, especially civil negotiations. For example, in large courts only 29 percent of judges who rate themselves average at negotiation report civil settlement discussions on their most common day, compared with 35 percent who rate themselves above average, and fully 59 percent who perceive themselves to be excellent. These differences persist across less common work days.

The direction of causality between judicial skills and work patterns is not fully clear; however, our observations suggest that the identification of judicial skills may *lead to* different work assignments. Courts do learn which judges are skilled at negotiation and try to assign more pretrial conferences to them.

Courts are likely to choose chief judges who are affable and skilled at community relations in order to project an effective image to the general public. To control and expedite the flow of cases, courts are likely to choose as supervising or calendar judges those who are skilled at administration.[27] In addition, judges themselves choose work consonant with their skills, when this is possible. Nearly all trial judges, of course, must adjudicate, but the degree to which they negotiate, do legal research, or are active in community relations usually is less determined. Judges who think they are better at a particular skill will seek work that draws upon that skill or even attempt to transform the nature of the tasks they are called upon to do. For example, judges who fancy themselves to be highly skilled at negotiation will see nearly every case as an opportunity to negotiate, no matter how intransigent the parties may seem.

## Summary

Trial judges express mixed reactions to their work environment. They are highly satisfied with courtroom personnel, tend to feel in control of their own work time, and like the variety of cases coming before them. Most important of all (to them), judges feel that their skills are well utilized in their judicial capacity. On the other hand, judges also feel too highly pressured by the flow of cases and substantially underpaid. There is no simple way to aggregate or weight these factors; their relative importance shifts from judge to judge. Indeed, many judges themselves probably cannot weigh the importance of each factor. Nevertheless, judges do seem to look for the positive aspects of their work, drawing satisfaction from elements of the work environment that are available in abundance in their own court.

Several variables play a key role in defining judges' perceptions of their work environment. Size of court affects judicial perceptions. Judges in intermediate-size courts feel best about their courtroom personnel and the variety of cases before them. Meanwhile, judges in smaller courts feel least under pressure to move cases, whereas judges in large courts perceive that their skills are most effectively utilized. No one size of court, then, is ideal in all aspects of the work environment; each has its advantages and drawbacks.

The perceived skills of attorneys also affect how judges assess their work environment. Judges who believe that they are surrounded by relatively skilled attorneys, especially in civil cases, generally reflect higher levels of morale. By contrast, the presence of court politics has a dampening effect on judicial morale. Where judges perceive that court politics has a substantial influence on assignments within their court, they are likely to feel less satisfied in nearly every area of the work environment, including skill utilization.

Trial judges are able to differentiate their skills at adjudication, administration, community relations, legal research, and negotiation. They feel highly confident in adjudication but substantially less so in the other areas. This should not be surprising, given traditional notions of what constitutes judging in trial courts and in view of the curriculum at state and national education programs for sitting judges. Substantive law is emphasized at these programs, typically to the exclusion of negotiation or community relations. Though judges themselves perceive community relations activities to be somewhat peripheral, they view negotiation to be central to the work of the trial judge.

Finally, there is a triangle of association among judicial job satisfaction, judicial skills, and hardworkingness. The hardworking judge—who works long hours and is involved in community relations and bar association activities—is more likely to be satisfied with his environment. Similarly, the hardworking judge is likely to see his own skills in a highly favorable light. This suggests the presence of a group of judicial "workaholics," men and women who thrive on work and who demand, and receive, much satisfaction from their work.

# Notes

1. For a discussion of the relationship between morale and performance among workers generally, see Ivar Berg, Marcia Freedman, and Michael Freeman, *Managers and Work Reform* (New York: Free Press, 1978); Waino W. Suojanen, W. William Suojanen, Mickey J. McDonald, and Gary L. Swallow (eds.), *Perspectives on Job Enrichment and Productivity* (Atlanta: Georgia State University Press, 1975); Marvin Dunnette (ed.), *Handbook of Industrial and Organizational Psychology* (Chicago: Rand McNally, 1976); and Victor Vroom, *Work and Motivation* (New York: Wiley, 1964).
2. T.R. Mitchell, "Expectancy Models of Job Satisfaction, Occupational Preference, and Effort: A Theoretical, Methodological, and Empirical Appraisal," *Psychological Bulletin,* 81 (1974), and Marvin Dunnette, J.P. Campbell, and M. D. Haskel, "Factors Contributing to Job Dissatisfaction in Six Occupational Groups," *Organizational Behavior and Human Performance,* 2 (1967).
3. Edwin Locke, "The Nature and Consequences of Job Satisfaction," in Dunnette (ed.). *Handbook of Industrial and Organizational Psychology.*
4. John R. Maher (ed.), *New Perspectives in Job Enrichment* (New York: Van Nostrand Reinhold, 1971).
5. See *Survey of Judicial Salaries in State Court Systems* (Denver: National Center for State Courts, 1977).
6. Our use of semantic differential scales is an adaptation of the original use by C. Osgood, G. Suci, and P. Tannenbaum, *The Measurement of Meaning* (Urbana: University of Illinois Press, 1957). For an extended discussion, including appropriate statistical applications, see Fred N. Kerlinger, *Foundations of Behavioral Research* (New York: Holt, Rinehart & Winston, 1964), pp. 564-580.
7. Alternatively, others have noted that some criminal court judges prefer a master calendar to avoid being identified individually with large backlogs. See Marcia J. Lipetz, Mary Lee Luskin, and David W. Neubauer, *Evaluation of LEAA's Court Delay-Reduction Program,* interim report, 1979, Chapter 6.

8. Feeley rejects this commonly advanced argument for lower (misdemeanor) trial courts. Based upon courtroom observations, he concludes that courts and courtroom participants want to finish their business quickly and move to other work or play, *regardless* of the volume of their caseload. See Malcolm M. Feeley, *The Process Is the Punishment* (New York: Russell Sage, 1979). Because the nature of the cases—the seriousness of the charges—is so different in felony and misdemeanor cases, however, we believe Feeley's argument is not applicable to felony courts.
9. An excellent case in point is the implementation and impact of the Ohio Rules of Superintendence, explicitly designed to reduce backlogs and decrease case processing time.
10. The predominant emphasis in the literature, however, has been upon the tedious and repetitive nature of judicial work, especially for criminal court judges. See, for example, Herbert Jacob, *Urban Justice: Law and Order in American Cities* (Englewood Cliffs, N.J.: Prentice-Hall, 1973).
11. See the discussion in Chapter 2 on variety of work days. Criminal assignment judges are much more likely to report only *one* type of work day.
12. This element of job satisfaction is perhaps the best example of the weakness of a question wording format built around "satisfaction." Most observers would attribute "dissatisfaction" on salary entirely to being underpaid. Yet some judges may feel a tinge of guilt from being "overpaid."
13. *Survey of Judicial Salaries in State Court Systems.*
14. The Pearson correlation coefficients (r) range from .21 to .33 among these three elements of job satisfaction.
15. Factor analysis of the six elements of job satisfaction unambiguously supports this conclusion.
16. For a fuller discussion of this issue, see Chapter 9.
17. In the question wording for effectiveness of courtroom personnel, we provided examples of whom we meant—bailiff, clerk, reporter, secretary. We intentionally excluded any mention of attorneys. See Figure 5-3 in Chapter 5.
18. Table 7-2 controls for the potentially confounding effects of size of court by restricting the analysis to large courts (twenty-six or more judges).
19. It is likely to be particularly damaging to younger and junior members of the bench who themselves more frequently attribute a "substantial" influence to court politics in their courts.
20. See, for example, Abraham S. Blumberg, *Criminal Justice* (Chicago: Quadrangle, 1967), p. 118.
21. Maureen Solomon, *Caseflow Management in the Trial Court,* American Bar Association Commission on Standards of Judicial Administration, Supporting Studies-2, 1973, and Eldridge Adams, *The Feasibility of Measuring and Comparing Calendar Effectiveness* (Springfield, Va.: National Technical Information Service, 1971).
22. This is true both before and after controls for size of court have been imposed. Note that in our discussion of judicial work patterns in Chapter 3, we could find only very limited effects attributable to calendar.
23. See, for example, the introduction of the Ohio Rules of Superintendence (note 9 above) in 1971, mandating an individual calendar.

24. The division of working hours into four groups is based upon figures that include lunch. For the distribution, see Figure 2-1.
25. The highest intercorrelation between any two skill areas is adjudication with legal research ($r = .35$); all other intercorrelations are smaller but still positive in direction ($r > 0 < .25$).
26. Jacob found that a much higher percentage of trial judges in highly urban areas attended "substandard" law schools, compared with their counterparts in less urban and rural areas. See Herbert Jacob, "The Effect of Institutional Differences in the Recruitment Process: The Case of State Judges," *Journal of Public Law*, 13 (1964).
27. Of course, not all courts act "rationally" in their selection of chief or supervising judges or in the assignment of work. For a look at the role of politics, see Chapter 9.

# PART IV

# Selective Views of Judicial Performance

# CHAPTER 8

# Styles of Negotiation: Judicial Participation in Plea and Settlement Discussions

JUDICIAL work is performed not only in different amounts and mixes of tasks but also with different styles. Nowhere is this more evident than in the work of negotiation, often viewed as the most controversial of all of the activities in which trial judges engage.

In this chapter, we look at *whether* and *how* trial judges are involved in the pretrial negotiation of criminal and civil cases. The nature, or level, of judicial involvement varies widely, even though most courts of all types rely heavily upon negotiated dispositions to move their dockets.[1] In some courts, attorneys are the primary actors in developing agreements in which the court (judge) then concurs. In other courts, judges themselves are active participants in the construction of an agreement. The role or style that a judge adopts in the negotiation setting is influenced by legally relevant cues; elements of the court structure; the skills, stability, and adversariness of attorneys; and the judge's perceptions of his skills and of the caseload pressures facing him. These factors assume different weights in criminal as opposed to civil cases, in part because the legitimacy of judicial participation is viewed quite differently in these two areas.

## Negotiation in Criminal and Civil Cases: Should the Trial Judge Participate?

Judicial participation in plea negotiations has frequently been criticized or condemned. Numerous federal and state court cases, state court rules, and commissions studying the administration of criminal justice have concluded, explicitly or by implication, that the trial judge should *not* participate in plea discussions between prosecutors and defense counsel.[2] Some of the arguments focus upon the likely coerciveness of a situation in which the judge moves from an "umpiring" or adjudicative role to an active negotiating role.[3] Will defendants be able to resist unattractive bargains to which the presumably neutral court has been a party? Other critics assert that inadequate safeguards exist, should the negotiations fail and the defendant ultimately go to trial.[4] For example, will the same judge who participated in plea discussions—at which inadmissible (but sentence-relevant) information was discussed—also conduct the trial? This question is particularly significant in courts that organize their work through an individual case assignment system where the same judge hears a case from beginning to end.

Arguments in favor of judicial participation in plea negotiations are advanced in less straightforward terms, and often with some reluctance. Judges, especially chief or supervising judges, may firmly believe that judicial participation is essential to moving criminal cases expeditiously. Public pronouncements to this effect, however, are not common. Similarly, appellate courts typically refrain from lauding either plea bargaining generally or judicial participation in the process, though they often uphold convictions to a plea of guilty where the judge was present or actively participated in discussions.[5]

Other rationales supporting judicial participation do exist, however, even if infrequently articulated. Perhaps the most compelling is that sentencing in criminal courts usually occurs in the plea negotiation process, and sentencing is clearly a judicial function.[6] Concurring in both charge and sentence agreements struck by counsel is not a significant judicial decision (unless the agreements themselves were made in light of a judge's sentencing preferences). Thus, if the trial judge is to be actively involved in most sentencing decisions, he needs to be present at, and participate in, plea discussions with prosecuting and defense counsel.

The appropriateness of judicial participation in civil settlement discussions is much more firmly entrenched. In part, this is because pretrial settlement of civil cases is less controversial than pretrial negotiation of criminal cases. There is no taint to settlement discussions and, accordingly, little guilt by association with the process. In large part, though, judges schedule and participate in civil settlement discussions because of less equitable relationships among competing parties, fewer incentives for defendants to settle, and the prospect of long delays and large backlogs.[7]

Where civil cases involve monetary claims resulting from personal injury, powerful and resourceful insurance company defendants are pitted against individual citizen plaintiffs. Such defendants have few or no incentives to settle quickly (they do not await trial in jail), and by threatening to go to trial in a substantial number of cases they can significantly affect an individual plaintiff's ability to get a trial date within a reasonable period of time. These factors encourage courts to adopt an aggressive stance toward cases once thought to be exclusively in the domain of private law. In a parallel way, judges come to represent a public interest in the pretrial settlement of other types of civil cases such as probate and domestic relations.

## Styles of Judicial Participation

In criminal negotiations, the decision by a judge to be present at plea discussions is itself significant. Once that threshold has been crossed, however, there are still a variety of roles a judge may assume. These range from "mere" presence to a full participation, and include passive, reactive, and initiating forms of behavior. Table 8–1 reports the proportion of judges who fall into one of four basic postures toward involvement in plea negotiations. The majority

TABLE 8–1. Trial Judges' Style of Participation in Plea Discussions[a]

| Which one of the following roles do you *most typically* assume with respect to plea negotiations? | PERCENT | NUMBER |
|---|---|---|
| "Attend plea negotiation discussions, and recommend dispositions to the D.A. and/or defense counsel" (Recommend) | 7.5 | (163) |
| "Attend plea negotiation discussions, and review recommendations of the D.A. and/or defense counsel" (Review) | 20.1 | (439) |
| "Attend plea negotiation discussions, but do not participate" (Attend) | 3.7 | (80) |
| "Do not attend plea negotiation discussions; only ratify in open court dispositions agreed to outside your presence" (Ratify) | 68.7 | (1505) |
|  | 100.0 | (2187) |

[a] Responses include only those judges whose *current* assignment involves the hearing of (some) criminal cases.

of judges—fully two-thirds—do not attend plea negotiation sessions between prosecuting and defense counsel.[8] Of the remaining judges, most do more than simply attend; they either take the lead in recommending dispositions to counsel or, more commonly, review and modify the recommendations of prosecuting and defense counsel. Let us examine each group of judges more closely, drawing upon our observational experiences.

Judges who only ratify agreements reached outside their presence may not remove themselves entirely from the plea bargaining process. For example, some judges may reject agreements (and thereby force counsel to try again) or may concur in agreements subject to a favorable presentence report. We never observed an instance where the judge—in open court—rejected an agreement proposed to him. We did see one judge in Los Angeles who consistently reserved final judgment until he saw a presentence report prepared by a highly professional probation department. Presumably, in a few cases this judge did later notify counsel that he could not concur, in view of the defendant's prior record or the recommendation of the probation department. Alternatively, some judges who only ratify agreements do wish to remove themselves entirely from the plea bargaining process. These judges may be uncomfortable making decisions about the liberty of another human being, as one Southern judge confided. In this judge's state, juries retain a significant voice in sentencing upon conviction at trial, leaving the judge who does not participate in plea discussions with little or no decision-making role in sentencing.

Judges who attend plea discussions passively and quietly are difficult to find. Very few judges in our survey and no judges whom we observed fall into this category. Most judges undoubtedly perceive this kind of passive participation as the worst of both worlds: Judicial impartiality may be tainted (by presence) and the opportunity to shape the final decision and, in so doing, to protect the rights of defendants is not taken.

Judges who respond to the initiatives of prosecuting and defense counsel represent the most common form of participation. In some instances, counsel may already have informally talked before a conference with the judge. One Chicago judge believed that this two-step procedure saved judicial time by forcing attorneys to be realistic with one another. Judges themselves responded differently to attorneys, depending upon the experience and sophistication of the counsel.

Timid prosecutors were, perhaps, the most common catalyst to initiating activity by judges—i.e., recommending dispositions before or during attorney "pitches." In both Chicago and Los Angeles we observed judges who suggested sentences where the prosecutor appeared timid, inexperienced, or simply unknowledgeable, but who sought (with interest) the recommendations of more experienced prosecutors. Thus, the line between recommending dispositions and reviewing recommendations is often thin. Nevertheless, the two postures appear to symbolize higher and lower levels of involvement respectively, as we shall see later in this chapter.

Type of assignment influences the choice of a negotiating style. Our survey data indicate that judges in criminal assignment are much more likely to participate in plea discussions than judges in general assignment. Almost 50 percent of judges who hear exclusively criminal cases recommend or review dispositions, compared with only about 25 percent of judges who hear both criminal and civil cases. Judges who hear only criminal cases are likely to be found in large courts where prevailing norms, especially the practices of attorneys, contribute to highly adversarial forms of plea negotiation in which the presence of a judge may be beneficial.

In civil negotiations, the prime issue is not whether but *how* a judge will intervene in pretrial conferences and discussions. Most civil judges become involved in formal or informal ways in settlement discussions, and these judges seek to find a style of behavior in which they will be comfortable and productive. Table 8-2 indicates the proportion of judges who report that they intervene aggressively, subtly, or not at all in civil settlement discussions.

The majority of judges—more than three-fourths—do participate in settlement discussions in order to produce a disposition. Most by far prefer to characterize their involvement in terms of indirect rather than direct pressure. Only about one judge in five allows counsel to try to reach an agreement entirely on their own. Let us again look more closely at each style, drawing upon our observational experiences.

Judges who intervene aggressively find ways to apply direct pressure on one or both parties to settle. This can take many forms. For example, some judges

TABLE 8-2. Trial Judges' Style of Participation in Civil Settlement Discussions[a]

| In (civil) settlement conferences, which one of the following roles do you *most typically* assume? | PERCENT | NUMBER |
|---|---|---|
| "Intervene aggressively—through the use of direct pressure" (Aggressive) | 10.3 | (261) |
| "Intervene subtly—through the use of cues/suggestions" (Subtle) | 67.9 | (1728) |
| "Do not intervene—allow the opposing counsel to try to reach a settlement on their own" (No intervention) | 21.8 | (556) |
|  | 100.0 | (2545) |

[a] Responses include only those judges whose *current* assignment involves the hearing of (some) civil cases.

prefer to negotiate *separately* with plaintiff and defense counsel, hoping to produce settlement by exaggerating the strengths of the other side's case. Obviously, this cannot be done effectively when both sides are present. The supervising judge of the pretrial division of one urban court used this technique of "separate consultation" vigorously. More frequently, judges apply pressure when both sides are present by challenging the standard defense counsel disclaimer ("my insurance company simply won't offer anything more"). Judges may do this either by having the defense attorney phone the top person in the claims department of the insurance company or by phoning that person himself. If either of these approaches is successful (as they often appear to be), plaintiff attorneys who have watched this scenario will feel pressured to get their clients to agree.

The most sophisticated use of direct pressure occurs when the judge has prepared so meticulously for a conference that he is in complete command of the facts of the case, the relevant law, and the likely outcomes if the case goes to a jury. We observed only one judge (in a suburban court) who was consistently able to operate in this way. This particular judge also varied the level of formality in the conference according to the types of lawyers participating. In all, he extracted settlements from the most intractable, confused, and even unpleasant of attorneys.

Judges who intervene subtly are characteristically more low-keyed in their approach to settlement. These judges do not like to "bludgeon" attorneys into settlement, perhaps because they empathize with the lawyers appearing before them when recalling their own trial practice days. But these judges do have techniques of their own—giving cues and suggestions to counsel about credibility of potential witnesses, possible rulings on motions, and likely jury behavior. Through indirect ways, they are able to provide counsel with enough reliable information to lead them toward the conclusion that settlement is in their own best interest. Judges who intervene subtly are much less likely to mention directly the court's interest in settlement ("we can save five or ten days of trial by settling"), though this consideration may be as important to them as to judges who apply direct pressure.

Judges who do not intervene at all are difficult to characterize, especially since we saw so few examples in the field. One Southern judge relied upon his "reputation" with attorneys for settlement pressure. Unfortunately, his reputation was one of enjoying jury trials. Furthermore, he served in an urban court where trial times for typical personal injury cases were low.[9] Another judge, in a suburban court, seemed highly uncomfortable with the interpersonal relationships that characterize informal discussions in chambers. He appeared so inept (in the one conference we observed, the parties left chambers shouting at one another after entering calmly) that he undoubtedly avoided involvement or intervention wherever possible.

Other judges whom we observed appeared to vary their level of intervention according to the type of case. One judge in a large urban court tried very hard to settle small claims cases so that he could spend his time enjoying well-argued medical malpractice and contract cases. Another judge in a different urban court took precisely the opposite perspective: He tried to settle a complex, but potentially interesting, products liability case to make room for "six or seven shorter cases deserving trial in a reasonable period of time." Still another judge settled a products liability case only to find himself hearing a routine bicycle accident claim which was next sent down by the master calendar. In short, some judges alter their level of intervention in order to accommodate their own personal case preferences or their philosophy about which kinds of litigants are most deserving of a trial.

Judges in different kinds of civil assignments report highly similar levels of intervention in settlement discussions. This is somewhat surprising, given that the "fear" of a jury trial can be present only in a few types of civil assignments. Judges sitting in chancery, probate, and domestic relations assignments virtually never hear jury trials but still intervene in pretrial negotiation at the same levels as judges in other civil assignments. Indeed, judges in domestic relations report the most frequent involvement in settlement discussions. Where mediation efforts were at one time directed toward conciliating the two parties and preserving the marriage, now negotiation efforts in domestic relations cases almost exclusively address disputes of alimony, child custody, and property.

Finally, how much if any transfer of negotiation role takes place when judges—in general assignment—move back and forth between criminal and civil cases? Are judges who actively intervene in civil settlement discussions likely to participate in plea discussions? Our survey data suggest a high level of transference in roles. For example, among those judges who do not intervene in civil settlements, only 9 percent recommend or review dispositions at plea discussions. That figure rises to 25 percent for judges who intervene subtly in civil cases, and to nearly 50 percent for judges who intervene aggressively in civil negotiations.[10] Thus, many generalist judges do *not* draw a significant distinction between the appropriateness of their participation in civil as opposed to criminal negotiation work.

## Variations in Judicial Styles: What Are the Causes?

There is substantial variation in the styles with which trial judges participate in plea and settlement discussions. This is clear both from our survey data and, even more vividly, from observational experiences. Is the variation attributable to "judicial personality" or to more concrete, measurable factors? In this section, we examine a range of variables that contribute to some of the variation in judicial styles. These include legally relevant cues, court structure, characteristics of attorneys, and judicial perceptions and self-attributions.

## LEGALLY RELEVANT CUES

State court systems have developed substantive, procedural, and administrative rules to guide the operation of trial courts.[11] In the rules of criminal procedure of seven states (Arizona, Arkansas, Colorado, New Mexico, North Dakota, Oregon, and Pennsylvania) and the District of Columbia, judicial participation in plea discussions is expressly prohibited.[12] The language is typically straightforward and unambiguous ("the trial judge shall not participate in plea discussions"). In most of these states, there is case law supporting the court rule (sometimes, a holding; more often, *dicta*).[13] What effect do these legal cues have upon judicial participation in plea negotiations? Table 8-3 presents these data, comparing judges in states with and without court rules prohibiting judicial participation.[14]

In states having court rules that prohibit judicial participation in plea discussions, judges are much less likely to get involved. Only about 8 percent of judges in these states, compared with 31 percent of judges in states without court rules, report participating in discussions. Court rules do not suppress all instances of judicial participation, but the number of noncompliers is quite low.[15] In no state does the proportion of noncompliers exceed 15 percent. Indeed, in both North Dakota and the District of Columbia, not a single judge reported any behavior other than ratification.

Our observations provide additional support for these data. In Pennsylvania we observed three judges who heard some criminal cases as part of their current assignment. In Philadelphia, both of the criminal court judges observed restricted their role to ratification of agreements; both judges mentioned the court rule as a reference point for their lack of involvement. In rural Pennsylvania we observed a general assignment judge to ratify seven guilty pleas in open court over the course of a week. During this time, we saw him present at (but not participating in) one informal plea session in chambers. Thus, we have every reason to believe that judges' self-reports of their role in this sensitive area parallel rather closely what they in fact do.

There are no analogous court rules of civil procedure that prohibit or attempt to discourage judicial participation in civil settlement discussions. Some states (e.g., California) actually mandate settlement conferences before a judge

**TABLE 8-3.** The Impact of Court Rules upon Trial Judges' Style in Plea Discussions

| Judicial Style in Plea Discussions | Court Rule Prohibiting Judicial Participation | No Court Rule |
|---|---|---|
| Recommend | 1.4% | 8.6% |
| Review | 6.8 | 22.6 |
| Attend | 4.8 | 3.4 |
| Ratify | 87.0 | 65.4 |
| Number | (353) | (1834) |

in civil cases meeting certain criteria (e.g., where there is a demand for jury trial or a trial time estimate of five days or longer). These conferences are typically conducted several months before the trial date in the chambers of a judge, who may actively intervene in the discussions.[16]

But what about possible spillover effects? Do judges in states with court rules against judicial participation in plea discussions tend to curtail their civil settlement role? Our data suggest not. Neither civil judges nor general assignment judges appear to be influenced in their civil negotiation role by legal guidelines applicable to a criminal negotiation role. Thus, a "role transference" model does *not* apply in states with restrictive rules of criminal procedure. In these states, judges draw a rather clear distinction between what they do in civil and criminal negotiation work.

Case law in the states is a more difficult legal reference point to measure accurately. Most states have case law that upholds the practice of plea bargaining generally. But only a few state supreme courts have spoken to the issue of judicial participation in plea bargaining. In states where court rules adverse to judicial participation already exist, the case law is typically supportive, directly or in *dicta*.[17] In other states, high courts have exhibited a tendency to comment that judicial participation may not be the best practice but that it is *not* inherently coercive.[18] The nuances of wording in many of these cases, however, preclude systematic analysis. We can only suggest that there is some correlation between existing state case law on judicial participation and the frequency with which judges in particular states participate in plea discussions.[19] Again, cues applicable to a negotiation role in criminal cases are not likely to be related to the negotiation style adopted by judges in civil cases.

## COURT STRUCTURE

Several elements of court structure bear decisively upon the role a trial judge adopts in negotiation. Size of court, as we would expect, is related to judicial style: In larger courts, judges are more likely to participate in both plea and civil settlement discussions. Figure 8-1 displays a summary of these relationships, by comparing the frequency with which judges recommend or review criminal dispositions and intervene aggressively or subtly in civil negotiations, across courts of different size.

The figure indicates a general rise in judicial participation in plea and settlement discussions as the size of court increases. For plea discussions, the sharpest increment occurs in courts with sixteen or more judges. The percentage of judges who take the lead in *recommending* dispositions jumps threefold. For civil settlement discussions, the most significant rise in the proportion of judges who intervene *aggressively* occurs in courts with twenty-six or more judges. These data generally conform to the relationships between size of court and the frequency and amount of time spent by judges in plea and settlement discussions.[20]

Why are judges more likely to participate in negotiations as the size of their

FIGURE 8-1. Frequency of Judicial Participation in Plea and Settlement Discussions by Size of Court

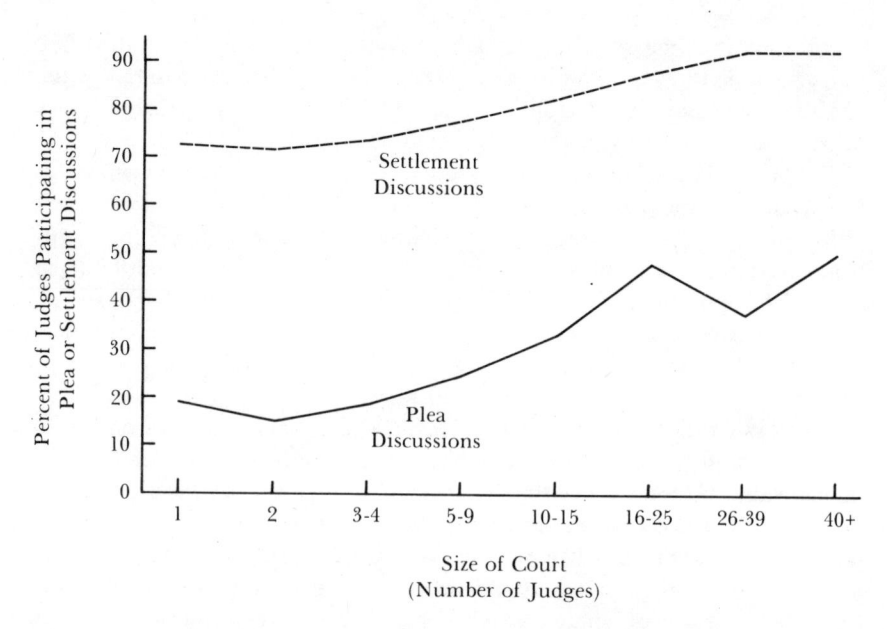

——— Recommend dispositions or review recommendations of counsel (n = 2156)
------- Intervene aggressively or subtly (n = 2509)

court increases? To a significant extent, the answer lies in the characteristics of the cases and procedures in larger courts, as well as the attorneys and judges who inhabit larger courts. These courts have, whether by choice or not, a work environment more conducive to adversarial negotiation. Larger courts are more likely to attract contentious attorneys, more likely to generate greater caseload pressures, and more likely to recruit judges who are—or who become—skilled at negotiation. We explore the relationships between these variables and judicial role in negotiation in the balance of this chapter.

A court's utilization of the master calendar is significantly related to the style that its judges adopt in *civil* pretrial negotiations. Where a master calendar is in effect, 20 percent of the judges intervene aggressively, compared with only 9 percent with an individual calendar. These differences become more pronounced in larger courts, which are better able to utilize judicial specialization.[21] For example, large courts typically feel comfortable in assigning many settlement conferences to a few judges. By contrast, in small courts the pressures or informal norms encouraging judges to carry a full trial caseload are greater.

The utilization of a master calendar may result in a more aggressive judicial stance in civil pretrial negotiations also because of the likelihood that the negotiating judge will not be the trial judge. As we mentioned earlier, mandatory settlement conferences represent a distinct stage in case processing, which occurs well before the actual trial date. When the trial judge himself attempts to negotiate a disposition on the trial date or during the trial, as often occurs, it is likely that he will not intervene quite so aggressively or directly. To do so would be to risk the appearance of his impartiality, or at least his willingness to hear both sides in an adversary forum.

Master calendar systems are also much more likely to establish work cycles conducive to intensive use of settlement conferences. Only one judge in ten sits in a court that sets aside one or more weeks entirely for settlement conferences, but most of these courts utilize a master calendar. While some judges hear only settlement conferences, other judges can hear trials so as to keep the court from grinding to an apparent halt. Such coordination can rarely be achieved when all judges have an individual calendar.

On the criminal side, the use of master calendars does not generate more judicial participation in plea discussions. The master calendar in criminal courts tends to break up, or prevent the formation of, the stable workgroups needed to encourage a system of plea bargaining in which the judge participates.[22] Familiarity with attorneys, especially with the prosecutor, is an important ingredient in judicial involvement in criminal negotiations.

Circuit-riding is another aspect of court structure that bears upon judicial style in civil (but not criminal) negotiations. Judges who ride circuit are *less* likely to intervene aggressively or subtly in settlement discussions. This remains true when circuit-riding judges and their stationary counterparts are compared in similar-size courts. Precisely how or why circuit-riding discourages aggressive judicial intervention in civil cases is not fully clear. Nor is the lack of impact on judicial participation in plea discussions readily explainable. Further research is needed to explore the interpersonal dynamics that characterize the life of the circuit-riding judge.[23]

## ATTORNEYS

The characteristics of practicing attorneys also contribute to the style a judge will adopt in criminal or civil pretrial negotiations. Such factors as the stability of attorney workgroup members, their skill at negotiation (as perceived by judges), and their level of adversariness influence judicial style in negotiations.

In criminal courts, attorneys are quite likely to become familiar with one another, and the judge, in turn, becomes familiar with them. This occurs primarily through the mechanism of assignment: Prosecutors and public defenders are often assigned to one courtroom for a period of time before being rotated to another courtroom (see Table 4-5). Eisenstein and Jacob find that the resultant familiarity among workgroup members is an important element in facilitating negotiated dispositions in urban felony courts.[24] Our survey data suggest some support, and some refinement, of this idea. We find a *curvilinear* relationship between stability of the prosecutor and judicial style

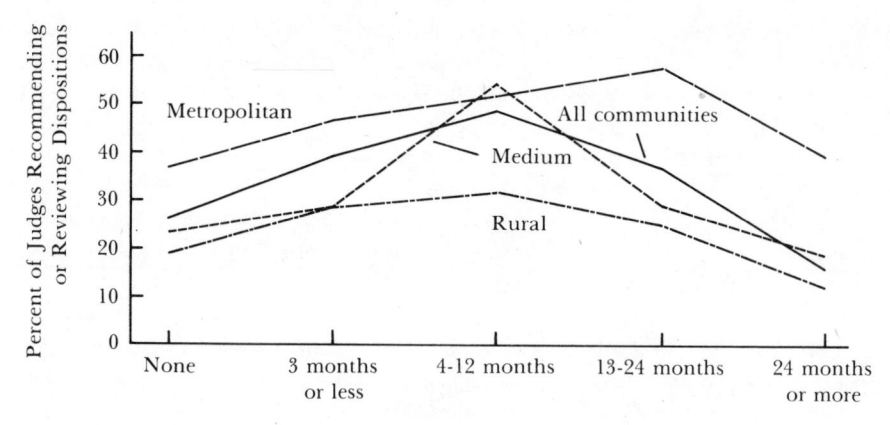

```
                    60
                    50    Metropolitan              All communities
                    40                    Medium
                    30                    Rural
                    20
                    10
                     0
                   None    3 months    4-12 months   13-24 months   24 months
                           or less                                  or more
```

Length of Prosecutor's Stay in Courtroom

```
──────────   All communities      (n = 2106)
── ── ──     Metropolitan only    (n =  503)
- - - - - -  Medium cities, etc.  (n =  957)
─·─·─·─      Rural only           (n =  597)
```

**FIGURE 8-2.** The Impact of Prosecutor Stability upon Trial Judges' Participation in Plea Discussions

in negotiation in criminal cases. A higher frequency of judicial participation in plea discussions—recommending or reviewing dispositions—occurs when prosecutors are assigned to the same felony courtroom for up to two years. Lower levels of judicial participation occur both when prosecutors are not regularly assigned to the same courtroom *and* when prosecutors are assigned to, or regularly appear in, the same courtroom for longer than two years. Figure 8-2 displays this curvilinear relationship, in all communities and in communities of different sizes.

Judicial participation in plea discussions increases as the stability of the prosecutor increases, up to a certain point. The peak of judicial participation typically occurs where prosecutors are assigned for a period between four and twelve months. In metropolitan communities, however, the peak occurs with more prosecutorial stability—between one and two years. Declines in the rate of participation are rather abrupt, especially among judges who report the same prosecutor(s) in their courtroom for two years or more. The substantial relationship between community size and negotiation style does not affect the relationship of prosecutor stability with negotiation style. In all types of community, this latter relationship is curvilinear: Judges reporting moderate stability of prosecutors are more likely to participate in plea discussions than those who report no stability or lengthy stability.

Judges are encouraged to participate in plea negotiations when a basis for interpersonal familiarity with the prosecutor exists. At some point when the prosecutor becomes so familiar with the judge that he knows—and perhaps internalizes as his own—the judge's sentencing preferences, it may no longer be necessary for the judge to be present at plea discussions. The trial judge and the prosecutor have become a "team," trusting in each other's judgment and knowing each other's mind.[25] The public defender or private defense counsel, by contrast, appears to be much less important to judicial behavior in plea discussions. Their stability is, at best, only slightly related to judicial participation in plea discussions, in a similarly curvilinear way. We generally observed defense counsel to be the least important link in the workgroup network, though this varied by attorney and by judge. Where defense counsel were viewed as dilatory (without good reason) or where judges were tough sentencers, prosecutor–judge teams flourished.

On the civil side, where stability of attorneys is primarily a function of community size, we find no relationship with judicial style in settlement discussions. Judges are not more likely to intervene where civil cases are concentrated among a smaller number of attorneys. Perhaps the needed increment in familiarity cannot be achieved in civil courts: The difference between working with forty-five as opposed to fifteen plaintiff and defense attorneys—for a group of fifty cases—may not be significant to judges. Both situations may preclude the kind of interpersonal familiarity present in criminal courts having one or two prosecutors and a few defense counsel.

It is the skill of civil attorneys at settlement—rather than their stability—that influences the style of the trial judge in negotiations. Where attorneys are more skilled at settlement (in the eyes of the judge), judges are *less* likely to intervene in settlement discussions. Table 8–4 presents these data. The percentage of judges who do not intervene in settlement discussions is highest (28 percent) where judges perceive attorney settlement skills to be "excellent." As judges' evaluations of attorneys' skills decline, so does the proportion of judges who leave settlement entirely to the attorneys. At the extreme, more than one-quarter of judges intervene aggressively when they perceive attorneys to be "poor" at settlement.

Trial judges respond to the skills of civil attorneys in negotiation work by

TABLE 8–4. The Impact of Civil Attorney Skill at Settlement upon Trial Judges' Style in Settlement Discussions

| Judicial Style in Settlement Discussions | Civil Attorney Skill at Settlement | | | | |
|---|---|---|---|---|---|
|  | Excellent | Above Average | Average | Below Average | Poor |
| Aggressive | 11.7% | 10.8% | 9.5% | 11.2% | 28.0% |
| Subtle | 59.8 | 65.4 | 71.2 | 70.3 | 60.0 |
| No intervention | 28.5 | 23.8 | 19.3 | 18.5 | 12.0 |
| Number | (137) | (899) | (1194) | (205) | (25) |

modifying both their own style of intervention and time spent in negotiations. Although judges who report average or poorer settlement skills in attorneys spend less time in settlement discussions (see Chapter 4), they are likely to intervene aggressively. Judges may not like to work with attorneys who are less skilled at settlement, but if circumstances dictate their presence they will try to apply some extra measure of pressure. In this way, judges can achieve a disposition if not the aesthetic pleasure experienced through working with skilled attorneys.

Finally, the level of attorney adversariness influences how active a judge will be in criminal and civil negotiation work. Where judges are confronted with contentious attorneys who require longer hours to complete a standard jury trial, judges become more aggressive participants in plea and settlement discussions. Table 8–5 presents the data for plea discussions.

There are large differences in estimated trial times for a typical armed robbery jury case, depending upon the judge's style in plea discussions. For judges who only ratify agreements, the average of reported trial times is 14.5 hours; but this figure jumps approximately two hours for each increment in judicial involvement in discussions. Judges who recommend dispositions to counsel in plea discussions face about one extra working day for each (armed robbery) jury trial. These large differences remain intact when controls for court size or community size are imposed. Thus, the prospect of long trials in criminal cases—usually generated by contentious attorney practices in a community—clearly induces judges to take a more active role in trying to insure a disposition without recourse to trial.

This same kind of influence also is at work in civil cases, though its effect is smaller. Table 8–6 presents these data. Differences in trial time estimates on the civil side are noticeably smaller: Only two and one-half hours separate the most and least active judges in settlement discussions, compared with nearly six hours in plea discussions. Nevertheless, the relationship is still sizable, especially between judges who do not intervene at all and other judges who do intervene. The small differences between those who intervene aggressively as opposed to subtly may suggest that "aggressive" and "subtle" are in fact characteristic of style rather than a substantive difference in the level of participation in discussions.

TABLE 8–5. The Impact of Trial Time Pressures upon Judges' Style in Plea Discussions

| Judicial Style in Plea Discussions | ($\overline{X}$) Hours Needed to Conduct Typical Armed Robbery Jury Trial | Number |
|---|---|---|
| Recommend | 20.2 | (146) |
| Review | 18.2 | (390) |
| Attend | 16.7 | (76) |
| Ratify | 14.5 | (1383) |

## TABLE 8-6. The Impact of Trial Time Pressures upon Judges' Style in Civil Settlement Discussions

| Judicial Style in Settlement Discussions | ($\bar{X}$) Hours Needed to Conduct Typical Personal Injury Jury Trial | Number |
|---|---|---|
| Aggressive | 16.1 | (222) |
| Subtle | 15.4 | (1474) |
| No intervention | 13.6 | (498) |

## JUDICIAL PERCEPTIONS

Trial judges' perceptions of their work environment also play an important part in shaping the style they will adopt in plea and settlement discussions. One key element of the work environment is caseload, an area where judges generally feel under too much pressure (see Figure 7–3). Judges who feel themselves surrounded by great pressure to move cases are more likely to be actively involved in negotiations. Though the differences are small with respect to plea discussions, they are sizable for settlement discussions. Judges who intervene aggressively on the civil side feel more case pressures ($\bar{x}$ = 5.2) than those who intervene subtly ($\bar{x}$ = 4.9) or not at all ($\bar{x}$ = 4.5). These differences remain equally large after controls for size of court and community.

Our findings on the impact of caseload pressure mirror those for trial time pressures, suggesting that these variables tap different yet related aspects of workload pressures. If attorney adversariness is a key component of trial time durations, it is also likely to influence how judges feel about case pressures generally. Judges, then, feel pressured to move cases when they and their courts "fall behind" because of contentious, highly adversarial attorneys.

A second area of judicial perceptions quite crucial to style of criminal and civil negotiation work involves self-attributions. Judges who perceive that they are skilled at negotiation are much more likely to participate actively and aggressively in plea and settlement discussions. Table 8–7 demonstrates the rela-

## TABLE 8-7. The Impact of Trial Judges' Skill at Negotiation upon Their Style in Plea Discussions

| Judicial Style in Plea Discussions | Judges' Self-Rated Skill at Negotiation ||||| 
|---|---|---|---|---|---|
|  | Excellent | Above Average | Average | Below Average | Poor |
| Recommend | 23.1% | 6.5% | 4.4% | 2.5% | 2.0% |
| Review | 25.3 | 28.0 | 17.2 | 9.9 | 6.1 |
| Attend | 3.7 | 3.1 | 4.2 | 4.0 | 6.1 |
| Ratify | 47.9 | 62.4 | 74.2 | 83.6 | 85.8 |
| Number | (320) | (675) | (801) | (202) | (49) |

TABLE 8-8. The Impact of Trial Judges' Skill at Negotiation upon Their Style in Civil Settlement Discussions

| Judicial Style in Settlement Discussions | JUDGES' SELF-RATED SKILL AT NEGOTIATION ||||| 
|---|---|---|---|---|---|
| | Excellent | Above Average | Average | Below Average | Poor |
| Aggressive | 29.4% | 14.3% | 3.4% | .8% | 1.8% |
| Subtle | 64.8 | 75.5 | 71.4 | 62.1 | 21.8 |
| No intervention | 5.8 | 10.2 | 25.2 | 37.1 | 76.4 |
| Number | (381) | (807) | (913) | (237) | (55) |

tionship for criminal negotiation work. The impact of judges' views of their own negotiating skill is substantial. About half of all judges who believe they are excellent at negotiation participate in plea discussions, either by recommending dispositions to counsel or reviewing their recommendations. The proportion who participate in plea discussions drops to one judge in three among those who rate themselves above average, one in five for judges who see themselves as average, and only one judge in ten for those who rate their negotiating skill as below average or poor.

The pervasiveness of the influence of self-perceived skill is perhaps best seen by examining judges in states having court rules prohibiting judicial participation in plea discussions. In these states, relatively few judges defy, or fail to comply with, their state court rule. But the few noncomplying judges disproportionately include those who see themselves as excellent or above average at negotiation. Thus, even where officially sanctioned cues to the contrary exist, judges sometimes participate in plea discussions if they believe they are skilled at negotiation.

The influence of trial judges' perceptions of their negotiating skill is equally dramatic in civil settlement discussions. Table 8-8 reports these data. The percentage of judges who intervene aggressively in civil settlement discussions rises substantially as judges evaluate more favorably their own negotiating skill. The range runs from a low of 2 percent among judges who feel they are poor at negotiating to 29 percent of those who feel they are excellent. Similarly, the percentage of judges who do not intervene at all rises dramatically as judges view their negotiating skills more critically. Fully three-fourths of the few judges who believe they are poor at negotiation do not intervene in settlement discussions.

Thus, the response of judges to their own general skill at negotiating appears to be parallel in criminal and civil cases. In both arenas, it is the judges who become involved in the "rough and tumble" of negotiation—assuming an activist posture in mediating disputes—who believe they are performing their work with the highest skill.

## PERSONAL AND PROFESSIONAL BACKGROUND OF THE JUDGE

The social background and professional experience of judges have very little influence upon the style they adopt in their negotiation work. It is not surprising that social characteristics—age, race, gender, and legal heritage—are unrelated, for there are no clear theoretical grounds on which to posit hypotheses about the effects of these variables upon judicial style in negotiation. More surprising is the lack of influence of variables reflective of the socialization or learning experiences of judges—specifically, years on the bench and teaching experiences in judicial education programs.

As judges grow in experience and maturity on the bench, one might expect that they would become more comfortable with an active posture in pretrial negotiation work. Newcomer judges, in particular, could be expected to experiment with different approaches before settling upon one normal style of negotiation. But such is not the case in either criminal or civil work. Though judges may quickly learn about the realities of plea bargaining[26] or about the techniques of civil negotiation, judges appear *not* to alter their basic style of negotiation over time. They may refine or improve their techniques, but the decision to participate or not to participate in plea and settlement discussions is determined by other factors, probably at an early point in the judicial career.[27]

Likewise, participation in teaching judicial education programs could be expected to socialize judges to a more activist role in pretrial negotiations. One general intent of judicial education courses—especially courses on administration—is to sensitize judges to the need for "court control" of the docket.[28] Presumably, some judges would associate court control with the need to take control of, or at least influence, plea and settlement discussions. But this is not borne out by our data. Judges who have taught in judicial education programs are neither more nor less likely to participate in plea or settlement discussions than other judges. Participation in the creative process of judicial education courses appears to make no difference in style of negotiation. It is quite likely, though we do not have comparable data, that mere attendance at judicial education programs also makes no difference in basic judicial style toward negotiation.[29]

Only one variable—immediate prior occupation—shows any relationship with judicial negotiating style. Judges who came to the bench directly from private practice are *less* likely to participate in plea discussions or to intervene aggressively in civil settlement discussions than judges who rose from a lower court. This lack of participation is especially characteristic of former private practitioners with a civil practice who now serve on the criminal bench and those from a criminal practice who now serve on the civil bench. These relationships conform quite closely to the impact of prior occupation on judicial time in plea and settlement discussions (see Table 6-7).

The general absence of relationships between personal/professional background characteristics of the judge and his style in negotiation may camouflage the real influences of personality, which are so difficult to measure. Some judges may choose a more active style of negotiation simply because they are, by nature, extroverted or aggressive human beings.

## Synthesizing the Causes of Variation in Judicial Negotiating Styles

We have described in this chapter a number of variables that are related to judicial style in criminal negotiations, civil negotiations, or both. These include legally relevant cues, elements of court structure, characteristics of attorneys, and judicial perceptions. But which of these are most important, that is, the ones that most influence trial judges' negotiating style? And how well do these variables, taken together, account for differences in negotiating style? These questions can most clearly be addressed through the use of multivariate statistical analysis.

Stepwise multiple regression determines the effect of each explanatory variable upon judicial negotiating style, controlling for the effects of many other variables simultaneously.[30] In previous analyses, we have examined a relationship controlling for one variable (often size of court or community). Through stepwise regression, we can control for the effects of *all* other explanatory variables (for which we have data). Thus, through this procedure we can assess the causes of variation in judicial negotiating style in a more accurate and statistically sound way. We shall also be better able to contrast the variables that influence the criminal and civil negotiating styles of judges.

Table 8-9 reports the summary of stepwise multiple regression indicating which variables, from among those included in the analysis, are significant predictors of negotiating styles, the relative weight (importance) of each variable vis-à-vis the others ("beta weights"), and the overall amount of variation in judicial styles accounted for by these variables ($R^2$). This analysis was performed first for judges who hear some criminal cases in their current assignment (for criminal negotiating style), then for judges who hear some civil cases in their current assignment (for civil negotiating style).

Table 8-9 closely confirms the earlier analysis in this chapter. Most of the variables that are related in an associational way to judicial participation in plea and settlement discussions remain causal predictors.

On the criminal side, five variables effectively predict variations in judicial negotiating style. The most important of these is the judge's perception of his own skill at negotiating; the next most important is the presence of a court rule prohibiting judicial participation. Three other variables are about equally important: attorney adversariness, attorney stability, and the judge's current assignment. Overall, these predictors together account for 18 percent of the

TABLE 8-9. Causes of Variation in Judicial Styles in Plea and Settlement Discussions: A Summary

| Judicial Style in Criminal Negotiations | Beta | Judicial Style in Civil Negotiations | Beta |
|---|---|---|---|
| Judge's negotiating skill (self-perceived) | .22 | Judge's negotiating skill (self-perceived) | .37 |
| Court rule prohibiting judicial participation | −.18 | Circuit-riding | −.08 |
| | | Attorney negotiating skill | −.08 |
| Judge's assignment[a] | .14 | Caseload pressures | .08 |
| Trial time pressures | .13 | Case assignment system[c] | .08 |
| Stability of prosecuting attorneys[b] | .12 | | |
| R = .42 | | R = .43 | |
| $R^2$ = 18% | | $R^2$ = 19% | |
| N = 1777 | | N = 1940 | |

[a] Criminal assignment coded high; general assignment coded low.
[b] Moderate stability (three months or less to two years) coded high; no stability or stability greater than two years coded low.
[c] Master calendar coded high; individual calendar coded low.

variation in negotiating style, suggesting that much of the variation is either random or accounted for by variables not included in our study.

On the civil side, five variables also are effective predictors of differences in judicial negotiating style. The relative importance of one variable, however, far outweighs the others. The judge's perception of his own skill at negotiating is probably more important than all of the other four variables taken together, as suggested by the wide disparity in beta weights. Overall, the five variables together account for 19 percent of the variation in negotiating style, again indicating that much of the variation is left unexplained.

Comparing the influences that affect the trial judge in criminal as opposed to civil negotiations, we note both similarities and differences. In both areas of negotiation, the judge's view of his skill at negotiation is important. In both areas, some form of case pressure—exerted either through the length of trials or in a more general way—is important. We attribute much of these pressures to attorney adversariness. But there are differences between criminal and civil negotiations. Court rules exist in some states to prohibit trial judges from participating in plea discussions, and these prohibitions have some effect. No such prohibitions exist on the civil side. Attorney stability and familiarity with the judge facilitate judicial participation in criminal negotiations but appear to have no influence or application on the civil side. By contrast, the presence of a master calendar and the absence of circuit-riding responsibilities each contributes to judicial participation in civil negotiations.

The one variable whose influence Table 8-9 masks is size of court. It is true that size of court does not remain a distinguishable predictor of variation in negotiating styles, but this is because the effects of court size are diffused across many variables. Court size and community size are "trigger mechanisms," which set in motion the panoply of forces that shape judicial negotiating style. These forces include negotiating skill of the judge (perceived to be higher in larger courts), attorney adversariness and case pressure (greater in larger courts), and type of case assignment system (more likely to be master calendar in larger courts). It is through these variables, and therefore indirectly, that the effects of organizational and community size occur.

## Summary

Negotiation is a subtle and often controversial aspect of a trial court's work. The judge's role in negotiation is at the core of this controversy, partly because there are several legitimate options available to the judge. Ranging from active through passive forms of participation to total lack of involvement, these options broadly reflect competing interpretations of the functions and purposes of the trial judge. Is he to be an umpire, referee, peace-keeper, dispute-resolver, or mover of cases? Each of these images suggests a slightly different way of approaching the work of negotiation.

We find that trial judges participate more often and more aggressively in civil pretrial negotiations than criminal. This reflects the greater legitimacy typically accorded judicial intervention in civil cases, where negotiation usually centers on money rather than individual liberty. This legitimacy is reinforced by court rules in seven states, the District of Columbia, and the federal jurisdiction prohibiting judicial participation in plea discussions, and by similar case law or *dicta* in a number of additional states.

Beyond legal cues, we find a number of other variables to be important in explaining differences in judicial participation in plea and civil settlement discussions. In particular, judges' perceptions of their own skill at negotiation are most important, for criminal and especially civil negotiations. On the criminal side, trial time pressures, the nature of the judge's assignment, and the stability of prosecuting attorneys in the judge's courtroom also exhibit a significant supporting influence. On the civil side, however, the judge's skill at negotiating is by far the most important influence. This reflects the presence of fewer constraints in processing civil cases. No court rules or case law comment, adversely or otherwise, upon judicial participation in settlement discussions, and requirements for speedy resolution of the civil docket have yet to be articulated or demanded by law. Thus, the trial judge's freedom of action in defining an appropriate role in negotiations is much greater in civil cases, enabling him to rely primarily on his own skills, interests, and preferences.

Other variables for which we do not have systematic data also help to shape judicial negotiating style. These variables probably include the personality of the judge, the norms of local courts, the beliefs of judicial colleagues and chief judges, and the behavior of public versus private defense attorneys. Our observations suggest that these variables do influence the style of negotiation that a judge will adopt, perhaps equally or more substantially than the variables we have been able to measure quantitatively.

Negotiation accounts for only a small portion of a judge's work day, but it is inherent in the work of criminal and civil courts. No courts can survive without a significant proportion of negotiated dispositions. Whether a judge ultimately comes to participate in this process or not, he will have to confront the propriety of his own participation. In doing so, he will be influenced by some of the same organizational and individual-level variables that shape his general work patterns.

# Notes

1. James Eisenstein and Herbert Jacob, *Felony Justice: An Organizational Analysis of Criminal Courts* (Boston: Little, Brown, 1977); Milton Heumann, *Plea Bargaining: The Experiences of Prosecutors, Judges, and Defense Attorneys* (Chicago: University of Chicago Press, 1977); and H. Laurence Ross, *Settled Out of Court* (Chicago: Aldine 1970).
2. Perhaps the most influential of all have been the American Bar Association's *Standards Relating to Pleas of Guilty*. The Standard 3.3(a), prohibiting judicial participation in plea discussions prior to agreement by counsel, has been widely quoted and referenced in the case law, in court rules, and in commission studies.
3. See, for example, Gerard A. Ferguson, "The Role of the Judge in Plea Bargaining," *Criminal Law Quarterly*, 15 (1972).
4. See the commentary accompanying Standard 3.3(a) in A.B.A., *Standards Relating to Pleas of Guilty*.
5. See, for example, *State v. Wolfe*, 46 Wis.2d 478, 175 N.W. 2d 216 (1970), and *People v. Montgomery*, 27 N.Y.2d 601, 261 N.E. 2d 409 (1970). Nevertheless, in states where court rules *prohibit* judicial participation, convictions pursuant to judicial involvement have been overturned, notably in Colorado (*People v. Clark*, 183 Colo. 201, 515 P.2d 1242, 1973) and in Pennsylvania (*Commonwealth v. Evans*, 434 Pa. 52, 252 A.2d 689, 1969).
6. For a discussion of sentencing as a judicial function, see the American Bar Association's *Standards Relating to Sentencing Alternatives and Procedures*. Standard 1.1 states that "authority to determine the sentence should be vested in the trial judge."
7. The length of delay and the size of backlogs is likely to be much greater on the civil side of a court's docket. See Thomas Church, Jr., Alan Carlson, Jo-Lynne Lee, and Teresa Tan, *Justice Delayed: The Pace of Litigation in Urban Trial Courts* (Williamsburg, Va.: National Center for State Courts, 1978).
8. This comports with the relatively low percentage of judges who report time spent in plea discussions (as discussed in Chapter 2).
9. Our survey data indicate that the average trial time for a typical personal injury case across all judges in this court is 14.8 hours, slightly below the national average ($\bar{x}$ = 15.1), and well below the average for metropolitan areas ($\bar{x}$ = 17.0).

10. Even more interesting would be comparisons between judges who move from a criminal to civil assignment, or vice versa. We do not have this type of data available, however, because our survey respondents were restricted in their answers to their current assignment.
11. For a recent analysis of the judicial rule-making process, see Charles W. Grau, *Judicial Rulemaking: Administration, Access, and Accountability* (Chicago: American Judicature Society, 1978).
12. See Ariz. R. Crim. P. 17.4(a); Ark. R. Crim. P. 25; Colo. R. Crim. P. 11(f)(4); N.M. R. Crim. P. 21(g)(1); N.D. R. Crim. P. 11(d)(1); Ore. Rev. Stat. § 135.432(1); Pa. R. Crim. P. 319(b)(1); D.C. R. Crim. P. 11(e)(1). The Federal Rules of Criminal Procedure provide for a similar ban; see Fed. R. Crim. P. 11(e)(1).
13. See *Rose* v. *Gladden*, 248 Or. 520, 433 P.2d 612 (1967); *People* v. *Clark* and *Commonwealth* v. *Evans*, (note 5 above).
14. Only in two other states do the rules of criminal procedure directly speak to the issue of judicial participation in plea discussions. In Illinois judicial *initiation* of discussions is prohibited. In Florida the commentary to the rules state that no ban on judicial participation is intended.
15. It is not clear whether mere attendance at plea discussions is to be construed as participation. State supreme courts have interpreted attendance in different ways; for example, compare *State* v. *Wolfe* (note 5 above) with *Commonwealth* v. *Evans*.
16. In some courts, the judge who conducts a mandatory settlement conference may *not* be the same judge who would conduct the trial, if settlement efforts fail. This is invariably true in California, where rules of the state judicial council mandate a master calendar for civil cases. See note 14 in Chapter 3.
17. See note 13 above.
18. See, for example, *State* v. *Johnson*, 279 Minn. 209, 156 N.W.2d 218 (1968), and *People* v. *Montgomery* (note 5 above).
19. For a more extended discussion, see John Paul Ryan and James J. Alfini, "Trial Judges' Participation in Plea Bargaining: An Empirical Perspective," *Law and Society Reveiw*, 13 (1979).
20. For plea discussions, our data in Chapter 3 suggested a *step-level* rather than linear relationship with size of court in which the primary jump occurs in courts with forty or more judges.
21. These findings dovetail very closely with the suggested impacts of a master calendar upon time spent in settlement discussions. See Chapter 3.
22. See Chapter 4 for an extended discussion of how master and individual case assignment systems impact upon the stability of prosecutors and public defenders.
23. One important question would focus upon the time spans (intervals) that typically occur between trips to the same courthouse (weekly, monthly, semimonthly).
24. See Eisenstein and Jacob, *Felony Justice* (note 1 above).
25. Whereas we easily observed prosecutor-judge "teams" in action when the judge actively participated in plea discussions, it was quite difficult to observe teams who worked only through shared assumptions—i.e., when the judge ratified agreements made in anticipation of his preferences.

26. Heumann, *Plea Bargaining* (note 1 above).
27. Our cross-sectional data preclude definitive treatment of this question, but the data are at least highly suggestive of the influence of other variables.
28. One major influence in the movement advocating "court control" has been the work of Ernest Friesen, Joseph Jordan, and Alfred Sulmonetti, *Arrest to Trial in Forty-Five Days* (Los Angeles: Whittier College School of Law, 1978). Friesen and his colleagues have addressed numerous audiences, including courses at the National Judicial College in Reno.
29. Very few courses in state or national judicial education programs focus upon negotiation in civil or criminal cases. Rather, the primary emphasis is given to substantive law and adjudicative skills, with secondary attention to court management (case scheduling, juror utilization, etc.). See *Survey of State Judicial Education and Training Programs, 1974-1976* (Washington, D.C.: American University Law Institute, 1978).
30. Our use of stepwise multiple regression is primarily intended to corroborate the bivariate analysis presented earlier in this chapter. There is much debate as to whether multiple regression should be performed on ordinal-level data (such as most of the independent variables in our analysis). Nevertheless, Ted Robert Gurr, *Politimetrics* (Englewood Cliffs: Prentice-Hall, 1972), p. 134, suggests that most ordinal data probably can be viewed as interval or ratio data, thereby making them amenable to higher-powered statistical tests. Sanford Labovitz, "Some Observations on Measurements and Statistics," *Social Forces,* 56 (1967), found that after empirical testing the use of ordinal data does not introduce significant biases in multiple regression analysis.

## CHAPTER 9

# The Social, Political, and Legal Environments of Courts: Judging in Chicago, Los Angeles, and Philadelphia

TRIAL judging is performed in a variety of settings within the confines of the larger social and political environment. No judge works as a "national trial judge." Rather, judges work in living communities surrounded by citizens, media, government, and politics. It is this important reality that needs to be captured in any national study of trial judges. In this chapter we examine the impact of community upon the work of judging in three large urban courts: Chicago, Los Angeles, and Philadelphia. We selected these particular courts because of their size (all have forty or more judges) and the availability of qualitative data from our observations.[1]

We first provide the political and social setting within which each city's courts are located. After a brief description of the three courts, their chief judges, and the visibility of the courts in the local community, we turn to a comparison of the recruitment and social characteristics of the judges. In particular, we emphasize the links between partisan politics in the community and the requirements of political apprenticeship for judges. Our primary focus in the chapter is upon the comparative work and work styles of judges in the three communities. Special attention is given to bench–bar relationships and to the influence of politics in the performance of judicial work.[2] Finally, we bring together the themes of attorney–judge relations and political influences in the context of case management and the problems of trial court backlogs and delay.[3]

## Three Cities and Their Courts

CHICAGO

To its inhabitants, Chicago is a city of striking heterogeneity and contrasts dramatized by a magnificently modern lakefront skyline, which hovers over the many racial and ethnic neighborhoods, barrios, and ghettos. For some of its affluent residents, Chicago is culturally and economically sophisticated and thriving, but for its many poor who depend disproportionately upon the mediocre level of the city's public services, it is simply a frost-belt slum.

To political historians, though, Chicago is no mixed metaphor. Whether viewed from the perspective of a St. Valentine's Massacre or the persistence of a political machine, Chicago is an understandable and straightforward phenomenon. The city has come to symbolize consummate partisan politics of the "blood and guts" variety: clout, connections, might makes right.[4] A large part of Chicago's contemporary political lore belongs to the late six-term Democratic mayor, Richard J. Daley. His two successors, in fact, battled each other for his ghost, invoking his name and memory at every opportunity in a closely contested primary election in 1979. To be sure, Daley was preceded by a long line of Democratic mayors, as far back as the early 1900s. Nevertheless, only in the Daley regime did the political–governmental nexus become complete: Daley alone served as mayor and as Cook County Democratic party chairman (a powerful patronage position).

It is within this rich but confining tradition that the judicial system and courts of Chicago are set. Physically, most of the city's criminal and civil courtrooms—which include countywide jurisdiction—are housed in three buildings: Civic (Daley) Center, Twenty-sixth and California, or Thirteenth and Michigan. Civic Center contains all of the county's major civil courts and some criminal courts, which hear mostly nonjury trials of bailed defendants having privately retained counsel. Twenty-sixth and California streets, a deteriorating commercial area isolated from downtown, is the site of an aging criminal courthouse and county jail, where judges hear mostly jury trials of jailed defendants represented by public defenders. Thirteenth Street and Michigan Avenue, a wholesale merchandising area nearer to downtown, is a recent addition to the complex of court buildings, and here too only criminal judges sit. Overall, the three buildings are two to five miles apart on routes not easily serviced by public transportation. In 1976 there were approximately 160 circuit judges in Cook County, the majority of whom were located in these three buildings.[5] Other circuit judges were sitting in neighborhood or suburban courts, hearing felony, misdemeanor, or traffic cases.[6]

## LOS ANGELES

Los Angeles is a city whose skyline is as recent as its political history. Growth in Los Angeles, both vertical and horizontal, is a contemporary phenomenon, mostly since World War II. It is home to the "youngest major American university" and the second home to a group of relocated Eastern sports franchises. Before the age of the jet, Los Angeles was truly part of the American frontier. Its only link to the larger society was through the movie industry, an image that (somewhat inappropriately) remains in the minds of most Americans today. While movies increasingly are filmed on location in side streets of New York or Chicago, Southern California residents move about their lives in much the same way and with much the same lack of glamour that characterizes Chicagoans or other urban and suburban dwellers.

Politically, however, Los Angeles is quite distinct from Chicago. Power and authority are as decentralized in Los Angeles as they are centralized in Chicago. In Chicago, the mayor overshadows and dominates second-level public officials to such a degree that they are largely unknown to the average citizen. In Los Angeles, second-level public officials develop power and constituent bases of their own, because there are no party slatemakers seeking to protect the base of the mayor. Furthermore, boards and commissions function much more independently in Los Angeles. For example, the board that appoints the police chief in Los Angeles screens, evaluates, and recommends candidates on the basis of written test scores as well as oral interviews. In Chicago, the police board merely conducts interviews with prospective candidates, thereby facilitating politically motivated interventions by the mayor. The result of these differences in the functioning of boards and commissions is apparent in the relative independence of the public officials selected. In retrospect, it is ironic that former Los Angeles mayor Sam Yorty's plea to a campaigning Senator Robert Kennedy that there was not much Yorty could do to improve trash collection in the black communities of Los Angeles was substantially true. Decentralization of power cuts many ways.

Los Angeles is also distinctively nonpartisan in its organization and delivery of public services. The Progressive era ethic that there is "no Democratic or Republican way to sweep the streets" is virtually institutionalized in Los Angeles, whereas in Chicago "regular" Democratic precincts are the first ones to have their streets plowed of snow. Most recent Los Angeles mayors have been Democrats, a feature of their background mostly incidental to their political beliefs or public policies. Sam Yorty, for example, was a four-term mayor in the 1960s and early 1970s who was constantly at odds with state and national leaders of his party. The present mayor, Tom Bradley, served in the city's police department for twenty years before becoming involved in electoral politics. Neither attempted to politicize, in a partisan way, the city's public services.

The Los Angeles County court system is geographically decentralized, reflecting the urban sprawl of the county itself. It is divided into nine districts, including a central district located in two buildings in a renovated area downtown. One older building—directly across the street from the Los Angeles Music Center—houses civil courts; this was the original county courthouse. A modern high-rise building stands a few blocks away and contains criminal courts. Criminal, civil, and general courtrooms are located in eight other districts, as far apart as Santa Monica and Pomona (50 miles) and also including Burbank, Long Beach, Norwalk, Pasadena, Torrance, and Van Nuys.[7] Slightly less than two-thirds of the county's 170 superior court judges sitting in 1976 served in the downtown central district; the remainder were dispersed fairly evenly among the other districts.[8]

PHILADELPHIA

Philadelphia is an Eastern city struggling to retain its identity and to recapture the vitality of its public life. It has several in-town universities and its own distinctive suburbs. It has its own media outlets, both newspapers and television stations. It is a city rich in political history, as reflected in the hosting of the American Bicentennial celebration. Yet Philadelphia remains overshadowed, physically and culturally, by its close neighbor, New York.

Politically, Philadelphia is more like Chicago than Los Angeles. Its mayor has institutional and informal powers akin to Chicago's, but the merging of political and bureaucratic resources—so effectively accomplished in Chicago—has never been complete in Philadelphia. Unlike most American cities, Philadelphia was governed by Republicans as late as the 1950s. Since then, a series of intraparty ideological squabbles have prevented the emergence of a unified Democratic party organization. As a result, Democratic mayors as different in ideology as Joseph Clark, James Tate, and Frank Rizzo have served. Philadelphia has both the schizophrenia of political personalities found in Los Angeles and the potential party machinery, patronage, and workers found in Chicago.

Philadelphia's courts, which have countywide jurisdiction, are located in several buildings in the downtown area of the city. Courtrooms are housed in City Hall and three other buildings, some of which are not within easy walking distance of one another. More peculiar, in many instances a judge's chambers and his assigned courtroom are in different buildings not necessarily near one another. One result is that judges use their chambers less than in other cities, preferring to have discussions with attorneys in the hallways or in "robing rooms" attached to the courtrooms. Some of these logistical problems may be alleviated by a proposed move of the civil courtrooms to the old federal building, now that a new federal courthouse shines above the downtown area. Despite these physical separations of one building from another, the Philadelphia courts are still centrally located and more proximate to one another than in either Chicago or Los Angeles. A "suburbanization" of the Philadelphia court system has not yet occurred. In 1976, eighty judges were sitting in the county's Court of Common Pleas.

## Three Chief Judges

The diversity of these cities is reflected in the position of chief judge and in the background of its occupants. The office of chief judge is becoming increasingly significant: In large and small courts alike, there is a recognized need for leadership and centralized management. Duties, responsibilities, and powers of chief judges vary from court to court, depending upon state court rules and the norms of the local court. Some chief judges are merely senior judges who act as liaison with the environments outside the court. Other chief judges, chosen for their administrative abilities, aggressively manage their courts. In the following section, we focus upon both the office and the three men who were serving as chief judge of the courts in Chicago, Los Angeles, and Philadelphia at the time of our field observations in 1976.

CHICAGO

John Boyle was the chief judge of the Cook County Circuit Court in 1976, as he had been since the Illinois court reorganization of 1964. At age seventy-six, he was also the court's patriarch. A graduate of DePaul University College of Law (a local Catholic school, which supplies fully one-third of the court's judges), Boyle served in key apprenticeships along his rise to judicial and political power in Chicago. Before ascending the bench, he was, in succession, assistant corporate counsel for the city, an assistant in the state's attorneys' office, alderman, and finally the elected state's attorney for Cook County. He served as chief judge of the criminal court before the consolidation of all courts in 1964. Judge Boyle's political credentials within the regular Democratic organization were impeccable: He served as an Illinois delegate to the Democratic national conventions of 1952, 1956, and 1960. His judicial credentials were viewed by some interest groups as far less than impeccable. The Chicago Council of Lawyers, a liberal activist group of lawyers, characterized Boyle as a "politician not judge" in their opposition to his retention on the bench in 1972. By 1978 more substantial groups came to oppose his retention (including the majority of the members of the Chicago Bar Association), and Boyle failed to capture the needed 60 percent affirmative vote in the retention election.

The powers of the chief judge in Chicago are considerable. He appoints the supervising judges of all divisions, assigns judges to divisions, and (by tradition) may even influence the distribution of work within divisions. Equally important, the chief judge typically can draw support from the Democratic organization because he owes his selection to the party. Though circuit judges formally "elect" their chief judge by secret ballot, the election is usually a ratification of the party's candidate.[9] The term of office is only one year, but by tradition the chief judge serves until he retires or is deposed by the voters or the party. Thus, his influence is a function of formal powers, political organization support, and lengthy tenure.

## LOS ANGELES

Robert Wenke was the chief judge of the Los Angeles County Superior Court in 1976, in the last year of his two-year term. Wenke's rise to power could not have been more different from Boyle's. A graduate of the University of Nebraska Law School and a member of its law review, he soon thereafter entered private law practice in Southern California. With no visible credentials, he was appointed by Governor Edmund G. Brown, Sr., in 1965 to the Long Beach municipal court, and elevated one year later to the superior court. (At the time of his appointment, Wenke was a registered Republican, but he changed to a Democratic party affiliation in 1968). Judge Wenke quickly developed a reputation for being the "judge's judge"—by extensive writings in the area of trial tactics, domestic relations, and judicial handbooks, and by affiliations and board memberships with national legal and court organizations. At age forty-eight, he became the court's chief judge, after serving the traditional two-year administrative apprenticeship as "assistant presiding judge."

The formal powers of the chief judge's office in Los Angeles are roughly analogous to those in Chicago: He appoints key leadership positions and assigns judges to divisions. Furthermore, there is a geographically wide range of locations to which he assigns judges. Unlike in Chicago, his tenure is fixed (two years) and nonrenewable. Also, he has no political party to call upon if he wishes to formally sanction an individual judge or to short-circuit the judges as a group. As a result, formal powers are exercised tamely and within a consensus framework. Leadership positions rotate frequently, and geographic exile is rarely imposed. Without the overriding presence of a one-party political organization, judicial power is more frequently and widely shared in Los Angeles.

## PHILADELPHIA

Edward Bradley was the chief judge of the Philadelphia Court of Common Pleas in 1976, serving in the second year of a five-year term. Like Boyle's, Bradley's educational and political roots lie in the local community; like Wenke, Bradley had a career in private practice. After graduating from the University of Pennsylvania Law School, Bradley entered private practice until tapped by Philadelphia's Democratic mayor Richardson Dilworth to be deputy city solicitor. Bradley served in that post for eight years, then was selected by Republican Governor William Scranton to fill an interim vacancy on the Philadelphia court in 1965. At age forty-seven he was selected by his colleagues to be President (chief) Judge of the Philadelphia court. Bradley is a lifelong Democrat whose family is well connected in city politics: His father had served as the Democratic party chairman in Philadelphia. Bradley was a beneficiary of a long-standing Northeastern tradition of "bipartisanship" in the appointment of judges.[10]

The chief judge's formal powers are weaker in Philadelphia. He does not appoint to key leadership positions, such as supervising judges of divisions (these are elected by judges serving in the division). The chief judge influences the distribution of work primarily through assignment of judges to divisions. Furthermore, an aggressive court administrator's office (headed by a judge, but relatively independent of the chief judge) operates in Philadelphia, and this office is actively involved in case assignment. By contrast, in both Chicago and Los Angeles the court administrator is institutionally weak and plays no significant role in case assignment and monitoring. For these reasons, the comparatively long term of office (five years) and the partisan political climate in Philadelphia become less important in shaping the office of chief judge. Though more than figurehead, Philadelphia's chief judge mostly engages in planning, community relations, and liaison with other public entities.

### Trial Court Visibility in Three Communities

A final focus in our overview of the three courts is their visibility in the wider community. We look at the sources of information about courts that are available to the citizenry: newspapers, investigative studies, research, and elections for judgeships. In particular, how much scrutiny of courts do these sources provide? Does the level of scrutiny differ significantly among the three communities?

To address these questions, we provide survey data based upon judicial perceptions about sources of information, as reported in Table 9-1. We also report our own perceptions of the level and type of court scrutiny, based upon field observations and general experiences in the three cities.

Newspaper and television coverage of court matters is widely perceived by most judges in all three courts. About four of every five judges in Chicago, Los Angeles, and Philadelphia agreed that media coverage is "extensive." We believe that such coverage is, at best, highly selective. Perhaps more important, coverage tends to be case-specific rather than general, though the balance

TABLE 9-1. Judicial Perceptions of Community Pressures in Chicago, Los Angeles and Philadelphia

| | % JUDGES REPORTING | | | | |
|---|---|---|---|---|---|
| | Extensive Newspaper or Television Coverage of Courts | Frequent Court-Watcher Projects | Local University Research Projects on Courts | Hotly Contested Elections for Local Judgeships | Number |
| Chicago | 78.9 | 85.9 | 49.3 | 63.4 | (72) |
| Los Angeles | 83.3 | 48.0 | 36.0 | 34.2 | (103) |
| Philadelphia | 79.6 | 69.4 | 40.8 | 65.3 | (50) |

shifts from city to city. In Chicago, for example, the two competing newspapers (*Sun-Times* and *Tribune*) focus heavily on the criminal courts, especially sensational or brutal cases. Analysis of court practices and administration is infrequent, except where partisan politics is involved, as in the selection of a new chief judge or in judicial retention elections. By contrast, the dominant Los Angeles newspaper (*Times*) is more frequent, consistent, and analytical in its coverage of the courts and criminal justice system. This is especially noteworthy in view of the lack of political intrigue surrounding the Los Angeles courts. The dominant Philadelphia newspaper (*Inquirer*) often crusades against individuals (e.g., a former district attorney) or entire institutions (e.g., the state supreme court). Its coverage of local courts is probably more characteristic, in style, of the *Los Angeles Times* than either of the Chicago newspapers, presenting a balanced proportion of news about individual cases and information on the court as an organization.

"Court-watcher" projects—where lay citizens observe courtroom activities—have become quite frequent in recent years. These projects are typically undertaken by a reform or "good government" organization, sometimes with federal funding. Trial judges in Chicago are much more likely to be cognizant of "court-watchers" than their colleagues in Philadelphia or Los Angeles. Most judges in Chicago (86 percent), the majority in Philadelphia (69 percent), but less than half in Los Angeles (48 percent) believe "court-watcher" projects are frequent in their court. Whether the frequency of such projects actually differs significantly from city to city, we do not know. It is clear, however, that judicial perceptions are different. The frequeny of, or at least the sting from, court-watcher studies was evident among Chicago judges. One Chicago judge whom we observed made an extended explanation (for the benefit of reporters in the courtroom) of why he would not be on the bench for the regular afternoon session of an ongoing trial. This occurred in response to a casual comment by the prosecutor about the judge "quitting for the day at noontime." Another judge was initially quite reluctant to allow our observer to witness "political" discussions in chambers. We attribute this sensitivity to scrutiny, in part, to one court-watcher report in 1975, which concluded that Chicago judges worked only a few hours per day, as well as to other studies that have highlighted the political nature of the Cook County bench. In contrast, judges in Los Angeles appeared comfortable with the observer and with any reporters nearby, and did not appear self-conscious on the few occasions when they left the courthouse very early in the day. We believe this is a reflection of the infrequency and tame posture of court-watcher studies in Los Angeles.

University research projects of faculty or students make different demands on courts and individual judges. Access to court files or response to interviews and survey questionnaires is often required, in addition to, or in lieu of, observation. The actual frequency of these projects is difficult to measure or even estimate. Again, however, more judges in Chicago perceive their court to be studied than in Philadelphia or Los Angeles.[11]

Finally, "hotly contested" elections provide a forum through which citizens can gain information about courts and the personalities and backgrounds of individual judges. Judges in both Chicago and Philadelphia are much more likely to report that heated contests occur than are their counterparts in Los Angeles. External evidence corroborates these perceptions. The only incumbent judge defeated or seriously challenged in recent history in Los Angeles is the one who decided that the city's school system must be desegregated by busing. By contrast, some incumbent judges in Chicago have been defeated in recent retention elections (including a chief judge and a supervising judge of the criminal division), while others have barely survived.[12]

In sum, the visibility of trial courts in the community differs from Chicago (high) to Philadelphia (moderate) to Los Angeles (low). Newspapers and television stations in all three cities cover the courts extensively (or selectively, depending upon whose viewpoint is taken), but the content varies significantly. Coverage tends to be much less sophisticated in Chicago, where a "court-watcher" project can command top headlines without analytic scrutiny, than in Los Angeles. Other sources of information, including court-watcher studies, university research, and hotly contested elections, are consistently perceived by judges to be most prevalent in Chicago and least prevalent in Los Angeles. External evidence, including our field observations, generally supports these judicial perceptions.

## Judicial Background and Experience

What kinds of background and experience do judges in Chicago, Los Angeles, and Philadelphia bring with them? Are they similar or dissimilar? In what ways are they a reflection of the local political and community environment?

The formal recruitment system is election in all three cities: partisan ballot in Chicago and Philadelphia, nonpartisan ballot in Los Angeles. In practice, the situation is complicated by the use of interim appointments. Chicago's judiciary is primarily an elected judiciary, with three-fourths of its judges first gaining the bench through election. Only one-fourth were initially appointed (by the state supreme court) to fill interim vacancies. Philadelphia's judiciary is about evenly divided between judges initially elected and those initially appointed by the governor to fill vacancies.[13] In contrast, the Los Angeles judiciary is almost exclusively an appointed one, with 90 percent of its judges initially selected by the governor to fill vacancies.

These differences in formal selection are reflected in the informal processes through which trial judges are recruited. Most notably, the prior occupational experience of judges in the three communities is substantially different. Table 9–2 presents these data. Perhaps the most striking finding is the degree to which the Chicago court draws upon political figures—from the elected and

TABLE 9-2. Immediate Prior Occupation of Trial Judges in Chicago, Los Angeles, and Philadelphia

|  | CHICAGO | LOS ANGELES | PHILADELPHIA |
|---|---|---|---|
| Private legal practice | 34.8% | 35.6% | 59.2% |
| Lower court judge | 20.8 | 49.5 | 4.1 |
| District attorney's office | 8.4 | 5.0 | 6.1 |
| Federal/local government lawyer | 5.6 | 2.0 | 14.3 |
| Other public official | 30.4 | 7.9 | 16.3 |
| Number | (72) | (101) | (49) |

appointed ranks—for its judgeships. Almost one-third of Chicago judges came directly from an elected or appointed public position, as against one judge in six in Philadelphia and one in twelve in Los Angeles. This is not because Chicago voters choose to elect many former politicians to the bench, but because they are typically able only to ratify the choice of the party slatemakers.[14] Thus, it is not surprising to discover that most of these former public officials served in politically important or sensitive posts to which they were appointed by Chicago's mayor. Examples include an administrative assistant to the mayor, chief and deputy city attorneys, a chief deputy tax assessor, and attorneys for the election board. Former elected public officials who reached the bench include city aldermen and state legislators.

The much smaller contingent of former public officials on the Los Angeles bench also includes elected and appointed positions. The elected positions are analogous to Chicago's (city council and state legislature), but the appointed positions from which judges are drawn tend to be more prestigious and less tied to *local* politics—e.g., directors of state agencies, commissioners (referees in the Los Angeles court), and members of the Workman's Compensation Appeal Board. Such backgrounds illustrate the dominance of California governors in making interim appointments without much regard to weak party leaders at the local level. In Philadelphia, all former public officials on the bench served in appointed positions—sometimes politically sensitive ones such as deputy city attorney or deputy attorney general, sometimes court-related ones such as deputy sheriff, deputy court administrator, or court administrator. Whether politically sensitive or otherwise, however, most Philadelphia judges were drawn from public offices relevant to the work of judging.

The courts are also quite different in the degree to which they recruit judges from the lower bench. Nearly half of all judges in Los Angeles rose from the municipal court; in Philadelphia, virtually none came from the justice of the peace court (most of whom have been nonlawyers). In Chicago and throughout Illinois, no lower trial court exists, but there is a lower level or class of judge—associate judge—which sometimes serves as a stepping stone to a circuit judgeship.[15] Interestingly, associate judges in Illinois are elected by the circuit judges of each court, giving rise to lobbying by some circuit judges on behalf of their favorite candidates.

The proportion of judges recruited from the private bar is modest in Chicago and Los Angeles, but much higher in Philadelphia. Lacking appropriate apprenticeships in the lower court and not relying significantly upon political officeholders, the Philadelphia court must look primarily to private legal practitioners and secondarily to public lawyers at the federal or local level. In all three courts, the district attorney's office rarely is a direct stepping stone to a judgeship.

Finally, it should be noted that the three chief judges were recruited from occupational paths quite prototypical for their courts. Judge Boyle in Chicago served various political apprenticeships, including city attorney, alderman, and, immediately prior to his election to the bench, state's attorney. Judge Wenke in Los Angeles was appointed from the municipal court, having no record of public office. And Judge Bradley in Philadelphia served in one appointed (but no elected) public position prior to his appointment to the bench.

The political party affiliation of judges in Chicago and Philadelphia is overwhelmingly Democratic (77 percent in each court) but in Los Angeles is evenly divided between the two parties. This, too, is related to selection systems. Partisan election and the Democratic majority prevailing on the Illinois state supreme court ensure a heavily Democratic bench in Chicago. Though gubernatorial appointment of interim vacancies is a much more frequent complement to partisan election in Philadelphia, Pennsylvania has had mostly Democratic governors or Republican governors who, like Scranton, appointed Democrats within the city. The result has been a similarly heavy Democratic majority on the bench. In Los Angeles, where gubernatorial appointment accounts for the selection of most judges, the alternating spirit of California voters for the office of governor (from Brown, Sr., to Reagan, to Brown, Jr.) has resulted in an equal balance of Democrats and Republicans on the trial bench. In sum, the Chicago bench is probably the most likely to retain its heavily Democratic character for years to come. The political balance of the Los Angeles judiciary, in particular, will be highly influenced by voter fluctuations at the gubernatorial level.

Finally, the social characteristics of the three trial benches are remarkably similar. In all three courts, judges average fifty-five years of age and are quite *unlikely* (compared with the nation as a whole) to report grandparents or parents with legal, judicial, or public service. Women appear to be in higher proportion on the Philadelphia bench (12 percent) than in Chicago (6 percent) or Los Angeles (7 percent).[16] Blacks appear to be more numerous in Chicago and Philadelphia (17 percent) than in Los Angeles (8 percent), though other minorities are also represented on the Los Angeles bench (6 percent).

The benches in Chicago, Los Angeles, and Philadelphia, then, are both similar and dissimilar in their backgrounds and experience. Their social backgrounds and characteristics are quite similar, at least in terms of the few variables for which we have data. By contrast, their professional background and experiences are distinctively different. The highly partisan political climate of Chicago recruits judges substantially from public office, elective or appointive. Furthermore, nearly all Chicago judges are reported to have political sponsors, often cultivated from less visible service to the party.[17] The more fragmented partisan political climate in Philadelphia permits the infusion of stronger norms of professionalism, resulting in a judiciary drawn from private practice, government law, or public positions in law enforcement or the court itself. The less partisan climate of Los Angeles results in a judiciary with substantial apprenticeship in the lower court, where judges have perhaps the best opportunity to learn the art and the detail of judging.

## Comparative Work Patterns

The work judges do in the three courts is very much a function of how each court chooses to implement specialization. The Chicago court is the most highly specialized, particularly on the civil side. There are distinct divisions of chancery (equity), probate, domestic relations, and civil—jury, among others, to which judges may be assigned and in which they will typically hear no other kinds of cases. The Philadelphia court has some of these specialized civil divisions (probate, domestic relations) but not others. The Los Angeles court also has some specialized civil divisions (family law, eminent domain) but not others. Both Philadelphia and Los Angeles courts have general civil divisions in which judges may hear a significant range of cases.

On the criminal side, the Chicago and Philadelphia courts have formal or informal divisions of jury and nonjury trial work. In Philadelphia, criminal cases are divided among a homicide division, a felony jury division, and a felony nonjury division. In Chicago, nearly all criminal jury trials are held in the old criminal courts building, whereas the criminal judges in the civic center hear mostly nonjury trials. In Los Angeles, there are no distinctions in the hearing of jury and nonjury criminal trials. Virtually all judges in the criminal division hear both in their current assignment.

Finally, some judges in Los Angeles and Philadelphia serve in a general assignment, hearing both criminal and civil cases at the same time. In Los Angeles this occurs predominantly in branch courts where the much smaller numbers of judges available necessitate a greater flexibility. In the central district, some judges in the civil division are drafted for an occasional criminal trial, which would otherwise be dismissed under the state's stringently enforced speedy trial rule. In Philadelphia all criminal judges are assigned two civil motions per week. Sometimes, these require mere *pro forma* decisions, but other times they necessitate significant reading or research. Because Pennsylvania also has a state speedy trial provision, civil division judges are occasionally asked to hear a criminal trial nearing or at the time deadline. In these ways, then, judges in Los Angeles and Philadelphia may come to do work equivalent to a general assignment. By contrast, judges in Chicago rarely if ever have a mix of criminal and civil cases in their work.[18]

This general picture of the specialization of work in the three courts is corroborated by the distribution of assignments reported in Table 9-3. The data suggest that the three courts differ substantially in the proportion of judicial resources allocated to criminal and civil cases. In Chicago, where all judges hear only criminal or only civil cases, the bulk of the resources are devoted to civil cases (by a ratio of 3:2). Philadelphia is at the other extreme: Most of its judges hear criminal cases (by ratio of 4:1), though a significant minority serve in a general assignment, where they may hear criminal and civil cases. Los Angeles falls in between: Its judicial resources are devoted about equally to civil and criminal cases. The reasons for this difference in court utilization of judges are not fully clear, though the allocation in Philadelphia is partly explained by the presence of an innovative and extensive arbitration program for civil cases under $10,000. This program is credited with disposing of 10,000 cases each year. Equally important, hundreds of local lawyers serve (with pay) on three-person arbitration panels in order to conserve judicial resources.

Specialization levels within the three courts, particularly on the civil side, are also apparent from Table 9-3. Large numbers of Chicago judges report hearing only one type of civil case: personal injury (jury), domestic relations, chancery, or probate.[19] In Los Angeles, with the exception of domestic relations, most civil-based judges hear a mixture of cases. The few Philadelphia judges hearing only civil cases seem to fall in between, more likely to be specialized than in Los Angeles but less likely than in Chicago.

The organization of work is substantially different in one other respect in these three courts: case assignment system. In Chicago the majority of judges

TABLE 9-3. Judicial Assignments in Chicago, Los Angeles, and Philadelphia

|  | CHICAGO | LOS ANGELES | PHILADELPHIA |
|---|---|---|---|
| General | 1.4% | 24.3% | 28.0% |
| Criminal | 38.8 | 33.0 | 54.0 |
|   Criminal |  | 33.2 | 29.1 | 48.0 |
|   Juvenile |  | 5.6 | 3.9 | 6.0 |
| Civil | 55.6 | 36.0 | 14.0 |
|   Civil—mixed |  | 18.1 | 28.2 | 8.0 |
|   Civil—jury |  | 15.3 | 1.9 | 4.0 |
|   Domestic relations |  | 12.5 | 4.9 | 2.0 |
|   Chancery |  | 9.7 | 0 | 0 |
|   Probate |  | 0 | 1.0 | 0 |
| Miscellaneous | 4.2 | 6.7 | 4.0 |
|   Number | (72) | (103) | (50) |

operate with an individual calendar. These include judges in the criminal and chancery divisions and some judges with civil—mixed assignments. On the other hand, judges in domestic relations, law-jury, and probate serve under a master calendar.[20] In Los Angeles only criminal division judges have an individual calendar; all civil division judges serve under a master calendar. In Philadelphia virtually all judges serve under a master calendar. These differences from court to court may not impact significantly upon individual judges' work. Rather, they reflect interest in, and sophistication about, management principles. The fluctuation in case assignment systems in Chicago, without apparent sound reason, reflects almost certainly the intrusion of court politics in subtle and highly localized ways.

## THE ENVIRONMENT OF WORK DAYS

Judges in the three courts work approximately the same amount of hours. Our observations indicated no visible differences from court to court. We observed five judges in Philadelphia to work an average of 7.5 hours and five judges in Los Angeles and Chicago to work 7.3 hours, over the course of a three-day period for each judge. Judges' reports of the length of their most common day also do not vary much across the three courts (from 9.5 hours in Los Angeles to 9.2 hours in Chicago). In all courts, judges' reports of their less common days reflect dropoffs in time worked, from one-half hour in Philadelphia and Los Angeles to one hour in Chicago. Taking these less common days into account, the exaggeration of work appears no greater in these three courts than elsewhere in the country. Of course, there is more to work than counting hours. Our subjective judgment is that the intensity of work was quite high among the judges we observed in all three courts. There was relatively little opportunity for extended socializing, politicking, or personal business once the judge arrived in chambers.[21]

## THE SUBSTANCE OF WORK DAYS

There is an underlying similarity in the nature of judicial work performed in the three courts. Because court size is the most effective discriminator of judicial work patterns, similarity from Los Angeles to Chicago to Philadelphia should not be surprising. There are, however, three areas in which judicial work is identifiably different in these courts: (1) the balance between jury and nonjury trial work, (2) time spent in plea discussions, and (3) frequency and time spent in preparing and writing decisions, judgments, and orders.

Judges in Chicago and Philadelphia are more likely to have nonjury rather than jury trial work on their most common day. In each court, about 53 percent report nonjury trials, but only 36 percent report jury trial work. Judges in Los Angeles, in contrast, are much more likely to have jury trial work (67 percent) than nonjury trial work (35 percent) on their most common day. The ratio of jury and nonjury work on less common days is roughly equal in all three courts, suggesting that there are real differences in the proportion of judicial resources devoted to jury and nonjury trial work in Chicago and Philadelphia compared with Los Angeles. It is probable that the organization of labor in the Chicago and Philadelphia courts (through jury and nonjury divisions) encourages and/or reflects more use of bench trials. In Philadelphia, in particular, bench trials may be the vehicle through which the court "encourages" defendants to plead guilty, given that a Pennsylvania court rule prohibits judicial participation in plea discussions. This is further supported by Paul Wice's contention that the Philadelphia court assigns its "tough" sentencers to jury trial work and "lenient" or "plea" judges to nonjury trial work.[22]

A second difference in work emphasis stems directly from the Pennsylvania court rule prohibiting judicial participation in plea negotiations. Philadelphia judges generally report behavior in compliance with this rule. Only about 20 percent of judges who hear criminal cases in their current assignment report any time spent in plea discussions on their most common day, compared with 80 percent of judges in Chicago and 50 percent of judges in Los Angeles. A similar lack of *participation* in plea discussions is reported by Philadelphia judges; only 14 percent report that they participate in plea discussions (by recommending or reviewing dispositions) as against about 80 percent of judges in both Chicago and Los Angeles. In essence, the sentencing role of Philadelphia judges is much diminished compared with their counterparts in Chicago and Los Angeles. Not only do Philadelphia judges not participate in the sentence negotiations implicit in plea bargaining, but many judges hear only nonjury trials where a sentence of probation is the norm in all but the most serious cases.

Finally, more judges in Philadelphia work at legal research—specifically, preparing and writing decisions. For example, about 70 percent of Philadelphia judges average more than one hour in this activity on their most common day; in comparison, only about 50 percent of judges in Chicago and Los Angeles report this activity on their most common day, averaging half as much time. The differences widen on the second most common day, where 70 percent of Philadelphia judges typically work almost *two* hours per day preparing and writing decisions. In contrast, less than one-half of Los Angeles judges and less than one-quarter of Chicago judges report this activity on their second most common day, typically for less than one hour. Thus, we find some support for the argument by Philadelphia criminal division judges that the assignment of two civil motions per week consumes a significant share of their time. Philadelphia's civil court judges also report more time in writing decisions than their counterparts in Chicago and Los Angeles, confirming widespread impressions that the culture of federal courts often spills over into state courts, or vice versa, in a local community.[23] In both levels of court, attorneys in Philadelphia have come to expect written decisions, and judges have become accustomed to writing them, with the assistance of their full-time law clerks.

In sum, there are only a few distinctions of work emphasis among judges in

Chicago, Los Angeles, and Philadelphia. Rather, their work is surrounded by a large layer of similarity. What distinguishes judging in these three courts is not so much the actual mix of tasks but rather the work relationships between attorneys and judges and the role of partisan politics in shaping judicial perceptions of work. It is to these two themes that we now turn.

## Bench–Bar Relationships

The working relationships between attorneys and judges in a given community constitute one important segment of the "local legal culture." In Chicago our observations suggest a highly symbiotic character to these relationships. Judges and attorneys look upon one another as part of the same legal fraternity, system, or club. Relations are friendly, amicable, and typically (though not always) without aloofness on the part of the judges. This is a striking phenomenon, particularly in the criminal courts. For example, we saw one instance where a public defender engaged in a shouting match with a Chicago criminal division judge over the enforcement of the speedy trial rule. Immediately afterward, the public defender rushed out to the judge in the hallway and assured him that it was really "mock anger" for the benefit of his client, nothing personal intended. The judge was relieved, after appearing surprised and flushed in the courtroom. We think this judge was surprised initially by the attorney's outburst because such expressions of emotion, mock or otherwise, are rare in Chicago courtrooms. It is a violation of the unwritten norm that lawyers and judges should always be proper and deferential toward each other in the courtroom, where clients, media, and the public at large may watch. More generally, we gained the impression that there was a "we–they" mentality in the Chicago courts. Lawyers and judges tended to see themselves as knowledgeable insiders and the public as sometimes foolish outsiders. This manifested itself in comtemptuous references in chambers to "oddball" jurors and spectators, in lack of concern about the inconvenience to witnesses resulting from frequent continuances, and even in lack of sympathy for some victims.

In Los Angeles we observed a quite different set of working relationships between attorneys and judges. Formality prevailed in the courtroom. More events take place in the courtroom, in full public view and hearing, rather than in whispered tones at the bench or back in chambers as in Chicago. Courtroom exchanges between attorneys and judges are sometimes intense or prickly, with no release of emotion or apology outside the courtroom. Judges in Los Angeles tend to see themselves as more aloof, part of an elite group separate from—and perhaps better than—the world of practicing lawyers. We heard many more complaints by judges about the quality or courtroom performance of criminal and civil attorneys in Los Angeles. One civil division judge, committed to a purist's idea of a well-argued trial, repeatedly admonished both attorneys not to ask leading questions of their witnesses. And a criminal division judge acknowledged that he had all but given up on the prosecutor's ability to ask properly worded questions. We also saw few examples of the "we–they" mentality characteristic of Chicago. Chambers discussions assumed a dignified informality, with few jokes at the expense of defendants or individual citizens. In sum, the social and professional distance between attorney and judge appears much larger in Los Angeles than in Chicago.

Relations between attorneys and judges in Philadelphia fall in between these two extremes. It is difficult to say exactly where, however, because of the peculiarities of the physical arrangement of the courthouses (located in different buildings from judges' chambers) and because of fewer opportunities to observe judge and attorneys together in plea discussions. We saw examples of judges who were quick to protect or defend the legal profession, as one judge who jousted with a young attorney quite critical of his fellow lawyers. Yet we observed another judge who actively sought to limit the number of cases that assigned counsel could take in his courtroom. This same judge was sufficiently empathetic with the nonprofessionals in court to institute the practice of anonymous jurors to protect them from possible retaliation. On balance, it is more difficult to generalize about attorney–judge relations in Philadelphia, except to say that they tend to be more formal than in Chicago. Similarly, the "we–they" dichotomy between legal professionals and the public, so noticeable in Chicago, is less noticeable in Philadelphia.

Our observationally based evidence on bench–bar relationships is fragmentary and at times little more than anecdotal. We do, however, have survey data that, by inference, support the picture of relationships already drawn. Consider the arena of negotiations and the role of the judge therein. Does the judge actively intervene in settlement discussions and in plea discussions, or not? In civil pretrial negotiations, there is a substantial difference in judicial style in the three courts, as Table 9–4 reports.

Trial judges in Los Angeles are much more likely to intervene aggressively in settlement discussions—"through the use of direct pressure"—than their colleagues in either Chicago or Philadelphia. We infer that a more aggressive judicial style is a response to greater case pressures (see Table 9–6), to a stronger commitment to case management, or to an unwillingness to leave to

TABLE 9-4. Trial Judges' Style in Civil Settlement Discussions in Chicago, Los Angeles, and Philadelphia

| Judicial Style in Settlement Discussions | Chicago | Los Angeles | Philadelphia |
|---|---|---|---|
| Aggressive | 14.6% | 44.8% | 15.0% |
| Subtle | 78.1 | 53.7 | 80.0 |
| No intervention | 7.3 | 1.5 | 5.0 |
| Number | (41) | (67) | (20) |

attorneys the "work of the court."[24] One Chicago civil division judge undoubtedly expressed the sentiment of many of his fellow judges when he remarked that he didn't like to "bludgeon" attorneys into settlement, because he recalled that he disliked such treatment as an attorney. Because Chicago judges remain psychologically and socially closer to the lawyers surrounding them, they are less likely to "get tough" with them.

The arena of plea negotiations is not a good area of focus for consideration of bench-bar relationships. The role a judge adopts—to participate or to ratify—is significantly determined by factors outside his control, including state court rules (as in Pennsylvania) and case law. That the majority of Chicago and Los Angeles judges participate in plea discussions while those in Philadelphia do not reflects the presence or absence of these constraints much more than their relationships with attorneys.

Judicial intervention in nonjury trials, on the other hand, is an appropriate forum to examine, because (like civil pretrial negotiations) judges have the freedom to adopt a variety of roles. Whereas jury trials require the judge to be circumspect for fear of prejudicing inexperienced lay persons, a nonjury trial offers the judge a more legitimate forum for activism. One type of judicial intervention in nonjury trials involves attempts to expedite the proceedings in order to be responsive to the growing backlogs of many courts. Table 9-5 presents judges' reports of their efforts to "encourage" counsel in the three courts to expedite presentation of testimony.

The most striking finding is the varying amounts of disparity between judges' behavior in the courtroom (in public) and in chambers (in private) from city to city. In Los Angeles and Philadelphia, judges are only slightly less likely to rebuke attorneys for "slow play" in public than in private. For example, the proportion of judges who would "never" ask attorneys to speed up

TABLE 9-5. Trial Judges' Level of Intervention in Nonjury Trials in Chicago, Los Angeles, and Philadelphia

| "Encourage counsel to expedite testimony" | CHICAGO | LOS ANGELES | PHILADELPHIA |
|---|---|---|---|
| *In chambers* | | | |
| Extensive | 10.9% | 13.0% | 8.5% |
| Moderate | 41.8 | 52.0 | 40.5 |
| Limited | 38.2 | 31.0 | 34.0 |
| None | 9.1 | 4.0 | 17.0 |
| Number | (55) | (100) | (47) |
| *In courtroom* | | | |
| Extensive | 1.7 | 8.1 | 2.3 |
| Moderate | 20.7 | 35.4 | 27.3 |
| Limited | 43.1 | 48.4 | 50.0 |
| None | 34.5 | 8.1 | 20.4 |
| Number | (58) | (99) | (44) |

rises only slightly in Los Angeles (from 4 percent to 8 percent) and Philadelphia (17 percent to 20 percent) when the forum shifts from chambers to the courtroom. In Chicago, by contrast, what judges are willing to do in private is greatly different from what they will do in public. Whereas only 9 percent would "never" privately encourage attorneys to speed up, fully 34 percent would "never" do so in the courtroom. This is perhaps the strongest evidence to support our observations of significant differences in the working relationships of attorneys and judges in the three communities.

It is somewhat paradoxical that while we characterize bench–bar relationships in Chicago as amicable, protective, perhaps "clubby," Chicago also experiences the most active and vigorous bar evaluation of judicial performance. Although the established bar, through its membership polling, supports the overwhelming majority of sitting judges in Chicago,[25] the mere presence of an evaluation mechanism serves to introduce tension into working relationships. More cynical observers might attribute judicial deference to attorneys to a threatening rather than protective institutional relationship.[26] Philadelphia, too, has a bar active in judicial evaluation efforts, including membership polling. By contrast, the Los Angeles bar has undertaken only weak efforts at judicial evaluation, not including polling. Furthermore, the political efficacy of evaluation efforts is hindered in Los Angeles because judges do not run on their record in a retention election. Rather, they seek reelection, usually unopposed. Thus, we cannot be certain that deferential relations between attorneys and judges are solely a product of local norms and preferences. Other factors, apart from the workings of interpersonal relationships, may also be involved,[27] including bar evaluation of sitting judges.

## Partisan Politics, Judicial Morale, and the Performance of Work

Partisan politics directly and indirectly influences the work of trial judges and their perceptions about the work environment. Judges in Chicago, Los Angeles, and Philadelphia view their work differently in ways that often can be linked to the political environment. Judges in these courts are also treated differently (or at least perceive that they are), sometimes on the basis of their political party affiliation.

### JUDICIAL MORALE

Judges in Chicago, Los Angeles, and Philadelphia view the work environment differently. Sometimes the differences are small, as in the areas of skill utilization, caseload variety, and control of work time. In the areas of caseload pressures, courtroom personnel, and salary, differences of perception are much greater. Table 9–6 reports these data. For each of the first three areas of the work environment, the differences among judges in Chicago, Los Angeles, and

TABLE 9-6. Judicial Perceptions of the Work Environment in Chicago, Los Angeles, and Philadelphia[a]

|  | CHICAGO | LOS ANGELES | PHILADELPHIA |
|---|---|---|---|
| Skill utilization | 5.5[b] | 5.8 | 5.7 |
| Case variety | 3.5 | 3.8 | 3.9 |
| Control of work time | 5.3 | 4.9 | 4.8[b] |
| Caseload pressures | 4.5[b] | 5.4 | 5.1 |
| Effectiveness of personnel | 5.5 | 6.0 | 5.1 |
| Salary | 2.1 | 3.3 | 2.2[b] |
| Number | (72) | (103) | (50) |

[a] Scores are means, based upon semantic differential scales ranging from 1 to 7. The higher the score, the more skill utilization, variety, control, pressures, personnel, and salary a judge perceives. See Chapter 7.
[b] Differences between Republican and Democratic judges > .5.

Philadelphia are small, but in the direction we would expect. For example, it is in the least partisan political environment (Los Angeles) that judges feel their skills to be best utilized, and in the most partisan political community (Chicago) that judges feel least well utilized. Differences in perceptions of case variety comport well with differences in the amount of specialization in the three courts. In the most highly divisionalized court (Chicago), judges are the most likely to perceive "too little" variety in their cases. Similarly, where the individual calendar is most extensively used (Chicago), judges are most likely to feel in control of their work time. In Philadelphia, where the master calendar is almost exclusively utilized, judges feel least in control of their own time.

In the areas of caseload pressures, personnel, and salary, the differences from court to court are substantially greater. Los Angeles judges, as a group, feel under the most pressure to "move cases"—somewhat more than judges in Philadelphia and much more than judges in Chicago. These differences in judicial perceptions may help to account for the large backlogs and longer delays in processing cases reported by the Chicago courts as compared with Los Angeles, especially on the criminal side.[28] We shall argue later in this chapter that the roots of these differences in perceived caseload pressures lie in the different uses and amounts of court politics and partisan politics in the three courts.

Differences in assessments of courtroom personnel parallel our discussions earlier in Chapter 5. Los Angeles judges view more favorably their relatively Spartan but civil service–selected supporting personnel than do their counterparts in courts where clerk and bailiff positions are political patronage. In fact, these data support our earlier observation that an overabundance of courtroom personnel can actually be counterproductive. Philadelphia judges have by far the *most* supporting resources in sheer numbers, but it is Philadelphia judges who are also least satisfied with the collective performance of their courtroom personnel.

Lastly, there is a large gap in satisfaction with salary between judges in Los Angeles (who are not too displeased) and judges in Philadelphia and Chicago (who are extremely displeased). Some of this can be attributed to actual differences in salary: Los Angeles judges were highest paid ($49,166) at the time of our survey (1977), and the most recently raised (September 1976). Chicago judges were lowest paid ($42,500) and least recently raised (July 1975). Philadelphia judges fall in between ($45,000), raised in July 1976.[29] Still, salary differences were not all that large; discrepancies in satisfaction with salary may also be tied to perceptions of other elements of the work environment.[30]

Overall, we conclude that Los Angeles judges feel better about most aspects of their work environment than do judges in Chicago and Philadelphia. Though some of these differences can be traced to a particular administrative structure (e.g., type of case assignment system or amount of divisionalization), other differences are related to the political qualities of the three communities.

## MORALE AND PARTISAN POLITICS

The influence of partisan politics is visible not only across the three communities but within communities as well. In the highly partisan communities, Democratic and Republican judges differ significantly in their feelings about some elements of the work environment. In Chicago it is the Democratic judges who feel that their skills are better utilized ($\bar{x}$ = 5.7 v. 4.7) and who feel under less caseload pressure ($\bar{x}$ = 4.4 v. 4.9) than Republican judges. Democratic judges also feel slightly better about the effectiveness of their personnel and control of their work time. One reasonable inference to be drawn is that the Democratic-affiliated judicial leadership rewards—tangibly or intangibly—judges of its own party. Some of the tangible rewards might include support personnel (Democratic judges do, in fact, appear to have more secretarial resources) or assignment.

In Philadelphia it is Republican judges who feel better about most aspects of their work environment, particularly control of their work time and salary. This is the case *despite* a Democratic chief judge. One partial explanation is that the chief judge in Philadelphia does not possess all of the formal and informal powers of the Chicago chief judge to reward and sanction. A second explanation may lie in the remains of the once-powerful Republican political organization in Philadelphia. Only since the 1950s have Democrats controlled City Hall; as a result, it was not until the late 1960s or early 1970s that the effects of Republican patronage in the courts could be entirely eliminated. Furthermore, the intra-organizational struggles for mayor and for control of the Democratic party organization probably deflected attention away from the courts, leaving them in a less politicized state than in Chicago. Though Republican judges are a small minority in Philadelphia (23 percent), they are clearly not a discouraged or oppressed minority.

Los Angeles appears to be relatively free of the influence of partisan politics in its courts. Republican and Democratic judges—who are about equal in numbers—view and assess their work environment and feelings of job satisfaction quite similarly. On the all-important measure of skill utilization, for example, the average scores are virtually identical.

## THE POLITICS OF ASSIGNMENT

The assignment of judges in urban courts is widely perceived as the likely arena for the interplay of partisan and internal court politics. The power of assignment is the most tangible and important reward or sanction at the disposal of the chief judge. This is so largely because judges, individually and as a group, have well-defined preferences for particular kinds of cases.

In Chicago we find evidence to suggest that judges are assigned, in part, on the basis of their political party affiliation. Eisenstein and Jacob asserted that Republicans are much less likely to be assigned to sensitive civil posts in Chicago.[31] "Sensitive" might include the chancery division, which hears injunctive matters concerning local governments and labor-management disputes, and the county division, which hears challenges to election procedures and outcomes. Our data support this contention: 33 percent of the Democratic judges in Chicago, but only 7 percent of Republican judges, were assigned either to the chancery division or a "civil-mixed" post in 1977. By contrast, a disproportionate share of Republican judges were sitting in domestic relations court and in the civil–jury division, which hears tort cases. Both of these assignments are viewed to be less sensitive, because cases involve individual litigants and no public policy questions are directly raised. Ironically, even the criminal division in Chicago is perceived to be less sensitive by the Democratic organization, though its work is actively scrutinized by the media. As a result, a higher percentage of Republican judges also serve in the criminal division. If Republican judges (who typically have their roots in the suburbs) are tougher sentencers than their city-based Democratic colleagues,[32] the chief judge can protect the court's reputation vis-à-vis a "soft on crime" charge while at the same time protecting the political party organization and city government in sensitive civil cases.

In Philadelphia the structure of divisionalization is such that potentially sensitive civil cases cannot be concentrated among a few judges. There is, for example, no chancery division and no division that hears only election disputes. The criminal division is the most identifiably important division. Thus, we would expect, and find, that a significantly higher percentage of Democratic than Republican judges (58 percent versus 33 percent) are assigned to the criminal division. Important civil cases may still be sent, on an *ad hoc* basis, to loyal Democratic judges who mostly, though, hear a wider range of civil cases.

In Los Angeles there are no significant differences in the assignments of Republican and Democratic judges. It is a reflection of the lack of partisan

**TABLE 9-7.** Trial Judges' Perceptions of the Influence of Court Politics on Assignments in Chicago, Los Angeles, and Philadelphia

| INFLUENCE OF COURT POLITICS | CHICAGO | LOS ANGELES | PHILADELPHIA |
|---|---|---|---|
| Substantial | 47.3% | 10.2% | 36.9% |
| Slight | 28.1 | 51.2 | 36.9 |
| None | 24.6 | 38.6 | 26.2 |
| Number | (57) | (88) | (38) |

politics and the suburbanization of the Los Angeles county court that the primary assignment sanction of the chief judge is geographic exile. Occasionally judges who cause some kind of trouble have been sent to branch courts as far from their homes as possible. For the most part, however, this has been a potential rather than frequently used sanction.

The influence of politics on judicial assignments is corroborated by judges' perceptions about the bases on which assignments are typically made in their courts. Table 9-7 reports judges' beliefs about the importance of court politics for assignments in the three courts. Judicial perceptions parallel quite closely our independent analysis of partisan politics and assignments. In Chicago and Philadelphia, where party affiliation is related to assignment, a large percentage of judges attribute "substantial" influence to the role of court politics.[33] Nearly half of Chicago judges, and more than one-third of Philadelphia judges, acknowledge such influences in assignments. To a large extent, "court politics" is synonymous with partisan politics in these two courts. In Los Angeles, on the other hand, the role of court politics is perceived to be much less substantial, and in this court there is likely to be little convergence between "court politics" and partisan politics.

If court politics play only a small role in assignments in Los Angeles, what other factors are more important? One is the technical expertise of the judge. Three-fourths of Los Angeles judges, but only about half of the judges in the other two courts, perceive technical expertise to be a "substantial" influence in assignments. The chief judge in Los Angeles appeared keenly sensitive to the importance of matching judicial interests with cases, in order to preserve the morale of the individual judge.[34] Yet at the same time there are countervailing pressures to specialization—particularly the perceived need to distribute dull cases among as large a group as possible. This need is reflected in the relative frequency with which Los Angeles judges are rotated, especially early in their judicial career. For example, 53 percent of Los Angeles judges on the bench three years or less report serving in at least one assignment prior to their current one; this compares with only 25 percent in Philadelphia and 22 percent in Chicago.

Another factor that accounts for assignments in Los Angeles and Philadelphia, but much less in Chicago, is the case disposition rate, or speed, of the individual judge. Table 9-8 reports judges' beliefs about the importance of

**TABLE 9-8.** Trial Judges' Perceptions of the Influence of Case Disposition Rate on Assignments in Chicago, Los Angeles, and Philadelphia

| Influence of Case Disposition Rate | Chicago | Los Angeles | Philadelphia |
| --- | --- | --- | --- |
| Substantial | 14.0% | 43.2% | 50.0% |
| Slight | 50.9 | 45.4 | 22.5 |
| None | 35.1 | 11.4 | 27.5 |
| Number | (57) | (88) | (40) |

this factor in the three courts. The perceived differences in the role of case disposition rate are very large. In Chicago, where case delay is reported to be great, only a handful of judges ascribe "substantial" influence to speed. In contrast, in Los Angeles, where case delay is a much smaller problem, many more judges believe speed of processing cases is a factor in assignments. Interestingly, Philadelphia judges are the most likely to believe that speed in processing cases is a substantial influence in assignments, though that court is nevertheless reported to have a major delay problem.[35] Overall, then, our data suggest a link among politics, management sensitivity, and court performance.

## Politics and Court Management in Three Cities

No court manages its operations and personnel entirely free of politics. If the amount of *partisan* politics is low, the influence of other kinds of politics (seniority, political philosophy, personality) may still be present. Equally, no court operates without some attention to the principles of management and administration separate from dominant political influences.

Nevertheless, the three courts we have examined—Chicago, Los Angeles, and Philadelphia—represent three different "models" in the relationship between politics and management. Los Angeles reflects the subordination of politics to court management. Partisan political affiliations make no difference in judicial assignments. Even court politics is perceived to be at a minimum by the judges themselves. What counts in Los Angeles is the technical expertise of the judge and concern for his morale, institutionally reflected in the wide distribution of different types of cases and in more frequent judicial rotation. Indeed, one result is that judges do come to view their work environment more favorably in Los Angeles. They feel that their personnel are highly effective, that they themselves are fairly compensated, and that their skills are well utilized. Nevertheless, they also come to feel under great pressure to move cases. Efficiency—the movement of cases—is the driving force in the Los Angeles court, *unhindered* by political considerations.

Chicago represents the subordination of court management to politics. Partisan affiliations do make a difference in assignments, and this is recognized by Democratic and Republican judges alike. The morale of the individual judge is a less important consideration in assignments (there is less frequent rotation in a more highly specialized court), and this is reflected in how Chicago judges come to feel about various aspects of their work environment. They feel they are underpaid, are surrounded by somewhat less competent courtroom personnel, and have too little variety of cases (Republicans perceive these problems more acutely). Interestingly, though, Chicago judges do not feel particularly pressured to move cases, nor do they perceive the ability to move cases to be related to the type of assignments received. It is as if case pressure is the political system's ultimate tradeoff. The politics surrounding the Chicago courts makes judging a less prestigious, more tainted occupation. In return for the cooperation or acquiescence of its judges, the system exerts minimal pressure to expedite cases.

Philadelphia represents a relatively equal balancing of politics and court management. Partisan affiliations do make a difference in assignment, as judges of both parties recognize. But other factors, most notably the disposition rate of the individual judge, are also important. The morale of judges—their satisfaction with various aspects of the work environment—is not high, but the differences between Republican and Democratic judges do not support a theory of "minority oppression." It is Republican judges who feel slightly better about their work environment, in the presence of a Democratic chief judge. Equally important, Philadelphia's extensive use of the master calendar reflects a determination to control the work habits of its judges. Our observations in Philadelphia suggest that the master calendar office is intrusive in its operation, continually looking for the available judge, checking up on the case status of its judges, and even calling judges back from vacation to handle "routine" emergencies. All this is reflected in judges' perceptions that they are under considerable pressure to move cases. Because the political organization is either too fragmented or benign in Philadelphia, the judicial leadership perhaps retains the margin of discretion necessary to demand that all judges do their work expeditiously.

## Summary

Judging does not take place in a vacuum. It is performed in living communities, each with its own distinctive politics, law, and social mores. The reflection of the community environment upon the nature of judging is exemplified by looking at cities as different from one another as Chicago, Los Angeles, and Philadelphia.

The occupational apprenticeships of judges reflect the communities from which they come. In Chicago judges are drawn heavily from the public-political sectors, where they have labored to achieve a reward or capstone to their professional career. For that matter, most of the judges who have come from other occupational paths (including private practice) have served the political organization. In Philadelphia judges come mostly from private practice, because the lower bench has historically been staffed by nonlawyers. In addition, partisan political loyalties have not been quite so important because of Philadelphia's fluid political climate over the last several decades. In Los Angeles judges come substantially from the lower bench, reflecting the norm of judicial apprenticeship wiedespread in most of the larger industrial states.

The actual day-to-day work of judging is not greatly different in the three courts, each of which has a similar jurisdiction. Judges in Philadelphia are most distinctive in what they do. A high proportion are assigned to criminal work, particularly nonjury trials, which may serve the function of slow pleas. Because Pennsylvania court rule prohibits judicial participation in plea negotiations, the Philadelphia judge's role in criminal sentencing is significantly diminished. Finally, Philadelphia judges in both criminal and civil assignment do more writing of decisions, as do the federal judges in Philadelphia. The work of judges in Chicago and Los Angeles is remarkably similar, save for the effects of institutionalizing a separation of nonjury from jury trial work.

It is the style of judging that is distinctively different from court to court. Judges are much more aggressive in their role in civil pretrial negotiations in Los Angeles. Similarly, Los Angeles judges are more active and interventionist in their conduct of nonjury trials than judges in Philadelphia and Chicago. Differences of style partially reflect the bench–bar relationships characteristic of each city. The greater professional distance between attorneys and judges in Los Angeles contributes to a judiciary with more freedom to manage cases actively, the inclinations of attorneys notwithstanding. The much closer professional and social relationships in Chicago encourage judicial deference to attorneys, especially in public, where the rebuke of attorneys is perceived to be damaging to individual lawyers or the bar as a whole.

Differences of judicial style are also related to a court's balancing of management and political influences. In Los Angeles, where politics is subordinated to management, incentives are clearly present for judges to take actions that will expedite the processing of cases. The result appears to be relatively rapid processing and disposition of cases. Incentives are present but weaker in Philadelphia, where reported backlog and delay problems are greater. And in Chicago incentives for judges to expedite cases are virtually nonexistent so long as the interests of management continue to be subordinated to those of partisan politics. The resultant delays are predictably large, with no diminution in sight.

## Notes

1. We observed five judges in each of these courts, including judges in criminal and civil assignments. In addition, our survey response rate was excellent in all three courts: Chicago, 67 percent; Los Angeles, 65 percent; and Philadelphia, 67 percent.

In this chapter we have excluded Chicago circuit judges, whose current assignment was not comparable to the work of Los Angeles Superior Court judges or Philadelphia Court of Common Pleas judges. Because Illinois trial courts are unified, circuit judges in Chicago may be assigned to misdemeanor, traffic, or small claims divisions, for example.

2. For a discussion of the influence of politics in courts, see Kenneth M. Dolbeare, *Trial Courts in Urban Politics* (New York: Wiley, 1967); James R. Klonoski and Robert I. Mendelsohn, "The Allocation of Justice: A Political Approach," in James R. Klonoski and Robert I. Mendelsohn (eds.), *The Politics of Local Justice* (Boston: Little, Brown, 1970); and James Eisenstein and Herbert Jacob, *Felony Justice: An Organizational Analysis of Criminal Courts* (Boston: Little, Brown, 1977).

3. See, for example, Thomas Church, Jr., Alan Carlson, Jo-Lynne Lee, and Teresa Tan, *Justice Delayed: The Pace of Litigation in Urban Trial Courts* (Williamsburg, Va.: National Center for State Courts, 1978).

4. For some contemporary political insights into Chicago, see Mike Royko, *Boss* (New York: New American Library, 1971), and Milton Rakove, *Don't Make No Waves, Don't Back No Losers* (Bloomington: Indiana University Press, 1975).

5. Since 1979 criminal court judges also sit at Eleventh and State streets, relatively near the downtown area.

6. Many of these judges were excluded from the analysis because of the nature of their assignment. See note 1 above.

7. Most but not all of these "suburban" districts in the Los Angeles county court system are in predominantly white areas. Nevertheless, the net result is still less courthouse separation of defendants by race than in Chicago.

8. Since 1976 a tenth district has been created in Compton to alleviate the burgeoning case pressures upon the central district. As a result, perhaps no more than half of the county's judges will be sitting in the central district in 1980.

9. The most recent election for chief judge—to choose a successor to Boyle—drew two candidates. The Democratic organization's choice, Harry Comerford, defeated the more independent Richard Fitzgerald by a wide margin, following intense lobbying by Democratic ward and precinct captains among the judges.

10. Feeley speaks of a "gentleman's agreement between party leaders to maintain an even balance" of judges in Connecticut. See Malcolm M. Feeley, *The Process Is the Punishment* (New York: Russell Sage, 1979), p. 63. In Pennsylvania, governors often defer to local party leaders in the filling of vacancies. Furthermore, there is some expectation that a judge who leaves the bench will be replaced by an interim appointment of a judge from the same party as the departing judge. These kinds of understandings between the two parties reflect the salience of partisan politics as well as the reality of a competitive two-party political system.

11. It is interesting to note that during the tenure of Chief Judge John Boyle, no federal funds for any court-related projects were sought or accepted by the Cook County Circuit Court. This was not true in Los Angeles or Philadelphia.

12. Under Illinois state law, a judge must receive a 60 percent or better affirmative vote in order to be retained in office. In Pennsylvania and other states where judges run in retention elections, only a 50 percent or beter affirmative vote is required.

13. Since 1973 Pennsylvania has used merit selection to fill interim vacancies.

14. In fact, former public officials were as likely to be selected by the state supreme court to fill vacancies as by the party slatemakers, whose selections voters ratify.
15. A number of unified state court systems utilize two "classes" of judge as a way of protecting upper-level judges from petty cases. In addition, the threat of assignment to a division that hears only petty cases (e.g., traffic or small claims) can be a powerful sanction against "troublemaking" judges.
16. These differences are sufficiently small to be eliminated if the proportion of nonresponding women judges were slightly different in the three courts. It is interesting to note that Cook argues that women are utilized in a much more gender-conscious way in Chicago than in Los Angeles. Assignments to domestic relations, juvenile, and probate divisions account for all women judges in Chicago, whereas in Los Angeles women judges also serve in criminal and major civil divisions. See Beverly Blair Cook, "Women Judges: The End of Tokenism," in Winifred L. Hepperle and Laura Crites (eds.), *Women in the Courts* (Williamsburg, Va.: National Center for State Courts, 1978).
17. See "Selection by Connection: The Cook County Judicial Monopoly," *Chicago Lawyer*, September 1979. This study found, among other things, that 51 percent of circuit judges sitting in 1979 in Cook County were once precinct captains or assistant precinct captains.
18. Illinois, too, has a speedy trial rule (160 days for defendants *not* in custody; 120 days for defendants in custody), but this is rarely treated seriously in the Chicago criminal courts. Courtroom actors seem willing to agree to continuances, which hold time in abeyance.
19. For some reason, no probate division judges in Chicago responded to our survey. Perhaps probate judges have the most "esprit de corps," or see themselves as least appropriately included in a definition of trial court judges of general jurisdiction. Otherwise, the distribution of assignments among our respondents parallels rather closely that of the Chicago court as a whole.
20. On January 1, 1978, the probate division switched to an individual calendar system. See "Where There Are Wills, There's Delay," *Chicago Tribune*, November 19, 1978.
21. In Los Angeles we discovered that a number of judges arrived at the courthouse quite early (7:30 or 8:00 AM), and went to a cafeteria upstairs to have coffee and talk about a variety of issues. The dispersion of buildings precluded this in Philadelphia. In Chicago, many of the criminal court judges at Twenty-sixth and California lunched together in the basement.
22. Paul B. Wice, *Criminal Lawyers: An Endangered Species* (Beverly Hills and London: Sage Publications, 1978), p. 39.
23. Federal District Court judges in Philadelphia write many more decisions than their counterparts in other districts. See Federal Judicial Center, *1969-1970 Federal District Court Time Study* (Washington, D.C.: Federal Judicial Center, 1971).
24. See David W Neubauer, "Judicial Role and Case Management," *Justice System Journal*, 4 (1979).
25. Two "alternative" bar associations in Chicago look upon sitting judges differently. The Chicago Council of Lawyers, a liberal activist group, scrutinizes the sitting judiciary much more critically. The Cook County Bar Association, a black membership bar, focuses upon ensuring continued black representation on the bench.

26. See "Judges Blamed for Case Delays," *Chicago Daily Law Bulletin*, August 17, 1979.
27. Wice, *Criminal Lawyers*, suggests that the Philadelphia defense bar is characterized by its "inbred nature" (most lawyers being raised and educated locally). Our observations suggest that this is quite characteristic of Chicago also, but much less so in Los Angeles.
28. A Chicago Crime Commission study of felony cases disposed in Chicago criminal courts in 1979 found a mean disposition time of 448 days. See "Excessive Trial Delays in County Courts Assailed," *Chicago Tribune*, August 17, 1979. This compares with a mean time of 132 days in Los Angeles for criminal felony cases filed in 1977; for these data, see Kathleen B. Brosi, *A Cross-City Comparison of Felony Case Processing* (Washington, D.C.: Institute for Law and Social Research, 1979), p. 55.
29. In December 1978, Chicago judges were increased to $50,000. Los Angeles judges received an increment to $51, 624 in July 1978.
30. Cost-of-living differences among the three cities in 1977 were negligible. The Index of Comparative Costs (based upon an intermediate budget for a four-person family) was 104 in Philadelphia, 101 in Chicago, and 100 in Los Angeles, with a national average of 100. See *U.S. Department of Labor News, Bureau of Labor Statistics* (Washington, D.C.: Government Printing Office, 1978).
31. Eisenstein and Jacob, *Felony Justice* (note 2 above), p. 112.
32. This is speculation; we have no quantitative data, nor are we aware of any, that support this.
33. Parenthetically, a somewhat higher percentange of Republican than Democratic judges find court politics to be a "substantial" influence in both Chicago and Philadelphia.
34. Personal conversation with Chief Judge Wenke.
35. Church et al., *Justice Delayed* (note 3 above), present data indicative of a significant delay problem in processing criminal cases in Philadelphia. The figures are not comparable to the mean disposition times reported in separate studies for Chicago and Los Angeles (note 28 above), but they did find Philadelphia to rank nineteenth in a twenty-one-city comparison. Only Boston and the Bronx (New York) fared worse.

# PART V

## Conclusion

# CHAPTER 10

## Judging in America's Trial Courts

TRIAL judges perform a wide variety of tasks, which call upon their skills as adjudicator, legal researcher, administrator, negotiator, community relations agent, and affiliator. Most judges spend time and psychic energy in each of these roles, either by their own choosing or at the request of their court.

Adjudication is the area where trial judges spend the bulk of their time. Jury trial work is the most time-consuming, but nonjury trials—which require the judge to assume the fact-finding role of a jury—are also frequent. Surprisingly, most judges rarely hear long or complex motions. By contrast, the flow of routine motions for continuances, discovery, subpoena of witnesses, and other matters is often unending.

Judges perform a mix of other functions. Of these, legal research is probably the most time-consuming. Keeping up with the law is a common activity for most trial judges, at least for a short time each day. This may involve reading new case law, becoming familiar with a new sentencing code, or keeping abreast of changing legal thought in a specialized area of interest. Preparing and writing decisions, judgments, and orders is a less widespread activity, but one that requires a substantial investment of judicial time. In some instances, this work is relatively routine, as in preparing divorce judgments. In other areas, such as products liability, mental health, and equitable relief the issues may be complex and quite challenging.

Judges perform administrative tasks on a frequent basis, though not usually for large amounts of time. Some administrative tasks are routine, mostly clerical in nature. Other work, notably docket management, has both an administrative and an adjudicative character; that is, managerial skills are required in the processing of cases. This blending of task areas is not easily captured in quantitative terms. Thus, if we define "calendar work" as adjudicative, we understate the amount of administrative work trial judges do. A few judges, usually chief or presiding judges, spend a large proportion of their time on administration, either in performing the court's liaison work with the sociopolitical environment or in managing the organization and distribution of work among judges in the courthouse.

Many, though not all, judges perform negotiation tasks, by being present at conferences between competing litigants or prosecutors and defense counsel, and perhaps by becoming involved in the formulation of an agreement. Negotiation activities do not typically consume large amounts of judges' time; nevertheless, they call upon the judge to choose a role. The diversity of roles adopted, ranging from active participation to passive ratification, reflect ambivalence about attorney–judge relationships in an adversary setting.

Community relations and affiliation work consume comparatively little time for most judges. Some judges consciously avoid community involvement, either on practical grounds or because of their philosophy about the role of a judge. Others find the community to be a relevant source of information about the values and opinions of political leaders or ordinary citizens. Similarly, some judges, by virtue of their personality and temperament, shun much affiliation with their judicial colleagues or courtroom personnel. Other judges do participate in socializing activities with attorneys and court personnel, either as a form of personal release or to maintain the cohesion and morale of the courtroom workgroup.

Judges work relatively normal hours, similar in duration to the hours of most American workers. Reports by judges themselves suggest an eight-hour working day (in addition to lunch). Our observations indicate a somewhat lower figure, perhaps six and one-half hours. Regardless of which figure is more accurate, most judges work a reasonably full day under a variety of physical, psychological, and interpersonal circumstances. The relationship between "hardworkingness" (our term for hours worked and involvement in community, bar, and teaching activities) and judicial productivity is another matter. For example, productivity is not easy to define or measure. Notwithstanding this and other problems, we have implicitly adopted the assumption that there is only a small (positive) relationship between the two phenomena, given what we know about the working world of trial judges. No matter how hard-working an individual judge may be, poor relationships with attorneys, ineffective courtroom personnel, or inadequacies of his own skills in a particular area of work (e.g., negotiation) may prevent his achieving a high level of productivity.

## Organizational Influences

We have demonstrated that organizational influences help to define the work of trial judges. Broadly speaking, these include court structure and management, the characteristics of attorneys, and the quality and availability of courthouse resources. The largest of these influences is court structure, especially size of court.

Judges perform quite different mixes of tasks, depending upon how many other judges sit in the same trial court. Though judges in all courts perform much adjudication, the balance between jury and nonjury trial work shifts sharply from smaller to larger courts. In larger courts, judges are much more likely to hear jury trials; in smaller courts, nonjury trials. This reflects, in part, the more highly adversarial character of larger urban courts, where attorneys are more combative and standard jury trials consume more time.

The frequency of negotiation sessions and the time spent by judges in them tend to be greater in larger courts. In pretrial negotiation of criminal cases, it is judges in the very largest courts who report more frequent conferences and discussions. On the civil side, there is a linear increase in the amount of time spent by judges in settlement discussions as court size increases. These relationships again reflect the adversarial character of attorney practices in larger courts. Agreement is not reached so easily between more contentious attorneys. This was especially observable in civil cases, where multiple attorneys and multiparty suits appeared to be the norm in big city courts. The relationships also reflect the greater caseload pressures that confront judges in larger courts. Judges perceive that their attentiveness to pretrial negotiation sessions will facilitate disposition of cases.

The mix of legal research tasks also fluctuates with size of court. As court size increases, judges report keeping abreast of the law more frequently while spending less time preparing and writing decisions, judgments, and orders. These relationships are a function of the different expectations of attorneys in larger and smaller jurisdictions and are facilitated by judges' different utilization of law clerks in large and small courts.

Finally, the contours of a judge's task environment change from smaller to larger courts. In larger courts, judges report longer working hours. These judges also indicate less variety in their work, in the types of cases heard and in the mix of tasks from one day to another. This restricted variety occurs in larger courts because specialization and utilization of expertise are more common. In sum, the work of trial judges appears more intense, time-consuming, and repetitive in larger courts.

Other elements of court structure and operations have only limited impact upon the work of trial judges. For example, the impact of circuit-riding is most visible in the extra-long hours worked by judges who ride circuit alone.

Statewide assignment judges also work longer hours, but they are less involved in community relations than their counterparts who are attached to one or more local communities. The impact of case assignment system is restricted to the area of negotiation: Master calendars promote or facilitate judicial involvement in civil settlement discussions but discourage or make more difficult such involvement in criminal plea negotiations.

The characteristics of attorneys have a broader impact upon judicial work than most elements of court structure. The skills of attorneys, as they are perceived by judges, shape which tasks judges emphasize in their work. Poor attorney skills sometimes lead judges to do more of certain tasks, such as preparing decisions, orders, and judgments. Conversely, when attorneys are highly skilled in trial or settlement work, judges also do more of these tasks. Secondly, the level of stability of attorney members of the courtroom workgroup impacts upon judicial work. Where criminal attorneys remain in one courtroom for a period of months or years, judges experience more frequent plea bargaining sessions and less jury trial work. The impact from stability of civil attorneys is less substantial, in part because civil attorneys never achieve the level of working familiarity with one another that some criminal attorneys do.

Finally, courthouse resources impact upon the work of trial judges. The overall efficiency of courtroom personnel (as perceived by judges) is related to the amount of time judges spend in their work. Efficient personnel shorten that time; inefficient personnel lengthen it. Interestingly, the number of courtroom personnel and their overall efficiency appear to be unrelated, perhaps even negatively correlated. This was painfully evident in our observations of three big city courts (Chicago, Los Angeles, and Philadelphia) and in the survey responses of judges in these courts. In our examination of individual courtroom personnel, the law clerk emerges as the most significant in shaping the work of trial judges. Where full-time or even part-time law clerks are present, judges report doing more legal research tasks. In large courts, law clerks assist judges in writing and researching decisions. In small courts, law clerks help judges to keep abreast of the law in the many areas with which judges must be familiar, given the characteristic diversity of their caseloads.

## POLICY IMPLICATIONS

Many of these organizational variables are relevant to policy-makers in the courts, because courts actively choose much of their structure, operations, and even resources. Sometimes these choices are made by local trial courts themselves; other times, they are dictated by state supreme courts or state court administrative offices. In both situations, however, decisions about the efficacy of particular structures or procedures are made, often without significant empirical input. Our findings provide one basis for more informed decision-making.

Nevertheless, we do not propose to make sweeping policy recommendations. Trial courts are diverse in their structure and operations, sometimes for good reason. Structures suited to the local sociolegal environment of one court may be quite inappropriate for other courts set in different local environments. In short, a growing body of research demonstrates that courts are most effective when they are sensitive to the distinctive characteristics of their local legal culture.[1]

We propose instead to address selected aspects of court structure, attorney characteristics, and courthouse resources in light of current policy questions in the management of trial courts. By doing so, we refrain from promoting an unthinking uniformity currently in vogue,[2] and at the same time acknowledge the genuine limitations in generalizing from data on the work of trial judges.

CIRCUIT-RIDING

Circuit-riding is a widespread phenomenon. In nearly every state, some trial judges ride circuit across county lines. Nationally, one-third of all trial judges in courts of general jurisdiction ride circuit. Furthermore, circuit-riding is not a vanishing creature, as some observers have suggested.[3] Few states have moved to eliminate it. As recently as 1977 judicial reformers in the state of North Dakota proposed to abolish stationary county judges, who serve part time, in favor of full-time "district associate" judges who would ride circuit within six multicounty districts, much as the upper trial court judges in that state do. Ironically, this "nineteenth-century" idea was proposed to facilitate modern reforms such as administrative unification of the state's trial courts and a more professionalized, legally trained judiciary.[4]

There are, however, costs as well as potential benefits to the proliferation of circuit-riding. About half (47 percent) of all circuit-riding judges report travel time on their most common work day, for an average of 1.5 hours. Additional judges travel on their less common days. Thus, travel is costly in judicial time. It is also costly in dollars of state and local money. Judges must use increasingly expensive gasoline to fuel automobiles to take them far enough from their homes to necessitate their staying in motels overnight.[5] Extensive travel may also impose physical and psychological strains upon judges. Though circuit-riding judges generally feel similarly to other judges on most dimensions of the work environment, circuit-riders are more critical of the efficiency of their courtroom personnel.

Whether the frequency or extensiveness of circuit-riding should be reduced is an issue that individual states may have to face sometime in the near future. The available options and existing resources will vary from state to state, dictating different resolutions. In particular, states should examine a major premise underlying the use of circuit-riding—that legally trained, full-time judges can be recruited in less populous locales only under a circuit-riding system.

STATEWIDE ASSIGNMENT

Statewide assignment of trial judges is the predominant method of assignment in nine states, including all of New England. No states are currently considering the adoption of a statewide assignment system (though many states are increasing their use of temporary assignments to attack backlog problems in urban courts). Some states are taking steps to minimize the traveling associated with a statewide assignment system. In addition to the traveling implicit in a circuit-riding system, statewide assignment presents the possibility that a judge will be assigned to cover an entire circuit far from his home. Both Maine and North Carolina have recently restructured regions, assignment patterns, or both in order to achieve a "modified resident judge" system.[6] Nevertheless, some states are severely limited in their ability to achieve this because their trial judges are appointed (by the governor) on a statewide basis, often without adequate consideration to their place of residence.

Like circuit-riding judges, those serving in statewide assignment systems incur significant travel time. Three-fifths (62 percent) report travel time on their most common day, for an average of 1.6 hours. Furthermore, judges in statewide assignment consistently report substantially longer hours worked on their most common day. These additional hours no doubt contribute to their perception of being more severely underpaid than judges in other states.

In light of the extensive traveling and the work habits and perceptions of judges in statewide assignment systems, the rationales underlying this organization of work need to be reconsidered. Judicial familiarity with local attorneys is a widespread, accepted, and often promoted state of affairs. Familiarity among members of the courtroom workgroup facilitates the disposition of criminal cases by introducing an element of predictability in sentencing.[7] It is probably more realistic to view cooptation and corruption of modern-day judges as the result of factors other than familiarity (partisan politics, personal political ideology, or greed). Statewide assignment systems, which continue to disperse judges far from their homes without a geographically based need to do so, should consider the real advantages and question the perceived drawbacks of judge–attorney familiarity.

MASTER VERSUS INDIVIDUAL CALENDAR

Both master and individual case assignment systems are commonly used in trial courts. In some courts, however, little or no administrative "choice" exists as to which shall be employed. In solo-judge courts, for example, an individual calendar is inevitable. Similarly, small courts having only a few judges lack the flexibility to specialize in ways required by a master calendar. Conversely, "moving courts," where judges ride circuit or serve in statewide assignment often result in master calendars, given the frequency and duration of assignments. It is in larger, multijudge courts where judges remain stationary that an actual choice exists. For these courts, we have little evidence to suggest that one assignment system is better than the other, at least with respect to the utilization of judicial time.

Trial judges under master and individual calendars generally work at similar tasks and mixes of tasks. The amount of "waiting time" judges experience is similar under both systems, as is the reported length of their work days. Even perceptions of the work environment are generally parallel on such dimensions as skill utilization, efficiency of courtroom personnel, caseload variety, and caseload pressures. Thus, with only a few exceptions,[8] judges in master and individual calendar systems appear to work, and to view their work, quite similarly.

Reformers who hope to create "docket consciousness" and accountability in trial judges by instituting an individual calendar may be disappointed.[9] Recent research on trial court delay also points to the probable lack of impact of case assignment system: Some courts utilizing a master calendar are slow, others are fast, and much the same is true for courts with individual calendars.[10] The likely conclusion from research on delay, from our survey data on judicial work, and from our own observations is that the choice of a case assignment system should be based upon the local environment rather than generalized philosophical arguments about the inherent value of the respective systems. One case assignment system may be superior in a given locale, but neither system appears consistently superior across all locations.

## COURT SIZE

The impact of court size upon judicial work is substantial, as we have highlighted in the summary above. Nevertheless, the implications for policy choices by courts are fuzzy, because court size is a variable determined by uncontrollable forces (e.g., amount of litigation, crime rate, community size and life-style). Furthermore, from the standpoint of the individual judge and his morale, it is not clear whether large, small, or intermediate-size courts are preferable. Each has its own advantages and drawbacks.

Viewed from another perspective, court size is actually a very crude variable which indicates little or nothing about how large courts, in particular, are organized. Most large courts are decentralized, to varying degrees, through the establishment or formation of courtroom workgroups.[11] These workgroups, especially in criminal courts, may develop the kind of interpersonal familiarity routinely found in small courts. Perhaps the most significant way in which courts can modify, if not transform, their size is through decentralization of work and authority. On the other hand, decentralization can lead to the development and institutionalization of different norms, including lack of uniformity or equity in decision-making.

## ATTORNEY SKILLS

Trial judges are generally quite sanguine about the skills of attorneys practicing in their courtrooms. Despite Chief Justice Burger's oft-repeated claim that in federal courts attorneys are ill-prepared advocates, state trial judges do not perceive this to be a widespread problem. Nevertheless, where attorneys are perceived to be poorly skilled—especially in case preparation and management—judges must often assume greater responsibilities, work longer hours, and endure the frustrations of more unconstructive waiting time.

How can attorney skills be improved? Some reformers have suggested certification of attorneys by area of specialization. Others advocate more clinically oriented law school programs. These kinds of solutions, however, are outside the domain of courts. Because attorneys are either "free-lancers" or belong to sponsoring organizations different from those of the court (judges), little direct training can be imposed. Courts could provide attorneys with easier access to a uniform set of administrative rules. But perhaps only through closer informal cooperation among prosecutors' offices, public defenders' offices, the private bar, and the court can judicial expectations of adequate attorney skill be better met, or readjusted. Some courts have found that increased communication among representatives of various sponsoring organizations can lead to improved court management, including better utilization of judge time.[12]

COURTHOUSE PERSONNEL

The availability of courtroom personnel varies widely. The individual state is the most important variable in determining level of secretarial and law clerk services. In a few states, all trial judges have access to the services of a full-time secretary and full-time law clerk. The significance of the law clerk in facilitating legal research by trial judges makes the distribution of this resource an important policy question. Our data indicate that the facilitative role of law clerks occurs most visibly in large and small courts (but not intermediate-size courts), suggesting that a more rational allocation policy would be based upon court size. But is this politically, or logistically, feasible?

In the few states where every trial judge has a full-time law clerk, the principle of equity is likely to override management considerations. Judges in these states undoubtedly come to believe that they are entitled to a law clerk, and few would voluntarily yield theirs. In states where only some judges have law clerks, the distribution appears to be rather haphazard, influenced by court size, internal court politics, the availability of nearby law students, and the presence of federal funds. We can only suggest that states and courts themselves look to the special needs of judges in small courts and small towns. These judges rarely have access to full- or part-time law clerks now, yet those who do have these resources utilize them in unusual and important ways—particularly as sounding boards, as surrogates for judicial colleagues. This is an important function, given the intellectual isolation of small-town judges and their generally diverse caseloads.

THEORETICAL IMPLICATIONS

Much of the literature on trial courts, particularly recent studies of criminal courts, addresses the viability of analyzing courts as organizations. But what kinds of organizations, with what characteristics? Are courts hierarchically managed in a routinized way, such that the label "bureaucracy" applies, as

Blumberg asserts?[13] Or are courts horizontally managed in a way that fosters idiosyncratic workgroups, as Eisenstein and Jacob assert?[14] Is a trial court one organization or a meeting ground for a number of different organizations?[15]

Our data cannot speak directly to these issues, because they involve matters of definition and perspective—value orientations that are superimposed on the real world of courts. Our data do demonstrate that the trial judge cannot be viewed or studied in isolation from the key actors with whom he comes in contact. Both attorneys and courthouse personnel, through their skills and actual performance of tasks, shape the work patterns and styles of trial judges. Given the focus of previous research, the area of attorney-judge interrelationships probably provides the best point of departure for an assessment of the theoretical implications of our data on judicial work.

ATTORNEY ADVERSARINESS AND JUDICIAL RESPONSES

Highly adversarial attorneys highlight the potentially different roles that trial judges can adopt. Combative, argumentative, procrastinating attorneys present judges with a problem. Are trial judges supposed to "umpire" disputes between advocates representing competing client interests? Or are trial judges supposed to move dockets, to manage the flow of cases before them in order to insure a speedy (or not too slow) resolution of disputes? In most locales, judges cannot perform both roles; they must choose to emphasize one role or the other. Interestingly, our data suggest that one of the key variables affecting a choice of judicial roles is the professional and social relationships between attorneys and judges. Observations and survey data from Chicago, Los Angeles, and Philadelphia indicate that these relationships and mutual role expectations are more important than the background, political philosophy, and perhaps even personality of the judge. In short, judges function within the boundaries of the political, social, and legal environments of their courts.

COURTROOM WORKGROUPS AND CASE DISPOSITIONS

Eisenstein and Jacob coined the term "courtroom workgroup" to refer primarily to prosecutors, defense counsel, and judges who regularly work together in criminal courtrooms.[16] Our survey and observational data confirm the presence of many such workgroups in criminal courts in metropolitan areas, smaller cities, and suburbs. In some courts, workgroups may be differently structured. Prosecutor–judge workgroups flourish where defense attorneys are too numerous to permit familiarity (e.g., where private counsel appear more frequently than public defenders), or when judges perceive prosecutors to be their "assistants" in moving the docket. Occasionally, but less frequently, public defender–judge teams develop, where defenders are assigned to the courtroom of a judge for a significantly longer period than prosecutors.

We also find support for the idea that the stability, or level of familiarity, of workgroups affects the mode of disposition. Eisenstein and Jacob concluded that more stable workgroups disposed of their cases more frequently through plea bargaining and guilty pleas, less frequently through trials (especially, jury trials).[17] Our data provide a striking parallel. Where attorneys are assigned to one courtroom for a period of time, judges are more likely to report participation in plea discussions, as well as a higher ratio of nonjury to jury trial work. Our data suggest a further refinement: Where prosecutors are assigned to the same courtroom for a very long period of time (typically, two years or more), judges come to participate in plea discussions *less* frequently. We conclude that when the prosecutor comes to know "his" judge well enough, in terms of sentencing proclivities, many judges no longer find it necessary to be present at plea discussions in order to implement their beliefs. The prosecutor and judge, in these instances, come to be of "one mind."

In civil courtrooms, it is much more difficult to identify workgroups. Civil attorneys are not assigned to courtrooms by sponsoring organizations; they "freelance" and, therefore, move in and out almost randomly. As a result, no handful of attorneys comes to dominate civil courts in the way that a few prosecutors and public defenders do in criminal courts. Still, judges report different levels of regularity among civil attorneys. Yet it remains to be determined whether any civil court judges work with a set of attorneys sufficiently regularly and repetitively to warrant the label "workgroup." Our data hint at this through the lack of substantial relationships between civil attorney stability and judicial work patterns. There may be more accurate ways to characterize the working relationships of attorneys and judges in civil courts than by the concept of workgroups. Indeed, the variety of civil courts suggests the need to study different civil courts before reaching any generalizations about the work of civil court judges or their relationships with attorneys.

## Individual Influences

We have also demonstrated that individual-level influences shape the work of trial judges.[18] Broadly speaking, these include the social background and characteristics of trial judges, their particular skills, and their perceptions of the work environment.

Several background variables influence judicial work; the most decisive is the age of the judge. Our data indicate that older judges are increasingly likely to be assigned to civil rather than criminal work, to have access to the services of a full-time law clerk, and to perform a somewhat different mix of tasks. Differences of assignment and resources appear to result primarily from age rather than seniority on the bench, suggesting that courts do not distribute rewards solely, or perhaps even primarily, on the basis of tenure.

Older and younger judges also differ in the types of work they perform, and the differences are not attributable to their level of resources or assignment. For example, older judges are much more likely to have jury trial work rather than nonjury trials. Older judges are less likely to do legal research, especially preparing and writing decisions. And older judges are much less likely to report tasks of an interpersonal nature—affiliation and case-related discussions with attorneys. Some of these differences in work emphasis are likely to be matters of personal choice, such as diminished interest in legal research and affiliation tasks. Others almost certainly represent adaptations by court systems to the real or perceived needs of aging judges, including the allocation of jury and nonjury trial work. Nonjury trials involve the judge in a more complete and possibly taxing role. Many courts that have the flexibility of size and a master case assignment system choose to spare their older judges the pressures of highly adversarial and complex nonjury trials, which often occur in civil cases.

Other background characteristics—notably the gender and race of the judge—affect the level of involvement of trial judges in their work. Women and black judges report working consistently longer hours on their various work days and appear to be more heavily involved in community relations and bar association activities than their male and white counterparts. The mix of tasks these judges perform is quite similar, however, suggesting that most courts utilize minority judges in much the same way as other judges.

The skills of trial judges influence what tasks they will perform. Judges who see themselves as skilled in a particular area of work are more likely to spend time in that area. The relationship is particularly marked for legal research and negotiation. Judges who believe that they are superior at legal research spend more time keeping up with the law and preparing/writing decisions. Likewise, judges who think they excel at negotiation spend more time in formal and informal discussions designed to reach agreement, especially in civil cases, where trial judges have more freedom to define their role. Furthermore, our observations suggest that courts come to learn which judges are skilled in specific areas (particularly negotiation) and draw upon those strengths, thereby reinforcing skills.

Finally, judges' perceptions of the work environment shape the amount of work they undertake. For example, judges who feel quite positive about their skill utilization report working longer hours and being more involved in community relations activities and judicial education programs. On the other hand, these same hard-working judges also perceive that their courtroom personnel are less effective and that they are less in control of their work time, under more pressure to move cases, and less well compensated. These latter perceptions are likely to be the result, rather than the cause, of longer hours worked.

## POLICY IMPLICATIONS

Individual attributes, perceptions, and background raise policy issues less directly than organizational variables. Local courts, for example, cannot control or modify the characteristics of the trial judges who are selected. For better or worse, the age, gender, racial composition, and skills of judges are either randomly distributed or the systematic product of the political environment within which courts are located. Nevertheless, the characteristics and skills of trial judges, and their relationship to the work environment, do generate policy implications at the state level.

## AGE AND MANDATORY RETIREMENT LAWS

There is a significant dispersion in the ages of sitting trial judges. Two-thirds fall between the ages of forty and sixty. Only a small percentage (7 percent) are under forty, whereas most of the remainder (26 percent) are sixty or older. But only a very small percentage (3 percent) are seventy or older. Thus, images of an old trial bench in the states are largely exaggerated. Most trial judges do not stay on the bench well into their seventies, unlike many U.S. Supreme Court justices who are familiar to the public. One reason for timely judicial retirements are the pension plans in various states which encourage (or induce) retirement, by reducing the benefits from a pension after a specified age (often seventy). Furthermore, most states now have a mandatory retirement age for judges (usually seventy).

There have been several challenges to the constitutionality of mandatory judicial retirement statutes (one in Illinois, another in Missouri). In each case, a court held that such laws are rationally related to a legitimate state interest.[19] Thus, as American society has begun to re-examine the desirability of early retirement for its workers generally, judges are increasingly required or encouraged to step down from the bench by the age of seventy.

Do older trial judges "pull their own weight," or are they less productive than their younger counterparts? From our data (where we define "older" judges to be sixty-five or above), we can say that older judges are given special considerations in assignment and resources (not always justified by seniority). In addition, older judges appear to be utilized disproportionately in tasks of adjudication, especially jury trials. On our measures of "hardworkingness," however, we find few differences between younger and older judges. Hours of work reported and involvement in community relations and bar association activities are comparable. Thus, our survey data are inconclusive. Observations only reaffirm the *diversity* in skill and work habits of older judges that are characteristic of all judges. Some older judges were hard-working and obviously capable of meeting the physical and mental demands of the job; other older judges appeared not quite so hard-working or capable. Even these latter judges, though, may offer their court unique contributions from experience that cannot easily be replaced. In sum, although many courts adapt to the perceived needs of aging judges, it is not clear that this adaptation is dysfunctional or undesirable.

## AFFIRMATIVE ACTION AND THE JUDICIARY

In one key area America's trial bench lacks diversity. Only a tiny percentage of judges in the states are either black (3 percent) or female (2 percent).

While President Carter made a determined effort to appoint minority candidates to federal judgeships,[20] few similar efforts have occurred at the state level.

Formal method of selection appears to make little difference in the proportions of minority candidates recruited for the trial bench. More important, at least in elective systems, is the constituency or geographic jurisdiction of the local court. For example, in Detroit, where the criminal court has only citywide jurisdiction and where judges therefore are elected only by city voters, the proportion of black judges is substantial. In other large cities where courts typically have countywide jurisdiction, the percentage of black judges is much lower. This kind of influence parallels the significance of constituencies in city council districts (ward versus at-large) for electing local black legislators.

The generally high involvement of women and black judges in their work provides a second basis of argument for proponents of affirmative action in the judiciary. To be sure, the trial bench should reflect the diversity of backgrounds in the nation. Also, however, black and women judges currently on the bench demonstrate a high standard of "hardworkingness" and community involvement. As more minority judges are selected, there is no reason to expect any diminution in the intensity of their commitment to the job.

## THEORETICAL IMPLICATIONS

Much of the early literature on judicial decision-making suggested that judges were heavily influenced by their personal background or political ideology.[21] Though most of these studies focused on appellate court justices, the transfer of intellectual models to trial courts soon followed. Our analysis indicates that the kinds of variables posited by these studies—political affiliation, prior occupation, selection method—are generally unrelated to the amount, variety, or mix of judicial work. Rather, the work of the trial judge is primarily a function of either organizational variables or individual-level influences, like age and skills, which courts can legally and morally use as the basis for allocation of work.

Our findings are also largely negative with respect to another individual-level variable currently popular in judicial research: socialization. Judges with more experience on the bench do not organize their work differently, nor do they avoid waiting time. In one sense, these findings are a logical extension of the studies that conclude that judges adapt to organizational constraints very early in a career on the bench.[22] On the other hand, our findings are at odds with studies that emphasize the evolution of judicial perceptions and orientations over long periods of time.[23] The impact of organizational influences upon the work of trial judges provides a clear alternative explanation. Elements of court structure, attorneys, courthouse personnel, and even state supreme court rules and case law all serve to surround the judge and to prevent him from being a "captive" of his background, imagination, or experience.

# Speculations About the Future of Trial Judging

## JUDGING AS A CORPORATE ENTERPRISE

There was a time in America when trial judging was mostly an individual enterprise. Judges in rural areas were responsible for the operations of the entire courthouse. In urban areas, each courtroom was something like a medieval fiefdom in which the resident judge ruled without interference from others. Accountability stemmed from the appellate courts, and then only with respect to the content of judicial decisions.

In the past twenty years, judging has increasingly come to take place within a more formal organizational context. In particular, judges have more colleagues, and as a result administrative decisions affecting the court as a whole must take into account a wider set of preferences. Small courthouses that could be managed by a series of autonomous judges have given way to large organizations, which clearly benefit from administrative cooperation.

Furthermore, the development of a science of management in the private sector of the economy has increasingly influenced public organizations, despite initial and sometimes persistent resistance. The call for both structural and management reforms in courts was initiated early in the twentieth century,[24] but it is only recently that the states and courts themselves have begun to respond. One currently popular structural reform is the unification or consolidation of many distinct trial courts into one trial court of general and/or limited jurisdiction. Thus, the autonomous police courts, magistrate courts, and city courts—to which judges were separately elected—are being replaced with one limited jurisdiction court typically governed by a chief judge with administrative authority to supervise and allocate the division of work.[25] A similar trend can be found in the upper-level trial courts, where probate, domestic relations, and juvenile courts are being merged into the general jurisdiction trial court. Such mergers seek to facilitate administrative flexibility, specialization, and accountability.

A parallel movement toward centralized management of the courts has also been taking place. Two important tools of centralized state management are court administration and the rule-making power.[26] The rise of state court administration is a very recent phenomenon, almost exclusively since 1960.[27] Its functions vary from state to state but generally include some effort at monitoring the disposition of cases in the local trial courts.[28] This occurs primarily through statistical reports whose data are collected at the local level. These collection efforts are routine yet not unobtrusive; most judges are well aware that their court and/or they themselves could look "bad" in the eyes of administrative supervisors. This knowledge can lead to alterations in behavior or reported practices. In some states, the state court administrator's office may have the power to do more than merely find out about "slow" courts or judges. Pressures may be exerted and sanctions threatened, including judicial reassignment on a temporary or even permanent basis.

State supreme court rule-making activities long predate the rise of state administrative offices. But the application of rule-making powers to administrative areas is a relatively recent phenomenon, initially encouraged by New Jersey, which in 1948 constitutionally authorized the chief justice to be the administrative head of all the state's courts.[29] Since then, other state high courts have adopted administrative rules regarding the superintendence of the trial courts, support personnel, the assignment of judges, courtroom facilities and security, and even time frames for the disposition of criminal cases (speedy trial rules).[30] Though such rules may, in the words of one observed judge, create a "blizzard of paperwork," they also create a framework within which courts and judicial personnel are expected to operate. Enforcement may not be uniform, but judges are directed to yet another source of administrative accountability.

The effect of these convergent trends—of increased court size, unification of trial courts, and tools of centralized management—is to decrease the professional independence and autonomy of the trial judge. He may still retain much discretion over the scheduling of his own work time, as judges in our survey indicate, but he is no longer the "entrepreneur of justice." Judging now takes place in an administratively rationalized, or corporate, setting, in which the characteristics of both collegial and power–dependency relationships are present. These latter relations, in particular, contribute to accountability by increasing significantly the risks of (slow) judging. In sum, individual trial judges no longer have the freedom to dispose of cases exclusively at their own pace. Increasingly, though in variable degrees, they will be held *accountable* either by state supreme courts, administrative offices, or their own chief judge.

## JUDGING AND POLITICS

If trial judges now face increased accountability, why do the problems of courts—notably backlog, delay, and inefficiency—persist?[31] One perspective, of course, is that these problems would be much worse without the response of structural reforms and centralized management. The increase in litigiousness and criminal behavior, together with expansion of constitutional rights, may simply outstrip the ability of human resources to do better.

A second perspective, however, might scrutinize the role which politics play in the administration of the courts. Politics can be viewed either as *partisan* politics or the court's own internal distribution of rewards and sanctions. Some courts may be an extension of the dominant political machine in their community. Other courts, located in relatively nonpartisan climates, create their own intrigue by permitting clashes of personality or political ideology to overtake larger management and policy goals.

Why some courts manage their affairs with less deference to politics than other courts is not an easy question to answer. If partisan politics is significantly involved, the nature of community politics will be important. The effects of partisan politics, for example, are more clear-cut in the Chicago courts, where a unified party organization has prevailed for a long time, than in the Philadelphia courts, where a fractionalized party assumed the reins of city government only within the last generation. In less partisan locales, variations in the influence of court politics are still more difficult to explain. We could speculate that, as in any organization, the mix of personalities may be important. For example, where most judges owe their job to the electorate, that mix may be more inflammatory than where a governor, in filling interim vacancies, may consider questions of collegiality. Alternatively, the presence or absence of court politics may simply reflect custom, prevailing norms.

Courts and judges have difficulty enough trying to accommodate the goals of "doing justice" and disposing of their caseloads.[32] When political considerations, too, need to be accommodated on a regular or even periodic basis, the interests of efficiency and substantive justice, as well as the morale of individual judges, are bound to suffer.

## THE PERSISTENCE OF TRIAL COURTS: A VIEW TOWARD FUTURE CONTROVERSIES

One scholar recently queried whether urban trial courts would "survive" the war on crime.[33] The implication was that the functions of a trial court and its central figure—judges—might dissipate in the face of pervasive plea bargaining. Others have pointed to neighborhood justice centers,[34] diversion programs,[35] and other forms of administrative adjudication or arbitration[36] as the wave of the future. Yet even if these alternative forums for dispute-resolution prove to be successful in diverting some of the work from formal trial courts, much work will still remain. Murderers, armed robbers, and burglars will still be processed in a criminal trial court. Injured parties and disputants to contractual matters will still find their way into the civil trial courts. And professional trial judges will remain at or near the center of case resolution and disposition in formal courts.

Diversity is certain to characterize the future working environment of trial judges as much as it reflects the current state. Trial judges will continue to serve in large and small courts, under different management philosophies and practices, and with skilled and not-so-skilled attorneys and courtroom personnel. It is unlikely that the mix of work that trial judges now perform will change dramatically in the years to come. What may change is the mix of skills and expectations that individuals bring to the office. Trial judges of the future will, of necessity, be more sensitive to administrative and management concerns. They will recognize the changing criteria by which judging is evaluated.

Controversies over the quality of judicial performance are currently edging onto the political agenda and are likely to intensify in the future. For once, recruitment and selection will take a back seat in these debates. Though the federal bench is in the throes of significant change in selection method,[37] states have spent most of their energies in selection reform. Rather, the question becomes: How do we evaluate and improve, where necessary, the quality of those already sitting on the bench? But which quality—administrative skill, fairness, legal competence, ethical propriety, political independence? Most observers would probably agree that all of these qualities are important to good trial judging. But which is most important or sufficiently important to warrant the attention of reformers? In which quality or qualities are trial judges currently most lacking?

Those who focus attention on bar polling tend to emphasize "legal competence." This is precisely because lawyers and the bar are perhaps best equipped to evaluate the legal ability of a judge. By contrast, good-government organizations who engage in "court-watching" are likely to focus on fairness and the quality of treatment accorded litigants and other members of the public in the courtroom, because these judicial traits are more readily observable. State discipline and removal commissions are most likely to hear complaints regarding judicial ethics, in part because deficiencies in some of these other qualities are not yet agreed-upon grounds for such strong actions as censure or removal.

After three years of studying trial judges, including six months of field observations, we think that these aforementioned reform efforts—like those centering on selection—may be slightly misplaced. Relatively few of America's trial judges are ill equipped to handle the legal tasks that confront them. We suspect, with less evidence, that relatively few judges lack basic fairness or a general sense of legal ethics. Many more judges, however, appear to lack sufficient independence from their sponsoring political parties, especially in a few large cities characterized by heavy-handed partisan politics. What the solution might be, we frankly do not know. By contrast, solutions to the lack of administrative or managerial skill among trial judges are much easier to visualize. Because judges are likely to be evaluated increasingly on their productivity—to be held increasingly accountable by their administrative superiors—trial judges will improve their managerial skills. This amounts to survival, to self-esteem and peace in their job of judging. In this search for administrative competence, other skills essential to judging should not be displaced or forgotten. In the final analysis, the qualities of trial judges may be "strainable"[38] but not easily balanced.

## Notes

1. See Thomas Church Jr., Alan Carlson, Jo-Lynne Lee, and Teresa Tan, *Justice Delayed: The Pace of Litigation in Urban Trial Courts* (Williamsburg, Va.: National Center for State Courts, 1978), and Raymond A. Nimmer, "A Slightly Movable Object: A Case Study in Judicial Reform in the Criminal Justice Process—The Omnibus Hearing," *Denver Law Journal*, 48 (1971)

2. See, for example, the American Bar Associations's *Standards Relating to Court Organization* (1974).

3. Ernest C. Friesen, Edward C. Gallas, and Nesta M. Gallas, *Managing the Courts* (Indianapolis: Bobbs-Merrill, 1971).
4. The North Dakota legislature defeated this proposal.
5. In an informal survey by the Oregon State Court Administrator's Office, one trial judge reported travel of 17,000 miles in 1979, and three other judges reported 12,000 miles or more. Numerous judges reported 7,000–8,000 miles traveled in 1977. See Oregon Office of the State Court Administrator, "Judicial Notices," December 22, 1978, p. 6.
6. See, for example, the order promulgated by the Chief Justice of the Supreme Judicial Court of Maine, January 2, 1979.
7. See James Eisenstein and Herbert Jacob, *Felony Justice: An Organizational Analysis of Criminal Courts* (Boston: Little, Brown, 1977); see also our suggestive data on the impact of attorney stability on judicial work patterns in Chapter 4.
8. The exceptions are negotiation tasks in criminal and civil cases (see earlier text in this chapter) and trial time estimates for armed robbery and personal injury jury trials (judges under master calendars report increasingly long estimates as size of court increases).
9. See the discussion in previous chapters of the Ohio Rules of Superintendence, instituted in 1971, which mandate the use of an individual calendar with the hope of reducing court delay.
10. Church et al., *Justice Delayed*, pp. 36–39.
11. Courts with individual calendars much more easily promote stable workgroups. See Chapter 4.
12. See Marcia J. Lipetz, Mary Lee Luskin, and David W. Neubauer, *Evaluation of LEAA's Court Delay-Reduction Program*, interim report, 1979.
13. See Abraham S. Blumberg, *Criminal Justice* (Chicago: Quadrangle, 1967).
14. See Eisenstein and Jacob, *Felony Justice*.
15. For the latter perspective, see Malcolm M. Feeley, *The Process Is the Punishment* (New York: Russell Sage, 1979).
16. Eisenstein and Jacob, *Felony Justice*, pp. 19–39.
17. *Ibid.*, 65–171.
18. Precise mathematical analysis of the comparative influence of organizational and individual-level variables upon judicial work would be impractical, given the range of our judicial work concerns (length, variety, substance and mix of tasks) and the imprecise or surrogate measures of many of these variables.
19. See Chapter 6, note 13, for case citations.
20. See Sheldon Goldman, "A Profile of Carter's Judicial Nominees," *Judicature*, 62 (1978), p. 248.
21. See, for example, Glendon Schubert, *The Judicial Mind: Attitudes and Ideologies of Supreme Court Justices, 1946–1963* (Evanston, Ill.: Northwestern University Press, 1965), and John D. Sprague, *Voting Patterns on the United States Supreme Court: Cases in Federalism 1889–1959* (Indianapolis: Bobbs-Merrill, 1968).
22. See, for example, Milton Heumann, *Plea Bargaining: The Experiences of Prosecutors, Judges and Defense Attorneys* (Chicago: University of Chicago Press,

1977), and Mary Lee Luskin, "Determinants of Attitude and Decision Behavior of Criminal Court Judges," Ph.D. dissertation, University of Michigan, 1978.
23. Lenore Alpert, Burton M. Atkins, and Robert C. Ziller, "Becoming a Judge: The Transition from Advocate to Arbiter," *Judicature*, 62 (1979).
24. Roscoe Pound, "The Causes of Popular Dissatisfaction with the Administration of Justice," address delivered at Annual Meeting of American Bar Association, 1906.
25. This consolidation movement is being accompanied by a professionalization of the judiciary. Most police court and city court judges, for example, were nonlawyers, whereas judges in a unified limited jurisdiction court are typically lawyers.
26. Russell R. Wheeler, "Broadening Participation in the Courts Through Rule-Making and Administration," *Judicature*, 62 (1979), p. 290.
27. See David Saari, *Modern Court Management: Trends in the Role of the Court Executive* (Washington, D.C.: Government Printing Office, 1970).
28. See Robert G. Nieland and Rachel N. Doan, *State Court Administrative Offices* (Chicago: American Judicature Society, 1979).
29. See Charles W. Grau, *Judicial Rulemaking: Administration, Access, and Accountability* (Chicago: American Judicature Society, 1978), p. 24.
30. *Ibid.*, 25.
31. The pervasiveness of these problems is viewed quite differently by court insiders (judges, attorneys, etc.) and the public at large. See *State Courts: A Blueprint for the Future* (Williamsburg, Va.: National Center for State Courts, 1978), pp. 50–54.
32. Eisenstein and Jacob, *Felony Justice* (note 7 above), p. 25.
33. Carl Baar, "Will Urban Trial Courts Survive the War on Crime?" in Herbert Jacob (ed.), *The Potential for Reform of Criminal Justice* (Beverly Hills and London: Sage Publications, 1974).
34. Daniel McGillis and Joan Mullen, *Neighborhood Justice Centers: An Analysis of Potential Models* (Washington, D.C.: Law Enforcement Assistance Administration, 1977); John C. Cratsley, "Community Courts: Offering Alternative Dispute Resolution Within the Judicial System," *Vermont Law Review*, 3 (1978); and Frederick E. Snyder, "Crime and Community Mediation—The Boston Experience: A Preliminary Report on the Dorchester Urban Court Program," *Wisconsin Law Review*, 3 (1978).
35. Earl Johnson, Valerie Kantor, and Elizabeth Schwartz, *Outside the Courts: A Survey of Diversion Alternatives in Civil Cases* (Williamsburg, Va.: National Center for State Courts, 1977), and Raymond T. Nimmer, *Diversion: The Search for Alternative Forms of Prosecution* (Chicago: American Bar Foundation, 1974).
36. See Austin Sarat, "Alternatives in Dispute Processing: Litigation in a Small Claims Court," *Law and Society Review*, 10 (1976).
37. For a description and analysis of the nominating commission established by President Carter's executive order, see Larry C. Berkson and Susan Carbon, The *United States Circuit Judge Nominating Commission: Its Members, Procedures, and Candidates* (Chicago: American Judicature Society, 1980).
38. For a discussion of the possible criteria of the good judge, see Maurice Rosenberg, "The Qualities of Justices: Are They Strainable?" *Texas Law Review*, 44 (1966)

# Appendices

# Appendix A

# Observing Trial Judges: A Note on Philosophy, Strategies, and Techniques

THE observational phase of this study was designed to gather qualitative data that would provide background for the development of a substantively grounded mail questionnaire. We therefore hoped that the observational data would not only confirm or disconfirm our working assumptions about judicial performance but also generate adjuncts to those assumptions.

The observations form a substantial body of information. We spent a total of 138 days observing forty judges in fifteen jurisdictions (eight states) and under virtually all work conditions—on the bench, in chambers, during meetings, inside and outside the courthouse, and at lunch. We participated in three to five days of a judge's work week, and we personally and extensively recorded daily activity from the judge's arrival at chambers until his departure from the courthouse. This record represents one of the few research attempts to focus observational methodology on trial judges in courts of general jurisdiction for this length of time.[1]

## Philosophy of Method

The philosophy of the observations lay in "participant observation," a term replete with different meanings. In the terminology of Schwartz and Schwartz,[2] we were "passive" participant observers; that is, we attempted to minimize our intrusion into the trial judge's working day and to be emotionally detached from the flow of events before us. Yet we were also "participants" in those events, in that we were physically present and visible, rather than viewing from behind a "one-way mirror." Thus, in Buford Junker's terminology,[3] we assumed the role of "observer as participant." He characterizes this role as one of "comparative detachment," suggesting that some involvement is indeed inevitable. For example, although we determined to intrude very rarely on the judicial behaviors observed, we found that asking questions of the judge from time to time was both necessary for clarity and important for the spontaneous extension of ideas. In addition, the immense variety in the ways different judges performed their jobs required that we be "trained human measurement or recording instruments," able to be flexible and take in the unexpected, pursue the explanation of the usual and unusual, and, indeed, draw some crucial inferences from assorted judicial actions. We felt in agreement with Bogdan and Taylor that qualitative research needs "imagination, sensitivity, creativity."[4] In short, we entered the field with working assumptions based upon previous research, our own courtroom and legal experiences, and consultation with judges, but we believed that the validity of our observations would correspond to how *wholly* we responded to the events of the judicial work day.

## Site Selection

The goal of site selection was to identify a wide range of courts in which to observe judges at work. Purposive sampling of courts was used to achieve substantial variance on a number of variables hypothesized to be related to the performance of judicial work.[5] These variables include: (1) original jurisdiction of the court, (2) type of case assignment system utilized by the court, (3) number of judges sitting in the court, (4) method of initial selection for trial judges, (5) scale and life-style of the community; and (6) state political culture. Thus, our fifteen locales reflect courts whose original jurisdiction includes all kinds of criminal and civil matters as well as locales whose trial court of general jurisdiction is restricted in subject matter by the presence of a number of separate, specialized courts of limited jurisdiction. The courts reflect all types of case assignment systems, including master, individual, hybrids, and mixes of these across different divisions. Courts of varying size are represented, ranging from large multijudge courts to solo-judge courts. Most methods of judicial selection are represented—partisan election, nonpartisan election, and merit selection. The fifteen courts are located within diverse political cultures reflecting variations in the degree to which a state has adopted tenets of the Progressive movement in the design and delivery of its public services. And finally, the courts are situated in communities of different size, ranging from metropolitan centers to rural places. In sum, we believe these fifteen jurisdictions represent a wide cross-section of American cultural, political, and judicial life (for a listing, see Table A-1 at the end of this Appendix).

The selection of sites, therefore, was not random. However, once a location was chosen, the selection of individual judges to be observed was (stratified) random, though affected by the choice of divisions and the refusal of some judges to participate. In courts with divisions, we sampled from at least the criminal division and a general civil division. Where courts were more specialized, as in Cook County, we sampled from those civil divisions which heard cases most common to trial courts of general jurisdiction (e.g., personal injury, equity). We generally avoided probate or domestic relations divisions, which are relatively uncommon across the entirety of general jurisdiction trial courts (see Table 2-1).

## Initial Access

We first needed to gain the cooperation of potential subjects. Although some researchers have successfully gained access to the courts without giving any advance notice, we chose to secure cooperation painstakingly and thoroughly, given the delicate nature of the observations and the geographic dispersion of sites.[6]

In multijudge courts having a presiding judge, we first telephoned that judge directly to enlist his support, or at least acquiescence, in our study and field plan. Every presiding judge agreed to support the study in his court, though some were more active or enthusiastic than others. We then contacted by mail the individual judges who had been randomly selected for observation in these courts and informed them of the purposes of the study and what would be required of participating judges (willingness to be observed in all settings for several days, completion of two sets of activity time logs to be described below, etc.). A number of these judges refused to participate, sometimes even after a personal telephone call on our part. Refusals occurred more frequently in courts where the presiding judge did not possess broad political or administrative support. In multijudge courts without a presiding judge (e.g., Houston) and in single-judge courts, we contacted the judges to be observed directly.[7] In none of these instances was there a refusal to participate.

In all, ten judges refused to be observed. This is a rate of approximately 25 percent, higher than we would have wished.[8] No judge, of course, objected to our observing in his courtroom, but access to chambers was a quite different matter for some. In addition, several judges complained of recent or current illness, either their own or on the staff, which could have created undue pressures during an intensive observation. One judge was in the midst of a hot campaign for a state appellate court seat during the time of the proposed observation. Otherwise, we know little more about these refusals. We did take an opportunity to observe briefly in the courtrooms of three judges who refused for reasons other than illness or campaign politics, during our visits to their locations to observe other judges. One judge was nearly eighty years old, and highly irascible and impatient with defendants. A second judge was much younger but also perturbable in court, especially by defense counsel. A third judge, in his sixties, seemed calm and placid during the very short time observed on the bench. All three judges either served in criminal court or heard predominantly criminal matters in their current assignments.

## Style and Strategies of Observation

The observational situation was an intensive experience for judge and observer. By focusing on one individual in the courtroom workgroup, rather than an amorphous process (e.g., case dispositions or plea bargaining), we were able to receive a glimpse into the private working, and occasionally personal, lives of forty trial court judges.

The context of the observations was shaped by their duration and substantive focus. We typically spent from three to five working days with each judge: three days with judges under a master calendar and five days with judges having individual calendars. Such a distinction was based on a belief, supported impressionistically by the literature, that judges with individual calendars are required to perform a wider variety of tasks and would therefore warrant a longer period of observational time to capture this variety.[9] We observed all kinds of tasks that judges performed, from the beginning of the judicial day to the end, wherever they occurred (except at home)—in chambers, in the courtroom, at bar association functions, at tax seminars, at civic gatherings and the like. One small city newspaper characterized our field observer as the "judge's shadow," which is precisely what we intended to be.[10]

We used a semistructured approach to the collection of qualitative data. Although we had working hypotheses about what we would see, we did not attempt to delineate a checklist of common tasks or judicial behaviors prior to the observations. Thus, we went into the field with loosely organized observational data sheets—open grids of wide spaces in which the observer recorded the nature of the task observed, the beginning and ending times for the task or interaction, the location where it occurred, and the actors present, including attorneys, courtroom personnel, and other judges (see Attachments at the end of this Appendix). For each judicial task or interaction noted, space was available for additional comments. Though not highly structured, this form provided a standardized format for different observers to approach the events before them.

In the judge's chambers, the observer typically sat quietly in a place where all activity could be seen and heard, but far enough away so that the judge could continue to work without the observer's being directly in view. In the courtroom, the observer usually sat in the "inner legal ring," reserved customarily for attorneys and personnel. Sometimes the observer occupied the chair of the clerk or bailiff or one nearby; other times, a seat in a vacant jury box. Wherever we sat in this "inner ring," we were almost always in clear view and hearing of all that occurred, including sidebars (if conducted outside the courtroom, we typically accompanied the parties outside).

We were occasionally asked to leave chambers by the judge for short periods of time, but this sort of exclusion was infrequent, usually for "personal" phone calls, and occurred only with some judges. More of a problem to continuous observation was the judge who moved quickly from chambers to hallway, to clerk's or secretary's office, and back again in the midst of assorted administrative chores. In these cases the observer would either remain stationary and ask the judge what had occurred once he settled again or attempt to follow after him as he moved, an activity sometimes fraught with humorous incidents of collision with other courtroom personnel on busy days. In most instances, we were afforded willing access to judicial activities, sometimes including informal or regularly scheduled meetings with other judges. Also, we received (or were given access to) much unsolicited information, including disposition statistics, work records, docket books, tours of the local jail, and introductions to other judges and court administrators.

## Rapport Development

One prime tenet of field work is to establish rapport with interviewees or observed subjects in order to win their trust and confidence,[11] to become privy not only to "public" information but to "confidential," "secret," and "private" information.[12] To establish rapport, we tried to adopt a mental set that conveyed both empathy and informed understanding of the judicial work environment. Some judges were initially wary because of past experience with ill-prepared researchers or unfavorable local newspaper publicity accompanying such research. Most of these judges became more open in their interactions with our observer after the first day, partly because frivolous researchers rarely show up for a second day, but mostly because judges came to view the observer as someone who understood judicial work and who could empathize with the judge.

The two observers who performed the bulk of the observations are social scientists, not lawyers, but this rarely proved a detriment to building rapport. Few judges expressed any reservations about our ability to understand judicial work. Some judges asked our evaluation of the rightness or fairness of their decisions (one such instance occurred in a mechanic's lien action where the observer was, in fact, thoroughly confused by the facts and law). Other judges sought our assistance in the formulation of a decision, usually in cases involving issues of social policy or human relations. Only one judge expressed astonishment that a nonlawyer could understand the workings of the court and the law, and this judge served not in civil assignment (where occasionally we *were* ignorant) but in criminal work. Gaining rapport with this particular judge proved impossible, notwithstanding the common ethnic-religious background of observer and judge—Irish Catholic. (At one point, the judge groused that his son attended some "radical, underground Catholic Church with guitar masses on the north side," probably the same place as the observer!)

Most judges came to view the observer as one who empathized with him and the work environment. Usually this interpretation was quite accurate. Weary observers were sobered by their own diminshed desire to see any more "justice done" when a case was assigned to a judge at 4:30 in the afternoon, especially if it were much like the previous cases. Similarly, the workload of some judges was so visibly overwhelming that we came to feel the same irritation with a tardy attorney. Our stance of empathy was not uncritical, however, As many researchers have noted, the quality of empathy or "social intelligence" does not necessarily involve sympathy.[13] Empathy involves the ability to recognize and understand another's point of view without losing one's own point of view.[14] The empathetic observer is able to understand events as those experiencing them do. The sympathetic observer becomes emotionally involved by taking the side of the person observed and by trying to convince himself or others of the appropriateness of that person's perspective. This distinction is important. We were frequently seen by the judge as a temporary judicial colleague or ally. For our research purposes, this impression was crucial, and in many instances we did become temporary colleagues, but "emotionally detached" ones. We were agreeable and understanding on the occasions when a judge asked us to leave chambers because he had a personal call to make, but we noted the frequency and duration of these occurrences.

With many judges, there was almost instant rapport. Some judges were highly self-confident and genuinely welcomed the opportunity for outsiders to view their skills. Other judges found personal interests in common with the observer—e.g., small children, political party activity, or golf. For example, in one court all judges except one "duty judge" and most of the regular attorneys vanished to golf courses near and far on Friday afternoon. There was no attempt to hide this activity. Indeed, attorneys and judges openly discussed various tee-off times and golf courses in chambers Friday morning, much to the envy of the observer, himself a golf addict.

Over the course of the observations, we also learned how better to project an empathetic attitude when confronted with some initial resistance. One judge from a smaller community, who had indicated that the observer could stay for only four days, as opposed to the requested five, not only allowed the observer to stay the fifth day but also remarked to one of his fellow judges: "They're going to write a report that will show how hard we work and give us some good publicity for once." Needless to say, we had promised or described no such report. This same judge seemed intent on concealing the length of his normal lunch hour. When the observer returned from lunch on the first day of observation, she noted no personnel around and the judge idling through such tasks as watering plants and wandering down the hall to check on the afternoon mail. Accordingly, the observer returned from lunch a half-hour "late" the second day, and even later the next day, offering a busy lunchroom one day and no excuse the next. By the fourth day, the judge was returning from lunch almost an hour later than the first day (and "as usual" according to the court reporter). This example illustrates an *ad hoc* attempt to encourage the judge to be comfortable with the observer, to conduct his day as he usually did. Finally, a metropolitan court judge initially excluded the observer from a number of chambers conferences with unidentified persons (not all of which were "personal business"). Looking and feeling very depressed at this turn of events, the observer dragged behind the judge toward the courtroom. Fortunately, the judge sensed something was wrong, and the observer was able to rearticulate and explain the need for unlimited access, to which the judge assented. Indeed, by the third day the observer was hearing the judge's phone calls to his mother.

Thus, in many but not all situations the observer tended to be accepted as an ally, someone in whom the judge could confide and to whom he could frequently complain. Observers heard judges' comments on the quality of the bar, on the quality of the bench, on the presence or lack of a smoothly running administrative procedure, a great deal about past case work, and sometimes (as we noted) serious or half-serious calls for assistance with current cases. This is not to say that the judge was betraying judicial confidences, but rather that the observer was regarded as a temporary legal or professional colleague—a participant, in one sense of that word—more times than not. By gaining this unusual access and rapport, with attendant insights into the "judicial mind," we were able to document and supplement the quantitative data that form the bulk of the text.

## Controlling Reactivity

A related aspect of gaining rapport is controlling the amount of subject reactivity, so that events occurring during the presence of observers "do not significantly differ from those which occur in their absence."[15] One remedy is the simple passage of time. Though we did not have the resources to stay with any one judge for a period of weeks or months, even the passage of a few days helped. Judges came to interact with the observer *less* after the first day and to return to their more normal work habits.

We also took other small but concrete steps to minimize reactivity and to develop alternative data sources as a check. In a brief exchange at the beginning of the observation period, each judge was assured that all information derived from observation (in the courtroom or chambers) would be reported either on an aggregate basis or without specific reference to, or identification of, individual judges. We further assured judges that the observer expected to see slow or slack days as well as busy ones, and that the observer would not distract the judge or others from the business at hand. We also discussed aspects of our study, including possible practical applications and results, if the judge expressed interest or curiosity.

Occasionally we were also able to engage in informal "chats" with courtroom personnel, with an eye toward confirming or disconfirming information from the judge or our own perceptions. Usually this was a part of general conversation about the individual's work, and it often occurred quite spontaneously. A direct question about the judge's work habits was typically met with unambiguous praise (the "brightest" and "fairest" judge in the building). A discussion about the clerk's long hours or the bailiff's sensitivity to the families of defendants, however, easily moved into a talk about the courtroom workgroup in general, including the judge. We had no definite plan or purpose in interviewing personnel, and such conversations were not conducted at every site.[16] But the information gleaned from these conversations was often enlightening. For example, in one urban court a very hard-working judge who started his day at 7:00 A.M. and frequently stayed until 6:00 P.M. or later abruptly informed the observer of a "personal matter" the following afternoon at 3:00 P.M., noting that the observer could, therefore, leave early. Noticing the mass of tennis awards and trophies displayed in the judge's office, the observer casually asked the clerk if the judge played tennis every Wednesday afternoon and learned that he regularly did.

Finally, we requested each judge to complete a one-week set of daily activity logs for two separate weeks after the observation period—one week later, and again four weeks later (see Attachments at the end of this Appendix). These logs attempted to elicit information parallel to what we recorded on our observation sheets, but in less detail. The purpose and importance of the logs were explained to each judge at the end of the observation period, and every attempt was made to enlist the judge's commitment to maintaining and returning them. In fact, 78 percent returned the first set of logs, 70 percent the second set—a relatively high response, which we attribute to the positive attitudes toward the study (and toward the observers) on the part of these judges. The logs are subject to some of the same kinds of biases as the observations (particularly, for example, with respect to total hours worked), but they nevertheless provide one additional data point against which the observations can be compared. Perhaps more important, the logs help place the observed period in more complete task context, especially in those courts with cyclical work patterns (e.g., jury and nonjury weeks).

Despite these various techniques to minimize reactivity, it was sometimes impossible to control or check it. This was particularly true for judges constantly on guard vis-à-vis the outside world (of which the observer was only a small part). Some of these judges may have been slightly paranoid about public perceptions of the appropriateness of particular kinds of work (e.g., professional committee work). Other judges were simply masters of "image projection," constantly seeking to improve the court's, or their own, image in the public limelight. For example, one judge in a large metropolitan court allowed a caravan of high school students to be brought into his chambers one day while they were visiting the courts. He spent a half-hour with the students, explaining the organization and work of the criminal courts, and fielding questions with skill and straight answers. At the conclusion of the session, the clerk who had escorted the students into chambers reminded them of the judge's name—and spelled it—and told them to tell their folks how nice this judge had been for taking time on their behalf.[17] Equally interesting, this judge abruptly ordered the observer to turn over a pillow on the couch in his chambers as the students entered, a pillow that the observer later noted had a slightly vulgar phrase embroidered on it. For such judges, it is nearly impossible even to estimate the nature and amount of reactivity, let alone to control it.

## A View Toward Reliability and Validity

We made a concerted effort toward standardization in the observer's framework, in the collection of data, and in the coding, collapsing, and analysis of data. All four authors participated in the observation of judges. We first engaged in a pretest of observational style and strategies by observing judges in the Chicago courts for four days, by exchanging experiences and ideas resulting from these observations, and by engaging in limited joint observation of the same judge. Throughout the formal observations that followed, we maintained a continuing dialogue about our approach and the completion of forms. Nevertheless, each of the authors possesses a somewhat different intellectual and disciplinary training; no amount of effort or practice can entirely eliminate these differences in "perspective."[18]

The collection and recording of data from the field in a standard way was facilitated by the limited structure of the observational data sheets. At a minimum, task, duration, location, and parties present were collected for each judge on every day of observation. It proved more difficult, however, for each observer to develop the same definition of the beginning and ending points of tasks or interactions. In part, this was the inevitable result of collecting data in an open-ended way, as opposed to categorizing activities on the basis of a precoded list.

Finally, qualitative data recorded on the observation sheets were coded into seventy-six discrete activities by a research assistant who had not participated in the observations. A sample of approximately 15 percent of these sheets were double-coded by one of the observers, to check for reliability of coding. An initial intercoder agreement of 70 percent was obtained; disagreements were explored, and a subsequent agreement rate of 85 percent was obtained. These numerous discrete activites were then collapsed, for comparative analysis, into the fourteen broader categories represented in the activities section of the mail questionnaire.

Validity is a more complex matter than reliability. We would like to think that our efforts to develop rapport and to limit the effects of reactivity make a substantial contribution toward this goal. Clearly, the presence of an outsider who recorded "everything" had an impact on the observed judge and those with whom he interacted. Nevertheless, we feel our data are rich in accurate flavor and detail. We saw judges with slack time; judges who left early or arrived late; judges who were unprepared for conferences or who snapped at attorneys, witnesses, or spectators; as well as judges who performed with skill, dedication, and patience in each of these areas. Although we cannot precisely determine how much personal business, socializing, or political activity judges generally do, we were aware and even participated in some of these behaviors with many judges. In short, despite probable and all-too-human wishes to provide us with a sterling judicial performance—as hard worker, researcher, negotiator, or whatever—we seemingly observed all varieties, qualities, and amounts of judicial work.

## Conclusion

We have attempted in this brief Appendix to provide detail on the methodology of our field observations. It is particularly important to articulate the philosophy defining the observational setting as well as the strategies, techniques, and tactics in doing these observations. Few researchers studying, observing, or "poking around" the courts have made explicit the basis on which their findings rest. It is testimony to this fact that *Streetcorner Society*[19] and *Tally's Corner*[20] remain, years later, among the most significant social science works that analyze, from a personal perspective, the researcher's intrusion into social settings. Yet courts may be no less difficult settings in which to do research than informal associations of human beings in ethnic neighborhoods. Courtroom workgroups, if they are as organized and stable as some suggest, probably develop mechanisms for coping with outsiders. Courts may not be as inscrutable as Dickens once thought,[21] but efforts to study their interpersonal essence require a heightened methodological sensitivity.

TABLE A-1. Listing of Fifteen Trial Courts Selected for Field Observation

| Locale | Jurisdiction |
| --- | --- |
| California | |
|   Los Angeles County | Los Angeles County Superior Court |
|   Orange County (Santa Ana) | Orange County Superior Court |
| Nebraska | |
|   Omaha | Fourth District Court |
|   Columbus (multi-county circuit) | Twenty-first District Court |
| Illinois | |
|   Cook County (Chicago) | Cook County Circuit Court |
|   DuPage County (Wheaton) | Eighteenth Circuit Court |
| Wisconsin | |
|   Milwaukee County | Second Circuit Court |
|   Dane County (Madison) | Ninth Circuit Court |
| Tennessee | |
|   Nashville-Davidson County | Tenth Circuit Court |
|   Anderson County (Clinton) | Twenty-eighth Circuit Court |
| Texas | |
|   Harris County (Houston) | Selected District Courts |
|   Potter County (Amarillo) | District Court |
| Pennsylvania | |
|   Philadelphia County | First District Court |
|   Cambria County (Ebensberg) | Forty-seventh District Court |
| Vermont | |
|   Statewide | Superior and District Courts |

TABLE A-2. Selection Criteria for Observations: Characteristics of Fifteen Trial Courts in 1976

| Family Prob. Locale | Number of General Jurisdiction Courts | Original Jurisdiction Juv. Family | Original Jurisdiction Prob. | Type[a] by Division Calendar- Cr. | Type[a] by Division Cv. | Type[a] by Division Gen. | Number of Judges | Selection Method[b] Init./Vac. | Type of Locale[c] | State Political Culture[d] |
|---|---|---|---|---|---|---|---|---|---|---|
| Los Angeles, CA | 1 | + | + | I | | M | 170 | NP/G | LM | P |
| Orange County, CA | 1 | + | + | | M | | 33 | NP/G | S | P |
| Omaha, NB | 1 | – | – | I | I | | 12 | M/M | IM | P |
| Columbus, NB | 1 | + | + | I | I | | 1 | M/M | R | P |
| Houston, TX | 1 | – | – | I | M | | 29 | P/G | LM | NP |
| Amarillo, TX | 1 | – | + | | I | | 4[e] | P/G | IC | NP |
| Nashville, TN | 3[f] | – | + | I | I | | 3/6/3 | P/G | IM | NP |
| Anderson County, TN | 2[f] | – | + | I | I | | 1/1 | P/G | R | NP |
| Milwaukee, WI | 1 | + | + | I | I | | 33 | NP/G | LM | P |
| Madison, WI | 2 | + | + | I | | | 4/6 | NP/G | IC | P |
| Chicago, IL | 1 | + | + | I | I/M[g] | | 160[h] | P/SC | LM | NP |

260

| | | | | | | | |
|---|---|---|---|---|---|---|---|
| DuPage County, IL | 1 | + | + | M | 7[h] | P/SC | S | NP |
| Philadelphia, PA | 1 | + | + | M   M | 78 | P/G[i] | LM | NP |
| Cambria County, PA | 1 | + | + | I | 4 | P/G[i] | R | NP |
| Vermont (statewide) | 2 | + | − | I   I | 8/14[j] | M/M | R | NP |

[a] Calendar Type (case assignment system): M = Master calendar, I = Individual calendar.
[b] Selection Method: NP = nonpartisan election, P = partisan election, M = merit selection (i.e., appointment, usually by chief executive, after screening by a nominating commission), G = appointed by governor, SC = appointed by state supreme court.
[c] Locale: LM = large metropolitan, IM = intermediate metropolitan, IC = independent (nonmetropolitan) city, S = suburban, R = rural.
[d] P or NP refers to Progressive versus non-Progressive political culture. See, for example, Daniel J. Elazar, *American Federalism: A View from the States* (New York: Crowell, 1966).
[e] One district judge in Potter county has been designated as judge of domestic relations court.
[f] Throughout most of Tennessee, there are two trial courts of general jurisdiction: circuit courts, with criminal and civil jurisdiction; and chancery courts, with civil jurisdiction only. But in Nashville, there are three trial courts—criminal, circuit (civil), and chancery. Tennessee Supreme Court Rules (as of 1975) do provide for the election of a local presiding judge with the power to assign cases, thus taking the first step toward a unified trial court structure.
[g] Variable, depending upon particular type of civil division. For example, civil—jury division has master calendar, whereas chancery division has individual calendar.
[h] In Illinois, there are two categories or classes of trial judges within the trial court of general jurisdiction: circuit judges, selected in partisan elections, and associate judges, selected by circuit judges of the given circuit. We observed and included in our survey only *circuit* judges, who are most comparable to "general jurisdiction" judges in other states.
[i] At present, there is a voluntary merit selection plan, by executive order—issued 1973, modified 1975—for interim appointments in Pennsylvania.
[j] Trial judges of general jurisdiction in Vermont serve on a *statewide* basis, rotating from county to county. At present, eight superior court judges and fourteen district court judges serve Vermont's fourteen counties.

# Notes

1. For examples of studies of trial courts utilizing an observational approach, see Maureen Mileski, "Courtroom Encounters: An Observation of a Lower Criminal Court," *Law and Society Review,* 5 (1971); Robert M. Emerson, *Judging Delinquents* (Chicago: Aldine, 1969); Abraham S. Blumberg, *Criminal Justice* (Chicago: Quadrangle, 1967); and most recently, James Eisenstein and Herbert Jacob, *Felony Justice: An Organizational Analysis of Criminal Courts* (Boston: Little, Brown, 1977), and Martin Levin, *Urban Politics and the Criminal Courts* (Chicago: University of Chicago Press, 1977). Most of these and other observational studies of courtroom or chambers activity focus on a variety of actors and a particular set of activities or procedures (e.g., plea bargaining, bail, etc.) in *criminal* courts. For a methodological discussion, see Lynn M. Mather, "Ethnography and the Study of Trial Courts," paper presented at the Annual Meeting of the Midwest Political Science Association, Chicago, 1976, and George McCall, *Observing the Law: Applications of Field Methods to the Study of the Criminal Justice System* (Washington, D.C.: National Institute of Mental Health, 1975).
2. Morris S. Schwartz and Charlotte Green Schwartz, "Problems in Participant Observation," *American Journal of Sociology,* 60 (1955), pp. 348-349.
3. Buford H. Junker, *Field Work: An Introduction to the Social Sciences* (Chicago: University of Chicago Press, 1960), pp. 32-42.
4. Robert Bogdan and Steven J. Taylor, *Introduction to Qualitative Research Methods* (New York: Wiley, 1975).
5. For a discussion of purposive sampling, see Earl R. Babbie, *Survey Research Methods* (Belmont, Ca.: Wadsworth, 1973), pp. 106-107.
6. Eisenstein and Jacob, *Felony Justice,* for example, simply appeared on the "doorstep" of the chambers of criminal court judges in Chicago on the morning of observation. Private correspondence with Herbert Jacob.
7. The selection of judges in one-judge courts was *not* random, since the courts were selected purposively according to external criteria.
8. We initially contacted between forty and forty-five judges, determining some of these judges to be inappropriate for observation because of their jurisdiction.
9. See, for example, Ernest C. Friesen, Jr., Edward C. Gallas, and Nesta M. Gallas, *Managing the Courts* (Indianapolis: Bobbs-Merrill, 1971), pp. 173-188.
10. *Wisconsin State Journal* (Madison), November 1, 1976.
11. Bogdan and Taylor, *Introduction to Qualitative Research Methods,* p. 45.
12. Junker, *Field Work,* pp. 34-35.
13. See, for example, Martin Feffer and Leonard Suchotleff, "Decentering Implications of Social Interactions," *Journal of Personality and Social Psychology,* 4 (1966); George Herbert Mead's classic study of the nature and development of decentering or empathy, *Mind, Self, and Society* (Chicago: University of Chicago Press, 1934); or an excellent overview of the concept of social intelligence as discussed in L. A. Stanley, Ronald E. Walker, and Jeanne M. Foley, "Social Intelligence," *Psychological Reports,* 29 (1971).
14. John H. Flavell, Patricia T. Bodkin, and Charles L. Fry, Jr., *Development of Role Taking and Communication Skills* (New York: Wiley, 1968).

15. Bogdan and Taylor, *Introduction to Qualitative Research Methods*, p. 45.
16. In some courts, regular courtroom personnel were on vacation; in other courts, some or all of the personnel rotated from courtroom to courtroom on a weekly or even daily basis. Such factors precluded obtaining reliable information about a judge.
17. This judge was *not* on the ballot in the election year (1976) during which the observations took place.
18. Two of the authors observed a total of thirty-five judges. Neither is a lawyer; one is a political scientist, the other, a social psychologist. The remaining five judges were observed by one of the other two authors, both of whom are lawyers. In actuality, then, the problem of interobserver reliability is lessened, because most observations were completed by only two different individuals, both of whom share a social science perspective.
19. William Foote Whyte, *Streetcorner Society* (Chicago: University of Chicago Press, 1955).
20. Elliot Liebow, *Tally's Corner* (Boston: Little, Brown, 1967).
21. "On such an afternoon, if ever, the Lord High Chancellor ought to be sitting here—as here he is—with a foggy glory round his head, softly fenced in with crimson cloth and curtains, addressed by a large advocate with great whiskers, a little voice, and an interminable brief, and outwardly directing his contemplation to the lantern in the roof, where he can see nothing but fog. On such an afternoon, some score of members of the High Court of Chancery bar ought to be—as here they are—mistily engaged in one of the ten thousand stages of an endless cause, tripping one another up on slippery precedents, groping knee-deep in technicalities, running their goat-hair and horse-hair warded heads against walls of words, and making a pretence of equity with serious faces, as players might."—from Charles Dickens, *Bleak House* (New York: Doubleday, 1953), pp. 1–2.

Observational Data Sheet

COURT _____ JUDGE _____ DATE _____ / PAGE _____

TASK

LOCATION
PERSONNEL

TIME
MISC.

# AJS Activity Log

NAME OF JUDGE _____ COURT _____

DATE _____ DAY OF WEEK: M  Tu  W  Th  F  Sa  Su

|  | Location[1] | Travel[2] | Detailed Nature of Activity[3] | Parties Involved[4] | Task Duration[5] (#Hrs) |
|---|---|---|---|---|---|
| **9** | | | | | |
| **10** | | | | | |
| **11** | | | | | |
| **12** | | | | | |
| **1** | | | | | |
| **2** | | | | | |
| **3** | | | | | |
| **4** | | | | | |

[1] Indicate where the task is performed—courtroom, chambers, other courthouse places (specify), or in the community (specify—e.g., university, state legislature, etc.).

[2] Indicate any significant (i.e., half hour or more) travel time incurred between locales in the performance of tasks. Round to the nearest *half* hour.

[3] List and describe all kinds of activity in any way related to the profession of being a judge in your community —including civic and political as well as legal-judicial tasks.

[4] List all judicial and non-judicial personnel, by *title*, or *position*, with whom you interact in order to complete a particular task.

[5] When indicating the time duration of a task, round to the nearest *quarter* hour.

# Appendix B

# The Development and Administration of a Mail Survey

A nationwide mail questionnaire was chosen to elicit detailed and representative information about the content of judicial work, organizational variables hypothesized to influence work (e.g., size, structure, resources, and specialization), judicial perceptions of the work environment, and a few baseline characteristics of judges (such as age, gender, and race). This focus reflected our primary questions, hypotheses, and interests regarding the work of trial judges, as they were refined by our observations.

## The Role of the Pretest

A pretest mail questionnaire was administered in February, 1977 to a small random sample of trial judges (n = 300). There were three specific purposes for the pretest. First, we needed to establish the viability of utilizing a mail survey. Would we receive an adequate response rate? Could we identify, with reasonable accuracy, the names and mailing addresses of the universe of trial judges in the states? How would we define the "universe" of trial judges? While there had been a number of localized mail surveys of trial judges,[1] no study had attempted a nationwide survey. Second, we needed to determine empirically how best to ask judges the way they allocated their time to a set of tasks. Our observations supplied us with a list of tasks, but we experimented with three different approaches for the allocation of time on actual or generalized work days. These are described in detail below. Finally, we wished to determine the interpretability and understandability of other questions in the survey. Given the variety of structures within which trial judging takes place, it was essential to develop a "common vocabulary" through which judges in any trial court could understand a particular question. Based upon the results of our pretest, we turn to a discussion of these three areas.

SAMPLING, ADMINISTRATION, AND RESPONSE RATE

We defined the universe of interest to be trial judges sitting in courts of general jurisdiction in the fifty states and the District of Columbia. For definitional purposes, we relied upon the distinctions of court jurisdiction drawn in the most authoritative study to date, LEAA's *National Survey of Court Organization*.[2] We actively chose to exclude trial judges serving in misdemeanor courts, justice of the peace courts, and magistrate courts. We also excluded trial judges serving in specialized jurisdiction courts such as juvenile, probate, or domestic relations. In many of these courts, judges do not serve full time, are nonlawyers, and are rarely if ever exposed to trials.[3] For these reasons, the work they do is not likely to be comparable—in time, intensity, or scope—to that of trial judges in courts of general jurisdiction.[4]

To draw a random sample for this universe, we used a computerized listing of trial judges made available by the National Judicial College in Reno.[5] The list did not purport to be a "fully accurate" one, given our purposes. That is, the list contained the names of judges who were retired as well as those who sat on courts other than of general jurisdiction. In all, there were 6,324 judges listed. Before proceeding with the mailing of the pretest instrument, we attempted to cross-check each name with other available sources to ensure that the judge was still on the bench and served in a court of general jurisdiction.[6] Having completed this, we drew a simple random sample of 300 judges and assigned every third judge to one of the three questionnaire formats (of judicial work) being tested.[7] We chose three hundred as a number large enough to permit limited statistical analysis but sufficiently small so as not to cut deeply into our universe.

In the administration of the pretest mailing, we included a questionnaire containing a cover letter on the first page, a return envelope, and a postcard-return. To maximize the candor of responses, we wished the survey to be anonymous. To facilitate efficient follow-up appeals, however, we needed to know which judges had and had not responded. Thus, a return postcard was included in order to identify which judges had responded to the survey, without jeopardizing the anonymity of responses.

The cover letter contained standard appeals but was aided by the institutional reputation of the sponsoring organization (the American Judicature Society) to which perhaps 20 percent of the sample belonged. Also, one special incentive to respond was included. We offered the lure of an expenses-paid trip to Florida, in the middle of winter, to one judge to be selected at random from among those returning the enclosed postcard verifying completion of the questionnaire. We dignified the trip by tying it to participation at an advisory committee meeting of the study, and no color brochures were enclosed. Nevertheless, the message was communicated effectively. (Numerous judges wrote on the return postcard that they would be anxious to attend the meeting!)[8]

To improve response rates, we engaged in a series of follow-up appeals. One week after the initial mailing, a reminder postcard was sent to all judges. One month later, a complete follow-up mailing (including a second questionnaire) was sent, but only to those judges not returning the postcard verifying completion of the survey. In the one-month follow-up, we experimented with two kinds of mail service: certified and first class. The literature on survey research techniques suggests that more expensive mailings call more attention to a survey, thereby producing a higher response rate.[9] We wished to test this idea in the relatively inexpensive setting of a small pretest.

We reached the basic finding that a nationwide mail survey was a potentially viable way of obtaining information on judicial work, if a more accurate method of obtaining lists of active trial judges were employed. Furthermore, follow-up mailings proved quite beneficial, though the class of mail service utilized did not make a difference. The response rate to the pretest was 53 percent with sharp variations depending upon format. One approach to asking about judicial work proved substantially superior in obtaining responses (66 percent), as we will discuss in the next section. The follow-up mailings were quite important. The response rate increased from 36 percent to its 53 percent level *after* the one-month follow-up. The inaccuracy of our techniques for identifying an up-to-date list of trial judges also emerged: More than 6 percent of the questionnaires mailed out were returned to us marked "undeliverable." This suggested that many judges had left the bench since the publication of sources that we used to validate the National Judicial College's computerized list. Thus we concluded that by developing a better list of trial judges and by using one particular format for inquiring about judicial work, we could achieve a very good response rate from an accurately defined universe of trial judges in state courts of general jurisdiction.

## ASKING JUDGES ABOUT THEIR WORK: THREE APPROACHES

We operationalized three different approaches to the measurement of judges' work time. Each reflected different assumptions about the interest, ability, and motivation of respondents, and each—in theory—would provide different problems of interpretation and analysis. All three approaches shared one important feature, though: A listing of eighteen discrete activities was provided as the basis for allocation of work time, with the option of an "other" category.

The first approach could be termed a "concrete log." Respondents were asked to list the tasks (from among those provided) that they performed for any five consecutive working days after receipt of the questionnaire. For each task performed, the judge was directed to (1) write the beginning and ending clock time, (2) check the location where the task was performed, and (3) enter the code number which (best) described the nature of the task. This format was a modification of a log used successfully by the Federal Judicial Center in its extended time study of federal district judges.[10] We also used a probe question to determine whether, and how, any of the five days for which the log was completed were "atypical." This was intended to elicit more information about the *patterns* of work days.

The second approach constituted a summary of a concrete log. Rather than detailing a chronological, quarter-hour-by-quarter-hour, daily account of tasks performed, the judge was asked to estimate the numbers of hours (and fractions thereof) spent on each of the same set of eighteen activities. In order to control for exaggeration in estimates, the judge was also instructed to total his estimates for each day. All of the other particulars were identical to the first format: Respondents were asked to complete this summary for five consecutive working days, to describe how (if at all) any of the days were "atypical," etc.

The third approach represented a sharp departure from the principles of analysis and assumptions of respondent ability underlying the first two approaches. We asked judges to abstract and generalize about their working days, to identify *patterns* of time allocations across their admittedly varied schedules. In this "typical work day" format, the judge was asked to identify the number of different types of work days encountered in his current assignment and to assign hours and fractions to the activities performed (again, from the same list of eighteen categories) on each of the different types of days. We provided spaces for up to five types of work days but noted in the instructions the idea that some judges might have only one type of work day whereas others might have several. We also asked the judge to indicate the *relative frequency*, over the course of a year, of each type of work day identified, by assigning a percentage number to each type of day to total 100 percent. The option of assigning some percentage for "random" days was provided. Finally, we attempted to gauge the respondent's own confidence level in completing this format through a closed-choice question.

We had initial working hypotheses or expectations about the efficacy and potential pitfalls of each approach. The first, the concrete log, seemed to have the most analytic value. In its ideal form, it would provide precise information about real days subject to the least amount of unconscious distortion. Yet it was also the most tedious and time-consuming format to complete, and we feared that the response rate might be perilously low. The third approach—"typical work day" format—would provide a wider range of information, subject to the limitations of judges' ability to generalize about the mix of tasks on their work days. This form, however, could be completed at one sitting, and we expected that the response rate would probably be satisfactory. The second approach, the summary of a concrete log, was a compromise between the other approaches, although falling much nearer the concrete log from an analytic point of view. We perceived that the summary approach would reduce the tedium in completing the concrete log (by eliminating chronology of events), without sacrificing either crucial information or a handle on "reality." We were uncertain about the response rate, because completion for five actual working days was required.

Our expectations and fears about response rate were largely confirmed. The typical work day format elicited a 66 percent response, as against 43 percent for the concrete log and 48 percent for the summary of a log. The difference between the response rate of the typical work day format and the other two forms was statistically significant in each case ($p < .001$).

The three approaches also differed considerably in the interpretability and apparent validity of responses. On the most basic measure of interpretability—whether the judge attempted to complete the section on judicial work or skipped it entirely—the three formats did not differ significantly: 12 percent of the judges responding to the typical work day form skipped the section on judicial work, as against 16 percent responding to the summary of a log and 18 percent for the concrete log. Other indices of interpretability were less straightforward but provided clearer clues to the comparative value of the formats. The concrete log yielded a larger number of judges (23 percent) who completed fewer than the five days requested. Most of these completed only one day, often writing in the margin that this was their "typical work day." In contrast, every judge who attempted to complete the summary of a log did so for all five days requested. Nevertheless, we had the uneasy (but difficult to verify) feeling that a number of respondents reported a profile of daily activities for some past (or even future) days. In some instances, recollections of specific past working days might be accurate, but in most instances they would be highly inaccurate.

The completion of the typical work day format was not subject to the same kinds of interpretations, since we had no way of knowing (or determining from responses to other questions) the accuracy or credibility of responses. Some judges, as we observed in the field, had only one type of work day, whereas other judges had several types of work days. We performed a subjective inspection to determine what percentage of respondents "understood" how to complete the section and concluded that approximately 75 percent understood. The remainder were confused either by the presence of five columns (misunderstanding that they must complete all columns) or by the abstraction involved (viewing the format as some kind of daily log).

The substance of the responses to the judicial work sections were extensively analyzed and compared, both from one format to another and against our own field observations. The summary log and typical work day formats yielded highly similar frequencies of task activity, but the concrete log elicited a rather different profile. When compared with our field observations, the summary log and typical work day formats conformed much more closely to the frequency and mix of tasks we saw than did the concrete log. Furthermore, the variety of tasks we observed in the field was better approached by the typical work day and summary log formats. The substance of responses in the concrete log yielded a pattern of oversimplification of the work day, one at variance with our field observations and not accounted for by any differences in the backgrounds or current assignment of judges responding to the concrete log.

We did not establish, *a priori,* any calculus for weighing the relative advantages and disadvantages of the three approaches. Fortunately, none was needed. Nearly all signposts pointed toward the typical work day format. The response rate of this approach was superior by a wide margin, and the interpretability of responses was clearly superior to the concrete log. The level of abstraction required of respondents completing the typical work day form was not beyond the comprehension of most judges. And comparisons of the substance of responses indicated clear validity problems with the concrete log, which elicited a different and oversimplified accounting of a judge's day, viewed against what we observed in the field.

Finally, we concluded that the inherent analytic flexibility and value of the data from the typical work day format was superior. *At best,* all that the summary of a log (or the concrete log) could provide was an accurate slice of *five* working days in the life of a trial judge. Even with supplemental information from responses to other questions, it was not possible to aggregate a representative profile of the work of any individual judge over a period of time. In this instance, "overlapping biases" do not wash out or melt away. Having data consisting of a jury week of one judge, a nonjury week of a second judge, and a mixture of jury and nonjury work for the week of a third judge does not solve the problem of *individual* representativeness; it merely adds to the problem. We wished to know not merely what the "average" of all trial judges do with their time (a statistical artifact), but how real, living, individual judges spend their work time. No causal analysis of factors influencing allocation of judicial work time could sensibly proceed within the confines of the former data set. In contrast, data from the typical work day format do provide profiles of the work patterns of individual trial judges.

For all of these reasons, then—response rate, interpretability of responses, validity of responses, and the analytic flexibility provided by generalizations about working days—we chose the typical work day format as the one best suited to yield meaningful data on judicial work.

## THE INTERPRETABILITY OF OTHER SURVEY ITEMS

Our pretest also served the more general purpose of guiding us in the development of question wording, category development, and the elimination of questions that proved unworkably difficult to operationalize.

We were able to develop and collapse categories on the basis of pretest results. For example, we turned an open question on size of court in the pretest ("How many judges are currently sitting in your local court?") into a closed question with categories of approximately equal percentages in the final questionnaire. The open-ended question also revealed the perils involved in asking for precise numbers of judges in large courts (inaccurate guesses, missing data, etc.). We also collapsed categories that yielded too few respondents, as in the questions on the frequency of rotation of judges, immediate prior occupation, and the activities list used in the section on judicial work. We developed new categories based upon responses to probes or open-ended questions. Thus, when asked to explain their participation in judicial education programs, judges cited also law school teaching and police training programs. In the final questionnaire we asked judges about their participation in all three types of programs. Finally, several unworkable questions were eliminated upon the analysis of pretest data or were sufficiently recast to be more comprehensible to the respondent. These included questions about courtroom personnel and the divisional structure (if any) of the local court. In particular, we found it difficult to establish a "common vocabulary" relating to divisionalization and specialization within courts.

Remarkably, many of the questions asked on the pretest did prove highly workable: Few respondents failed to answer, few bothersome comments portending misunderstanding were written in the margin, and a distribution of responses indicative of a variable rather than a constant emerged. Thus, we affirmed the utility and learning experience of our field observations in helping to frame questions for the pretest.

## Administration of the Final Questionnaire

In light of problems encountered in using available lists of judges, we solicited directly each of the state court administrative offices to gather up-to-date information. These offices, with rare exceptions,[11] were happy to supply us with the lists of judges for the courts we requested. As a result, we obtained the most recent available information on the names of trial judges in courts of general jurisdiction (usually as of January 1, 1977).

We made a crucial decision to "sample" all judges in the defined universe, despite some warnings about incurring unnecessary costs. We did so for two basic reasons: (1) to ensure in data analysis the flexibility of a very large data base, and (2) to facilitate within-court analysis. We anticipated the need to perform statistical routines utilizing one or more control variables. To draw a random sample of, say, 50 percent or 25 percent would reduce significantly our ability to perform second-order, or possibly even first-order, controls. Having sampled the entire universe, we still sometimes "ran out" of cases in a few cells because of colinearity problems. Second, we wished to do some contextual analysis of trial judges and courts, by looking in-depth at a few big-city courts.[12] The use of simple random sampling would yield too small a number of judges in these courts to permit statistical analysis. We could have employed a "stratified" random sample by surveying all judges in these courts, but this would have introduced other problems. For example, size of court proved a decisive determinant of many key variables (including judicial work patterns). As a result, a complex system of weighting would have been required in order to reach frequency distributions unbiased by the effects from stratified sampling.

Once the decision to survey the universe was made, we mailed questionnaires to all trial judges in courts of general jurisdiction within a one-week period in May 1977. The mailing paralleled that of the pretest in content. We then pursued a series of follow-up appeals based upon our successful pretest experiences. A reminder postcard was sent to all judges one week after the conclusion of the mailing. One month later, an entire follow-up mailing was employed (including another questionnaire). Lastly, a second follow-up mailing, which included a new cover letter and a humorous return postcard, was undertaken.

The resultant response rate to this initial mailing and two follow-up appeals was 63 percent. There were some variations by state, but in every state (except New Jersey) at least 50 percent of the universe of judges responded. Also, there were modest differences across regions, with the response rate highest in the West (71 percent) and lowest in the Northeast (58 percent). No clear-cut biases arose from these differential response rates, though. Some populous states responded well, others did not; some rural states responded

TABLE B-1. Response Rate by State and Region[a]

| STATE | (REGION)[b] | RESPONSE RATE | NUMBER |
|---|---|---|---|
| Alabama | (S) | 59% | 60 |
| Alaska | (W) | 72 | 13 |
| Arizona | (W) | 73 | 47 |
| Arkansas | (S) | 65 | 35 |
| California | (W) | 65 | 320 |
| Colorado | (W) | 83 | 74 |
| Connecticut | (NE) | 54 | 22 |
| Delaware | (S) | 90 | 9 |
| District of Columbia | (S) | 66 | 25 |
| Florida | (S) | 56 | 150 |
| Georgia | (S) | 55 | 45 |
| Hawaii | (W) | 71 | 10 |
| Idaho | (W) | 79 | 19 |
| Illinois | (NC) | 65 | 215 |
| Indiana | (NC) | 67 | 99 |
| Iowa | (NC) | 73 | 54 |
| Kansas | (NC) | 74 | 51 |
| Kentucky | (S) | 74 | 60 |
| Louisiana | (S) | 51 | 65 |
| Maine | (NE) | 50 | 6 |
| Maryland | (S) | 58 | 46 |

**TABLE B-1.** (Continued)

| STATE | (REGION) | RESPONSE RATE | NUMBER |
|---|---|---|---|
| Massachusetts | (NE) | 57 | 25 |
| Michigan | (NC) | 67 | 105 |
| Minnesota | (NC) | 65 | 43 |
| Mississippi | (S) | 69 | 43 |
| Missouri | (NC) | 64 | 68 |
| Montana | (W) | 70 | 19 |
| Nebraska | (NC) | 79 | 34 |
| Nevada | (W) | 65 | 15 |
| New Hampshire | (NE) | 67 | 8 |
| New Mexico | (W) | 78 | 28 |
| New York | (NE) | 50 | 183 |
| North Carolina | (S) | 50 | 22 |
| North Dakota | (NC) | 89 | 16 |
| Ohio | (NC) | 60 | 181 |
| Oklahoma | (S) | 67 | 38 |
| Oregon | (W) | 85 | 57 |
| Pennsylvania | (NE) | 70 | 184 |
| Rhode Island | (NE) | 69 | 11 |
| South Carolina | (S) | 56 | 14 |
| South Dakota | (NC) | 64 | 23 |
| Tennessee | (S) | 60 | 64 |
| Texas | (S) | 52 | 114 |
| Utah | (W) | 79 | 19 |
| Vermont | (NE) | 50 | 9 |
| Virginia | (S) | 59 | 59 |
| Washington | (W) | 73 | 69 |
| West Virginia | (S) | 70 | 40 |
| Wisconsin | (NC) | 63 | 109 |
| Wyoming | (W) | 58 | 7 |
| Total |  | 63% | 3032 |
| Region |  |  |  |
| Northeast (NE) |  | 58% | 448 |
| South (S) |  | 59% | 889 |
| North Central (NC) |  | 66% | 998 |
| West (W) |  | 71% | 697 |

[a] New Jersey has been excluded, because that state's Administrative Office of the Courts prohibited judicial response to questionnaires. Despite the ban, we sent our mail questionnaire to the state's trial judges but received a response of only 9 percent, prior to follow-up appeals (which we chose not to pursue). Those few responses received have not been included in any data analysis.
[b] Region definitions are those of the U.S. Department of Commerce, Bureau of the Census.

well, others did not. Table B-1 presents the response rate by state and region.

The potential biases resulting from nonresponding judges are more difficult to assess. Approximately one-third of the universe did not respond. What might these judges be like? We have no direct way of knowing or determining this, but we can make some inferences from judges who responded after protracted appeals. If there are any differences at all, late-responding judges are probably more like nonresponders than are early-responding judges. In fact, our analysis indicates that there are very few differences between early- and late-responding judges across a wide range of variables. Their perceptions of the work environment are highly similar; their backgrounds are quite similar; they are located in a similar range of court structures. Even their (perceived) workload is quite similar with one exception: Late-responding judges actually report less time worked on their most common and subsequent days. Late-responding judges are not highly pressured or unusually overworked, as one might hypothesize; on the contrary, they may be slightly less involved in their work. Overall, however, we infer from the few differences between early- and late-responding judges that nonresponding judges are likely to be similar to those who have responded, given our premise that late-responders would have been nonresponders but for the last follow-up appeal. Thus, we conclude with some confidence that the biases resulting from nonresponse are minimal.

## Summary

The development and administration of a nationwide mail survey is a painstaking and detailed process of data collection. Nonetheless, the effort is more straightforward than observational methodology. Much literature has been written on survey research techniques generally and mail questionnaires in particular. In most instances, we have followed the explicit or implicit guidelines of this literature in developing and administering our mail survey. A sample of the final mail questionnaire can be found in Appendix C.

## Notes

1. See, for example, Bancroft C. Henderson and T. C. Sinclair, *The Selection of Judges in Texas: An Exploratory Study* (Houston: University of Houston Press, 1965), and Maurice Rosenberg, "Comparative Negligence in Arkansas: A Before and After Survey," *New York State Bar Journal*, 36 (1964). These and other studies are summarized in Theodore L. Becker, "Surveys and Judiciaries, or Who's Afraid of the Purple Curtain?" *Law and Society Review*, 1 (1966).
2. *National Survey of Court Organization* (Washington, D.C.: Law Enforcement Assistance Administration, 1973). Based upon our field observations and the survey's discussion, we included the District Courts in Vermont because they handle, in practice, almost the entire range of criminal cases except capital cases. In one-tiered systems having two levels of judges (as, for example, in Illinois), we included only the upper-level trial judges (only circuit judges in Illinois). This pro-

vided the most comparability with the identification of trial judges in miltitiered state court systems.
3. See American Judicature Society and The Institute for Court Management, *Misdemeanor Court Management Research Program, Part I* (Washington, D.C.: Law Enforcement Assistance Administration, 1978).
4. Of course, a few such judges in general jurisdiction courts are assigned to domestic relations, juvenile, probate, or even misdemeanor work, but they will have the opportunity to serve in other assignments during their judgeship.
5. This list was an updated version of NJC's *Directory of State and Local Judges* (Reno: National Judicial College, 1975).
6. Such sources included a few up-to-date lists of judges, which we had begun to assemble from state court administrators, as well as state legal directories published by the Legal Directories Publishing Company in Los Angeles. *The American Bench* (Minneapolis: Reginald Bishop Forster, 1979), an impressive attempt to catalog sitting judges, was not available at the time.
7. One variation from random sampling was employed. To test the potential effects of "collegiality" or "small group contamination," we sampled the universe of trial judges in one intermediate-size court (Des Moines). By mailing (on the same day) only one format to all nine judges of the court, we attempted to simulate the potential impact of the final mailing in larger, multijudge courts. We wished to explore effects on response rate and on the substantive patterning of responses. Although working with small numbers, we could find no striking effects.
8. The winning judge was unable to attend the meeting because of a snowstorm that covered much of the Midwest in January 1978. Most of the project staff successfully weathered the elements.
9. See Herbert H. Blumberg, Carolyn Fuller, and A. Paul Hare, "Response Rates in Postal Surveys," *Public Opinion Quarterly*, 38 (1974), pp. 114–115.
10. Federal Judicial Center, *The 1969–1970 Federal District Court Time Study* (Washington, D.C.: Federal Judicial Center, 1971), p. 96.
11. The Administrative Office of the Courts in New Jersey refused to cooperate and asserted that it had imposed a statewide ban on the completion of questionnaires by its trial (and other) judges. The office felt that too many surveys were being distributed in that state, taking valuable time away from individual judges.
12. We identified the state of responding judges by a stamping of the state's name at the end of the mail questionnaire. In a few states where we wished to ensure the possibility of analyzing separately the responses of judges in a large urban court, we utilized a different color of questionnaire. The stamping of the state was visible to all respondents; the use of color-coded questionnaires was not. Nevertheless, neither step significantly jeopardizes the anonymity of individual responses.

# APPENDIX C

# The Questionnaire

I. JUDICIAL STYLES

From our field observations, we have found that different trial judges adopt different roles in bench trials, and in settlement and plea negotiation conferences. The questions below ask you to identify the manner in which you actually perform these activities.

1. To what degree (if at all) do you involve yourself, in presiding at criminal and/or civil non-jury trials, in each of the following activities (assume for the purpose of responding that the competence of the trial lawyers is "average").....?

*(IF NO NON-JURY TRIALS, WRITE "NA")*

*(CHECK ONE FOR EACH OF a-e)*

|   | | EXTENSIVE | MODERATE | LIMITED | NONE |
|---|---|---|---|---|---|
| a. | Taking notes . . . . . . . . . . . . . . . | ( ) | ( ) | ( ) | ( ) |
| b. | Questioning witnesses. . . . . . . . . . . | ( ) | ( ) | ( ) | ( ) |
| c. | Encouraging counsel (in chambers) to expedite testimony . . . . . . . . . . . . | ( ) | ( ) | ( ) | ( ) |
| d. | Encouraging counsel (in courtroom) to expedite testimony . . . . . . . . . . . | ( ) | ( ) | ( ) | ( ) |
| e. | Interrupting counsel during legal argument to expedite, question, clarify or advise . . . . . . . . . . . . . . . . . | ( ) | ( ) | ( ) | ( ) |
| f. | Other (specify) _____ . . . | ( ) | ( ) | ( ) | ( ) |

2. Which one of the following roles do you most typically assume with respect to plea negotiations?

   *(CHECK ONLY ONE)*

   ( ) Attend plea negotiation discussions and recommend dispositions to the DA and/or defense counsel

   ( ) Attend plea negotiation discussions, and review recommendations of the DA and/or defense counsel

   ( ) Attend plea negotiation discussions, but do not participate

   ( ) Do not attend plea negotiation discussions; only ratify in open court dispositions agreed to outside your presence

   ( ) NA (civil, chancery court)

3. In (civil) settlement conferences, which one of the following roles do you most typically assume?

   *(CHECK ONLY ONE)*

   ( ) Intervene aggressively -- through the use of direct pressure

   ( ) Intervene subtly -- through the use of cues/suggestions

   ( ) Do not intervene -- allow the opposing counsel to try to reach a settlement on their own

   ( ) NA (criminal court)

## II. VIEWS OF SELF, COURT, AND BAR

1. In your judicial capacity, to what extent are you able to utilize your skills and preferences effectively?

   *(CIRCLE ONE NUMBER)*

   Effective                              Ineffective
   Utilization 7  6  5  4  3  2  1  Utilization

2. To what extent (if any) do you experience too much or too little variety in the cases coming before you?

   *(CIRCLE ONE NUMBER)*

   Too Much                              Too Little
   Variety  7  6  5  4  3  2  1  Variety

3. To what degree do you feel in control of how you spend your work time?

   *(CIRCLE ONE NUMBER)*

   Full Control 7  6  5  4  3  2  1  No Control

4. For each of the following tasks which you perform in your current assignment, rate the "efficiency" of your work time -- i.e., how much is accomplished per hour of time spent:

   *(FOR EACH OF a-d, CIRCLE ONE NUMBER OR WRITE "NA")*

   a. Plea negotiation discussions

   Efficient 7  6  5  4  3  2  1  Inefficient

   b. Settlement conferences (civil)

   Efficient 7  6  5  4  3  2  1  Inefficient

   c. Non-jury trials

   Efficient 7  6  5  4  3  2  1  Inefficient

   d. Jury trials

   Efficient 7  6  5  4  3  2  1  Inefficient

5. How effective are the personnel in your courtroom (bailiffs, clerks, reporter, secretary) in facilitating your work?

   *(CIRCLE ONE NUMBER)*

   Effective 7  6  5  4  3  2  1  Ineffective

6. How do you feel about your current judicial salary?

   Overpaid 7  6  5  4  3  2  1  Underpaid

7. Under how much pressure to move cases do you feel?

   *(CIRCLE ONE NUMBER)*

   Too Much                              Too Little
   Pressure 7  6  5  4  3  2  1  Pressure

8. Which one of the following areas of your work is the most important to your overall level of satisfaction?

   *(CHECK ONLY ONE)*

   ( )  Skill utilization
   ( )  Variety of caseload
   ( )  Control of work time
   ( )  Task efficiency
   ( )  Effectiveness of courtroom personnel
   ( )  Salary
   ( )  Caseload pressure

   ( )  Other (specify)_____

9. How many hours are required to complete a jury trial in your courtroom, in a typical case, from voir dire to verdict, in the following areas?

   *(WRITE "NA" IF YOU DO NOT HANDLE JURY TRIALS IN THESE AREAS)*

   a. Personal Injury
      (auto accident)          _____ hours

   b. Armed Robbery            _____ hours

10. How would you rate your <u>skill</u> in each of the following work areas?

*(CHECK ONE FOR EACH OF a-e)*

|   | | EXCELLENT | ABOVE AVERAGE | AVERAGE | BELOW AVERAGE | POOR |
|---|---|---|---|---|---|---|
| a. | Adjudication | ( ) | ( ) | ( ) | ( ) | ( ) |
| b. | Administration | ( ) | ( ) | ( ) | ( ) | ( ) |
| c. | Community Relations | ( ) | ( ) | ( ) | ( ) | ( ) |
| d. | Legal Research | ( ) | ( ) | ( ) | ( ) | ( ) |
| e. | Negotiation | ( ) | ( ) | ( ) | ( ) | ( ) |

11. On balance, how would you rate the quality of the local practicing bar in your community -- i.e., those attorneys appearing before you most frequently?

*(CHECK ONE FOR EACH OF a-g)*

| CIVIL BAR | EXCELLENT | ABOVE AVERAGE | AVERAGE | BELOW AVERAGE | POOR | NO BASIS FOR JUDGMENT |
|---|---|---|---|---|---|---|
| a. Preparation of decrees/orders | ( ) | ( ) | ( ) | ( ) | ( ) | ( ) |
| b. Case preparation & management skills | ( ) | ( ) | ( ) | ( ) | ( ) | ( ) |
| c. Settlement skills | ( ) | ( ) | ( ) | ( ) | ( ) | ( ) |
| d. Trial skills | ( ) | ( ) | ( ) | ( ) | ( ) | ( ) |
| **CRIMINAL BAR** | | | | | | |
| e. Case preparation & management skills | ( ) | ( ) | ( ) | ( ) | ( ) | ( ) |
| f. Plea negotiation skills | ( ) | ( ) | ( ) | ( ) | ( ) | ( ) |
| g. Trial skills | ( ) | ( ) | ( ) | ( ) | ( ) | ( ) |

---

## III. COURT STRUCTURE

1. Which one of the following <u>best</u> characterizes your current assignment?

   *(CHECK ONLY ONE)*

   ( ) Criminal and Civil
   ( ) Criminal only
   ( ) Juvenile only
   ( ) Chancery only
   ( ) Domestic Relations only
   ( ) Probate only
   ( ) Civil-Jury only
   ( ) Civil - mixed (i.e., more than one above)

   ( ) Other (specify)_____

2. How many consecutive months (years) have you been in this assignment?

   _____yrs    _____months

3. How many years have you served as a judge in a court of <u>general</u> jurisdiction?

   _____yrs

4. How many judges (including yourself) are currently sitting in your local court of <u>general</u> jurisdiction?

   *(CHECK ONE)*

   ( ) 1         ( ) 10-15
   ( ) 2         ( ) 16-25
   ( ) 3-4       ( ) 26-39
   ( ) 5-9       ( ) 40 or more

5. Do you currently hold one of the following administrative positions in your court?

   *(CHECK ONE)*

   ( ) Chief/Presiding Judge
   ( ) Administrative (Assignment) Judge
   ( ) Presiding/Supervising Judge of one division within a multi-division court
   ( ) None above

6. What kind of secretarial services (if any) do you have in your current assignment?

   *(CHECK ONE)*

   ( ) Court reporter, clerk, or bailiff acts as secretary
   ( ) Shared, in secretarial pool
   ( ) Part-time personal secretary
   ( ) Full-time personal secretary
   ( ) None

7. What kind of law clerk services (if any) do you have in your current assignment?

   *(CHECK ONE)*

   ( ) More than one full-time law clerk
   ( ) One full-time law clerk
   ( ) More than one part-time law clerk
   ( ) One part-time law clerk
   ( ) One (or more) law clerk(s) shared with other judges
   ( ) None

8. Are prosecutors assigned to your court for some period of time so that the same prosecutors try most/all cases in your courtroom?

   ( ) Yes
   ( ) No
   ( ) NA (civil, chancery court)

   If yes, for how long a period of time do the same prosecutors typically stay in your court?

   *(CHECK ONE)*

   ( ) 3 months or less   ( ) 1-2 years
   ( ) 4-12 months        ( ) 2 years or more

9. What kind of counsel is typically provided for indigent defendants in your court?

   *(CHECK ONE)*

   ( ) Public defender
   ( ) Private (assigned) counsel
   ( ) NA (civil, chancery court)

   Do one or a few counsel defend most/all indigent cases in your courtroom?

   ( ) Yes
   ( ) No

   If yes, for how long a period of time do these same defense counsel appear in your courtroom?

   *(CHECK ONE)*

   ( ) 3 months or less   ( ) 1-2 years
   ( ) 4-12 months        ( ) 2 years or more

10. For the most recent 50 civil cases concluded in your court, approximately how many different plaintiff lawyers and defendant lawyers appeared before you?

    *(IF CRIMINAL COURT JUDGE, SKIP QUESTION)*

    a. Plaintiff Lawyers

    *(CHECK ONE)*

    ( ) 46-50
    ( ) 31-45
    ( ) 16-30
    ( ) 1-15

    b. Defendant Lawyers

    *(CHECK ONE)*

    ( ) 46-50
    ( ) 31-45
    ( ) 16-30
    ( ) 1-15

11. What kind of calendaring principle predominates in the assignment of cases in your current assignment?

    *(CHECK ONLY ONE)*

    ( ) Cases are assigned to a judge at an early stage and remain with the same judge until final disposition
    ( ) Cases are assigned to a judge only for one (or more) particular stage(s) -- e.g., motions, settlement, trial...
    ( ) NA (single-judge court)

    If assigned only for one or more stages, how many cases -- at the "ready for trial" stage -- are typically assigned to you at the same time?

    *(CHECK ONE)*

    ( ) Only 1 case
    ( ) 2 or more cases
    ( ) NA (discovery/pre-trial work only)

12. Does your court have any of the following work cycles or procedures?

    YES NO

    ( ) ( ) Months or weeks set aside as jury or non-jury terms
    ( ) ( ) Months or weeks set aside as criminal or civil terms
    ( ) ( ) Week(s) set aside exclusively for settlement conferences
    ( ) ( ) Day(s) of the week (M-F) set aside to hear certain types of proceedings
    ( ) ( ) Active use of commissioners, referees, arbiters, pro-tem judges, etc.

13. Which (if any) of the following jurisdictional descriptions applies to you?

    YES NO

    ( ) ( ) Multi-county jurisdiction requiring circuit-riding among locations
    ( ) ( ) Multi-county jurisdiction, but you sit only in one location
    ( ) ( ) Statewide jurisdiction; you sit in different locations throughout the state, by assignment

    If statewide jurisdiction, for how long are you typically assigned to one location?

    *(CHECK ONE)*

    ( ) 2 months or less   ( ) 7-11 months
    ( ) 3-5 months         ( ) 1 year
    ( ) 6 months           ( ) more than 1 year

14. Which one of the following descriptions best characterizes the community(ies) in which you currently sit?

    (CHECK ONLY ONE)

    ( ) Large city only (500,000+)
    ( ) Large city and suburbs (1M+)
    ( ) Medium-sized city and suburbs (250,000 - 1M)
    ( ) Smaller city in non-metropolitan area (50,000 - 250,000)
    ( ) Suburban only
    ( ) Rural

15. Is your local community significantly involved in court matters through any of the following ways?

    YES  NO

    ( ) ( ) Extensive newspaper or television coverage of courts
    ( ) ( ) Frequent "court watcher" projects
    ( ) ( ) Local college or university research projects on courts or judicial personnel
    ( ) ( ) Hotly-contested elections for local judgeships
    ( )     Other (specify)_____

- - - - - - - - - - - - - - - - - - - - - - - - - - - - - - - - - - - - - - - -

Questions 16, 17, 18, and 19 are directed to judges sitting in multi-judge courts which have divisions -- i.e., courts which assign judges to hear only certain types, or stages, of cases for a period of time. For example, many courts have a criminal division and one general civil division; or several civil divisions -- e.g., probate, domestic relations, etc. Other courts have a different kind of divisional structure -- one or several calendar judges (hearing motions in criminal or civil cases) and a general trial division in which judges hear both criminal and civil cases.

(IF YOUR COURT HAS DIVISIONS, ANSWER Qs 16-19; IF NO DIVISIONS, WRITE OR CHECK "NA")

16. Which one of the following descriptions best approximates the divisional structure of your local court of general jurisdiction?

    (CHECK ONLY ONE)

    ( ) Criminal division and one general civil division
    ( ) Criminal division and two or more different civil divisions (e.g., probate, domestic relations, equity, etc.)
    ( ) One or more calendar (motions) judges and one general trial division (criminal and civil)
    ( ) NA (no divisions)

17. How frequently, in practice, are judges typically rotated from one divisional assignment to another in your court?

    (CHECK ONE)

    ( ) Every six months (or more frequently)
    ( ) Once per year
    ( ) Once in two to five years
    ( ) Almost never
    ( ) No discernible time pattern
    ( ) NA (no divisions)

18. To what extent (if at all) do each of the following factors influence the assignment of judges to divisions in your court?

    |   | SUBSTANTIAL INFLUENCE | SLIGHT INFLUENCE | NO INFLUENCE |
    |---|---|---|---|

    (CHECK ONE FOR EACH OF a-e)

    a. Case disposition rate of judge    ( )    ( )    ( )
    b. Court politics                    ( )    ( )    ( )
    c. Regular rotation                  ( )    ( )    ( )
    d. Sentencing philosophy of judge    ( )    ( )    ( )
    e. Technical expertise of judge      ( )    ( )    ( )

19. Have you served in any divisional assignments other than your current one?

    ( ) Yes
    ( ) No
    ( ) NA (no divisions)

    If yes, please list your most recent two divisional assignments and the number of years served in each.

    |              | Division | Number of Yrs Served |
    |---|---|---|
    | Most recent  | _____ | _____ |
    | Next . . .   | _____ | _____ |

## IV. SUMMARY OF TYPES OF WORK DAYS

Below, we ask for information on what your work days are typically like. For some judges, each day may be almost exactly like the next with respect to the <u>relative amount</u> of time spent in trial, conferences, research, administration, etc. These judges would have only <u>one</u> type of work day, and would fill in time estimates only in the first blocked column in Q2 -- under "MOST COMMON WORK DAY." For other judges, some days may be quite different from others -- e.g., some days spent mostly in jury trial, while other days require different mixes of time in non-jury trials, motions (calendar), conferences, etc. These judges would have <u>two</u>, <u>three</u>, <u>four</u>, or even <u>five</u> different types of work days, and would fill in time estimates for each different type of work day in the appropriate columns provided -- their most common type of work day in the first column, their second most common type of work day in the second column, etc.

1. How many <u>different types</u> of work days do you have in your current assignment?

   ( ) 1     ( ) 2     ( ) 3     ( ) 4     ( ) 5     *(CHECK ONLY ONE)*

2. Write, in the spaces provided, the amount of time you spend (if any) on the activities listed <u>for each of the types of work days</u> which you encounter (in your current assignment).

*PLEASE READ THE LIST OF POTENTIAL ACTIVITIES BEFORE FILLING IN TIME SPENT, IF ANY.*

**TYPES OF WORK DAYS**
*(ESTIMATE TO NEAREST 1/4 HOUR)*

| | MOST COMMON WORK DAY | 2ND MOST COMMON WORK DAY | 3RD MOST COMMON WORK DAY | 4TH MOST COMMON WORK DAY | 5TH MOST COMMON WORK DAY |
|---|---|---|---|---|---|
| Reading case files................ | ___hrs | ___hrs | ___hrs | ___hrs | ___hrs |
| Keeping up with the law (reading reporters, statutes, court rules, journals, books, etc.) | ___hrs | ___hrs | ___hrs | ___hrs | ___hrs |
| Preparing/writing decisions, judgments, orders | ___hrs | ___hrs | ___hrs | ___hrs | ___hrs |
| General administrative work and correspondence | ___hrs | ___hrs | ___hrs | ___hrs | ___hrs |
| Plea negotiation discussions (criminal).... | ___hrs | ___hrs | ___hrs | ___hrs | ___hrs |
| Settlement discussions (civil)......... | ___hrs | ___hrs | ___hrs | ___hrs | ___hrs |
| Socializing with attorneys, court personnel, etc. | ___hrs | ___hrs | ___hrs | ___hrs | ___hrs |
| Case-related discussions with attorneys (<u>not related</u> to plea or settlement)..... | ___hrs | ___hrs | ___hrs | ___hrs | ___hrs |
| Waiting time -- for attorneys, court personnel, jurors, witnesses, case assignment, etc.... | ___hrs | ___hrs | ___hrs | ___hrs | ___hrs |
| Travel time (circuit-riding, etc.)....... | ___hrs | ___hrs | ___hrs | ___hrs | ___hrs |
| Lunch.......................... | ___hrs | ___hrs | ___hrs | ___hrs | ___hrs |
| Presiding at non-jury trial.......... | ___hrs | ___hrs | ___hrs | ___hrs | ___hrs |
| Presiding at jury trial............ | ___hrs | ___hrs | ___hrs | ___hrs | ___hrs |
| Civil or criminal calendar (motions, defaults, arraignments, prelim. hearings, guilty pleas, sentence hearings, etc.)............ | ___hrs | ___hrs | ___hrs | ___hrs | ___hrs |
| Other (specify)_____ | ___hrs | ___hrs | ___hrs | ___hrs | ___hrs |
| DAILY TOTALS | ___hrs | ___hrs | ___hrs | ___hrs | ___hrs |

*PLEASE ADD THE HOURS AND FRACTIONS FOR EACH TYPE OF WORK DAY TO INSURE THAT YOUR ESTIMATES ARE APPROXIMATELY ACCURATE*

3. How often, over the course of a year, does each type of work day occur?

*(FILL IN A PERCENTAGE NUMBER FOR EACH TYPE OF WORK DAY IDENTIFIED IN Q2, AND FOR RANDOM DAYS, IF ANY, TO TOTAL 100%)*

Most Common _____ %
2nd Most Common _____ %
3rd Most Common _____ %
4th Most Common _____ %
5th Most Common _____ %
Random _____ %

TOTAL   100  %

4. Given the recognized difficulty in characterizing "types of work days" how confident are you in your responses to Questions 2 and 3?

*(CHECK ONE)*

( ) Fully confident
( ) Reasonably confident
( ) Somewhat confident
( ) Not at all confident

## V. PROFESSIONAL BACKGROUND AND EXPERIENCES

1. How were you <u>initially</u> selected for the court of general jurisdiction?

   *(CHECK ONE)*

   ( ) Elected -- partisan ballot
   ( ) Elected -- non-partisan ballot
   ( ) Selected by state or local legislature
   ( ) Appointed under merit or Missouri plan
   ( ) Appointed by governor
   ( ) Selected by other judges
   ( ) Other (explain): _____

2. What occupation did you hold <u>immediately prior</u> to your current judgeship?

   *(CHECK ONE)*

   IMMEDIATELY
   PRIOR

   ( ) Lower court judge
   ( ) District attorney's office
   ( ) Federal/local government lawyer
   ( ) Other public official (specify) _____
   ( ) Private legal practice
   ( ) Other (specify) _____

   If "private legal practice," what was your specialization?

   ( ) Criminal
   ( ) Civil
   ( ) No specialization

3. What is your current political party registration or affiliation?

   *(CHECK ONE)*

   ( ) Democratic    ( ) Republican
   ( ) Independent   ( ) Other _____

4. Since becoming a judge, have you ever <u>designed</u> or <u>taught</u> courses in any of the following settings?

   YES  NO

   ( )  ( )  Law school courses
   ( )  ( )  Judicial education programs for new or sitting judges
   ( )  ( )  Police officers' training

5. How many hours <u>per month</u> do you currently spend on community relations -- i.e., speeches, interviews, civic meetings, etc.?

   *(CHECK ONE)*

   ( ) 0          ( ) 5 - 8 hrs
   ( ) 1 - 2 hrs  ( ) 9 - 12 hrs
   ( ) 3 - 4 hrs  ( ) 13 hrs or more

6. How many hours <u>per month</u> do you currently spend on bar association meetings and activities?

   *(CHECK ONE)*

   ( ) 0          ( ) 5 - 8
   ( ) 1 - 2 hrs  ( ) 9 - 12 hrs
   ( ) 3 - 4 hrs  ( ) 13 hrs or more

7. Have (are) any members of your immediate family been lawyers (L), judges (J), or elected public officials (P)?

   *(CHECK AS MANY AS APPLY; THEN, CIRCLE APPROPRIATE LETTER(S) FOR EACH CHECK)*

   ( ) Grandparents    L    J    P
   ( ) Parents         L    J    P
   ( ) Brother/Sister  L    J    P
   ( ) Spouse          L    J    P
   ( ) Children        L    J    P
   ( ) None

8. What is your present age? _____

9. What is your sex?

   ( ) Male          ( ) Female

10. Which of the following applies to you?

    ( ) Black         ( ) Indian
    ( ) Hispanic      ( ) Oriental
              ( ) White

# Selected Bibliography

Adams, Eldridge. *The Feasibility of Measuring and Comparing Calendar Effectiveness.* Springfield, Va.: National Technical Information Service, 1971.

Alpert, Lenore, Burton M. Atkins, and Robert C. Ziller. "Becoming a Judge: The Transition from Advocate to Arbiter," *Judicature*, 62 (1979): 325–335.

Alschuler, Albert W. "The Trial Judge's Role in Plea Bargaining, Part I," *Columbia Law Review*, 76 (1976): 1059–1154.

American University, Criminal Courts Technical Assistance Project. *Survey of State Judicial Education Programs, 1974-1976.* Washington, D.C.: American University Law Institute, 1978.

Balbus, Isaac D. *The Dialectics of Legal Repression: Black Rebels Before the American Criminal Courts.* New York: Russell Sage, 1973.

Berkson, Larry C., Steven W. Hays, and Susan Carbon (eds.). *Managing the State Courts.* St. Paul: West, 1977.

Blumberg, Abraham S. *Criminal Justice.* Chicago: Quadrangle, 1967.

Botein, Bernard. *Trial Judge.* New York: Simon & Schuster, 1952.

Church, Thomas, Jr., Alan Carlson, Jo-Lynne Lee, and Teresa Tan. *Justice Delayed: The Pace of Litigation in Urban Trial Courts.* Williamsburg, Va.: National Center for State Courts, 1978.

Cook, Beverly Blair. "Women Judges: The End of Tokenism," in Winifred L. Hepperle and Laura Crites (eds.). *Women in the Courts.* Williamsburg, Va.: National Center for State Courts, 1978.

Dolbeare, Kenneth M. *Trial Courts in Urban Politics.* New York: Wiley, 1967.

Eisenstein, James, and Herbert Jacob. *Felony Justice: An Organizational Analysis of Criminal Courts.* Boston: Little, Brown, 1977.

Federal Judicial Center. *The 1969-1970 Federal District Court Time Study.* Washington, D.C.: Federal Judicial Center, 1971.

Feeley, Malcolm M. *The Process Is the Punishment.* New York: Russell Sage, 1979.

Friesen, Ernest C., Edward C. Gallas, and Nesta M. Gallas. *Managing the Courts.* Indianapolis: Bobbs-Merrill, 1971.

Gignoux, Edward. "A Trial Judge's View," *Massachusetts Law Quarterly*, 50 (1965): 100–107.

Heumann, Milton. *Plea Bargaining: The Experiences of Prosecutors, Judges, and Defense Attorneys.* Chicago: University of Chicago Press, 1977.

Jacob, Herbert. "The Effect of Institutional Differences in the Recruitment Process: The Case of State Judges," *Journal of Public Law*, 13 (1964): 104–119.

Jacob, Herbert. *Urban Justice: Law and Order in American Cities*. Englewood Cliffs, N.J.: Prentice-Hall, 1973.

Jacob, Herbert (ed.). *The Potential for Reform of Criminal Justice*. Beverly Hills and London: Sage Publications, 1974.

McLauchlan, William P. *American Legal Processes*. New York: Wiley, 1977.

Nardulli, Peter F. *The Courtroom Elite: An Organizational Perspective on Criminal Justice*. Cambridge, Mass.: Ballinger, 1978.

Neubauer, David W. *Criminal Justice in Middle America*. Morristown, N.J.: General Learning Press, 1974.

Neubauer, David W. "Judicial Role and Case Management," *Justice System Journal*, 4 (1979): 223–232.

Rosenberg, Maurice. "The Qualities of Justices: Are They Strainable?" *Texas Law Review*, 44 (1966): 1063–1080.

Ryan, John Paul, and James J. Alfini. "Trial Judges' Participation in Plea Bargaining: An Empirical Perspective," *Law and Society Review*, 13 (1979): 479–507.

Salter, Robert. "The Quality of a Judge's Experience," *American Bar Association Journal*, 65 (1979): 933–935.

Saltzburg, Stephen A. "The Unnecessarily Expanding Role of the American Trial Judge," *Virginia Law Review*, 64 (1978): 1–81.

Sarat, Austin. "Studying American Legal Culture: An Assessment of Survey Evidence," *Law and Society Review*, 11 (1977): 427–488.

Skogan, Wesley G. "The Politics of Judicial Reform: Cook County, Illinois," *Justice System Journal*, 1 (1975): 11–23.

Solomon, Maureen. *Caseflow Management in the Trial Court*. American Bar Association Commission on Standards of Judicial Administration, Supporting Studies-2, 1973.

Uhlman, Thomas M. *Racial Justice*. Lexington, Mass.: D.C. Heath, 1979.

U.S. Department of Justice, Law Enforcement Assistance Administration. *National Survey of Court Organization*. Washington, D.C.: Government Printing Office, 1973.

Wheeler, Russell R., and Whitcomb, Howard P. (eds.). *Judicial Administration: Text and Readings*. Englewood Cliffs, N.J.: Prentice-Hall, 1977.

Wice, Paul B. *Criminal Lawyers: An Endangered Species*. Beverly Hills and London: Sage Publications, 1978.

Wyzanski, Charles A. *A Trial Judge's Freedom and Responsibility*. New York: Association of the Bar of the City of New York, 1952.

# Index

Alpert, Lenore, 137, 138, 139
Attorneys
   adversariness of, 81–83, 97, 186–87, 235
   and judges' work, 80–81
   skills of, 84–90, 97–98, 157–59, 166, 185–86, 230
   skills and their policy implications, 233–34
   stability in courtrooms, 90–91, 98, 230; (civil), 95–97, 185, 236; (criminal), 91–95, 183–85, 235–36

Bailiffs: *see* Court personnel
Blumberg, Abraham, 235
Bogdan, Robert, 250
Botein, Bernard, 4, 5
Boyle, John, 200, 206
Bradley, Edward, 201, 206
Bradley, Tom, 198
Brown, Edmund G., Sr., 201, 206
Brown, Edmund G., Jr., 206

Carp, Robert, 136
Case assignment system
   and attorney stability in courtrooms, 92–93
   in Chicago, 208–209
   description of, 55–57
   and job satisfaction of judges, 149–50, 160
   and judges' work, 71–74, 134–35, 182–83
   in Los Angeles, 209
   in Philadelphia, 209
   policy implications of, 232–33
   and size of court, 56–57
   and statewide assignment, 56–57
Caseload pressures of judges, 147, 150–51, 154–55
   and attorney skills, 159
   in Chicago, 214–15
   and court politics, 159–60
   and judges' work, 187
   in Los Angeles, 214–15
   in Philadelphia, 214–15
   and size of court, 156–57
Caseload variety of judges: *see* Judges' work, variety of
Chicago courts
   bench-bar relationships in, 211–14
   chief judge, 200
   and community politics, 197–198
   court personnel in, 103–104
   location of, 197
   management of, 219–20
   media coverage of, 202–203
Chicago judges
   gender, 206
   job satisfaction of, 214–17
   and jury trials, 209–10
   length (hours) of work day, 209
   morale of: *see* job satisfaction of
   and nonjury trials, 209–10, 213–14
   and plea discussions, 210
   political affiliation of, 206, 216
   and preparing or writing decisions, 210
   professional background of, 204–206

Chicago judges (*Cont.*)
  race, 206
  selection of, 204
  and settlement discussions, 212–13
Circuit-riding
  and court personnel, 113
  description of, 53–54
  and judges' work, 47, 183
  policy implications of, 231
  and size of court, 61–62
Clark, Joseph, 199
Clerks: *see* Court personnel
Control of work time of judges, 147, 149–50, 154–55
  and attorney skills, 158
  in Chicago, 214–15
  and court politics, 159–60
  in Los Angeles, 214–15
  in Philadelphia, 214–15
Cook, Beverly Blair, 131
Courts: *see* Trial courts
Court personnel
  and attorney skills, 158–59
  bailiffs, 102–105
  in Chicago, 214–15
  and circuit-riding, 113
  clerks, 102–105
  and court politics, 112, 159–60
  description of, 102
  efficiency of, 112–16, 153–55
  and judges' work, 230
  law clerks, 105–10, 116, 132, 230
  in Los Angeles, 214–15
  in Philadelphia, 214–15
  policy implications of, 234
  rotation of, 104–105
  secretaries, 110–12
  and size of court, 157
  and statewide assignment, 113
  variations across courts, 102–104
Court politics
  in Chicago, 217–20
  and court personnel, 112, 115
  description of, 52–53
  and job satisfaction of judges, 159–60
  in Los Angeles, 217–20
  in Philadelphia, 217–20

Daley, Richard J., 197
Dickens, Charles, 258
Dilworth, Richardson, 201
Divisions within courts
  in Chicago, 207–208
  description of, 49–53
  and judges' work, 75
  in Los Angeles, 207–208
  in Philadelphia, 207–208
Dolbeare, Kenneth, 10

Eisenstein, James, 8, 91, 93, 95, 98, 183, 235

Federal Judicial Center, 270
Freedman, Monroe, 82
Friesen, Ernest C., 17

Gallas, Edward C., 17
Gallas, Nesta M., 17
Gignoux, Edward, 4, 5

Heumann, Milton, 8, 135, 136, 138, 139

Individual calendar: *see* Case assignment system

Jacob, Herbert, 4, 5, 8, 91, 93, 95, 98, 183, 235
Judges: *see also* Chicago judges, Los Angeles judges, Philadelphia judges
  and affirmative action, 238–39
  age of, 127–29, 131–35, 138, 141–42, 236–38
  of civil assignment, 23, 131–32, 160

of criminal assignment, 4, 23, 131–32, 160
diversity of, 3–4
evaluation of, 5
family background of, 129–30
gender, 128, 130–31, 141, 237–39
of general assignment, 22–23
job satisfaction of 8, 10, 148–62, 166–67, 237
morale of: *see* job satisfaction of
political affiliation of, 126–27
professional background of, 124–26, 136–37, 189–90
race, 128, 130–31, 141, 237–39
retirement of, 238
selection of, 122–24
socialization of, 135–42
tenure of, 138–39, 189
Judges' work: *see also* Negotiation style of judges
adjudication, 6, 38–39, 162–63, 227
administration, 6–7, 31–32, 38–39, 64, 76, 111–12, 162–63, 227–28
affiliation, 7, 32, 64, 132–33, 228
bar association activities, 41
calendar call, 18, 32, 35, 133–34
in civil assignment, 19–21, 33–34, 65, 134
community relations, 7, 41–42, 69–70, 130–31, 162–64, 228
in criminal assignment, 18–19, 33–34, 37–38, 68
discussions with attorneys, 32
diversity of, 242
in domestic relations, 21
environment of, 10, 240
in general assignment, 21–22, 33–34
jury trials, 30–31, 33–34, 36–37, 40, 63, 66–67, 69, 75, 82–83, 90, 93–94, 134, 186–87
keeping up with the law, 31–32, 62–63, 107–109
legal research, 7, 38–40, 75–76, 162–65, 227

length (hours) of, 26–28, 42–43, 62, 69–71, 89, 115, 130–31, 209, 228
negotiation, 7, 38–39, 136, 162–63, 165, 228
nonjury trials, 30–31, 33–35, 37–38, 40, 63, 69, 75, 90, 93–94, 134
plea discussions, 32–33, 64, 72, 75, 93–95, 136–37, 181–92
preparing or writing decisions, 66, 87–88, 106–107, 133
reading case files, 31–32
settlement discussions, 33–34, 66, 72–73, 75, 136–37, 181–83, 185–92
travel time, 35, 53, 55
variety of, 24–26, 40, 42, 62–63, 147, 151–52, 154–56, 159–60, 214–15
waiting time, 32, 35–36, 62–63, 66, 71–74, 89–90, 114–15
Judicial education, 6, 135–36, 140–41, 189
Junker, Buford H., 250


Kennedy, Robert, 198


Law clerks: *see* Court personnel
Lawyers: *see* Attorneys
Los Angeles courts
bench-bar relationships in, 211–14
chief judge, 201
and community politics, 198
court personnel in, 102–103, 105
location of, 198–99
management of, 219
media coverage of, 202–203
Los Angeles judges
gender, 206
job satisfaction of, 214–17
and jury trials, 209–10
length (hours) of work day, 209
morale of: *see* job satisfaction of
and nonjury trials, 209–10, 213–14
and plea discussions, 210

Los Angeles judges (*Cont.*)
  political affiliation of, 206, 217
  and preparing or writing decisions, 210
  professional background of, 204–206
  race, 206
  selection of, 204
  and settlement discussions, 212–13
Luskin, Mary Lee, 139

Mail survey of judges
  administration of, 273–76
  pretest of, 267–73
Master calendar: *see* Case assignment system

National Judicial College, 268
Negotiation style of judges
  and attorney adversariness, 186–87
  and attorney skills, 185–86
  and attorney stability in courtrooms, 183–85
  and case assignment system, 182–83
  and case law, 181
  and caseload pressures, 187
  in Chicago, 210
  and circuit-riding, 183
  in civil cases, 174–75, 177–79, 191–92
  and court rules, 180–81
  in criminal cases, 174–77, 190–92
  and judicial skills, 187–88
  in Los Angeles, 210
  in Philadelphia, 210
  and professional background of, 189–90
  and size of court, 181–82, 191–92
  summary of, 192–93

Observations of judges
  entree, 251–52
  rapport development in, 253–55
  and reactivity, 255–58
  reliability of, 257–58
  and role of observer, 249–50, 252–53
  and sampling, 250–51

Personnel: *see* Court personnel
Philadelphia courts
  bench-bar relationships in 212–14
  chief judge, 201–202
  and community politics, 199
  court personnel in, 103–104
  location of, 199
  management of, 220
  media coverage of, 202–203
Philadelphia judges
  gender, 206
  job satisfaction of, 214–17
  and jury trials, 209–10
  length (hours) of work day, 209
  morale of: *see* job satisfaction of
  and nonjury trials, 209–10, 213–14
  and plea discussions, 210
  political affiliation of, 206, 216
  and preparing or writing decisions, 210
  professional background of, 204–206
  race, 206
  selection of, 204
  and settlement discussions, 212–13
Prosecutors: *see* Attorneys
Public defenders: *see also* Attorneys
  and attorney stability in courtrooms, 92

Reagan, Ronald, 206
Rizzo, Frank, 199
Rosenthal, Douglas, 81

Salary of judges, 147–48, 153–55
  in Chicago, 214–16
  and court politics, 159–60
  in Los Angeles, 214–16
  in Philadelphia, 214–16
Schwartz, Charlotte Green, 249

## Index

Schwartz, Morris S., 249
Scranton, William, 201
Size of community: *see also* Size of court
   and attorney stability in courtrooms,
     92; (civil), 96
   and court personnel, 102–103
   and judges' work, 94–95, 140–41
Size of court
   and attorney adversariness, 83
   and case assignment system, 56–57
   and court personnel, 113–16
   description of, 48–49
   and divisions, 51
   and job satisfaction of judges, 156–57, 166
   and judges' work, 47, 61–68, 74, 181–82, 229
   and law clerks, 106–10
   policy implications of, 233
   and secretaries, 111
   and skills of judges, 164–65
Skill utilization of judges, 147–49, 154–55, 163–64
   and attorney skills, 157–58
   in Chicago, 214–15
   and court politics, 159–60
   in Los Angeles, 214–15
   in Philadelphia, 214–15
   and size of court, 156
Specialized courts: *see* Divisions within courts

Statewide assignment
   and case assignment system, 56–57
   and court personnel, 113
   description of, 54–55
   and judges' work, 69–70
   policy implications of, 232

Tate, James, 199
Taylor, Steven J., 250
Trial courts
   and case disposition methods, 43
   centralized management of, 240–41
   the future of, 242–43
   and politics, 241–42
   types of, 58–61

Wenke, Robert, 201, 206
Wheeler, Russell, 136
Wice, Paul, 210
Work cycles
   description of, 57–58
   and judges' work, 73–74

Yorty, Sam, 198

Ziller: *see* Alpert

| DATE DUE | | | |
|---|---|---|---|
| JUL 6 '81 | | | |
| AG 1 Z '81 | | | |